A CITY THAT
DARED
TO FIGHT

Peter Taaffe and Tony Mulhearn

*To the working people
of Liverpool*

Cover design and cartoons by Alan Hardman

Liverpool

A CITY THAT DARED TO FIGHT

Peter Taaffe and Tony Mulhearn

Fortress

The authors have received help from many comrades and friends, too numerous to mention here. However, the following deserve special acknowledgement for their encouragement, work, criticism and advice, without which this book would not have seen the light of day: Liz Floyd for her self-sacrifice and unflagging energy in typing the many manuscripts. Kevin Parslow for his devotion to exacting research, checking and verification of facts and events. Without his intrepid qualities this book would certainly not have been produced at an early date. Kevin Ramage whose energy and drive have ensured publication. Margaret Edwards and Ginny Armstrong for editorial assistance and the reading of the manuscript. Ted Grant and Lynn Walsh for their most valuable comments and criticisms. We would also wish to thank all our Liverpool comrades whose sterling work over the years, devotion to the cause of socialism and the working class made this book possible. We would particularly like to thank Richard Venton, Dave Cotterill, Terry Harrison and Sam Bond for their comments and suggestions and Tony Aitman for putting at our disposal his historical knowledge and documents relating to the history of the Liverpool labour movement. Last but not least a special word of thanks to those comrades whose technical skills and labour ensured that we published on time.

Liverpool—A City That Dared To Fight
By Peter Taaffe and Tony Mulhearn

First Edition January 1988

ISBN No 1 870958 00 4 (Paper)
1 870958 01 2 (Hardback)

Published by Fortress Books, PO Box 141,
London E2 0RL

Typeset by Eastway Offset Ltd (TU)

Printed by Bath Press, Lower Bristol Road,
Bath BA2 3BL

Single copies available from Fortress Books,
PO Box 141, London E2 0RL

Trade Distribution by Central Books,
14 Leathermarket, London SE1

Contents

Preface

SINCE 1979 the conditions and rights of working people appear to have been crushed by the Thatcher juggernaut. In reality, the working class has put up ferocious opposition to the Tory government. This reached its height in the titanic year-long miners' strike of 1984-5 and in the stand of the Liverpool City Council between 1983-7.

But whereas the miners' strike has been the subject of detailed examination and comment, mostly of a superficial and facile character by capitalist journalists, a veil of silence has been drawn over the drama which unfolded in Liverpool. Much abuse, verbal and written, has poured down on the heads of the 'Liverpool Militants.' But until now not one account has been published which seeks objectively to appraise the mighty sweep of events which surrounded this embattled city. One academic, though useful, work—Michael Parkinson's *Liverpool on the Brink*, mainly dealing with the financial aspect, was published in 1985. And yet here is a city of half a million, formerly the major seaport of the mighty 'British Empire', which witnessed a convulsive movement of the working class and compelled the 'Iron Lady' to beat a retreat in 1984. No other section of the British working class, apart from the miners in 1981, humbled the government in such a fashion. Moreover, as the press has never ceased to remind us, the leadership of that movement involved adherents to the ideas of *Militant*, the Marxist wing of the labour movement. How did *Militant* supporters like Tony Mulhearn and Derek Hatton come to wield such influence in Liverpool?

Capitalist commentators either ascribed the rise of *Militant* in the city to an 'aberration' or alleged that it was the product of some sinister 'coup'. The more serious strategists of capital, however, were shaken by the upheavals in Liverpool. They were confronting a mass movement, but one in which the strategy and tactics deployed by the leadership were more than a match for their own. All the forces at their disposal, which unfortunately included the right wing of the labour and trade union movement, were marshalled in order to crush the 'Liverpool experiment'.

However, their plans were to founder again and again on the rock solid support which the Liverpool working class extended to the city council, the Liverpool District Labour Party (DLP) and to its leadership. It is a historical fact that not one city wide council or general election in Liverpool was lost by Labour from 1983 to 1987. On the contrary, support for Labour was immeasurably stronger in 1987 than it was at the outset of the struggle. It was not the will of the population of Liverpool which led to the eviction of 47 councillors from office in March 1987. This was only achieved by the deployment of the full panoply of the capitalist legal system.

At the same time, the possessing classes attempted with all the enormous means at their disposal through the media to heap one slander upon another in order to deflect attention from the real achievements in housing, health, education, as well as in the heightened political awareness of the working class of Liverpool. It is the task of the authors to rescue these achievements from the mountains of lies and vilification, particularly those piled on the leaders of the struggle, and bring them before the attention of conscientious readers who are prepared to study and learn from the experiences of Liverpool.

While we desire the widest readership possible, we are above all concerned to capture the attention of the working people, particularly of the guiding layers of the working class in the shop stewards' committees, the trade-union branches, among the socialist youth, blacks, and the exploited working-class women. These are for us 'the salt of the earth', the layer of the population which will ultimately shape the future of the mighty British labour movement and thereby the fate of British society. It is for this reason that we have not burdened our text with numerous notes which would only bother and distract working-class readers in particular. Needless to say, every fact which is quoted has been verified by the authors while the sources of quotations are given in the text. Insofar as we refer to ourselves it is in the third person.

The authors have been passionately involved in the struggles of the working class of Liverpool: Tony Mulhearn was vice-president of the Liverpool District Labour Party for 8 years, then its president for 5 years and a city councillor from 1984 until his removal by the District Auditor in 1987. Peter Taaffe has participated, as a writer editing *Militant* since its inception in 1964, and as a political collaborator for over 20 years of those who were in the leadership of this struggle.

It is possible, if not inevitable, that this work will meet with perhaps as much vilification from the opponents of Marxism as the leadership of the Liverpool labour movement itself. No doubt we will be attacked for a lack of 'impartiality' which, it is claimed, is the hallmark of 'real history'. Trotsky, co-leader with Lenin of the Russian Revolution, long ago answered such objections:

> The serious and critical reader will not want a treacherous impartiality, which offers him a cup of conciliation with a well-settled poison of reactionary hate at the bottom, but a scientific conscientiousness, which for its sympathies and antipathies—open and undisguised—seeks support in an honest study of the facts, a determination of their real connections, an exposure of the causal laws of their movement. That is the only possible historic objectivism, and moreover it is amply sufficient, for it is verified and tested not by the good intentions of the historian, for which only he himself can vouch, but by the natural laws revealed by him of the historic process itself. *(History of the Russian Revolution)*

It is up to the reader to judge how far we have met Trotsky's criteria. Our aim is to give not just a simple narrative of events, although that in itself is of historic interest, but to show the hidden processes which in the welter of publicity were hidden from view and have been smeared over by bourgeois journalists, writers and their shadows in the labour movement. Our aim is to show that the growth of a powerful Marxist tendency within the city was not at all an accident or the result of the takeover of 'moribund' Labour Parties. The growth of *Militant* was rooted in the collapse of British capitalism, which was expressed in a particularly extreme fashion in the early 1980s on Merseyside.

However, it takes more than just economic and social collapse to rouse the working people to their feet in their tens of thousands as in the Liverpool drama. The city experienced one mass demonstration, one mass meeting after another, and a number of partial or general strikes over a four-year period. Not since the time of the colossal 1911 transport strike had the city witnessed such mass involvement. Without an authoritative leadership which can gather the opposition of the working masses together, provide clear direction, tactical adroitness, and organisational forms through which the working class can express itself, mass discontent can be very easily dissipated. It was the interlacing of the objective factors with the 'subjective factor' of a Marxist leadership which invested the struggle in Liverpool with such tenacity, and which provided its tremendous sweep and elan.

Both in the ascendant phase from 1983-5 and in the period of partial retreat in 1986-7, the ruling class and the right wing of the labour movement were time and again wrong-footed by the Liverpool labour movement. The premature political obituaries both of the Liverpool working class, and particularly of *Militant* and its supporters, were written and rewritten many times. But time and again the strategists of capital and the right wing of the labour movement were out-manoeuvred. Gradually it was borne in on them that they were confronting something different from what they had faced in the past. This is what accounts for the venom which was unleashed against the leaders of the Liverpool workers, which outdid in its class spite even that deployed against the miners' leadership during their epic struggle.

But they were not able to break the spirit nor check the growth of *Militant* within Liverpool. It is true that the right wing of the labour movement, under the whip of the bourgeois press, have managed laboriously to construct what they now consider to be a 'safe' Labour council and Liverpool District Labour Party. But this is not due to any change in the consciousness either of the advanced workers or of the mass of the working class: it is the result of a crude purge combined with bureaucratic machinations to exclude 'undesirables' from the labour movement. Compare this with the esteem in which the 47 disqualified councillors are held both in the Liverpool labour movement and throughout the country. The weekly donations of workers to pay off the £348,000 fine and costs is witness to this fact.

The struggle of the 47 councillors has added a new chapter to the rich history of the Liverpool working class, which goes back over a period of more than 100 years. As we have only been able to touch on the main highlights in our introductory chapters we intend to produce a fuller account at a later stage.

The bureaucratic and police mentality—and the Liverpool labour movement has had more than its fair share of these in the past—believes that by manoeuvres and administrative fiat the position of the right wing can be shored up for ever. But more than once the movement of the Liverpool workers has elbowed the conservative officialdom aside and begun to transform their organisations. There will be ebbs, in which the conservative stratum which dominates the summits of the labour movement will appear to strengthen their grip. But in periods of upsurge, when faced with the mass movement this layer has been as helpless as a leaf in high wind.

The Liverpool workers, as well as working people throughout the country, are digesting the experiences of the last ten years, particularly of the miners' strike and the events of 1983-7 on Merseyside. The collapse of British capitalism, which was partially obscured by a credit boom prior to the 1987 General Election, will be enormously compounded by the coming world recession. This in turn will result in a sharp deterioration in the living standards of big layers of the British working class. In their millions they will move to defend their rights and conditions. They will also seek to transform their organisations into fighting instruments. In this process they will turn—particularly the new, fresh and energetic layers—for inspiration to the past struggles of the working class. In the miners' strike and above all in the study of the Liverpool experience these workers will find the weapons to carve out a new world. We hope that this account of Liverpool's struggle can play its part in the rearming of the British working class for the mighty battles to come.

Peter Taaffe
Tony Mulhearn

December 1987

1.
Roots

IN THE 1980s the city of Liverpool has become synonymous with 'militancy'. This is recognised not just in Britain, but also internationally. The Tory Prime Minister Margaret Thatcher was greeted with chants of 'Liverpool! Liverpool! Liverpool!' by demonstrating students in Bandung, Indonesia, in 1984. And they were not referring to the famous football team!

The banner of the labour movement which was held by Glasgow—'Red Clydeside'—in the aftermath of the First World War and during the 1920s has now passed, for the time being, to Liverpool. Capitalist commentators seek an explanation for the Liverpool phenomenon by delving into the mysterious 'character' of the city and the Merseyside area. But this cannot explain the titanic struggles with the Tory government between 1983 and 1987, which have marked out Liverpool as something special. Nor has Liverpool 'declared political UDI', as shallow capitalist commentators have suggested.

Nevertheless, all cities have special characteristics. Liverpool is no exception. Its geographical position, which marked it out in the past as one of Britain's most important sea ports, shaped its complex economic and social history, thereby moulding the character of the area. The city was transformed from a sleepy village nestling on the banks of the Mersey, with a population of less than 1000 in the late seventeenth century, into a bustling port, with a population of 78,000 by 1801. In the next 40 years there was a further threefold increase.

This transformation had been wrought by the slave trade. The powerful Liverpool capitalists made their fortunes through the inhuman trade in black skins. PJ Waller, writing in *Democracy and Sectarianism, a Political and Social History of Liverpool*, pointed out that by 1840 'Liverpool contained sixteen docks. By 1900 forty

Mersey docks covered 1600 acres, with 35.5 miles of lineal quay space...The docks and warehouses seemed as monumental as the pyramids.' The labour which built these modern pyramids and worked them was supplied from the wave of immigrants, primarily Irish, but also Welsh and Scots who flooded into the city. This racial and social mix earned the port the title of 'the Marseilles of England'.

The terrible Irish famine of the 1840s provided the impetus for the human flood of immigrants which swept into Liverpool. Some 500,000 Irish entered Liverpool before July 1848. Many re-emigrated, but over 105,000 remained. The bourgeois complained, 'This increase was not one of the people of all classes, but of the poor.' It is the rapid transformation of the living conditions of the masses which provides the fertile soil in which radical and revolutionary ideas take root. The uprooting of the rural population and the drawing of them into the towns and the maelstrom of industry furnished the base for the growth of revolutionary Chartism in the early labour movement. Mostly driven from the land by hunger, the Irish immigrants transferred their hatred of English landlords to the Liverpool capitalists. The capitalists feared, not without justification, that 'rootless Irishmen would turn into revolutionary Chartists'.

Chartism in Liverpool, however, was a tender plant. While Chartists meeting in other manufacturing towns witnessed crowds of 200,000 and 300,000, a meeting in Liverpool's Queens Square in June 1839 drew no more than 15,000. Nevertheless, one of the leading Chartist orators, William Jones, was a native of the city. The Liverpool Chartists called the city 'this seat of corruption' after the 1830 General Election. Bribes were freely offered at £5 a vote and £80,000 was spent in securing votes by bribes.

Hostility to the English was carried on into second and third generation Liverpool Irish. They considered themselves as more 'Irish' than English. This undoubtedly was a factor in fashioning the fiery temperament of the Liverpool labour movement. Leon Trotsky commented that running through the veins of the British working class is not a little Scottish, Irish and Welsh blood, which has contributed revolutionary temper and quite a few of its leaders.

The Liverpool capitalists adopted the methods of 'divide and rule', already tried and tested in Ireland. The ruling class was to employ this weapon in the city for over 100 years. Indeed, the fumes of sectarian poison were to be dissipated only in the period after 1945. The idea was cultivated that 'Irishmen depressed wages.' The slums according to one commentator, bred a 'congenital urge to fight' which usually took the form of a battle between 'green and orange' rather than against the capitalists. The casual nature of dock work, making it difficult for the young trade unions to organise, reinforced this. The capitalists played off one group against another. Competition for jobs on the docks resulted in a drop of real wages for many of the Merseyside working class between 1850 and 1875, despite the rapid expansion of capitalism in that period.

Early Struggles

Long before this, however,Liverpool experienced strikes and violent clashes between labour and capital. The first recorded strike in the city was by shoemakers in 1756. A far more serious clash developed between the shipowners and sailors in 1775. The strikers, carrying a red flag and with red ribbons in their bonnets, stormed the Exchange, which doubled as the Town Hall, after the employers' armed guards had fired on an unarmed crowd. In 1833, a strike of building workers took place in Liverpool and Birkenhead from April until October, when they were forced back to work in defeat.

The ebb of the revolutionary wave which swept Europe in 1848 coincided with a long economic revival of capitalism. The ten year cycle of capitalism, analysed and described by Marx, resulted in periodic crises. But the basic trend in this epoch was for a colossal development of the productive forces. Britain's monopoly of the world market allowed it to give certain concessions to a layer of the working class, creating what Engels called 'the aristocracy of Labour'. Trade unionism in the main was restricted to the skilled trades, who jealously guarded their position and privileges.

The National Union of Elementary Teachers was founded in Liverpool in 1870. This became the National Union of Teachers in 1889. The forerunner of the National Association of Local Government Officers (NALGO) grew out of the Liverpool Municipal Officers Guild, founded in 1896. NALGO was established in 1905. These organisations began as 'professional associations'. The founder of NALGO was Principal Agent of the Conservative Party between 1924 and 1927! It is one of the ironies of history that Derek Hatton, scourge of the Thatcher government, first built support in NALGO eighty years after it was established by a Tory!

The loss of English imperialism's monopoly of world trade, and the challenge posed to it by emerging German imperialism, compelled the British capitalists to attack the conditions of the working class. The privations of the unemployed, the low paid and unskilled workers led to riotous demonstrations in London in the mid-1880s. These privations also 'turned Liverpool dockers from hungry men into angry men'.

The Liverpool Trades Council was revived in 1888 to unite 'for the protection of Labour'. First set up as the Liverpool Trades Guardian Association in 1848, it had entered into a period of decline about 1860. The 3000 membership of the Trades Council was restricted primarily to the skilled workers: printers, tailors, saddlers, bookbinders, railway workers, gilders, cabinet makers etc. It also proscribed 'party or political matters unless bearing upon Labour questions'.

The more politically active workers bypassed the Trades Council. Liverpool's first 'working-class' councillor, JG Taggart, was an Irish nationalist who, together with Thomas Kelly remained the only standard bearer of labour in the council right up to 1905. Nevertheless, the Trades Council increased its membership to more than 10,000 within a year of its revival. But the greatest impulse for union organisation came from the lower depths of the proletariat, the unskilled, particularly the despised seafarers and dockers upon whose labour the wealth of the city had been built.

The spark for this movement had been laid by the strikes of the dockers, matchgirls and other workers in London. The National Union of Dock Labourers (NUDL) had been founded in Glasgow in 1889. In June and July 1889 strikes of seafarers broke out, followed by the dockers in February and March 1890. The 'new unionism' also searched for a political expression. The NUDL proclaimed in its 1891 Annual Report that:

> For the first time in the history of the labour world, distinctions of nationality and religious creed and political party and colour of skin were set aside, and the common brotherhood of the workers

asserted and vindicated...the utter helplessness and uselessness of capital without labour.

By 1891 the Trades Council had 121 delegates representing 47 trades and 46,000 members, which made it the largest Trades Council outside London. The Tory leader Forwood warned that 'dangerous doctrines were being preached by the new school of trade unionists—the Burns, Mann and Tillett type of demagogue'. There were more than enough causes which sustained and built the unions and the emergent labour movement. Slums and terrible housing were a feature of Liverpool, as with most large cities. Liverpool had first given the world the term 'Jerry-building' in the 1880s.

The towering figure of James Larkin, born in Liverpool in 1876, symbolised the rise of the Liverpool labour movement at the beginning of this century. While Larkin became famous for his leadership of the Irish labour movement at a later date, particularly of the titanic 1913 Dublin lockout, he possessed the qualities which the best of the Liverpool workers' leaders have all shown. Those working-class forces and individuals which did battle with the Tory government between 1983 and 1987 were cast in the same mould.

Tony Mulhearn, Derek Hatton and the supporters of *Militant* on Merseyside stood on the shoulders of Larkin, but had the immense advantage of a worked-out Marxist programme, perspectives and tactics. Larkin evinced those qualities which have given a special quality to the 'militancy' of Liverpool. That tradition was continued by others, perhaps not as well known, but who played a crucial role in the local labour movement, keeping the torch of Marxism alight and passing it on to the new generation.

The first steps of the British workers towards independent political representation separate and in opposition to the Liberal Party, found some of its most ardent champions in the city. The first Liverpool branch of the Independent Labour Party (ILP), which included James Larkin among its founder members, was set up in June 1892, six months before the ILP's first national conference.

The severe worsening of the conditions of the working class nourished the growth of socialism and the labour movement. Unemployment had risen from 2 per cent in 1890 to over 7 per cent in 1893. At the beginning of the new century the tide began to turn in favour of Labour. Keir Hardie was elected to Parliament. The Labour Representation Committee, linking socialists and trades unionists, was formed in 1900. This in turn laid the foundation for a Parliamentary Labour Party. In the same year, John Morrissey was the first Liverpool socialist to be elected to a public position, that of Public Auditor. Larkin assisted in his campaign but was destined to play a greater role in the trade-union field.

The 1906 general election was a triumph for the Liberals, but it also brought a significant increase in Labour representation in Parliament. Shortly afterwards, the death of the sitting MP for Kirkdale, David MacIver, forced a by-election. Liverpool Labour threw itself energetically behind their candidate, John Hill, secretary of the Boilermakers Union. Some 100 open air meetings were held in Liverpool before polling day, 27 September. Nearly twenty Labour MPs appeared, including Ramsay MacDonald and Arthur Henderson. The by-election was described as the 'biggest fight in Labour's history'. The *Protestant Standard* declared that socialism would mean 'absolute infidelity, the grossest immoralities', and—anticipating Enoch Powell—'rivers of human blood'. Labour was defeated, but it put up a creditable performance: Hill received 3300 votes to Charles M'Arthur's 4000.

The events of 1905-6 and particularly the strikes of seafarers and dockers were the dress rehearsals for 1911, the year of Merseyside's greatest industrial battle. The strike wave of 1911 represented the emergence of the Merseyside working class as a powerful, combative force.

The period 1910—14 was one of the stormiest in British history. Lenin commented, 'the shadow of revolution hung over Britain'. Transport workers, the miners, the mighty movement of the Dublin workers in the 1913 lock out, the movement of the suffragettes, as well as the threat of civil war over the issue of Ireland all convulsed Britain. But it was the strike of the transport workers in 1911, which was ignited by the strikes in Liverpool, which started the movement.

Paradoxically, the spark for this movement came from the revival in industry and the economy in 1911. A similar process in Russia was analysed by Trotsky at this time. He was the first to point out that it is neither a recession nor an economic upswing which necessarily radicalises the working class or results in strikes. It is the change from one period to another, argued Trotsky, which furnishes the basis for a strike wave or a radicalisation of the working class. Thus after a recession, a revival in industry, sometimes a small and partial upswing, can lead to a drop in unemployment and imbue the workers with a greater confidence. This in turn can lead to a movement with the aim of recapturing what was lost in the recession. This was the major factor which gave a mighty push to the workers' movement in 1911. It combined with the emergence of a new generation of younger workers who were impatient both with the ossified trade-union leadership and the seemingly impotent Parliamentary Labour Party. This 'anti-parliamentarianism' was reflected in the growth of syndicalist ideas and the popularity of leaders like Tom Mann and Ben Tillett.

The 1911 Dock Strike

In the decade before 1911, real wages had dropped by 10 per cent. The upswing in production and the growth in the profits of the capitalists fuelled the opposition of the working class. Together with Ben Tillett, Tom Mann had formed the National Transport Workers Federation, which brought together some 30 bodies into a loose trade-union federation. On 31 May this body called a 'monster demonstration' which gathered on the Eastern Plateau by St George's Hall.

The two seafarers' unions, the National Union of Ship Stewards, Cooks, Butchers and Bakers and the National Sailors and Firemens Union, were shaping up for a battle with the notorious Shipowners Federation. The seafarers' main demands were for a conciliation board, a minimum rate of wages and an end to the degrading medical examination by doctors privately appointed by the Shipowners Federation. The shipowners rejected the demands of the seafarers. They were confident that there would be no strike. But the crew of the White Star liner, *Baltic*, when they docked in Liverpool, immediately put in for an increase of £1 a month. This was turned down and all the firemen refused to sign articles for the next voyage. By 14 June 500 men of the *Baltic*, *Teutonic* and the *Empress of Ireland*, refused to sign on and the strike began.

Tom Mann arrived in Liverpool and immediately convened a

dockside meeting under a banner which proclaimed: 'War
Declared: Strike for Liberty'. Two to three thousand attended
the meeting at Canning Place, addressed by Tom Mann. The
Daily Post quoted a trade unionist who said, 'It's like striking one
match of a box which can very easily set fire to all the rest.'
Prophetic words! This is precisely what happened in the
following months. The strike was 100 per cent successful.

Strikes spread like wildfire throughout the rest of Britain. The
dockers showed splendid solidarity, refusing to unload a ship,
The Pointer, which was being worked by blacklegs. On 26 June
the dock labourers struck against firms refusing to recognise the
seafarers' union. Action was also being considered in the United
States of America and Europe. Non-unionists were drawn in
behind the unionised seafarers. In the heat of the battle
sectarianism began to be pushed aside. The dockers were mainly
Catholic and the carters were mainly Protestant. The flood of
non-unionists into the unions meant a dramatic increase in
overall strength. As a result of the struggle, the dock labourers'
union gained 8000 new members during the dispute, the
stewards 2500 new members and the sailors and firemen 4500.
It was now claimed that 99 per cent of Liverpool shipping was
sailing under union conditions.

Alarmed by these developments, the government began to
prepare for military intervention. Shipping firms had agreed to
recognise the union, but began to stall on the question of wages
and conditions. The strike committee had achieved the aim of
recognition of the union, but a majority of the dockers rejected
the settlement because of the lack of progress on wages. It
seemed as though the strike was going to disintegrate. Tom
Mann and the strike committee launched a series of mass
meetings to explain the issues to the men. They won the
argument and there was a general return to work. But there was
a dramatic increase in the confidence, cohesion and
membership of the unions.

No sooner had the dockers returned, however, than others
began to come out, mill workers, brewery workers in favour of
'union ale', and 250 women at Walton rubber works, all struck in
the wake of the dockers' successful action. Tramway workers
were drawn into the campaign for unionisation, and wage rises
were conceded. But these strikes, important as they were,

merely foreshadowed another titanic struggle, which was now about to unfold.

The 1911 Railway Strike

Over 500 porterage staff at the North Dock goods station of the Lancashire and Yorkshire Railway first threatened strike action over pay and conditions. This was opposed by the Executive of the Amalgamated Society of Railway Servants, who ordered that the men take their grievances to the conciliation board. But already bitter from their experience with the conciliation board, 1000 goods porters from the Lancashire and Yorkshire Railway went on strike on 5 August right along the line of the docks. Their demands were for a 50-hour week (a reduction from 60) and a two shillings a week pay increase for all grades.

The strike wave was spreading far and wide. From the lowest depths of the working class one section after another joined in. But the bourgeois were shaping up for an outright confrontation with the workers. Troops were drafted into the city. Together with the police, they were openly used as strikebreakers. The troops were issued with live ammunition. The strike committee called for a 'monster demonstration' for Sunday 13 August on St George's Plateau.

Forty thousand workers were expected, but in the event 100,000 turned up to listen to 40 speakers on four separate platforms. While militant, the meeting was extremely peaceful. Then a small incident involving a section of the crowd and police was seized on by the massed ranks of the police to launch a vicious assault on the demonstration.

The police charged repeatedly for half an hour. After the crowd was dispersed the area was strewn with broken glass, stones, pieces of timber and other missiles, 'and other silent witnesses of the savage spirit in which the warfare had been waged'. A contingent of soldiers from the Warwickshire Regiment appeared on the scene, taking up stations at the north end of the plateau. The Riot Act was read twice. Fighting continued north of Lime Street, where 'behind barricades, residents withstood the police for 36 hours'. Commenting on the events of the day Tom Mann said:

This afternoon's happenings will certainly not cow our men, and whilst we shall keep within the necessary limits, the spirit of genuine fight on recognised lines is immmensely stronger now as a result of the dastardly behaviour of the police than it was 24 hours ago.

The police brutality on 'Bloody Sunday' only served to intensify the anger of the working class. Two days later 3000 workers attacked prison vans containing arrested 'rioters' and two men were killed by the police, 'one after the sergeant he was attacking shot him in the head'. This further inflamed the workers. Tram cars were wrecked and barricades were erected in parts of the city. Lord Derby forwarded to the Home Secretary, Winston Churchill, the Lord Mayor's cry that Westminster should realise that 'a revolution was in progress.'

The bourgeois took fright at developments in Liverpool, *The Times* (16 August) declared: 'Labour agitation gone mad.' The press reported: 'Walton jail was full. Shops and public houses were shuttered, but determined looters checked only when troops assumed the firing position.' The reactionary magazine *Porcupine* proclaimed 'The crimson flag of anarchy was let loose in Liverpool.' Another declared: 'A nightmare for civilisation.' The shipowners, as expected, locked out the dockers, affecting 20,000 men.

Before the outbreak of police violence at the demonstration on the Sunday, Tom Mann had warned: 'If they [the employers] refuse to take action with a view to an honourable settlement, then we shall declare a general strike for the whole of Liverpool.' The strike committee now prepared to put that threat into practice. Liverpool took on the appearance of a city subject to full-scale military occupation. The cruiser, *Antrim*, was anchored in the Mersey with its guns trained on the city centre. On the evening of 14 August the strike committee called a general strike.

The funerals of the workers who had been shot, one a Protestant carter, the other a Catholic docker, was an occasion for sectarianism to be swept aside in a display of working-class solidarity. The working class responded magnificently to the strike call. Dockers, sailors and firemen, cooks and stewards, railway workers, coal heavers and tugboatmen, flatmen, canalmen and bargemen, all came out. More than 66,000 workers were on strike.

A situation of virtual dual power existed in Liverpool at this stage. The power of the capitalist state was challenged by the joint strike committee, which issued permits for the transportation of certain goods. Businessmen and tradesmen were approaching the committee, and sometimes, in response, bread was 'set free' and hospitals exempted. One Liberal was quoted as saying, 'Labour is out of hand for the moment.'

This movement came from below and revealed to one bourgeois commentator the 'absolute powerlessness of the trade union leaders to guide their followers [which] is the most unfortunate feature of the struggle.' As a result of the pressure in Liverpool, the right-wing leaders of the four railway unions were forced to come to Liverpool and in effect to ratify the national rail strike that had already broken out.

The capitalists began a recruiting drive for special constables. More significantly, Territorial Army members in Liverpool were forced to surrender their rifles and ammunition, allegedly 'for the use of the regular army'. The bourgeois were obviously terrified that the radicalisation of the working class would infect even part-time soldiers. Tom Mann, speaking at a mass meeting in Bankfield Street, declared that:

> He was not the sort of man to be cowed by the soldiers, even if there were a million of them. A very big percentage of the military, he was genuinely convinced, had hearts that beat in sympathy with the strikers, for they knew that when their period of service was over they would be pitchforked onto the market of labour, to subsist on the same low wages and to suffer the same hardships as the workers who were on strike...a great percentage of the police too, in spite of their dastardly work on Sunday, were, he believed, in sympathy with the men, and he would be the last man to encourage unwarrantable bitterness against the police force. (*Daily Post*, 16 August 1911)

Tom Mann was later imprisoned, following the publication of his *Open Letter to British Soldiers* during the 1912 miners' strike.

By 19 August 200,000 were on strike. The Liverpool employers fulminated against the strikers with words which could be borrowed from the speeches of Thatcher. They particularly denounced 'The system known as "peaceful picketing", under which, as carried out, many thousands of our employees who are wishful to work are prevented from doing so

by the threats of, and intimidation of strikers.' The radicalisation
of the masses on the other hand had affected even Labour MPs
of the day like GM Barnes who declared that: 'The only solution
of their troubles was to do away with the damnable system of
capitalism.'

The Liberal government, faced with the determined mood of
the transport workers, rushed in a mediator. He called for both
sides to resume work with no dismissals. This meant that the
railway company's secret agreement was finished. The union
leaders accepted, but the rank and file accepted only with great
reluctance and suspicion. The workers went back on 22 August,
conscious that they had scored a great victory. The bourgeois,
gnashing their teeth, thirsted for revenge. Tory leader Sir
William Forwood, in a letter to *The Spectator* wrote:

> In my native city of Liverpool Tom Mann and the strike committee
> have ruled supreme during the last week. Their orders have been
> despotic. No cart could move along the streets unless it bore a
> placard stating that it was 'under the auspices of the strike
> committee' or under a convoy of cavalry and even the presence of an
> escort has not always prevented an attack from the mob.

Tory leader Chamberlain was also to declare a year later, 'We
shall never have settled peace until one struggle at least has been
fought out to a finish.' The 1911 railway strike had established
Liverpool as a bastion for the working class. The ruling class's
fear of the labour movement in the city really dates from this
time. The unions were now an immense power and Liverpool
was a 'hotbed of militancy'.

This tradition was sometimes to sink into the background,
particularly in periods of economic upswing, only to return later
with even greater force. The 1911 strike inspired workers
throughout Britain. In 1912 the miners called a national strike
and in 1913 the Dublin lockout won enormous support from the
working class throughout Britain. There was a massive increase
in union membership from 2.2 million to over 4 million by the
outbreak of war in 1914.

In the wake of the strike the Liverpool labour movement
turned to the political plane. In 1910-11 Labour's vote in the
municipal elections rose from 4129 to 12,231. It dropped back
in the two succeeding years. A vicious slander campaign was
conducted by the Tories and Liberals against Labour

candidates. In the Breckfield ward, Petrie, the Tory leader, advised women that 'if the socialist candidate was elected to imagine their husbands coming home on Saturday, with their free love and no wages'.

Once more sectarianism, in the wake of the heightened conflict in the north of Ireland, was to become an obstacle to the development of the labour movement. Sir Edward Carson, the Conservative and Unionist leader, organised the 100,000 strong 'Ulster Volunteer Force' and in 1914 British officers at the Curragh Barracks revolted against any 'Home Rule' being implemented by the Liberal government.

These developments found an echo in Liverpool. The reactionary barrister and MP for Walton, FE Smith, who was later to become a Tory Cabinet Minister, promised Carson that 10,000 Liverpudlians in three ships were ready to join him. Reports indicated that there were also 3000 'Irish Nationalists' who had received military training ready to counter the Ulster Volunteer Force.

With the outbreak of the 1914-18 war class issues were muffled by the roar of cannon and shells, but they broke out with even greater ferocity in the post-war period. The workers linked the carnage of the war, from which there was a profound revulsion, to capitalism. As John Maclean the Scottish socialist put it, the capitalists were 'dripping from head to foot' with the blood of the working class.

The Revolutionary Wave of 1917-19

The Russian workers, by breaking with landlordism and capitalism and establishing a workers' democracy in the revolution of 1917 blazed a trail which others attempted to follow. The German workers attempted to make a revolution, only to find that it was the leaders of their own organisations, the German Social Democrats (SPD) and the Independents (USPD) who were the main obstacle. The Hungarian workers took power for a short period, but were overthrown by a bloody counter revolution.

The reverberations from the Russian Revolution were felt in Liverpool, as in the rest of the country. The young John Braddock, at that stage a fiery left winger and soon to be a founding member of the Communist Party, hailed the revolution: 'There had been many revolutions in Russia, but this was *the* revolution. The workers were in power!' In wave after wave and in one country after another, the masses battered at the foundations of capitalism.

The high-water mark of this revolutionary wave was undoubtedly the year 1919. The onrush of the masses under the impetus of the Russian Revolution was so great that Lenin and Trotsky raised the theoretical possibility that European capitalism could be swept away even before the creation of mass parties armed with a clear programme, strategy and tactics. Their hopes were not borne out by the march of events. But even in Britain, not the worst affected country, the bourgeois were terrified by the movement of the working class.

The 1919 Police Strike

One of the most remarkable incidents at this time was the police strike. The very fact that an important arm of the capitalist state could be infected with the spirit of revolt was a reflection of the crisis facing capitalist society. The National Union of Police and Prison Officers was founded in August 1918 to fight for the interests of 'workers in uniform'. Many of the members were ex-servicemen and the union found itself pushed rapidly towards the left, gravitating towards the labour movement.

The union was first organised in London and began to demand wage increases and recognition of the union. Under tremendous pressure the government conceded an enquiry. But while this was deliberating, disaffection in the Metropolitan Police worsened when PC Spackman was dismissed for 'insubordination'. This triggered off a mood of real hostility to the government, and the union decided to hold a ballot on the issues of strike action, recognition, a pay increase, and reinstatement of all dismissed constables.

On 6 June 1919 the government announced plans to cut across the union by establishing a 'police association'. This was incorporated in the police bill published on 16 July. While the national Labour Party leaders, led by dockers' leader and MP Sexton, welcomed the pay rise in the House of Commons they showed only token opposition to the government's prohibition of policemen belonging to a proper trade union. But on 31 July, delegates from the Metropolitan Police Union met to consider their response to the Police Bill. They decided to call a strike from the following day, with a demonstration from Tower Hill to Downing Street.

Many workers in Liverpool had indicated that they would come to the side of the police, which showed their sound proletarian instinct. This was despite many vivid memories of the beatings and shooting they had suffered at the hands of the police in 1911. The workers, if not their national and local leaders, understood the importance of supporting the police strike as a means of pulling them towards the labour movement.

The strike was most successful in the Liverpool area. The government claimed that only 1056 strikers from a force of 19,000 had come out in the London area. But in Liverpool, out of a force of approximately 2000, 95 per cent were in the union. Over 700 came out on the first day of the strike and attended a mass meeting on St George's Plateau. Some of the police marched to the meeting in military fashion. The Bootle police union claimed that 69 out of 70 officers were out on strike.

There was an instinctive rallying of rank and file trade unionists to the police. The Liverpool branch of the Postmen's Federation telegrammed: 'Compliments. Fight the good fight. Civil and citizens rights, with full recognition. With other unions will consider practical sympathy, if necessary.' The Tory Home Secretary, Shortt, denounced the police strike as 'an act of mutiny'. The Merseyside police were considered by the national and local authorities as a key centre. At least 2500 troops arrived in Liverpool. Four tanks were stationed at St George's Plateau, and warships anchored in the Mersey.

The absence of police on duty resulted in what the *Post* (4 August) described as 'an orgy of looting and rioting' over the August Bank Holiday weekend. One rioter was shot. He later died in hospital. Baton charge after baton charge was made in an attempt to end the disturbances, and the dock gates were set on fire. The London Road—Scotland Road area became a 'war zone'. The Riot Act was read and according to one account the shops and pubs were plundered to the tune of £150,000. In Birkenhead the Riot Act was also read. A mass meeting of trade unionists in support of the police passed a resolution which stated:

> This meeting of Liverpool trade unionists declares common cause
> with the National Union of Police and Prison Officers and
> determines in order to give immediate and necessary assistance, that
> a 'down tool' policy to be forthwith declared. All trade unionists in
> the city and district are, therefore, urged to cease work at once owing
> to the attack made by the government on trade unionism...That as
> rioting conferred a pretext for military interference, Liverpoool
> men were asked to act so as not to put their brothers in the force in a
> false position. (*Post*, 4 August 1919)

The police by themselves could not possibly succeed because
of the 800,000 ex-servicemen, many now unemployed, who the
government were busily recruiting into the force. The success or
otherwise of the strike depended upon whether the heavy
battalions of the labour movement would come to the support of
the police. The local workers' leaders instinctively gravitated in
the direction of supporting the police. But the national
leadership of the unions began to distance themselves. On 6
August the National Union of Railwaymen Executive turned
down calls for a sympathy strike and urged those members
already on strike to return to work. Reluctantly, the Liverpool
branches accepted the decision, but demanded that all strikers
be reinstated. On the same day, under Sexton's pressure, the
dockers decided not to take any action.

The lack of support from the national trade-union leaders
weakened the resolve of police in other areas, and sections
began to leave the union. The bourgeois, feeling they had the
upper hand, completely rejected the possibility of reinstatement.
Recognising that they were being betrayed by the leaders of the
labour movement and desperate to retain their jobs in the teeth
of the widespread recruitment of blacklegs, branches of the
union in Bristol, Chester, Bradford, Nottingham and Salford
resigned from the union. Realising that they had been isolated,
many police beat a frantic retreat in a desperate attempt to
regain their jobs. Their isolation drove them to the right and led
them to beg for help from their 'betters'.

A resolution was passed at a meeting of the Liverpool police
which declared: 'This meeting, representing the major portion
of the city police now on strike, have realised the mistake made,
and discovered that we were misled, and regret the step we took
on 1 August 1919.' It also stated: 'we give an undertaking to

abandon the Police and Prison Officers' Union'. Despite this grovelling supplication to the Watch Committee, the police were isolated, and most of them never got their jobs back.

The police strike of 1919 indicated the colossal ferment which affected all layers of society after the First World War. The perfidious character of the right-wing trade-union leaders was laid bare. Lloyd George considered that the defeat of the 1919 police strike was 'perhaps the turning point in the labour movement', redirecting it 'from Bolshevist and direct actionist causes to legitimate trade unionism'.

Many police strikers were victimised and never reinstated. Nevertheless, three police strikers stood as Labour candidates in Liverpool in the 1919 municipal elections. Two were elected, and Labour as a whole made great progress, with ten gains. This brought the number of Labour councillors up to 20.

But with the ebb of the revolutionary wave, sectarian tendencies reappeared in the following years, particularly with the election of Protestant councillors. Yet Liverpool in the early 1920s was in the grip of recession and unemployment. According to John Braddock: 'Roughly one in nine of the population of Liverpool was unemployed. And because a man might—and often did—have seven children, that meant destitution for more than half the 800,000 in the city.'

The continuing mass unemployment in the early 1920s led to the formation of the National Unemployed Workers Movement, with the young Communist Party in the leadership. Demonstrations of 30,000 and 40,000 unemployed marched through Liverpool demanding 'Work or Full Maintenance'. When they occupied the Walker Art Gallery in 1921, the police meted out savage beatings—workers' blood ran down the steps of the gallery. But in general the police were circumspect in their handling of demonstrations—these unemployed were ex-servicemen who marched in military fashion. Indeed, the police more than once had to request the unemployed to slow down because they had difficulty in keeping in step!

The city council had a crushing Tory majority of 150 to Labour's 15. Yet so effective and threatening were the demonstrations that Salvidge, the Tory leader, called in John Braddock for negotiations. Braddock describes the almost autocratic power exercised by this representative of the Liverpool capitalists:

Salvidge said: 'I want to talk to you about the mess we've got into with the unemployed.'

'But you're not a member of the Board of Guardians,' I reminded him.

He looked at me hard. 'Are you going to act your age, Mr Braddock?' he asked.

'Yes,' I said, 'You're telling me that you and I can reach an agreement, and that agreement will be carried out by the three boards of guardians?'

'That's what I'm telling you,' he smiled.

The fact that boards of guardians were separately elected bodies, administering a special law, with their own statutory powers, owing no allegiance to the council, bothered him not a bit. He had the town well sewn up.

'Have you the proposals?' I asked.

'Yes, I have,' he told me. 'I'm proposing that the scales paid at the labour exchanges to those entitled to unemployment pay, generally called the dole, shall be paid to all on poor relief.'

I went on: 'If you'll undertake that the three boards of guardians will start paying unemployment scales of relief, in money, I'll undertake to accept it.'

I went back to the committee and told them, and they said: 'That'll do.'

The government warned Salvidge that he had no authority to do this and that he was breaking the statutory regulations, but he ignored them. He was the boss. (Jack and Bessie Braddock, *The Braddocks*).

There is a striking parallel here between Salvidge's behaviour and that of Tory Minister, Jenkin, when he made concessions to Labour in 1984. In both cases it was 'extra-parliamentary' activity which brought the ruling class to heel. The right wing of the Liverpool labour movement who, when necessary, will invoke the image of the 'moderate' Braddocks—conveniently pass over this 'militant' episode.

The 1920s in Liverpool were characterised chiefly by the struggles against unemployment: The unemployed organisations worked with the Trades Council. Up to this time many catholic Liverpool workers supported the Irish Nationalists, who even had an MP in Liverpool for many years. Likewise many protestant workers voted for Conservative and Unionist candidates. After the partition of Ireland in 1921, the Irish Nationalists declined as a force in Liverpool, and in March 1923 Labour elected its first MP in Liverpool, winning a by-election in Edge Hill.

Liverpool in the 1926 General Strike

A council of action had been convened in 1925 in preparation for the confrontation which was expected to develop from the miners' struggles and between the labour movement and the government. The majority of the Liverpool working class responded magnificently to the call, in May 1926, for a general strike. Of the heavy battalions of the working class only the tramway and the electricity workers failed to come out. Havelock Wilson also refused to bring the seafarers out. The government, now wary of Liverpool's involvement in any struggle, put two battalions of troops into Liverpool and two battleships arrived in the Mersey. When the national leaders called the general strike off while it was still spreading, the advanced workers, a large minority of the Liverpool Trades Council, condemned the TUC's abandonment of the miners. Moreover, several hundred workers in the Liverpool flour milling industry who had come out in support of the strike were not reinstated afterwards.

In the aftermath of the general strike trade union membership on Merseyside dropped by a quarter. But the municipal elections that followed the strike saw the representation of Labour on the council increased to 19. This growth was sustained by the terrible distress caused by the unemployment which was endemic in Liverpool even before the onset of the 'Hungry Thirties'. The West Derby Board of Guardians was, for instance 'overdrawn in its account of current expenses by £650,000 by 1925'. By 1930 the number of unemployed had reached a staggering 72,518 in Liverpool and Bootle. On one famous occasion in 1929 the Garston Exchange had to close when insufficient money had been drawn from the bank to meet the claims.

Despite mass unemployment the labour movement was the rising force in the city. By 1929, 'Labour inspired what enthusiasm there was, Margaret Beavan (a Tory councillor) likened their devotion to that of Crusaders: 'They are willing to make any sacrifice—week in, week out—for socialism.' These pioneers of the labour movement in Liverpool are separated by a chasm from the present national right-wing leadership of the labour and trade-union movement. The average Labour Party member in Liverpool, and particularly *Militant* supporters, have the same spirit of self-sacrifice and conviction which motivated the pioneers.

Nor were the upheavals in the Liverpool Labour Party of the 1980s unknown to those who built the labour movement in the city in the 1920s and 1930s. Three councillors in Great George Street and one in Vauxhall, in an action like that of the SDP in 1981, split from the Labour Party in the 1930s calling themselves 'Democratic Labour'. At the same time, an ILP candidate, Bob Tissyman, one of the victimised leaders of the 1919 police strike, was victorious in a by-election in the Edge Hill ward. This was one indication of the radicalisation of the working class that was taking place in the city.

The betrayal of Labour by Ramsay MacDonald in 1931, when he split away while Labour Prime Minister and joined with the Liberals and Tories to form the National government, had its repercussions in Liverpool. One Labour MP, Hall Caine, followed MacDonald into supporting the National Government and was accordingly vilified as a 'twister and traitor'. In the general election of 1931 Labour lost every Liverpool seat except the Scotland seat in which David Logan MP was to remain entrenched for 40 years.

The 1930s were characterised by a further growth of unemployment and increased misery for tens of thousands. There were 110,000 unemployed in Merseyside in 1931-2. Fully one-third of males were unemployed.

The 1932 Birkenhead Riots

In September 1932 the anger of the unemployed boiled over in riots which erupted in Birkenhead. A demonstration led by the Communist Party leaders to the house of the Chair of the Public Assistance Committee was ambushed by a large contingent of police. The ensuing battle resulted in barricades being thrown up in parts of Birkenhead. Bootle and South Wales police were mobilised, but they were held at bay for a period of three days.

The movement spread to Liverpool and another riot broke out. As a result of this demonstration, John Braddock was sentenced to 16 months' imprisonment allegedly for leading it, although other councillors testified that he was elsewhere at the time. He was released from jail after a successful appeal, even the police having to admit they had mistaken him for somebody else.

The slump in the world economy, with a consequential collapse of world trade, had a devastating effect in Liverpool. The port lost an average one per cent in trade a year between 1919 and 1939. The complete dependency of the city on the port and its unskilled labour was shown by the fact that only 37 per cent of Liverpool workers were engaged in production, compared with the 63 per cent national average. The only escape route for many of the thousands of unemployed was the armed services. Yet 50 per cent of the 3692 Liverpudlians seeking to join the armed forces in 1935 and about 30 per cent of the 6000 who attempted to follow the same route in 1936 failed to meet the medical or physical standards! Moreover, the council provided no help to reduce unemployment; the corporation in fact cut the health and education administration by £5 million in 1932.

The decade of the 1930s ended for Liverpool as it began with demonstrations of the unemployed. Faced with the horrendous 80,000 unemployed considered by experts to be 'normal', the unemployed organised a 'lie down demonstration' in Lime Street. In August 1939, one month before the outbreak of the Second World War Huyton tenants struck against rent increases and women 'picketed with perambulators'.

The Origins of Trotskyism in Liverpool

The late 1930s saw the first beginnings of a Marxist force which was to play such a decisive role in the labour movement in the 1980s. Trotskyism—the genuine continuation of the ideas of Lenin and the Russian Revolution—originated in Liverpool not from the Communist Party, but from the Independent Labour Party and to some extent from the Labour Party.

Tommy Birchall and Jimmy Deane were two of the pioneers of Trotskyism in the city. The Deane family in particular had a long tradition of struggle, along with Jimmy Deane, his brothers Arthur and Brian, and his mother Gertie were all in the Trotskyist movement. Gertie Deane's father Charles Carrick had been one of the first Labour councillors in Liverpool. Both Jimmy Deane and Tommy Birchall still adhere to the ideas of their youth, are firm supporters of the *Militant*, but through

Ted Grant (left) and Jimmy Deane, 1945.

ill-health are no longer able to be fully active in the labour movement. (see Appendices 4 and 5 for interviews with Tommy Birchall and Jimmy Deane). In 1938 they came into contact with Ted Grant, who at that time was—and still remains—the theoretician and principal leader of Trotskyism in Britain.

It is on the shoulders of these pioneers, as well as many others who are too numerous to mention, that the present generation of Liverpool militants stand. Their work laid the foundations for a powerful Marxist force in the city, without which the mighty movement of the Liverpool working class would not have reached such a pitch.

2.
Labour in the Boom

THE REVOLUTIONARY wave that swept Western Europe at the end of World War II was, if anything, greater than that which followed the First World War. Capitalism, however, was saved by the reformist and Communist Party leaders who in Italy and France linked up with capitalist parties in Popular Front governments. This created the political pre conditions for the economic upswing of 1950-75.

In Britain, the radicalisation of the masses was reflected in the coming to power of the first majority Labour government in 1945. The working class, particularly the mass of soldiers returning from the war, were determined never again to return to the privation and misery of the inter-war years. In Liverpool, Labour won eight out of eleven parliamentary seats. In the Scotland division Davey Logan was one of the only three candidates in the whole of Britain who was actually unopposed.

However, in the 1950 general election, with the disappointment at the retreats of the 1945-50 Labour government, the Tories recovered. They remained the dominant power in the parliamentary field in Liverpool until 1964 when Labour gained four seats, with a spectacular 8 per cent swing. By 1955 Labour controlled the Liverpool council for the first time. The Liverpool labour movement at this stage was dominated, as with the Labour Party and the unions nationally, by the right wing. The upswing of capitalism had reinforced the hold of the reformists, both over the Labour Party and the trade unions.

A feature of the 1950s was the rebuilding of the inner-city areas and the transference of some of their inhabitants to the overflow towns like Kirkby and Skelmersdale. This tended to break down sectarian divisions. This process was reinforced by the general prosperity, which benefited the great majority of working people. Protestant councillors were still returned to the council even as late as the early 1970s, but their prominent spokesperson, Longbottom, was a fading force and a pale echo of what he had been in the past.

The Liverpool Labour Party was under the iron grip of the 'Braddock machine'. Bessie Braddock was elected the MP for Exchange in 1945 while John Braddock became the leader of the Labour group on the council in 1948. Former Communist Party members, they both moved far to the right during the boom years, assembling a ruthless apparatus around themselves in the Labour Party. Membership was deliberately kept small; workers applying to join were told that they could not become members because the party was 'full up'. Simon Fraser, the Liverpool Trades Council and Labour Party's secretary at that time, has conceded that 'the organisation was poor and intentionally kept poor to keep out the "wrong sort of candidate".'

It was only in the Walton constituency that Marxism had any appreciable success in Liverpool at this stage. Year after year they argued the case for the general programme of socialism, both at the level of the Liverpool Trades Council and Labour Party, which was then a joint body, and also at the national conferences of the Labour Party. In 1955 Ted Grant was selected as the parliamentary candidate for Walton. However, in an anticipation of what happened in the 1980's, he was manoevered out by the officials backed by the right-wing dominated National Executive Committee.

Walton Labour Party remained a stronghold for the forces of Marxism in the late 1950s. In 1959, George McCartney, a supporter of *Socialist Fight*, the forerunner of *Militant*, was selected as Labour's Prospective Parliamentary Candidate for Walton. In this battle he easily defeated Woodrow Wyatt, then a supporter of *Tribune* but now a rabid right winger. Unfortunately, the 1959 general election, against all expectations, was a victory for the Tories. Despite a tremendous campaign, Labour failed to win Walton.

Among those who joined Walton Labour Party in 1957, thereby coming into contact with the ideas of Marxism, was Keith Dickinson, one of the five *Militant* Editorial Board members expelled from the Labour Party in 1983. He recalls how even in the difficult period of the 1950s, the Marxists on Merseyside saw youth as the key to the future transformation of the labour movement:

> Walton Labour Party Youth Section had started producing *Rally* at the end of 1957. I was made the business manager. Walton Youth Section was the only one that existed on the whole of Merseyside if not in Lancashire at this time, the Labour League of Youth having been wound up as a national organisation by the right-wing dominated NEC in 1956.
>
> Walton Youth Section was attended by people from all over the Merseyside area, and the editorial board of *Rally* reflected this. Pauline Knight, who later married Pat Wall, was on from the beginning. Pat Wall who had been secretary of Garston CLP at the age of 16 back in 1952, was in the army at the time and came onto the *Rally's* editorial board later. Other prominent people were Beryl Deane, who was the editorial and organisational driving force behind the magazine, and Don Hughes who was the main political guiding hand from Walton itself. The *Rally* rapidly built up sales which were significant considering the difficulty of the period, during the years of the long post war boom, for the forces of Marxism. A large number of copies were sold in Liverpool itself, with a large distribution also in London, Tyneside and Swansea. (Interview with the Authors)

The main task for Marxists at this time was to defend their programme and ideas against reformism and ultra-leftism. The forerunners of *Militant*, gathered round the journal *Socialist Fight*, argued against the ultra lefts on the outskirts of the labour movement who had written off the Labour Party because it was dominated by the right wing. Marxism predicted the inevitable decline of capitalism, and with this the intensification of the struggle between the classes. This in turn would be reflected in the growth of the left in the Labour Party and the trade unions.

Militant in the 1960s

The harbinger of this movement was the 1960 apprentices' strike. One hundred thousand young engineers struck nationally for improved conditions and a shortening of the period of apprenticeship. Terry Harrison, the secretary of the Apprentices Committee on Merseyside, was already a supporter of the ideas of Marxism. Ted Mooney, the Vice-Chair of the committee, relates how he was drawn into activity:

The Young Socialists in Liverpool actively helped the apprentices, but they were only a handful of people. I took a leaflet into work to circulate. A mass meeting of apprentices was organised and they called for a strike. The mood was euphoric. The apprentices began touring the factories and shipyards *en bloc* and the strike on Merseyside really took off, strike committees were set up, and I became the Merseyside strike committee chairman. After two weeks of strike action, a substantial rise of 17 shillings (85 pence) a week and other concessions were won. The young workers clearly understood the nature of the strike and had to organise collections for the payment of hardship money. They had an instinctive understanding of the need for organisation. (Interview with the Authors)

This understanding led Ted Mooney to become involved in the Walton Young Socialists, where he became attracted to the ideas of Marxism. Both Terry Harrison and Ted Mooney have over the subsequent decades played an important role in building support for the ideas of *Militant* in the city. Other young workers, such as Tony Mulhearn, were won to *Militant's* ideas by long standing Marxists in the printing industry.

Contrary to the usual experience of Marxist groups in their formative periods, in which intellectuals and students usually play a predominant role, the rebirth of Marxism in Liverpool was soundly based on young workers. Right from the start, *Militant's* supporters, although not known yet by that name, had a firm basis within the trade unions. With small forces they were able to lead a number of important strikes. In 1964 another apprentices strike broke out, under the leadership of *Militant* supporters in Liverpool. Upwards of 10,000 apprentices in Liverpool and Manchester came out in a week long stoppage which resulted in increases in wages and concessions on the length of the apprentices' training. This was particularly the case in unions such as the printers, the building workers, and the electricians. It was from these forces that *Militant* drew its support when the paper was founded in October 1964. At this stage, the main task was one of propaganda and agitation for the ideas of socialism and Marxism within the labour movement. Whereas on a national plane *Militant* supporters worked first of all in the Labour Party Young Socialists, in Liverpool this was to run parallel with extremely successful work in the Labour Party and in the trade unions.

The main pole of attraction for the Liverpool working class was to change at each stage in the struggle. In the 1960s, particularly in the battles against the Wilson government's attempts to shackle the trade unions through its 'In Place of Strife' measures, it was the Trades Council which played a key role in organising one-day strikes and other opposition.

Tony Mulhearn became a delegate to the Liverpool Trades Council in 1964, shortly after the election of the first Wilson government. During the following months and years sharp debates and clashes took place over the direction being taken by the Labour government. Bill Sefton, who in 1963 had assumed the leadership of the Labour group on the city council on the death of Jack Braddock, became president of the Trades council and Labour Party after the previous president Eric Heffer had been elected to parliament. Sefton strenuously defended the policies of the government on devaluation, import controls, incomes policy, etc.

In 1964 Labour also took control of the Liverpool City Council. A financial crisis was smouldering, which three years later was to explode around the issue of council rents. Discovering a large deficit in the housing revenue account, Sefton proposed that this be bridged by substantial rent increases of 10 shillings (50 pence), a 25 per cent increase in some cases.

When the news of the proposed rent increases reached the hard pressed council tenants a howl of protest went up. They already paid about 25 per cent of their average income in rents, the highest figure in Western Europe. The question for the left was how to give the mood of anger organised expression.

The Executive Committee of the Trades Council and Labour Party agreed to organise the tenants. Meetings of the tenants were held all over the city. Eddie Loyden led the opposition in the Labour group and, together with Tony Mulhearn, addressed many of the tenants' meetings. Thousands of tenants were drawn into the struggle. The Trades Council and Labour Party was divided with a majority voting against the rent increases. Eventually Sefton was compelled to retreat, the rents were increased but by far smaller amounts than originally proposed. *Militant* supporters played a key role in organising the tenants, assisting them in setting up tenants' associations, and drawing them towards the labour movement. These events proved to be an important dress rehearsal for the struggle against the Tories' Housing Finance Act in 1971-3. In a development which reflected the tenants' disillusionment with right-wing Labour, the Liberal Party got a foothold in Liverpool politics in the 1973 council elections.

The Bus Strike

1968 marked a new development in the leadership of the Trades Council and Labour Party. Eddie Loyden had been elected president for a third consecutive term, and the Wilson government was initiating a drive for cuts in public expenditure. Transport was one of the targets. The Liverpool bus workers were told one-man operation of buses would have to be accepted for a wage increase of 50 pence a week. The management claimed that they were prevented from offering more by Labour's Incomes Policy.

For the first time since 1926 they took strike action. All Liverpool's 3000 bus workers were out. The Trades Council Executive, on which *Militant* supporters now had an important influence, met to see what support could be given. A resolution calling for a 24-hour all-out Liverpool strike in support of the bus workers was carried. The following day Tony Mulhearn addressed a mass meeting of the striking bus workers in the Liverpool stadium. He conveyed the decision of support and received warm applause. The day of the strike saw an estimated 50,000 workers take some form of action in support of the busmen. A demonstration of 8000 marched through Liverpool. The strike was in its ninth week, with enormous pressure being brought to bear on the employers, the Tory controlled council, to reach a settlement. Two weeks later the management withdrew the ultimatum to impose one-man buses and agreed to negotiate. The bus workers returned to work having secured what they saw as a great victory.

A major battle opened up in August 1969, when GEC−AEI−EEC announced 3,000 redundancies on Merseyside. Two *Militant* supporters, Ted Mooney and Tony Aitman, were on the Joint Action Committee along with Tony Byrne, which called a one-day strike on 13 August, bringing 10,000 workers out. The workers were eventually defeated, with two of the three factories on Merseyside being closed.

In Place of Strife

By 1969 British capitalism found itself retreating on the world markets, profits were being squeezed. Ninety per cent of strikes between 1960 and 1968 had been unofficial. Succumbing to the pressure from the baying hounds of Fleet Street and the Confederation of British Industry, the Wilson government produced a White Paper entitled 'In Place of Strife'. This proposed making unofficial industrial action a criminal offence.

The publication of the White Paper by Labour Minister Barbara Castle provoked uproar in the workplaces. This opposition was reflected on the Liverpool Trades Council and Labour Party, which received a deluge of resolutions calling for organised opposition to the White Paper.

Mass meetings of shop stewards and demonstrations were organised. Eddie Loyden, as president, addressed numerous meetings. *Militant* supporters produced resolutions and statements articulating the opposition to the White paper, but also explaining theoretically how the crisis of capitalism compelled the right wing down the road of attacking the unions.

In March 1969 a demonstration of 20,000 marched through Liverpool demanding the withdrawal of the White Paper. Such was the pressure from below that the TUC General Council was forced to come out against the White Paper. Eventually, in June, the government abandoned its proposed anti-union legislation. The significance of the retreat was not lost on the ruling class, who blasted out in the *Daily Mirror*: 'Power resides, not in 10 Downing Street, but in the headquarters of the TUC.'

As if to prove again the axiom that history repeats itself, first as a tragedy and then as a farce, behind the scenes of these great events the right wing on the Labour Party NEC were working to sabotage the Trades Council and Labour Party. These moves foreshadowed the right-wing attack on the Liverpool District Labour Party sixteen years later.

Acting on a bogus complaint made in 1962-seven years earlier-they moved to split the joint body, hoping thereby to remove the pressure of the radicalised unions away from the Labour Party. The resistance in the Liverpool labour movement, like in 1985, was almost unanimous, but the right wing ignored the voice of the membership. By bureaucratic, blackmailing manoeuvres, they forced the delegates to accept the separation—on pain of placing themselves outside the labour movement. As with the attacks in the 1980s, the right wing welcomed the split believing it would ensure their control of the city council and a period of calm. Events rudely shattered these illusions. They were to learn that while right-wing sabotage may slow down or derail the movement of the working class for a time, the will of the labour movement, if correctly organised, will eventually reassert itself.

As a result of the Wilson government's actions in attempting to placate the representatives of a diseased, crisis ridden capitalism by attacking workers' wages, conditions and their organisations, the Tories were swept to power in June 1970, against the forecasts of the opinion polls. A Labour majority of 96 was converted into a Tory majority of 30. When pressed to explain the result, Wilson said: 'People could not tell the difference between Tory and Labour.' By then unemployment had reached 600,000.

The Fisher Bendix and Lucas Occupations

In December 1971, the Thorn Engineering Combine announced the closure of its Fisher Bendix plant in Kirkby, which employed 600 workers. The workers decided to fight by occupying the plant. The Trades Council immediately moved to organise support and a statement prepared by Tony Mulhearn and Terry Harrison was presented to an all-Liverpool mass meeting of shop stewards. This statement called for industrial and financial support and linked the Fisher Bendix workers' struggle with the need to defeat the Tory government. The statement was enthusiastically supported by the delegates and shop stewards. Collections throughout Merseyside were begun and workers began picketing the plant. Months of intense activity, during which Fisher Bendix became a *cause célèbre*, ended in victory: the plant was saved by a new owner.

The occupation at CAV Lucas, a motor component plant employing 1600 workers, lasted for four months in 1972. The determination of the workforce was unfortunately not matched by the leadership nationally, although people like Hugh Scanlon and Jack Jones were giants compared to the trade-union leaders of the 1980s. The company was determined to succeed, and after a heroic fight the CAV workers were compelled to accept defeat.

Tory Prime Minister Edward Heath represented the hard nosed business wing of the Tory Party, and was determined to curb the trade unions and to cut back public spending. The main vehicles for securing these objectives were the Industrial Relations Act and the Housing Finance Act. Like its forerunner, Barbara Castle's In Place of Strife, the publication of the Industrial Relations Bill provoked a storm of protest throughout the labour movement, particularly on Merseyside.

In a foretaste of the differences in the 1980s, *Militant* supporters came into conflict with Communist Party members on the Trades Council,who opposed linking of the campaign against the Bill with the call for the defeat of the Tories and the return of a Labour government committed to a socialist programme.

In February 1971 a demonstration of 25,000, the largest at that time since 1945, marched through the streets of Liverpool to a rally at the Pier Head. Under such pressure from Liverpool and many other industrial areas, the TUC General Council was pushed into calling the greatest demonstration in its history, 250,000 workers marched from Hyde Park to Trafalgar Square on 21 February 1971. The government was compelled to retreat in 1972, releasing dockers who had been imprisoned under the Industrial Relations Act. This capitulation was brought about by a mass demonstration converging on Pentonville Prison, with the TUC General Council even calling for a one-day general strike Later in 1972 three building workers, the 'Shrewsbury Pickets' were jailed under ancient conspiracy laws.

Running parallel with the campaign against the Tory laws was the battle being waged against the Housing Finance Act. To a greater extent than the movement of 1967-8, council tenants in their thousands moved into action against the Tory government's proposals to double rents over a three-year period.

Again the Trades Council moved into action. Ted Mooney prepared a pamphlet repudiating point by point the Tory argument on 'Fair Rents'. The Trades Council and the Tenants' Associations jointly arranged meetings throughout the city to explain the implications of the Tory proposals. The Liverpool

Tom Mann addressing strikers, 1911.

Part of the huge demonstration, Bloody Sunday 13 August 1911.

CITY OF LIVERPOOL.

PUBLIC WARNING.

I, the Lord Mayor and Chief Magistrate of the said City, hereby warn and urge all persons not having any business to transact in the centre of the City, to keep away from those parts of the City, especially the neighbourhoods of St. George's Hall, Lime Street, Christian Street, Scotland Road, and any other parts where trouble has taken place or is likely to take place. Especially do I request all women and children to remain at home as much as possible during the disturbed condition of the City.

Large numbers of persons have assembled in the disturbed streets for the purpose of seeing what is going on, and I warn all such persons that if the Authorities are called upon to act, innocent citizens are as likely to be injured as those against whom any drastic measures on the part of the Police or the Military are directed.

S. M. HUTCHINSON,

Lord Mayor.

14th August, 1911.

C. Tinling & Co., Ltd., Printing Contractors, 53, Victoria Street, Liverpool.

Proclamation posted the day after Bloody Sunday.

HMS Antrim anchored in the Mersey, 1911.

The Police Strike, August 1919. Tanks on St George's Plateau.

Soldiers take over the city during the 1919 Police Strike.

Demonstrating unemployed workers occupy the Walker Art Gallery, 1921.

Trades Council was the body which organised and drew together the tenants' associations and the organs of the Labour movement. Reflecting this pressure, the Liverpool Borough Labour Party, although controlled by the right wing and virtually dormant for three years, came out against the Bill.

When the vote for implementation of the Act took place in the council chamber, 27 Labour councillors voted with the Tories in favour, 21 Labour councillors voted against. Such was the revulsion against the right wing that the 21, including Ted Mooney and Eddie Loyden, formed their own Labour group and began meeting separately. The campaign to defy the Act continued, culminating in the imprisonment of some Kirkby tenants.

But the end of the Heath government was in sight. In 1972 the miners struck over wages and achieved a great victory. In the winter of 1973-4, faced with a second miners' strike, Heath went to the electorate on the slogan of 'who runs the country' and lost the election. One of Harold Wilson's first acts on becoming Prime Minister, recognising the consciousness of the labour movement, was to repeal the Housing Finance Act and the Industrial Relations Act.

The decade between 1964-74 was a turbulent period of struggle for the Merseyside labour movement during which *Militant* supporters and close allies on the left made a powerful impact on events. This prepared the basis for the historic events of 1983 and after. Another factor in the struggle of the decade 1973-84 was the rise of the Liberals in Liverpool. They became the largest party in the city council in 1973, the year after Labour's right wing joined with the Tories to implement the Housing Finance Act.

The 1974-9 Labour Government

With the onset of the world economic recession of 1974-5, the Labour government of Harold Wilson came into conflict with workers. Instead of carrying out socialist policies, the Labour leadership, attempting to manage capitalism in a period of crisis, embarked on attacks on workers' living standards, in particular through a series of pay policies.

In the winter of 1977 the firefighters came out on strike in what became a bitter dispute, with the army being used as strike breakers. A number of firefighters were attracted to Marxism on Merseyside during the dispute, including Terry Fields.

The following year saw another important dispute for the development of *Militant's* role. The closure of the Western Ship Repairers yard in Birkenhead led to a picket by the workforce. *Militant* supporters in the area were actively involved from the outset and effectively led the dispute. The position raised by *Militant* supporters was adopted by the action committee and the workers at mass meetings. This included the demand for the Labour government to nationalise the yard, under workers' control and management, to protect jobs.

Many mass meetings were held, and two demonstrations were organised through Birkenhead. The right-wing Labour leadership, however, refused to act. Although the yard was not saved, the role played by *Militant* supporters in the dispute, and the taking up of *Militant's* ideas by the workers in struggle, marked a qualitative development of the intervention of Marxism in industrial disputes on Merseyside.

At the 1978 Labour Party Conference a young Liverpool worker, Terry Duffy, the delegate from Wavertree Labour Party, moved the crucial resolution which for the first time clearly committed the Labour Party Conference to reject policies of wage restraint.

In the general election the following year, Tony Mulhearn was selected as Labour's candidate for the Tory seat of Crosby. Despite the Tories' sweeping victory nationally, he polled over 15,000 votes, a creditable 26 per cent of the poll.

As a result of the experiences of the working class of Merseyside, which felt the onset of economic downturn before it seriously affected other parts of the country, Marxism began to grow through the 1970s within the labour and trade union movement. A new generation came onto the scene in the late 1970s, prominent amongst them being Derek Hatton. A perspective was then worked out for the likely course of developments within the labour and trade union movement, in which it was concluded that the city council and the District Labour Party would play a crucial role. Only the Marxists had a worked-out programme and perspective that could prepare the Liverpool working class for the mighty events that were about to unfold in the 1980s.

3.
The Road to Power

THE SEEDS of the Liverpool conflict were sown with the coming to power of the Thatcher government in May 1979. A central plank of its programme was to cut public expenditure and, in particular, to slash local government spending. British capitalism demanded that the Tories should hold down working-class living standards as the precondition for boosting their flagging profits. One aspect of Thatcher's monetarist policies was to squeeze wages. Another was to cut down the so-called 'social wage', that is, expenditure on housing, social services, education, etc.

In doing this Thatcher was able to build on the retreats of the Labour government of 1974-9. It was Anthony Crosland, as Minister of the Environment under the Wilson government, who proclaimed: 'The party is over.' This marked the abandonment of the Keynesian philosophy of Labour's right wing. Yet Crosland had himself been prominent among the reformists who had written books attempting to prove that increased public expenditure was a means of softening the contradictions of capitalism and eliminating the cycle of booms and slumps.

Marxism had, on a theoretical level, refuted these ideas many times, in works such as Ted Grant's *Will There be a Slump?* But it was the harsh reality of the Wilson-Callaghan government which dealt a crushing blow to Labour's right-wing theoreticians. With its demands for draconian cuts, the team from the International Monetary Fund (IMF) in 1976 effectively sealed the fate of Crosland-Healey reformism. The present leadership of the Labour Party conveniently glosses over the fact that in 1977 it was Labour who carried through the biggest single cut in government expenditure, a total of £8000 million. Denis

Healey, as Chancellor of the Exchequer, pre-dated Thatcher in his advocacy of 'sound money'. Through their policies during 1974-9 the Labour leaders paved the way for Thatcher.

Liverpool, already one of Europe's most deprived cities, was to suffer more than most under the iron heel of Thatcher and her acolytes in the Department of the Environment. In the first phase of resurgent Toryism, from 1979-83, various coalitions of Tories and Liberals held power in Liverpool. Contrary to their later claims, the Liberals were more than willing accomplices in Thatcher's onslaught against Liverpool. The slashing of the city's grants from central government had a devastating effect on the lives and conditions of hundreds of thousands of working people. Within months of Thatcher's victory, experts warned the government that rather than cutting local government expenditure, massive amounts needed to be pumped in, in order to break the cycle of deprivation which had become so evident in the 1960s.

Most big cities over the previous 20 years had suffered a population loss, which in turn had cut their income from rates. Liverpool had experienced a 33 per cent drop, compared for example to a 17.5 per cent drop in the population of London. The more mobile and affluent were able to escape to the suburbs, leaving in the inner city the old and the poor who were even more dependent on the resources of the council than in the past.

Through a variety of schemes, successive governments since the 1960s had attempted to bribe the capitalists to invest in and regenerate the inner city. Millions of pounds had been pumped into the coffers of firms who, after a few years, escaped to lusher pastures.

Toxteth Explodes

Between 1974-9 conditions worsened considerably. While there was a vital need for increased public-sector expenditure, the actual income of the city declined dramatically. Total income fell by 18 per cent in this period, while income from rates fell by 25 per cent. The total real net expenditure fell by 14 per cent from the peak level of 1975-6. In the cycle of falling population, loss of income and increased social deprivation, Liverpool was like a tinderbox. By 1981 the number of people unemployed in

Merseyside was almost equal to the number of unemployed in the whole of Wales.

In July 1981 a part of the city, Toxteth, exploded. For the first time outside of Northern Ireland, CS Gas was used by the police against a riot which was far more desperate, wider in scope, and more furious than the earlier uprisings in St Pauls in Bristol and Brixton in South London. Black and white youth joined together in fighting against police harassment and oppression. But the causes of the riot lay in the area's terrible social conditions, which typified Liverpool as a whole. Unemployment affected both black and white youth. In fact, unemployment of youth in Croxteth, an almost totally white area, was greater than in Toxteth. In the conflict between the police and rioters, one young man was killed by police. Since then, the area has virtually become a 'no-go' area for the police, with the total alienation of the population from the police.

The Liberals resorted to typical 'red scare' tactics, backed up by the media in Liverpool and nationally. *Militant* supporters, and members of the Liverpool Labour Party Young Socialists, were singled out as the instigators of the riot! Clare Doyle, a member of the *Militant* Editorial Board who had played a prominent role in the Labour Committee for the Defence of Brixton set up in the wake of the Brixton riots, was pictured by the gutter press as 'Red Clare'.

Her fleeting visit to Liverpool to speak at a meeting was exploited as the pretext for portraying her as an incendiarist, visiting the city to throw fuel on the fire. But riots have never been the method of Marxists. As Martin Luther King put it: 'riots are the voice of the voiceless'. They express the inchoate rage and despair of an alienated section of working class youth, particularly of black youth. The method of Marxists, however, is to develop a class-conscious, politically aware working class.

A Minister for Merseyside

In the wake of the Toxteth riots the ruling class took fright. Thatcher sanctimoniously condemned the rioters, denying any link between the uprising and social conditions. Nevertheless, Michael Heseltine, then the darling of the Tory Conference, was rushed to Merseyside as a new Minister for the area. Millions of pounds were poured into the area-but with little or no effect in terms of jobs for native Liverpudlians. In 1981 Liverpool, amongst other cities, was given the 'benefit' of an Enterprise Zone. Companies were offered relaxed planning requirements, exemption from rates for non-domestic property, and 100 per cent capital allowances for industrial and commercial properties. Liverpool's Development Officer at this time declared: 'With no rates to pay, it is a tremendous bargain'. Those who benefitted were mostly 'out of town' contractors with their own specialised labour. Patches of green field were laid down throughout the Toxteth area and plenty of trees were planted. Liverpool wags commented that it was mostly the dog population which benefited from Heseltine's spell in Liverpool.

Moreover, what was given with the one hand was more than cancelled out with the other. The housing charity Shelter commented in its journal *Roof*: 'There has been something ludicrous in Mr Heseltine's professions of concern about the problems he has seen on Merseyside, when it was he who savaged the Housing Investment Programme and re-calculated the Rate Support Grant to favour the shire counties at the expense of inner cities.'

Under the auspices of the Liberals, Heseltine attempted to coax the building companies to regenerate the inner city. Before the Tories' U-turn, Heseltine had been eagerly wielding the axe against local government spending. Liverpool's Liberal-Tory coalition had been an eager accomplice. In 1980 Liverpool was expected by Heseltine to make 'savings' of £12.7 million. In the three months after the Liberals took effective control in May 1980, they had slashed spending by £7.5 million. Trevor Jones, Liberal council leader, boasted 'We did this before Michael Heseltine's letter arrived.' (*Sunday Times*, 27 July 1980) The Liberal-Tory coalition set about dismantling all the conquests of the Liverpool labour movement in the field of local government. In house-building and repairs, employment , and the care of the elderly and sick, there was an all-out offensive.

Flushed with their victory in the 1980 local elections, and backed from Westminster, the pro-capitalist parties considered they had a mandate for their 'counter-revolution'. The 80,000 council tenants were the first to feel the 'firm smack' of Liberal-Tory rule. Despite furious protests from Labour's ranks and indignation from council tenants' leaders, a 34 per cent rent rise was steered through the council. The architect of this increase, Richard Kemp, resigned as Chair of Housing as a 'personal protest' for being 'compelled' to act as Heseltine's butcher. But after making this gesture, the 'martyr' was soon back in the same saddle. Kemp voiced the Liberals' deep loathing for council housing and for the city's poor inhabitants. Expressing concern at the 'class and social balance', he declared in March 1981: 'Really, we ought to be building houses for rich people. What Liverpool needs above all is more wealthy inhabitants. The dominance of council tenants only fosters the ghetto mentality' (*The Times*, 5 March 1981).

In propounding their political credo, Liberal spokesmen revealed the brutal reality of their position. Just before the demise of Liberal rule Richard Kemp declared: 'We are not ashamed of the fact that 4500 jobs have gone from the city council'. Sir Trevor Jones, their leader, earlier declared: 'We are proud of the fact that we have reduced jobs in the city council...we think we can reduce still more.' No wonder the Tory Leader, Reg Flude, remarked: 'We don't need the majority on the city council-the Liberal Party are carrying out our policies'. The Tories even tried to present themselves as being to the left of the Liberals: 'The Liberals are more reactionary than the Tory Party', claimed John Lee, a leading Conservative.

These statements were used like clubs by Labour who attacked the Liberals and their Tory cohorts in a series of brilliant propaganda news-sheets and leaflets. The District Labour Party's *Liverpool Labour News* and *Not the Liverpool Echo* were distributed to every household in the city. Using facts and figures and arguments this material undoubtedly played a key role in preparing the way for Labour's victory in the 1983 elections.

Not only the council tenants, who, prior to 1983, were paying the highest rents in the country outside of London , but also the householders suffered under the Liberal-Tory coalition. In 1981, on the casting vote of Sir Trevor Jones, the city increased rates by 21.5 per cent for the following year. In contrast to the position under Labour from 1983 until 1987, the average householder was forced to pay massive rate increases as the Liberals passed on the Tory government's draconian cuts.

Later it became a theme of Liberal-Tory propaganda that Liverpool's plight was due to the 'dogmatism' of the *Militant*-inspired city Labour Party in refusing to work in 'partnership with big business and the Tory government'. But what was the result of all the Liberals' special pleading to the Tories and business interests? In reality, the government turned a deaf ear. The Tories only listened to Liverpool's demands when the city was roused into a mass campaign of opposition by the incoming Labour council.

In virtually every department, there was little difference between the Liberals and the government itself. The government's plan to abolish county councils was enthusiastically supported by the Liberal leader, Sir Trevor Jones: 'I think the Environment Minister is moving along the right lines. His ideas support our view that the Merseyside County Council is a disaster and the sooner it is demolished the better.' (*The Times,* 27 August 1981) One of the effects of the abolition of the county council was a massive 50 per cent increase in fares and a catastrophic deterioration of public transport throughout the Merseyside area.

Liberal 'Allies' and Opponents

In the aftermath of their defeats in 1983 and 1984, the Liberals were to form an unholy alliance with the so-called Black Caucus-a completely unrepresentative group of mostly middle-class elements who lived mainly in the suburbs while claiming to be 'community leaders' in the Liverpool 8 area. Among their ranks were to be found people with a violent past. But it had not always been sweetness and light between these two allies.

In 1982 the Liberals announced that they intended to cut the grant to the Charles Wootton Centre in Toxteth and to the Vauxhall Law Centre. Indeed, at one stage the Liberals were intending to withdraw completely the Law Centre's £26,000 grant. Their hand was only stayed by a demonstration of the Black Caucus and others, and a noisy disruption of council business. This anticipated the methods the Black Caucus were to use subsequently in attempting to prevent the appointment of Sam Bond as Race Relations Officer by the Labour-controlled council.

At the same time, the Liberals tried to muzzle criticism from the opposition. Labour Party members, including councillors, who attempted to expose the reality of Liberal rule, were met with the threat of legal action for libel. Around election times especially, Liberal lawyers, notably Rex Makin, threw writs out almost as if they were confetti.

The 1981 County Council Elections

All the dirty tricks subsequently used by the Liberals up and down the country, from Bermondsey to Knowsley North, in a bid to climb to local prominence and eventual power, were first tried out in Liverpool against the Labour Party, specifically against *Militant* supporters. In Liverpool, however, Labour demonstrated that by taking the Liberals head on, their accusations could be refuted and Labour could get its policies across to the working class. The basis for this was the clarification of methods for fighting government cuts which were thrashed out in the Liverpool Labour Party as a consequence of the 1980 budget set by Labour.

In 1980, when Labour held a tenuous minority control, the government had imposed swingeing cuts. The response of Labour's right wing had not been to confront the government, but to opt, albeit reluctantly, for a 50 per cent increase in the rates to avoid further cuts in local services. The Marxists had been implacably opposed to such a course of action. In the debate on the 1980-1 budget, Derek Hatton in the Labour Group and Tony Mulhearn in the District Labour Party, pressed for rate increases no greater than the rate of inflation plus a small amount to pay for the promised reforms in Labour's programme.

This policy was rejected by the right wing. When it went to the council the main opposition to the Labour leadership was provided not by Liberals and Tories, but by Derek Hatton, who moved an amendment in the chamber. This provoked outrage from Labour's right-wing leaders. In their own cynical fashion, the Liberals contrived a 'division of labour' among themselves to allow the 50 per cent rate increase to go through. Some, like Trevor Jones, abstained in the vote: others voted with the Tories to oppose the budget. Later, they claimed to have opposed Labour's massive rate-increasing budget.

The Marxists warned that Labour would pay a heavy price in subsequent polls, and this was unfortunately borne out. In the 1980 elections Labour lost 6 seats-at that time, the highest loss by any party in the city since 1964. But as Lenin once said, 'an ounce of experience is worth a ton of theory.' Labour's ranks fully digested the debacle of the 1980-1 Budget. The arguments of the Marxists were reinforced and became the centrepiece of Labour's campaign in the next two years, leading to the advances made in 1982.

Accusations from the press, the Liberals and, of course, the Tories, that Labour was a party of 'extremism', were answered nationally by Labour's right-wing with a campaign of witch-hunts and expulsions. This was a gift to the capitalists. The constant refrain of the press at that stage was that *Militant* was 'an electoral albatross' around Labour's neck, and the right wing seized on this as the excuse for a campaign against the left-wing.

But at every turn, not just in Liverpool but in other areas of Britain, the performance of *Militant* supporters standing as Labour candidates contrasted very favourably with that of right wingers. Brighton Kemptown, for instance, was a stronghold of *Militant* support at that time, and the Parliamentary candidate was Rod Fitch, a well-known *Militant* supporter.

In the 1981 county council elections in Brighton Labour scored a spectacular 14.3 per cent increase in its vote. This was the biggest swing to Labour in the south of England. Yet in Cardiff South-East, the stronghold of ex-Prime Minister James Callaghan, there was a swing against Labour of 5.3 per cent. In Liverpool there was a 10 per cent swing to Labour in Wavertree, where the activities of *Militant* supporters led by Tony Mulhearn and Derek Hatton were already having an effect.

The contrast between the performance of *Militant* supporters and the right wing could not have been more striking. The same picture was to emerge in the 1982 elections and particularly in the crucial municipal and general elections of 1983.

1982-The Liberal Lie Machine

The Liberals, feeling the ground slip from beneath their feet, engaged in a desperate scare campaign in the run-up to the 1982 local elections. Under the slogan of 'Marxists Out-Liberals In', Trevor Jones and his supporters brought up all the old shibboleths. They dragged in the monarchy, attempted to whip up religious sectarianism, and, above all, played on the memory

of 1980, threatening the Liverpool population with massive
Labour rate rises.

The Liberals, desperate to prevent Labour's advance, flooded
the city with a series of leaflets under such lurid slogans as
'Trotsky lives inside Britain's Labour Party'. Pictures of the
Queen were featured in their leaflets under the headline: 'They
even say: "The Queen must go".' This was alongside entirely
false statements attributed to Derek Hatton, who allegedly
endorsed 'civil war and bloodshed'. The clear intention was to
connect the Marxists with the idea that *Militant* favoured
violence against the monarchy.

Militant demands the abolition of the monarchy, on the
grounds that it is a reserve weapon of the ruling class to be used
in the future, particularly against a left Labour government.
The ruling class has been very careful to preserve the
monarchy's powers of veto. This was shown when they were
used in November 1975 in Australia-through Sir John Kerr, the
Governor-General appointed by the Queen-to dismiss the
Labour government led by Gough Whitlam. In the same way in
Britain the monarchy still formally has the power to select who
should be the prime minister and the government. Repeating
the lies of the *Echo,* the Liberals stated in one leaflet: 'They want
to ban religion in favour of *Militant* atheism'. To be fair to
Trevor Jones and his crew, they adopted a non-sectarian
position in their onslaught against Labour and *Militant*. They
carried photographs of Catholic and Protestant churches
together on the same leaflet, claiming 'that means the closure of
local churches and church schools'.

In another leaflet they claimed that *Militant* supporters wanted
to 'let the city burn'. Labour canvassers pointed out that it was
Liberal-Tory policies which resulted in the 1981 riots and the
burning of a part of the city. Intending to make electors' flesh
creep, one Liberal leaflet declared 'How could anyone let this
Militant mob run their affairs?' Featured prominently in the
photograph were Derek Hatton and John Hamilton.

As an example of *Militant* support for violence, they stated:
'Last week, on hearing at the Policy and Finance Committee that
a Liberal councillor had had his finger bitten off by a dog,
councillor Hatton moved a motion of "Congratulations to the
dog"'. Harking back to the 1980 budget, they proclaimed: 'Vote
for *Militant* Labour and double your rates'.

A complicating factor for Labour in Liverpool was the sabotage by Labour's right wing with their constant attacks on the left and particularly on *Militant*. On their leaflets the Liberals even produced a tear-off slip which people were urged to send to Labour leader Michael Foot, calling on him to disassociate himself from *Militant* and demanding 'an urgent decision on the inquiry [the *Hayward-Hughes Report*] into the Militant Tendency'. Throughout the saga of Liverpool the statements of Labour's right wing would be continually used as a weapon by Labour's opponents to divide and weaken the struggle against the Tory government.

Prominent supporters of the ideas of *Militant* rigorously defended the right of *Militant* and its supporters to be part of the Labour Party. In leaflets distributed to the households of constituencies for which they were parliamentary candidates, Derek Hatton, Tony Mulhearn and Terry Harrison consistently explained *Militant*'s real ideas and policies:

> The Fleet Street press, who attacked the railwaymen and health workers during their struggle for decent wages and conditions, also pour out poison about socialists in the Labour Party. In particular, they are trying to interfere in Labour Party affairs by campaigning for the expulsion of supporters of the socialist newspaper *Militant*.

Leaflets went on to demand:

> *Militant* supporters campaign alongside other Labour Party members for a Labour government. But we believe the next Labour government should introduce measures in the interest of the working class, not just repeat the disastrous policies of wage restraint, cuts in services, increased nuclear arms spending and rising unemployment which led to the defeat of the 1974-9 Labour government. *Militant* supporters call for Labour to introduce a 35-hour working week to create 1 million jobs, a £90 minimum wage to end poverty-a massive scheme of public works to build homes, hospitals and schools...
>
> *Militant* supporters support every democratic right-the right to vote, free speech, right of assembly, the right to strike. We fight for an end to the grip of the five millionaires who own the press, controlling what goes into the papers, and for public ownership and full access to the press for all organisations. Join the Labour Party and help ensure it becomes a mass workers' party, committed to socialist policies. Make sure the

right wing in the Labour leadership do not succeed in wrecking Labour's chances by splitting the Party from top to bottom, in their campaign to expel rank and file socialists. Help build a mass, campaigning Party which fights against the Tories, unemployment and poverty.

The growth in *Militant*'s support did not drop from the sky. It was a product of the catastrophic material conditions in Liverpool and Merseyside as a whole. *Militant* supporters in most of the constituencies in the area were not just tolerated but enthusiastically welcomed as energetic workers for Labour. One right winger commented in 1982 to the *Financial Times* correspondent, Margaret Van Hattem:

> They are very hard workers. They lick stamps, fold pamphlets, canvass tirelessly for the Party, speak at all sorts of meetings. Whenever there is an industrial dispute, they are in there from the start, picketing, lending support, drawing up resolutions for the workers. But they are a bit intense. They attract a lot of young people...Two of the leading *Militant* activists in Liverpool have already fought unwinnable seats for the Labour Party—Mr Tony Mulhearn, Chairman of the General Management Committee in neighbouring Wavertree fought the seat of Crosby in the last General Election; and Mr Terry Harrison, a full-time *Militant* worker, fought the seat for Liverpool in the European election last year.

Not a whimper, not a hint of any demands to expel *Militant* supporters when they were fighting unwinnable seats and doing the 'donkey work' of the Labour Party. Indeed, in what was then the Wavertree constituency, Tony Mulhearn and Derek Hatton were extremely energetic activists in the 1979 general election campaign where the Labour candidate Roy Morris, in the words of Derek Hatton, 'was solidly right wing; we knew that his commitment to the Labour Party was very tenuous. Nevertheless we energetically campaigned for him in the 1979 General Election, and two weeks after the election he defected to the Social Democratic Alliance.'

The right wing of the Labour Party, were prepared to tolerate *Militant* as election workhorses, even to turn a blind eye to the political influence exercised by *Militant* supporters in the Labour Party Young Socialists. But once *Militant* supporters began to be selected as parliamentary candidates they began to foam at the mouth. A frenzied campaign was whipped up against alleged 'entrism' and 'infiltration' into the Labour Party on Merseyside and elsewhere.

The 1979 European Elections

A hint of this was given when Terry Harrison was selected as the candidate for the European elections in 1979. He fought a spirited campaign in what was in general a lacklustre event. In contrast to the right wing who echoed the ideas of the ruling class, and most of the left who opposed entry into the Common Market (EEC) on a nationalist basis, Terry Harrison opposed the Common Market, but at the same time fought for a Socialist United States of Europe. In his election material he stated:

> While I stand in total opposition to the EEC, I do this not as a nationalist, but as a fighter in favour of workers' internationalism. Faced with massive multinational companies, I believe that now more than ever, it is crucial for the Labour movement of Europe to link up and fight together on key issues if the employers and their system are to be defeated. The campaign for a 35-hour week is an example of what needs to be done. The launching of a European campaign by the European TUC is a step forward in this regard and needs to be followed up on the question of fighting unemployment, improved wages and other issues which face the workers of Europe.

He pointed out that the workers in Europe face a common enemy, the top 200 companies which dominate the British economy, and the 350 largest European firms which control over 50 per cent of industrial production. He pointed in particular to the need for the working class, through the trade unions, to link their struggles on an all-European basis. For the first time in an election, the idea of Labour representatives receiving no more than the average wage of a skilled worker was raised:

> For them [members of the European Parliament] to seriously fight in the interests of working people, they must be aware of the day-to-day problems faced by workers and their families. How can they possibly do this if their salary is so high that most workers can only dream of having such amounts? Therefore if selected I undertake to take only from my salary the average wage of a skilled worker, and donate the rest back to the labour movement. All my expenses, I believe, should be vetted and questioned by the labour

movement, and I will ensure that this is done. For too long, our representatives have been cut off from the problems facing working people.

This idea of 'a workers'MP on a worker's wage' was to be repeated in other elections on Merseyside and send shock waves of fear through the ranks of the careerist right who dominated the Parliamentary Labour Party . The local press (the *Post* and the *Echo*) tried out in this election the methods that were subsequently to be employed on a massive scale in the slanderous campaign against *Militant* on Merseyside and in particular against the Liverpool City Council. They harped on the theme of Terry Harrison being 'a Trotskyist'. Desperate attempts were made to crowd out the socialist message which he was bringing to working people.

This produced confusion which was sometimes expressed in the most unexpected fashion. Befuddled by the campaign against 'Trotskyism', one elderly woman declared to a Labour canvasser: 'Oh, I don't know whether I can support him, he's a transvestite isn't he?' Such was the hate campaign whipped up that at one stage a gunman fired on Terry Harrison from a tower block while he was canvassing in the Lee Park area of the city. The windscreen of his car was shattered by the shot, narrowly missing him in the process. Less lethal but equally poisonous weapons were to be aimed at *Militant* and its supporters on Merseyside by the media in the following years.

As in all elections, the aim of the Marxists in the European election campaign was not just to turn out the vote, but to touch the workers with ideas and to raise their level of political understanding. Within the limits of the issue, the campaign succeeded admirably in explaining the socialist internationalist ideas of *Militant*. However, Terry Harrison was defeated on a very low poll.

The mass of the workers on Merseyside were indifferent to the outcome of the election. The national results seemed to be a foregone conclusion, with the Tories and the right wing of the Labour Party, backed up by the media, whipping up the prospect of even greater unemployment and impoverishment if Britain ever came out of the EEC. In a unique event for an election, in one polling district in Vauxhall Ward not a single vote for any candidate was recorded! But defeat for Terry Harrison in this election did not check the growth in support for *Militant* amongst the Party rank and file.

Resurgence of the Left Wing

The Tory Government's onslaught against the rights and conditions of the working class, together with the revulsion felt at the policies of the right-wing dominated Labour government of 1974-9, had resulted in a marked shift towards the left within the Labour Party. This was particularly evident on Merseyside.

The resurgent left within the Labour Party and unions gathered around the figure of Tony Benn in the battle over the election of the Deputy Leader of the Labour Party under the new 'electoral college' system in 1981. Tony Benn was only defeated by a handful of votes of those who subsequently defected to the SDP. In the nationwide campaign of meetings conducted by Benn and the left at this time, Merseyside was a bedrock of support. The ecstatic support which Tony Benn received from the Liverpool workers on more than one occasion prompted him to make his famous declaration that the area was 'the graveyard of British capitalism and the birthplace of socialism'.

The enormous shift towards the left in the Labour Party was a challenge to the predominantly right-wing group of MPs who represented Labour in Liverpool at this stage. Toxteth, West Derby and Kirkdale constituencies were represented respectively by arch right wingers Richard Crawshaw, Eric Ogden and Jimmy Dunn. In the well-worn tradition of Labour right wingers, having lost the argument on policy, they then stabbed the labour movement in the back, joining the SDP. Crawshaw and Dunn jumped before they were pushed. Eric Ogden, a 'man of principle', only decided to abandon ship after he had lost a reselection battle by one vote. The party rank and file in two of the three constituencies subsequently selected Marxists as parliamentary candidates, Tony Mulhearn in Toxteth and Terry Fields for Kirkdale. They were joined by Terry Harrison, selected for Edge Hill, held by the Liberal David Alton since the death of Labour right winger, Sir Arthur Irvine, and Derek Hatton, who was selected for Wavertree.

This development was greeted with hysteria by the press: 'Revolution, if ever it comes to Britain, will surely flare first on Merseyside where Labour politics are virtually controlled by the Trotskyist hard men.' Occasionally a sober comment would appear, which would give an inkling of the reasons why *Militant* supporters were being selected as parliamentary candidates:

> Significantly perhaps the six *Militant* supporters share a working-class background and a strong conviction that their own kind have been largely ignored and cheated by those they have elected to represent them in the past. They do not have much time for the trendy middle-class intellectual left, nor for those working- class MPs on the centre and right whom they see as having been corrupted by the taste of power and distanced from their roots by the upper- class atmosphere at Westminster. (*The Times*, 10 December 1981).

These developments were taking place at the same time as the national full-time officers of the Labour Party were conducting an 'investigation' into *Militant*. The then General Secretary of the Labour Party, Ron Hayward, with David Hughes, National Agent, subsequently submitted a report which was accepted by the Labour Party Conference. This set up a register of 'acceptable groups' in the Labour Party. *Militant* was specifically excluded from this register, and this in turn opened the door to the expulsion of the *Militant* Editorial Board in 1983.

The charge of 'entrism' against *Militant* supporters who had been members of the Labour Party for decades, was repeated *ad nauseum* by the press. It is only the press and their right-wing shadows within the Labour Party who can entertain the idea that the ordinary workers who make up the Labour Party membership are like putty to be manipulated by small, secretive, conspiratorial groups of Marxists. In answer to the campaign of the press Wally Edwards, the Liverpool Party Secretary, not a *Militant* supporter, and described by the *Guardian* as 'a Labour official of the old school', stated that 'the four are not entrists or infiltrators, but have been on the local political scene for some time. They are not Johnny-come-latelys.' (*Guardian*, 8 November 1982).

The ruling class had already identified Merseyside as the area likely to cause them the most concern. Even in 1982, Tom King, Local Government Minister, foreshadowing the sentiments of Thatcher at a later stage, declared 'We must stop them [*Militant*] because they are unfit for office and would destroy our country.' The fear of the Marxists by the Tories and the ruling class was well-founded. The economic havoc which had been wreaked during the crisis of 1979-81, together with the measures of the Thatcher government, prepared the near extinction of the Tory Party as a viable force in the area. Anthony Steen, right-wing Tory MP for Wavertree until 1983, when pressed to support the Dunlop workers' fight to keep their factory open replied, 'It is impudence for Mr Eddie Loyden (Labour candidate for Garston) and the Action Committee to come along and demand that the factory stays open.' Such statements were to prepare the political grave for the Tory Party in Liverpool in the election of 1983.

Notwithstanding the forecasts, *Militant* supporters continued to make significant advances. They spearheaded an enormous revitalisation of the labour movement in the area. Speculation was in the air of a general election within the next year. The approach of the Marxists represented a complete break with the pedestrian, low-key approach of the right and sometimes of the left wing in organising and preparing election campaigns.

The right wing had taken the support of the workers for granted. In one canvass of Wavertree a man told Derek Hatton that in 20 years of living in the area no one from the Labour Party had knocked on his door before! A mass campaign to win workers to the Labour Party and to prepare for a general election was launched in all the constituencies.

The mass door-to-door canvassing in Wavertree in 1982 was typical of the local campaigns carried out at this time.Two hundred, predominantly Young Socialists, converged on the area. Three quarters of the constituency was canvassed in a weekend! The same approach was adopted in other Liverpool constituencies. Thousands of new members were won to the party. Connections were cemented with the shop stewards and active workers in union branches by the tireless work of the parliamentary candidates and councillors in support of workers fighting to prevent redundancies etc. Even Dick Crawshaw in one of his rare frank moments was forced to declare 'Many of the Militant Tendency in Toxteth are, I believe, motivated by a genuine desire to change our society for the better.'

The opponents of Labour were taken aback by the sweep, the verve and the elan that was generated in these campaigns. Like tributaries these were to converge into one huge river in the elections both to the council and to Parliament in 1983. The campaign launched in the parliamentary seats were undoubtedly test runs for the spectacular campaigns organised between 1983 and 1985.

The May 1982 Council Elections

Labour's refusal to bow before the avalanche of hostile propaganda from the media and the Tories and Liberals, paid rich dividends in the 1982 elections. In contrast to the dismal performance of Labour in other regions, Labour triumphed in Liverpool. These elections took place during the Falklands War. The 'Falklands factor', so evident in the 1983 General Election, was already exercising an influence. Thatcher, in her conflict with the Argentinian junta over the Falklands, was able to draw on the relics of Britain's past imperialist role.

The memory of former glory, when Britain controlled one quarter of mankind, was drawn on heavily by the ruling class in this conflict. The petit-bourgeois strata, together with certain politically backward sections of the working class, were enraptured by the prospect of a return to some long-lost 'Golden Age'. There was the illusion that just as Britain 'beat the Argies', so the economic and political problems besetting the nation could somehow be conjured away by Thatcher's new imperial grand design. With the Labour leadership providing no serious alternative this potent drug—for a very short period—was able to have a certain effect. The 'Falklands factor' then played a significant part in the 1982 council elections. But even so it was striking that where Labour went out and campaigned on the real issues facing working people and explained a class alternative to the Falklands war, it was possible to cut across this process. In Islington in London, for instance (a left, campaigning party in which *Militant* supporters played some role), the SDP's stranglehold on the council was broken. Every ward was canvassed, sometimes several times over. Even on the eve of the poll, when the SDP brought out a last-minute leaflet, the Labour Party was able to bring out a quick reply and deliver it to every house in the borough. Unfortunately, Islington was the exception to a general rule of Labour indolence and inactivity.

When the votes were counted in Liverpool on 6 May, the Liberals suffered a heavy blow—from which they have still not recovered to this day. The *Echo* (7 May) declared: 'All eyes had been on the City—the only Liberal-controlled city in the country— as being a likely place for a Liberal-SDP Alliance victory'. Sir Trevor Jones had been consistently predicting a total of 48 Liverpool seats, with perhaps another 3 coming from their uncertain allies in the SDP, which would have pushed them over the 50 mark to give them an overall majority.

However, as the Echo commented: 'City voters clearly rejected his anti-Marxist campaign, much to the delight of Labour and Tory chiefs who had branded it as a smokescreen.' It went on: 'In a crushing disappointment for Liverpool Liberals and their SDP Alliance partners, the city took two steps to the Left in the local elections. Labour gained a net two seats from the ruling Liberals, and the SDP lived up to its cruel nickname the "Sudden Death Party"—by being completely wiped out.'

The modest overall advance in terms of seats—a net gain of only two—disguised the real scale of Labour's victory. The Liberals had suffered an absolutely stunning blow with the loss of Smithdown ward, the birthplace of the Liberal revival. This was the ward which first sent 'Boy Wonder' David Alton to the city council, which he used as a springboard to grab the parliamentary seat of Edgehill in 1979.

Moreover, while Labour did very well throughout the city, where *Militant* supporters stood they did spectacularly well. In Wavertree, for instance, where a particularly vicious campaign was launched against Paul Astbury, a Labour Party Young Socialist, all the Labour votes increased and he was elected onto the council. Even where Labour was not completely successful, the votes of the Liberals fell dramatically. In Kensington in the Edgehill constituency, the Liberal vote decreased from the 1980 election by 1000 votes and their majority was reduced to only 65 votes. In Picton, which was the safest Liberal seat in the country, the Liberal vote was also reduced by over 1000.

One of the best results was in Dingle ward in the Toxteth constituency, where Labour, increasing its vote by nearly 300, won the seat from the Liberals. This was undoubtedly a product of a fighting, active campaign by the Labour Party, particularly since Tony Mulhearn had been selected as Labour's prospective parliamentary candidate for Toxteth. In Broadgreen, anticipating its success in the 1983 general election, Labour achieved a spectacular increase in its vote. In some wards, before *Militant* supporters became dominant, there had been no canvassing for more than 12 years. So desperate were the Liberals in this election, that they even accused Labour of trying to confuse the voters in one of the wards by standing a candidate with the same (uncommon) name as the Liberals' candidate—Smith!

Despite their success, Labour did not attain a majority on the city council. They now had 42 seats, but the Liberals and Tories between them still commanded a majority with 57 seats. The District Labour Party (DLP) therefore took a decision not to take the chair of Council committees, a step which, lacking overall control, would have involved carrying out Liberal-Tory policies of cuts, redundancies and rent rises. Instead, the DLP saw the 1982 elections as a springboard for a massive campaign to achieve majority control the following year. The new campaign was to be more energetic and spread even wider. Significantly, it would embrace important layers of the council workforce.

No Labour Party anywhere else in the country had mapped out a campaign of such scope. It was to reach practically every group of workers who had been alienated by Liberal-Tory rule, hit by the collapse of industry, and affected by cuts in social services, and who were looking for a new era under Labour. Labour's 1983 victory was conditioned by the catastrophic economic and social conditions on Merseyside. But the scale of this victory would have been impossible without the guiding hand of the *Militant* supporters and their strategy and tactics at each decisive stage in the struggle.

The rise to prominence of *Militant* and its supporters was long in its gestation, as we have seen. For more than 40 years, Marxism had been an oppositional current within the Merseyside labour movement, only occasionally able to lead a section of the working class in mass struggle. Now the ideas of *Militant* were to be put to the test. Merseyside was to be a laboratory in which the ideas of both *Militant* and its opponents would be tested. How would *Militant* conduct itself in leading a mass movement? When faced with a decisive test, would these ideas crumble in the face of the combined resistance of the ruling class, the reformist right, and of the soft left within the

Labour Party? Would the Marxists be capable of gathering wide layers of the working class behind the banner of a militant labour movement, to educate and steel them, not just for the current battles but for the long-term struggle to change society?

Marxists approach work on the councils in a similar fashion to work in Parliament. First and foremost the council is seen as a platform from which to raise the political consciousness of the working class. This involves not just propaganda, but the need to take whatever measures are possible within the framework of local government to improve and ameliorate the conditions of the working class. Given the vice-like grip which had been imposed on local government spending, this of necessity would require the mobilisation of the majority of the population to bring mass pressure to bear on the Tory Government.

Contrary to what their opponents have argued, the Marxists do not make 'utopian' demands in the knowledge that they are 'unrealisable'. Whether they are realisable or not, depends on the struggles of the working class. It is not entirely ruled out that under certain conditions the ruling class, as events in Liverpool were to show, can be compelled to take a step backwards and to give concessions.

Reformists demand very little from the government and the capitalists, and their reward is invariably less than nothing. This had been the brutal experience under Liverpool's Tory-Liberal coalitions throughout the 1970s and early 1980s. As the Marxists consistently pointed out, however, even when gains *were* made, any concessions would be purely temporary and on the terms of capitalism. When confronted with an unfavourable relationship of forces, the British ruling class, with its long experience of bending to hostile winds, take a step backwards, wait for a more favourable period, and then takes back, the concessions—with interest.

Another guiding principle of *Militant* supporters was to tell the working class the truth. Engaging in manoeuvres or attempting to cover up unpalatable truths could only result in deceiving the working class and lowering its level of understanding. It was necessary to explain to the widest layers of the working class the reality of the situation confronting Liverpool and what a Labour council would mean to the city.

4.
A Historic Victory

GIVEN THE attacks of the Tory government almost from its inception in 1979, local government was bound to be one of the major battlegrounds between Labour and the Tories. Organically suspicious of any 'extra-parliamentary' movement which could disturb the polite parliamentary minuet with the Tory front bench, Labour spokespersons endeavoured to keep opposition to the government within safe bounds. At a conference of local authority Labour groups in July 1979, Roy Hattersley declared that outright confrontation with the government over cuts would be a 'tactical error'. Any council which broke the law and became 'another Clay Cross', he claimed, 'would enable our enemies to focus attention on the behaviour of one or two councillors and thus divert interest from cuts in services endured by millions of families.'(*Financial Times*, 9 July). This was to be the constant refrain of Labour's front bench.

But it was more than just 'one or two councillors' who came into collision with the government. A number of metropolitan councils were compelled—in a faltering and tremulous manner, it is true—to take a half step into 'illegality'. But only in Liverpool, with the backbone that was provided by *Militant* supporters, was the labour movement prepared for the battle which opened up after 1983. Liverpool, it seems, is 'unique'. Yet equally bad, if not worse, social conditions can be found in Glasgow, Newcastle, Bradford, parts of London such as Hackney, and other inner-city areas. What was distinctive and unique in Liverpool was the character of the labour movement, its combativity, and the leadership provided by *Militant* and its closest supporters within the District Labour Party (DLP) and the Labour group.

The forms of organisation through which all the vital forces of the Merseyside labour movement gathered, had changed and developed in the struggle over the previous 20 years. At one stage, opposition to the measures of Tory and right-wing Labour governments gathered around the Trades Council and Labour Party, then a joint body. At another stage, it was the Trades Council which provided the focal point of opposition.

In the 1980s, the DLP became the movement's main forum of debate and the focus of working-class struggle. The Trades Council became an inconsequential body, with very little participation in its deliberations by the major trade unions. It concentrated on secondary issues, which were of vital concern to the squabbling sectarian grouplets which dominated its proceedings but which left the working class cold. This body was elbowed aside by the DLP, which now provided the leadership in all the main working-class struggles in the area. No strike, no picket line, no movement of a local working-class community, no occupation, took place in the area without the conscious intervention of the DLP and its leading figures such as Tony Mulhearn, Derek Hatton and Eddie Loyden.

Save Croxteth Comprehensive

A battle which stood out in that period was the heroic struggle of the workers of Croxteth to maintain their comprehensive school. The Liberals and Tories were determined to close it down. The school was occupied by local parents and sympathetic teachers from August 1982. In a city suffering social blight, Croxteth was one of the worst affected areas, with an unemployment rate of about 40 per cent and something like 98 per cent of 16 to 19 year olds without work. Only with the determined support and financial backing of the labour movement was the school to be kept going.

The council, controlled by the Tories and Liberals, refused to pay the school's heating bills or waive rates amounting to £1000 a month. In January of 1983 they slapped a £20,000 rates bill on the three organisers of the school's action committee. The Liberals, supposedly exponents of 'community politics', combined with the Tories to try and crush this example of a working-class community attempting to preserve a lifeline for its children out of the misery and hopelessness which surrounded it. The decisive support provided by the labour movement, particularly by *Militant* supporters, won the general support of those engaged in this battle, many of whom became new adherents to the *Militant*.

The Lady at Lord John Dispute

Another famous battle which unfolded at that time was the dispute at the Lady at Lord John store in the city centre. The battle revolved around a vital issue for working- class women. Young members of the staff complained to the manageress, Audrey White, a long-standing *Militant* supporter, about sexual harassment by the area manager. Audrey energetically took up these complaints, involving her union, the Transport and General Workers Union (TGWU). For her pains she was sacked by the upper echelons of management.

The TGWU then engaged in a systematic campaign of picketing and organised a boycott of the firm's stores. *Militant* supporters were prominent throughout the strike, which lasted several months. Terry Fields, Derek Hatton, Tony Mulhearn and many others appeared on the picket line. The police arrested eight pickets during the dispute, including an 18-year-old schoolgirl who was strip-searched while held in custody. This intimidation and harassment proved ineffective in the face of the determination of these young working-class women and the trade unionists who were supporting them to win the struggle.

The management eventually conceded defeat in September 1983, and Audrey White was reinstated as manageress. Alongside her, however, was the area manager, whose conduct provoked the strike, and the manageress who ran the store during the dispute. With the support of her union, Audrey took her complaint to an industrial tribunal, with the assistance of the Equal Opportunities Commission. She claimed victimisation under the Sex Discrimination Act. Eventually an agreement was arrived at which involved the removal of the area manager and two others. Moreover, charges against the eight arrested pickets were dismissed in court and costs awarded against the police.

This successful struggle established a precedent and became

famous not just in Liverpool but throughout Britain. The dispute has now been dramatised in a major feature film, *Business as Usual*, directed by Lezli An-Barrett with Glenda Jackson playing the character based on Audrey White. *Militant* supporters are often falsely accused of ignoring the claims of women, of standing aside from the struggle for 'women's liberation'. Yet it is a fact that on this major issue affecting working-class women, *Militant* supporters have played a prominent, and rightly celebrated, role.

The Council Typists' Dispute

There were two other important disputes in the run-up to 1983. Both involved sections of the local authority workforce, and they had a crucial effect in crystallising the final and complete alienation of council workers from the Liberal-Tory administration. The first involved a section of NALGO (National Association of Local Government Officers) workers, the typists, who were in dispute with the administration for nine months in 1982. Events at local and national level had played a key role in the radicalisation of white-collar workers and particularly of NALGO.

NALGO began in Liverpool as little more than a benevolent society, firmly wedded to a 'non-political' approach under the sway of chief officers for years. But processes were at work that would undermine this. From Selwyn Lloyd's pay policies of 1961 right up to the Labour government of 1974-9, holding down the wages and conditions of public sector white-collar workers had become 'an easy option' to that of challenging the power of manual workers. This, however, tended to result in a radicalisation of the white-collar unions.

Other factors also pushed the white-collar unions in the same direction. The deindustrialisation of capitalism, evident throughout the post-war period but speeding up enormously in the 1970s and 1980s, closed the traditional path into engineering and manufacturing industry taken by working-class youth, boys in particular. In so far as they got jobs in Liverpool and other major cities, they were increasingly pushed into local government and the civil service. They brought with them the traditions and heritage of militancy which were formerly the preserve of blue-collar workers. Moreover, the tendency towards factory-like conditions, with large, open-plan offices and repetitive routines, also assisted in breaking down the 'Uriah Heep' mentality traditionally associated with clerks and white collar workers.

As part of their cost cutting exercise, the Liberals introduced regrading for secretarial staff, which would have effectively held down wages. The typists came out on strike, disrupting the work of many council departments. There was a legacy of bitterness which more and more undermined the Liberals' support among council workers.

The Fight Against Privatisation

The local authority workers' Joint Shop Stewards Committee (JSSC) was set up after the election of the Tory government in 1979. Within a few months the Liberal-Tory coalition in control of Liverpool City Council announced 2000 redundancies. The JSSC called a mass meeting which was attended by thousands. An all-out strike was called for the day of the council meeting which was to agree the redundancies. Fifteen thousand workers struck and 10,000 lobbied the meeting forcing a 'no-redundancy' agreement out of the council.

In November 1982 another bitter dispute broke out over the issue of the planned privatisation of the cleansing department. This brought the Liberals into a head-on confrontation with the General Municipal Workers Union (now GMBATU), the most powerful and militant section of the 30,000 council workforce. *Militant* supporters, led by Ian Lowes, had built up a powerful position of leadership within this union, particularly in the key Branch 5.

The Tory-Liberal council had deliberately run down the cleansing services. In 1982, there were over 200 unfilled vacancies in the Cleansing Department alone. Outdated equipment and run down bin lorries were the norm. Sir Trevor Jones and his acolytes did everything they could to discredit the Cleansing Department, in preparation for handing over city cleansing to their friends in private industry. The Liberals and the *Echo*—which at times became almost an 'in-house' Liberal journal—systematically complained about the alleged 'filthy' character of the city. But the roots of this lay in Liberal-Tory measures prior to 1983.

The campaign against privatisation launched by the manual workers led by Branch 5 was a model: it both informed the workforce and prepared them for the battle. Examples were used like nearby Wirral, where redundancies carried out by the Tory administration had resulted in increased costs of £500,000 in redundancy pay alone. Moreover, the selling off of council property such as bin lorries, equipment, and depots at knock-down prices, would have undermined the resources of the city and, as subsequent experience in other boroughs has amply shown, such measures would not have resulted in a more effective cleansing service.

There were 8000 members of the GMBATU at this stage. The GMBATU convenors consciously saw themselves as the vanguard of the workforce. The GMBATU members were divided up into 11 branches. Cleansing, with 1200, was the largest, with only 100 in the TGWU, mostly drivers. The GMBATU stewards considered that before they could call upon other unions to take action they would need to prepare their own members thoroughly. A well-researched leaflet was therefore written by the stewards and distributed to all GMBATU members. The next stage was to call a shop stewards' meeting: 100 out of 120 GMBATU stewards attended. A coordinating committee of three from each branch was then organised, including three full-time officials responsible for the council branches.

While attempting to draw support from the official apparatus of the unions, both at local and at national level, the stewards put their faith in the workforce. The full-time officials were at best ambivalent in sanctioning action against privatisation. The stewards wrote to the GMBATU National Executive Committee asking for support for action, if it proved necessary, against privatisation—in line with GMBATU Conference decisions. The NEC replied that, first of all, the workforce should try to negotiate with the council to seek a 'success' similar to the GMBATU agreement in Birmingham.

But that deal had involved the union negotiating 250 redundancies and cuts in wages as the price of avoiding privatisation! This advice was rejected and instead, the stewards decided to call a mass meeting. The GMBATU Executive, however, then informed them that they could not have a mass meeting because official backing would be forthcoming only if an individual ballot was held. After a very heated debate by the committee it was agreed by a majority to request permission to ballot all members.

The full-time union officials, especially GMBATU officials at regional and national level, deeply suspicious of any movement from below, were to play the role of a fire hose throughout the Liverpool struggle. From hampering and restricting before 1983, they would by September 1985, become open strike-breakers. Since 1985 they have not hesitated to tell the most bare-faced untruths about the implications of the cuts embodied in the so-called *Stonefrost Report*. The local GMBATU stewards however trusted the workers. The ballot was accompanied by a series of section meetings involving the most oppressed strata of workers, such as refuse collectors and street sweepers.

At the same time, the issue was taken to the Joint Shop Stewards Committee. As usual, the 'Communist' Party members and their co-thinkers were hesitant. They suggested that a compromise could be achieved with the council to avoid privatisation—an approach which was no different from that of the full-time trade-union officials and was a dress rehearsal for their role in future events.

This was completely rejected by the GMBATU stewards, who pushed for a vote on a resolution calling for an all-out strike by all council workers to coincide with the council meeting called to take a decision on privatisation. It also demanded that if the council went ahead with privatisation, the strike was to continue indefinitely. A declaration for action was carried by the JSSC. On paper at least, this committed every union to call mass meetings to put the proposals to their members.

The idea of selective action was floated but rejected. The experience of GMBATU members on Merseyside, particularly in the 1979 'Winter of Discontent' was that selective strike action could actually undermine the struggle. Key sections of workers had taken action on the basis of financial support from others. But these front-line workers bore the brunt of the attacks from the media, and felt all the odium, while other workers, with minimal involvement, just paid a limited amount of cash each week to keep the strike going. An enormous campaign was then launched by the GMBATU stewards to explain the issues, which also involved the Labour councillors who supported them at every step. The union reciprocated by donating £1000 to the

District Labour Party to put out a news-sheet on privatisation. Meanwhile, the Liberals offered a new bonus scheme which would mean the loss of 400 jobs and up to £15 loss of earnings. The full-time officials recommended acceptance of this 'new deal' to a mass meeting of over 1000 refuse workers and street sweepers. One angry shop steward commented: 'Full-time officials take the view that if you have 1000 workers and you agree to 250 redundancies to avoid privatisation, you save 750 jobs. What we say is that you haven't saved 750 jobs, but you've lost 250—and we are not in the business to sell our members' jobs!' When the vote was taken, the officials' recommendation was overwhelmingly defeated, with only about 12 votes in favour. The *raison d'être* of such full-time officials is to avoid struggle at all costs, even if it means presiding over the slashing of jobs. The theme of the GMBATU stewards' campaign was that those who were fortunate to be in work had no right to sell jobs. They were temporary custodians of jobs which had to be passed on to the next generation.

A feature of the campaign was the involvement of youth in the colleges whose facilities were threatened with privatisation. Joint leaflets were issued between the GMBATU and college students, who in turn took strike action and supported demonstrations against privatisation. The battle was seen as a long-term struggle for the future of Merseyside, particularly for young people. This was one of the reasons why the campaign generated such enthusiastic support from the youth of the city.

Despite all the obstacles, the majority of the workers voted in favour of strike action. On 27 April 1983, just before the council elections, 20,000 Liverpool City Council workers struck in response to the Joint Shop Stewards Committee's call for action against privatisation. Thousands lobbied the council's finance meeting. Their anger was directed at Trevor Jones, who was virtually mobbed and was only able to enter the meeting after the intervention of shop stewards. Faced with an all-out, indefinite strike ten days before local elections, Trevor Jones backed down. When the Tories moved that privatisation be introduced, the Liberals voted with Labour to beat the Tories. Trevor Jones' intention was to buy time, work for victory in the May elections, and then to recommence an all-out offensive against the workers.

Into the 1983 Local Elections

The council workers were equally conscious of the temporary
character of their victory. The shop stewards urged the workers
to turn out to campaign in the forthcoming elections. So vital
was the issue that many took holidays to participate in the
campaign. Upwards of 100 stewards were involved at times in
leafletting, canvassing, and organising meetings. As a
consequence of the battles they had been involved in many local
authority workers saw the importance of becoming involved in
the Labour Party. This went hand-in-hand with preparations for
a general election: speculation about the imminence of one
being called was rife at the time. This campaign involved not just
the council workforce but spread throughout the private
sector.

One indication of the degree to which the District Labour
Party had penetrated wide layers of the advanced workers was
the support given by the Transport and General Workers'
Union. In February, 80 TGWU stewards, branch secretaries,
district representatives and officials had met with Labour Party
members in Transport House to discuss preparations for a
Labour victory. Such enthusiasm and commitment could only be
generated by the kind of ideas and fighting spirit displayed by
Labour in Liverpool at this time.

The Liberals were not going to give up their hold on power
easily. Their vilification of Labour exceeded their previous
efforts. Their methods were comparable with the infamous
'Zinoviev letter' red scare campaign, by which the Tories
climbed back to power in 1924. Labour councillors were the
object of a vicious hate campaign which hysterically distorted
what they stood for.

The Liberals distributed a leaflet in Melrose ward which
purported to show that Pauline Dunlop was a 'communist' and a
'Stalinist totalitarian'. Their leaflet deliberately gave the
impression that it was produced by *Militant*, with the *Militant*
masthead and a sub-heading: 'The Marxist voice of Labour'. It
went on to say: 'rates and rents will rocket. Labour candidate
Pauline Dunlop is a leading member of the Militant Tendency.
She previously stood as a Communist candidate in Bootle.'

Another Liberal leaflet, issued in Vauxhall ward with the
heading 'Why no Catholic can vote Labour on Thursday',

carried a picture of the Pope with the statement: 'Who would have thought that just twelve months after the Holy Father's historic visit, the Labour Party would want to close our Christian schools.' Certainly not the workers of Liverpool who voted the Liberals out of power! It went on: 'The Archbishop said at first he thought it was a hoax...But [the leaflet pronounced] it's true!'

To underline the contrast between the wicked *Militant* Marxists and the Liberals, a photograph of the Liberal candidate with his children in his arms carried the imposing message: 'That's why no self-respecting Christian should ever vote Labour again. Labour's Militants not only want to close our schools but would ban religion as well.' This example of gutter politics, especially disgraceful given the history of religious sectarianism in Liverpool, rebounded on them. Several nuns told Labour canvassers that they had come out to vote Labour, because the Liberals 'dared to insult His Holiness by using his name for cynical manoeuvres'!

On 'Chaos' and 'Violence'

Once again, the Liberals set out to identify *Militant* with 'chaos'. One leaflet stated: 'Yes Militants believe in chaos. For as Karl Marx foretold out of chaos comes revolution.' This dish, with various different additives, has been served up to the voters of Liverpool in every election since 1982. It completely distorts the aims and methods of *Militant*. The 'chaos' is a product of the capitalist system itself. Marxism merely describes the workings of the laws of capitalism, of the inevitability of booms, slumps, overproduction and, at a certain stage, mass unemployment.

It is not the task of Marxism to foment 'chaos'. Capitalism itself, without intervention by the Marxists, provokes periodic eruptions and social earthquakes from which flow the chaos and dislocation complained of by the Liberals. Witness the riots in the 1980s, which the serious capitalist commentators had to recognise were the product of conditions in the inner-city ghettos, not the work of 'agitators'. Marxism seeks to explain and analyse the workings of the capitalist system. Its purpose is to replace the chaos of capitalism with a planned, organised and harmonious socialist society.

The twin themes of 'chaos' linked with 'violence' were the chicken's legs on which the Liberals built a tower of misinformation, distortions and outright lies about *Militant* and the Liverpool labour movement. The false charges of 'violence', 'thuggery' and 'intimidation' were the hallmark of opponents incapable of answering real arguments. Marxists welcome violence as little as they would welcome plague. In a widely misreported speech in 1982, Pat Wall, then prospective Labour candidate for Bradford North, pointed to the possibility of the capitalists resorting to violent measures to suppress the labour movement. Under lurid 'rivers of blood' headlines, the press portrayed him as a wild-eyed 'revolutionary' with a knife between his teeth. He was, they alleged, an advocate of 'civil war'.

But all Pat Wall had done was to draw the necessary conclusions from the frightful decay of capitalism. Faced with the refusal of the working class to accept the burden of 'irreversible decline', the inevitable reaction of the British bourgeois would be to move in the direction of limiting and attempting to destroy democratic rights. In reality it is the representatives of capitalism who threaten civil war in the event of the left ever seriously threatening to change society. The statement of Ian Gilmour, a former member of Thatcher's cabinet, in his book *Inside Right*, published in 1977, makes this clear:

> Conservatives do not worship democracy. For them majority rule is a device...majorities do not always see where their best interests lie and then act upon their understanding. For Conservatives, therefore, democracy is a means to an end and not an end in itself. In Dr Hayek's words, democracy 'is not an ultimate or absolute value and must be judged by what it will achieve'. And if it is leading to an end that is undesirable or is inconsistent with itself, then there is a theoretical case for ending it.

Moreover, the real history of Britain is riddled with examples of the ruling class threatening or resorting to force whenever its position was seriously threatened by the labour movement and the working class. As Leon Trotsky pointed out, not one serious reform in the franchise from 1830 right up to the period of the Russian Revolution was granted by the British bourgeoisie without the threat of revolution in Britain or abroad. On all occasions the British ruling class applied the dictum of 'reform from the top in order to prevent revolution from below', so long as the real levers of economic power and the means of moulding public opinion, the press and other media, remained concentrated firmly in their hands. Marxists are like good doctors who on the basis of a sound diagnosis can predict that certain abnormalities in the human body, if left unattended, will result in a catastrophe. Imagine a surgeon, who diagnoses cancer at its inception—only to be accused by quacks of promoting the development of cancer in human beings.

Yet with regard to 'violence', this absurd method is used by the ruling class and its acolytes. Marxists advocate violence, according to them, because they predict violence as inevitable, given the processes at work within capitalist society. On the contrary! They advocate a bold, socialist programme which can win the support and confidence of the overwhelming majority of the working class and draw behind it the middle class. Far from provoking violence, this would make possible a peaceful, socialist transformation in Britain.

The reformists, through irritating the ruling class while failing to satisfy the aspirations of the working class, produce the worst of all possible worlds. Tinkering with the capitalist system allows the ruling class to regroup its forces. With the real levers of economic power still in their hands, the bourgeoisie is able to sabotage the economy, undermine left governments and alienate the middle strata from the labour movement. They can use this middle strata, at a certain stage, as a basis upon which to stage a military coup to bring down a left-wing government. Is this not the history of Chile, written in the blood of 50,000 workers murdered by Pinochet? Chile has been turned into one gigantic torture chamber for the proletariat. Nevertheless, after 14 years the working class is rising from its knees again and throwing off the chains of reaction.

It is the reformists, if they continue to dominate the labour movement, and not the Marxists, who will be responsible for terrible suffering and possibly bloodshed in Britain. Weighed on the scales of history, the Russian Revolution was entirely justified. It ended the blood and carnage of the First World War, when five million Russians were killed or wounded. The accession of the Bolsheviks to power in October 1917 was carried out in a relatively peaceful fashion with very few victims, at least in Petrograd. The bloody civil war, with its countless victims and suffering, arose from the attempt of the dispossessed property-owning classes backed up by 21 imperialist armies of intervention, to overthrow the workers' and peasants' government.

In Germany, the refusal of the Social Democratic and Communist Party leaders in 1933 to forcibly bar the coming to power of Hitler resulted in the decimation of the German proletariat. This paved the way for the Second World War, with at least 50 million victims. The path to socialism will be less painful, the victims far fewer, provided Marxism becomes the guiding philosophy of the advanced workers and the broad labour movement. Whenever the Marxists have faced this hysterical charge of 'violence', they have countered it by sober explanation, outlining their demands and their long-term perspectives.

Labour Landslide

The steadfast approach of the Marxists to all the smears, lies and attacks of the ruling class was completely vindicated in the historic May 1983 council elections in Liverpool. In a brilliant victory, Labour gained 12 seats, ten from the Liberals and one from the SDP. Not a single Labour seat was lost. The Tory leader, Reg Flude, lost his seat to Labour in Warbreck. This in a city dominated by the Tories up until 1964! Labour's vote increased by an astonishing 40 per cent—22,000 extra votes.

Foreshadowing what was to happen a month later in the general election, the turnout in the Broadgreen constituency was 44 per cent and Labour's vote increased by 50 per cent. In the Broad Green ward, Labour gained a seat from the Liberals, winning an extra 1000 voters—a 60 per cent increase. In Old Swan, another Labour gain, Labour's vote increased by 800. Even where Labour did not score a victory, as in Childwall, one of the more affluent middle-class areas of Broadgreen, the Labour vote shot up by 60 per cent. In Kensington, where both the Labour and Liberal vote rose by 500, Alan Fogg just failed to take the seat by 24 votes. This ward had been the arena for a Liberal versus Labour poster war with over 800 requests for Labour posters.

In Dingle, where *Militant* supporters and local authority workers turned the party outwards into a campaigning branch, the Labour vote rocketed from 1839 to 2917 with the gain of a seat. All those who had valiantly supported Croxteth Comprehensive were given an enormous boost when Labour gained Clubmoor in which the school is situated. There was an outburst of joy and celebration that night, with dancing in the streets.

5.
A Workers' MP on a Worker's Wage

IN EQUAL measure, the ruling class, the Tories and Liberals in Liverpool and the right wing of the Labour Party, were flabbergasted at Labour's victory. All their calculations had been upset. Trevor Jones declared: 'I am disappointed for the city. Many members of Militant Tendency have been elected.' It had been repeated *ad nauseam* by Labour's right that *Militant* was an 'electoral albatross'. The events of May 1983 were a crushing answer to the critics of Marxism—though successive election victories in Liverpool have not deterred them from repeating such claims.

The issue of *Militant* had been made a central feature of the anti-Labour campaign waged by the capitalist media and the Liberals in particular. By their own benchmark, therefore, the Liverpool victory was a triumph for Marxism and *Militant*. The result of the local elections was all the more outstanding when compared with a poor performance by Labour nationally. Above all, where the right wing predominated, Labour's results were disappointing. In Birmingham, which was firmly in the grip of the right wing, the swing to Labour compared with the disastrous results of 1979 was only two per cent, whereas in Liverpool it was seven per cent. A similar picture emerged from Labour's poor result in Grimsby, where Austin Mitchell MP has long been prominent among those who spend more time abusing the Marxists than attacking the Tory-Liberal-SDP enemy. In Rochdale a right-wing Labour group presided over the loss of two Labour seats to the Tories and one to the SDP!

Stunned by the Liverpool results, dissembling bourgeois and right-wing Labour commentators tried to explain them away. The strategists of capital pressed the panic button. Meanwhile the real message was clear: 'militancy pays'.

Militant, in the traditions of the great teachers of Marxism going back to Marx himself, recognised that participation in elections and winning battles in this sphere, was a test of the viability of their programme and perspectives. Their strategies had nothing in common, however, with 'parliamentary cretinism'. It was recognised that the struggle in Parliament must also be supplemented by the most determined 'extra-parliamentary' methods on the part of the working class to back up any steps taken in Parliament. Parliament is only one field of struggle, and not always the most decisive. It is, of course, a barometer of the relationship between the classes, one indication of the mood of the working class. Elections, however, represent only one moment in history.

There have been occasions when the ruling class has taken an election victory as a mandate for harsh measures against the proletariat. In turn, however, this has provoked a furious reaction by the working class, leading to the most serious form of 'extra-parliamentary' action—the general strike. In 1926 the British workers moved in reaction to attempts by the ruling class to impose the burden of Britain's collapse onto their shoulders. The working class pushed the tops of the trade union leadership into sanctioning, at least in words, a general strike. Nevertheless, elections, particularly in the period through which we have just gone, are one of the best tests of ideas and programmes.

For Marxism the Liverpool result was important from another very significant point of view. For the first time in decades the ideas of Marxism were tested out in action at the level of a major city council. This came at the turn of a long historical tide which, through the upswing of capitalism and the reinforcement of reformism, had isolated Marxism for over three decades. Now history was, in the words of Trotsky, 'picking up the revolutionary threads and tying them together'. The terminal decay of British capitalism, and its extreme manifestation in the 1960s and 1970s in Liverpool, prepared the ground on which the ideas of Marxism could grow.

For the Marxists, Liverpool was never seen in isolation from the general struggle of the working class. It was seen as a springboard for galvanising the opposition of other councils and for defeating the Tory government's onslaught against services and jobs. To fulfil this task, it was necessary to proceed energetically to implement Labour's programme.

Labour in Power—The Early Days

The beleaguered Croxteth Comprehensive was first to benefit from the Labour victory. 'Like the arrival of the US cavalry,' commented the *Guardian* (9 May), 'Labour's victory in last Thursday's council elections has come just in time for the rebel parents running the Croxteth school.' Using the same analogy, only in a negative sense, Neil Kinnock was to declare at the Labour Party Conference two years later, that no Labour government would act 'like the Seventh Cavalry'.

In the spring of 1983, despite their fears, the Labour leaders were forced to recognise the advances made in Liverpool. At the National Executive Committee, party leader Michael Foot congratulated 'the comrades in Liverpool', saying 'all honour to the Liverpool Labour Party, they fought back and they fought well'. Internationally, too, the Liverpool result was followed attentively. The Swedish Social Democratic Party's daily Stockholm paper, *Tidningen* (10 May) commented:

> The most interesting development is exactly what will happen in one specific council, namely Liverpool, where Labour took power and where the Party is dominated by its Trotskyist wing. Not least from outside, this test of what a radical council leadership can and cannot achieve will be interesting to follow.

After their debacle, the Liberals, of course, looked for any excuse to explain away their defeat. Rosemary Cooper, who lost her seat to Labour by 481 votes in the Broad Green ward, claimed that extremists using 'strongarm tactics' posed as voters to swing a vital Labour victory (*Post*, 23 May). 'Left-wing heavies' were accused of casting crucial false votes and 'tough-looking men wearing Labour rosettes threatened electors when they turned out to vote'.

The decision to abolish the Lord Mayor's position and to put in cold storage the medieval lumber of gold chain, coach and horses, not to mention the Rolls Royce, provoked the first manifestation of middle class fury from the Liberals. There was to be much more of the same over the next three years. Tony Mulhearn declared: 'Possibly the gold chain will be put in a museum, along with the defeated Liberals.'

Trevor Jones, Liberal leader, declared that this was the beginning of 'a Trotskyist tide'. He conveniently forgot that in

1972 the Liberals had produced a pamphlet denouncing the expense of the Lord Mayor's office. Now, according to this worthy, a 'Comrade Commissar' was to be installed in place of the Lord Mayor. The *Daily Star* (11 May) claimed that the newly elected Labour council, in doing away with the Lord Mayor's parade, was intending to replace it with 'a Kremlin-style march-past'. *Militant* ironically commented: 'Yes, but will the fur hats, and row upon row of gleaming tank squadrons and missile carriers, have to be paid for by the rates, we ask?'. Even the relatively uncontroversial proposal to set up a low cost funeral service provoked the indignation of the *Post* (28 May):'Labour plans funeral takeover.'

No sooner were the election results declared, than Trevor Jones was predicting mayhem and disaster. During the election the Liberals had repeated the claims of the *Echo*, (26 April): 'The Labour Party's revival programme for Liverpool would add up to £5 per week to ratepayers' bills, according to the City Treasurer.' Spicing up the dish somewhat, a Liberal advertisement in the *Echo* claimed:

> Every householder, including council tenants, will pay at least £4 per week or between £200 to £400 per annum extra, and some will pay considerably more according to rateable value. Although all council tenants have been offered a £2 per week rent reduction, their rates would rise by £5 per week in order to pay for it...Businesses would collapse and the city would suffer.

In warfare the first casualty is always the truth—and a bitter class war was being fought in Liverpool. Labour had made it quite clear that they were not going to pay for their programme through increasing rates. Nevertheless the Liberals constantly harped on the theme of a doubling of the rates, or more, under a Labour council.

The speedy implementation of parts of Labour's programme, including the cancellation of the redundancies which the Liberals had in the pipeline, actually increased support for the council. This was undoubtedly one of the factors in Labour's triumph in the general election a month later. But it must be remembered that the council election in Liverpool was exceptional. Nationally, there had been a swing to Labour of less than one per cent against the disastrous election results of May 1979. Throughout the country Labour had lost and the Liberal-SDP Alliance had stood still or gone backwards.

The General Election Campaign

Seizing the favourable conjuncture provided by the victory in the Falklands, Thatcher decided to 'go to the country'. The campaign was seen as a crusade against the left. Speaking to Scottish Tories Thatcher declared that 'the choice facing the nation is between two totally different ways of life and what a prize we have to fight for...no less than the chance to banish from our land the dark divisive clouds of Marxist Socialism'. But whereas in much of Britain the Tories could look forward to success on 9 June, the omens were not at all good in Liverpool.

In the local elections the Tories had received only 21 per cent of the vote, the lowest in the city this century. The prospect of success in Liverpool, however, did not exactly fill the Labour leadership with joy! As David Alton, the Liberal MP, correctly stated, obviously reflecting gossip in the House of Commons tea room : 'They [the right wing] have effectively put Liverpool into political quarantine.' Alton declared: 'Mr Fields and others would have been expelled from the Labour Party if this election hadn't happened.'

The campaign launched by Liverpool Labour in the 1983 general election was undoubtedly the most successful in its history. In no other city was there the same degree of mass involvement. Nowhere was there such systematic and organised canvassing, such big public meetings, or such enthusiasm generated. All parts of the city were drawn in, but Broadgreen was the most outstanding example of the prevailing spirit. Reminiscent of the pioneering period when the Labour Party was originally built, enormous numbers of workers turned out to canvass. A minimum of 200 canvassers were involved over weekends, with the average being about 250. On election day, 500 workers from Liverpool and other parts of the country worked in the Broadgreen constituency.

Such commitment and enthusiasm could not have been generated unless these workers had believed that they had a candidate and a programme which would make a decisive difference to their lives. With the exception of the Marxist Pat Wall in Bradford North however, no other candidate in Britain faced such a systematic and organised campaign of vilification as Terry Fields. The election address of the Tory candidate, Danny

Dougherty declared: 'If the Socialist Militant wins this seat, it will not encourage new employers to come to Liverpool.' But the slanders were answered on the doorstep.

Traditionally Labour conducts campaigns more as opinion polls. The canvasser is advised by 'professional agents' merely to obtain the voting intentions of the elector. Canvassers are told not to 'waste time' on Tories, Liberals, SDP, or even the 'doubtful'. In contrast, the Broadgreen campaign started off with the understanding that only through a campaign of explanation, discussion and attempting to convince people through argument would it be possible for the seat to be won. Sometimes canvassers were asked into houses or were kept for 20 or 30 minutes on the doorsteps discussing political issues. A massive campaign of political education took place, with tens of thousands of workers understanding the issues clearly by the end of the campaign. The main demands of Terry Fields' campaign carried in *Broadgreen Labour News* were:

★ A crash programme of public works to build houses, schools, etc. and to provide jobs.
★ The immediate introduction of a drastically shorter working week, without loss of pay, to create jobs. This to be coupled with a national minimum wage.
★ The repeal of all anti-trade union legislation implemented by this Tory government.
★ An end to the scandal of council rents of £25 to £30 a week while the council has to pay 85p back to the money-lenders for every £1 collected in rent, and where home-buyers are having to pay the highest mortgage repayments in history.
★ The necessity for a police force which can effectively detect and prevent crime is essential, and the democratic accountability of the police to elected representatives of the community is vital.
★ These demands will be linked to the call for the public ownership of the nation's wealth and resources—democratically managed and controlled—which is being sold off by the Tories to their rich backers or invested abroad to the tune of £7000 million each year, while industry is being starved of investment.

Special leaflets were produced and appeals made to the youth and to working-class women to draw them into the campaign. A central feature of the campaign was the call for a 35-hour working week. This was official Labour Party policy but, although in the election manifesto, it was never featured by the leadership running the national campaign.

There was deep scepticism as to how a Labour government would pay for its promised reforms. Moreover, many workers were searching for an explanation of the difficulties that would confront a Labour government working within the framework of capitalism.

The modern working class is more cultured than in the past, has much wider horizons because of the television and other mass media, and sees what is happening to the labour movement in other countries. Workers pointed to the inadequacies and the retreats of the French Socialist-Communist government. How would a Labour government avoid treading the same path? The right wing of the Labour Party, and also some on the left, contemptuous of the capacity of working people to understand an analysis, completely failed to give any explanation of the processes at work in society.

In contrast the Marxists in Broadgreen did not restrict their campaign to a few slogans, but sought to raise the level of understanding and to prepare a bastion of working-class consciousness for future battles, no matter what the outcome on 9 June. Above all Labour's candidate, Terry Fields, never hesitated to explain that within the confines of capitalism any limited concessions won by Labour for workers could be snatched back by the capitalists at a later stage. Only a socialist planned economy, the idea of which is enshrined in Clause 4 Part IV of Labour's constitution, would eliminate the mass poverty and suffering which scars the Broadgreen constituency and Britain as a whole.

A Workers' MP on a Worker's Wage

One demand which separated Terry Fields not only from his political opponents but from other Labour candidates , was his promise to be a 'workers' MP on a worker's wage'. The slogan was displayed in thousands of leaflets and posters throughout the city. This generated colossal enthusiasm amongst workers, who were convinced that 'one of their own' would enter Parliament and would not be separated from them in his lifestyle or outlook. One woman commented: 'If Terry lives on a worker's wage he would be the first one I've known of since Bob

Tissyman [a Liverpool strike leader] who came out of politics worse off financially than he went into it.'

Desperately attempting to counter the effect of this slogan, Labour's opponents went in for cheap imitations. Liberal candidate Richard Pine, a personnel manager, fancifully proclaimed: 'a worker, a winner'. The Tory candidate Danny Dougherty implausibly dubbed himself 'a friend, a fighter' while other Tories warned of a 'Marxist takeover in Broadgreen'. One of Mrs Thatcher's strongest weapons in the 1983 election was the line-up of ex-Labour prime ministers, James Callaghan and Harold Wilson, who either scored timely 'own goals' or directly assisted the enemy in attacking Labour. Wilson told that purveyor of Sunday 'morality', the *News of the World* (29 May): 'I would sling them [*Militant* supporters] out on their neck. Their only aim is to wreck the country and bring it to a standstill.'

So effective was Terry Fields' campaign that the Liberal candidate confessed it was 'unlike anything he had seen in the country, even in by-elections'. The esteem in which Terry Fields, an ex-firefighter, was held by ordinary workers was reflected in financial donations to the campaign from branches of the Fire Brigades' Union (FBU). Moreover, groups of uniformed firefighters from Merseyside, Cheshire, Manchester, and even Strathclyde canvassed in Broadgreen.

The depth of support was also reflected in the *Echo*, which showed a photograph of an elderly street cleaner putting up an election poster supporting Terry Fields. He was so enthusiastic that he plastered lampposts in other constituencies with Terry Fields' leaflets! He told the *Echo*: 'Terry's a good working-class man. All the senior stewards have decided to go around canvassing for him.'

Terry Fields spoke at more than ten factory-gate and canteen meetings. At a bin depot about 200 drivers waited from 6.30 am to 7.30 am for a gate meeting before their hard day's work. Numerous small meetings were held throughout the constituency, although one of the major features of the Broadgreen campaign was the number of mass meetings called by the Labour Party. Liverpool was the scene of one mass meeting after another. Two thousand gathered on 17 May for a North-West Regional Labour Party rally at St George's Hall, where Michael Foot spoke alongside seven Labour parliamentary candidates. There was great enthusiasm for Michael Foot when he hailed the local election victory:

> Labour's success in the city council elections last week has been a timely boost. It was tremendous the way Liverpool has set the standard in the local elections just before the general election. It was very fitting that just before we cleared the Tories out of Westminster, we here in Liverpool should have such a wonderful success in the council elections. (*Post* 18 May)

But it was Terry Fields who really caught the mood of the meeting when he declared:

> The only alternative to the Tories and the Liberals is for the Labour Party nationally to take a leaf out of the sort of campaign waged in the local elections by the Liverpool Labour Party. Go out to the working class and explain the ideas of socialism!

Unfortunately, this was not done by the Labour Party nationally, nor in most areas of the country where the right wing still held sway. In Liverpool, however, and especially in Broadgreen, a clear explanation of the crisis was spelt out, and the demand for a socialist programme to be implemented by a Labour government was hammered home. The response was impressive. Where else could a meeting be called at 5 pm and attract over 300 people, many still in overalls having come straight from work? This was the scene for Tony Benn when he spoke on 26 May at the National Union of Railwaymen Club in Kensington. He said he was proud to be on a platform with Terry Fields and generated tremendous enthusiasm with his declaration that 'once confidence flows back into the working class in Britain then no power on earth can stop us'.

The atmosphere in the hall was electric, with the speakers frequently interrupted by applause and shouts of approval. Alongside Tony Benn were Terry Fields, Derek Hatton and Pat Phoenix, star of the television series *Coronation Street* who holds a special place in the memories of Liverpool socialists for the support she gave to Terry Fields. There was even greater enthusiasm at a meeting addressed by Arthur Scargill on a local estate, with 450 people present. The atmosphere was like that of a football match, with workers standing with their arms raised high in sheer class determination. In a prophetic speech, Arthur Scargill pledged 'industrial action if the new coal boss, Ian

MacGregor, axed pit jobs'. He warned of the pressures which would be exerted on a new Labour government: 'There is only one reason why Labour has lost elections. It is because they have failed to put into practice real socialist policies.' He also warned a future Labour government: 'We are electing you, but at the same time making you accountable to produce socialism and ensure that never again will there be a Tory government.'

The campaign was sinking roots for a mass party. Caught up in the atmosphere were the most unlikely supporters. A poster was put up in a stained glass window by one priest. A Franciscan monk bought a copy of *Militant* and made a donation to the Fighting Fund. He would have liked to take a poster, but said the other monks would not let him put it up!

There was complete unity within the party behind all the Labour candidates. It was the enemy, particularly the Liberal-SDP Alliance, which was divided against itself, with separate candidates standing. Nationally, however, Labour presented a picture of a divided and split party and this had disastrous results. The attack on the Labour candidate in Bermondsey for example had virtually handed the seat to the Liberals in the February 1983 by-election, especially since the day before polling day the NEC had finally carried through the expulsion of the *Militant* Editorial Board, after protracted witch-hunting proceedings. This would also undoubtedly have had an effect in weakening and undermining Labour in Liverpool but for the effectiveness of Labour's campaign. Liverpool vindicated *Militant*'s argument in opposition to the witch-hunt.

Marxism Victorious

On the night of 9 June, the contrast between the mood of the Liverpool Labour workers and the rest of the country could not have been greater. Hundreds of party workers danced and cheered in Labour committee rooms in Liverpool as a stunning victory was chalked up. While nationally the biggest swing in post-war elections went to the Tories, in Liverpool there was a 2 per cent swing *from* the Tories *to* Labour.

The greatest cheer was reserved for the victory of Terry Fields in Broadgreen. Broadgreen was a new constituency, created by the recent parliamentary boundary revision. From recalculation of the 1979 results on the new basis, the BBC classified the seat as a Tory seat with an estimated majority of 600. It was the only Tory seat that was won by Labour in the election. It was won with a handsome majority of 3800. The turnout was 72 per cent, exactly the national average: yet the calculated swing to Labour was 4.5 per cent. The bedrock of the campaign had been precisely those policies of *Militant* which the right wing had consistently argued were 'election losers'.

Initially the right wing were dumbfounded. Their response was to try to conceal the real meaning of the Liverpool results under a cloak of silence. Not so the local press. Readers of the *Post* and *Echo* were well aware that these journals had worked energetically for a Labour defeat in the city. Above all, the scalp they were looking for was that of Terry Fields. In the immediate aftermath of the election, therefore, they were compelled to admit the advances made by Labour, and particularly by *Militant*. Ian Craig, an enemy of socialism and of *Militant* made some very telling points:

> The election of Terry Fields is an embarrassment to members of Labour's National Executive who have tried for months to throw *Militant* supporters out of the Party. *Militant* supporters in Liverpool were last night openly contemptuous of such moves. And they had every right to be...No longer can Labour moderates and right-wingers condemn the rantings of *Militant* supporters and candidates. Terry Fields has defied their opposition and is now one of their back-benchers. And if that might give Peter Shore, Roy Hattersley, Denis Healey and John Golding a few sleepness nights it will give Mrs Thatcher and her new Cabinet nightmares. The Mersey Militants are on their way. (*Echo*, 10 June 1983.)

One of the most enduring features of the campaign was the building of a powerful mass base in the area. Ninety-nine people joined the Labour Party in the Tuebrook ward alone. Such was the enthusiasm of some Labour voters for Terry Fields that one girl hitched from Newcastle to Liverpool just to vote! Workers were enthusiastic that class fighters such as Terry Fields and Dave Nellist in Coventry South-East were entering Parliament to espouse their cause.

Terry Fields remarked that one of the most touching experiences during the campaign was a conversation with a teacher: 'Just promise me one thing—you won't change.' He replied: 'Many have said it before, but there's no way I'll change.

I've got no pretentions to enhance my own life style on the backs of working people, when you see the conditions and the support that they've given me.' The day after the election, Dick Crawshaw, the ex-Labour MP and defeated SDP candidate ruefully commented in a radio interview: 'It's rather ironic that the first *Militant* to win was against me in Broadgreen. I left the Labour Party to fight the Militants. I devoted 30 years of my life to fight the Militants. It would appear, on the face of it, I might have failed.' After listening to Terry Fields' powerful maiden speech, the strategists of capital would probably echo Crawshaw's sentiments.

Terry Fields represented the new mood that swept throughout Merseyside. Up until 1964 Liverpool could be described as a 'Tory city'. Apart from a period just after the war, it had mainly been represented by an assortment of Tory and Liberal MPs. Now, in an election where the Tories had won a landslide nationally, there was not a single Tory MP in the city for the first time in 100 years.

The bitterness, the class loathing, which the majority of workers on Merseyside felt for the Tory victors was voiced in Terry Fields' maiden speech in Parliament. By convention, these are supposed to be uncontroversial. New members of the House of Commons are expected to introduce themselves, heartily congratulate opposition speakers, and wish well to their retiring or defeated constituency rivals. Indeed, one new Labour MP, Dr Norman Godman from Greenock and Port Glasgow heaped praise on his predecessor, the Labour renegade Dickson Mabon who had defected to the SDP. The Tories endorsed his sentiments.

But such pleasantries were cast aside when Terry Fields rose to speak. He made it clear he was there to represent the Liverpool workers. They had elected him to fight the Tories, not to go around congratulating the likes of Dickson Mabon who betrayed the labour movement. He was there not to appeal to the ruling class, but to express the real feelings of the working class against this government and the system they represent. Terry Fields' speech, which is included in full as an appendix, stands out as a rare note of reality in the Mother of Parliaments.

A cynical journalist in the *Guardian* (22 July) described Terry Fields as 'an angry young man in a leather jacket', awarding him the 'Jimmy Porter award for best angry young speeches'. But the more serious representatives of capitalism understood that both Terry Fields and Dave Nellist, Labour MP for Coventry South-East, would combine to use Parliament as an effective platform to assist and further the struggle of their comrades in Liverpool.

The rich capitalist backers of the Tory Party appeared to be celebrating their victory with a new round of closures and redundancies on Merseyside. They seemed to be taking revenge on the Liverpool workers for daring to vote for Labour and for Terry Fields. One family (featured in *Militant*'s pages at the time) typified the anger and bitterness which fuelled Liverpool's revolt. The Hayes family included three unemployed workers. The father Philip had worked for Union Cold Storage for many years, but since the factory had been run down he had been out on the stones for four years. Of the three sons, Brian had been fortunate enough to get an apprenticeship as a fitter with the council, but at the end of his time he had also been put out of a job. Under Labour's new rule, no apprentice was to be sacked at the end of their training period. Another brother was thrown out on the stones when his factory announced redundancies one week after the election.

On the very day that Terry Fields made his Commons speech, Cadbury-Schweppes announced the closure of their factory. When United Biscuits announced the rundown of their Crawfords factory the workers were stunned. The workforce, mainly women workers, were in tears as news spread around the factory: 'Some people feel suicidal', commented one shop steward. A woman worker graphically described in *Militant* the decline of industry in the area. *Militant* commented:

> Walk around the United Biscuits factory and it is a monument to the industrial decay. Within a stone's throw the industrial hopes of Meccano, Pattern and Calvert, and Wingrove and Rogers can be seen shattered. At the nearby Plessey factory you see massive job losses. Ten years ago at 4.30 pm you couldn't move on Edge Lane, now there's hardly anyone around.

There were workers in the factory who had voted for the Tories in the election. One commented: 'I voted for Thatcher, I thought I was safe.' The Managing Director of United Biscuits was Hector Laing, one of Thatcher's 'business advisers', yet examples of management bungling and inefficiency at United

Biscuits were legion. Workers gave many examples, one of which was that £2 million was lost when biscuits were sent to Saudi Arabia in Marks and Spencer wrappers!

The fear with which big business viewed developments in Liverpool, particularly the growing influence of *Militant*, was revealed in a letter to *Militant* (16 September 1983):

> Dear Comrades, *Militant* seems to be gaining readership in high places. On his recent visit to United Biscuits, Ashby, Company Chairman, Sir Hector Laing, was touring the shop floor shaking hands and exchanging pleasantries with some of the workers. However, when he got to me he pointed his finger and said, 'You wrote a letter to a certain newspaper about my involvement with other companies, didn't you?'. This was a reference to my article in *Militant* No 658, so I said, 'Yes, that's right.'
>
> He then lectured us on how it was good for business for him to be on boards of other companies as he would secure orders that way. If you're reading this Sir Hector, I'd just like to say that your work and that of your colleagues on various boards hasn't done much good for UB workers at Liverpool or Osterley. My article was not an attack on you personally—rather it was an example of the way capitalism works (or does not work, more accurately).

More than one commentator was to point out that the government was more intimately involved in developments in Liverpool than in any other city. No other city warranted a special Minister in the Cabinet. The Department of the Environment, and teams of civil servants and advisers, monitored down to the last detail the events, the changing mood and the major political forces at work in the city.

Like the miners in 1984-5, Thatcher viewed Liverpool as a dangerous foe that had to be beaten into submission if the government was to survive. This was to prove a difficult task however, and she and her Minister, Patrick Jenkin, were to be forced to beat a retreat before a favourable opportunity arose to crush the movement—an opportunity given to them by the national leadership of the Labour Party and the trade unions.

Liverpool was the only force, alongside the miners in 1981, which compelled the government to grant concessions. How was this achieved? How was it possible for one city, in isolation and in the teeth of opposition from all sides to launch such a successful campaign which was to humble the 'Iron Lady' herself?

From the outset, the new Labour council's campaign for more resources was unique in its involvement of working-class organisations and its arousal of mass participation. Like no other city, Liverpool saw a series of magnificent one-day strikes and mass demonstrations. In a conversation in 1919 with the English writer, Arthur Ransome, Lenin commented: 'When I was in England I zealously attended everything I could, and with a country with so large an industrial population public meetings were pitiable, a handful on a street corner...a meeting in the drawing room, the school class...pitiable.'

No such thing could be said about the events in Liverpool during 1983-7. Implacable opponents of *Militant*, like the Communist Party on Merseyside, grudgingly admitted, after the event, that 'the belligerent fighting stance of Labour councillors touched a popular nerve. There is no doubt whatever that the politics of the financial crisis electrified the people in a way that was simply never there before. Everyone knew about it, everyone had an opinion.' (Tony Lane, *Marxism Today*, January 1986.)

In an enormous cover-up operation, the ruling class and its journals later sought to hide the real situation which faced the Labour administration when it took power in 1983. They fostered the legend that *Militant* deliberately exaggerated the scale of the problem. The impression has been given that it was the 'wicked Marxists' who were responsible for the social plight of Liverpool, rather than the government. Some in the labour movement have argued that, if only a more 'moderate tone' had been adopted in negotiations with the government, then in some way the city's colossal social problems could have been conjured away. These sages conveniently forget that the Tory government turned a deaf ear to all special pleading prior to 1983. The Tory government would only understand the force of mass struggle.

The lessons of Liverpool were a book sealed with seven seals as far as Labour's right wing were concerned. They saw the general election defeat as being entirely due to the 'unrealistic', supposedly 'socialist policies' which had formed the basis of the Manifesto. Their analysis corresponded closely to that of the demoralised rump of the so-called 'soft left'. Drawing heavily on the analysis of the 'Communist' Eric Hobsbawm, the professor of pessimism, they attributed Thatcher's victory to a move to the right by the British working class itself. Thatcher won, seemingly, because of the 'appeal' of council house sales to a layer of the working class. The trade unions were impotent against a resurgent Thatcherism. Hobsbawm, an organic sceptic and veiled social democrat masquerading as a Marxist, even suggested a coalition with the traitors who formed the SDP.

Soon after the election, a veiled counter-revolution against the gains on policy registered in the Labour Party between 1979 and 1982 was set in train. Even the selection and reselection of Labour MPs was to be challenged by the right, with only lukewarm opposition from the 'soft left'. Many of the soft left had fervently supported Tony Benn in the contest for Labour's deputy leadership in 1981. Many of them had attacked, in hysterical terms, the refusal of Kinnock and others to vote for Benn. They were the 'careerist left' who had hoped, through a Labour victory, to get their share of the state pie. They had hoped to ride to power on Tony Benn's coat tails. Now they heaped scorn and sometimes outright abuse on their former idol.

Neil Kinnock became the new totem of these ex-lefts, now travelling to the right at the speed of light. All the conservative forces within the Labour Party—the place-men and self-seekers, the Party's own officialdom, and the union leadership—looked for a figure to front their counter-revolution. Kinnock had been sounding out this layer in the period before the election and in an energetic campaign afterwards. The support which he got from the unions came from the right and the nominal 'left'.

Alan Tuffin, the right-wing leader of the Union of Communication Workers, was one of the first to fly Kinnock's colours in the expected leadership contest following the June 1983 defeat. He formed a block with Clive Jenkins, leader of ASTMS (Association of Scientific, Technical and Managerial Staffs). Once a member of the Communist Party, and still an inveterate opponent of Trotskyism, Jenkins was undoubtedly a driving force behind Kinnock's attack, two years later, on *Militant* and Liverpool City Council.

Kinnock had all the attributes required by the conservative, privileged stratum which became ascendant in the Labour Party in the aftermath of the election defeat. He still claimed to be on the left, although he had distanced himself from Benn and had voted for the expulsion of the *Militant* Editorial Board in March 1983. The election of Roy Hattersley as the leader, rather than deputy leader, would have enormously complicated the task of shifting the axis of the labour movement to the right. Roy Hattersley, at the Labour Party Conference two years later, publicly recognised this when he said the party had chosen correctly when it elected Neil Kinnock in 1983. Hattersley is not known for false modesty. His statement expressed an understanding that only somebody with left credentials could become the stalking horse for the policies of the right wing.

Central to the right's campaign to carry through a counter-revolution was the campaign for the expulsion from the party of *Militant* supporters. With all the votes duly counted beforehand, the five members of the *Militant* Editorial Board were graciously conceded five minutes each at the Party's Annual Conference in Brighton in October 1983. The majority of delegates gave the five Editorial Board members a standing ovation when they left the hall despite the vote of roughly 5 million to just over 1 million in favour of their expulsion. This was the prelude to many later expulsions of *Militant* supporters and others which was to culminate in the expulsion of Tony Mulhearn, Derek Hatton and seven other Liverpool Marxists in 1986.

In the period 1983 to 1987, the Liverpool drama was to unfold with all its vicissitudes. During this struggle as in the miners' strike, are to be found the germs of future mass conflicts which will convulse the whole of Britain in the next decade. In their response to events in Liverpool, all the forces of the old society, the strategists of capital, the Labour and trade-union leadership, and the so-called 'soft left', were to be put to the sternest test. With the single exception of the Marxists around *Militant*, all were to be found wanting. The strategy and tactics of the leadership of the Liverpool labour movement, of *Militant*, despite some mistakes which were openly recognised, were vindicated in the course of this momentous struggle.

6.
Cut or Fight ?

AFTER ITS outstanding victory in May 1983 the new Labour council, with a majority of only three, was faced with a simple choice; obtain significant financial concessions from the Tory government, or abandon the programme upon which it was elected. The financial position was dire and Labour was forced to operate within the budget introduced by the Liberals just before the election. This proposed expenditure of £218 million. But the limit for the city's spending set by the government was £212 million. The Liberals therefore included in their budget so-called 'unallocated cuts' of £6 million, which they intended to make in the following year.

Since 1979 the government had stolen £270 million in grants from the city. The successive cuts and deliberate underspending which had been made under Liberal-Tory administration meant that Liverpool's level of spending had fallen way behind the average for comparable local authorities and even government guidelines. This in turn meant that the financial targets set by the government for 1983-4 were lower than for other cities such as Manchester. To remain within the constraints of government spending limits and the Liberal-Tory budget, Labour would have to completely abandon its programme of creating 1000 new jobs, reducing rents by £2 per week, and introducing a minimum wage and a 35-hour week for council workers. In addition the council would either have to have sacked 5000 workers or increase rates by 170 per cent in order to balance the books.

There were to be many attempts, both by the government and the tops of the labour movement, to argue that 'Militant was falsifying the figures' or 'deliberately exaggerating' in order to bring about a confrontation with Thatcher. Local government finance with its lending and borrowing on a daily basis is a very complicated moving picture only understood fully by specialists. The contradictory and rapid alterations in local government legislation and frequent changes in the basis of the grant system has complicated it even further in the 1980s.

But no matter how 'creative' or 'innovative' the attempts to interpret the finances of Liverpool City Council were at the time Labour took control, one stark fact stood out: there was a gap of about £25 million between what Labour intended to spend and its projected income. The council, together with all wings of the labour movement, decided that this gap could only be filled by forcing the Tory government to grant concessions. Wiseacres, of course, pontificated: if the Argentine dictator Galtieri could not humble Thatcher, then what chance would one council like Liverpool have? The same narrow and ossified outlook was also displayed towards the miners' struggle: 'They could not win', intoned the right wing Labour and trade-union leaders.

To be sure, they only dared to state this openly after the miners' strike had ended. But, to paraphrase Napoleon, 'First engage in struggle—and then see what happens.' Regrettably the right-wing labour leadership consider that a guarantee of victory must be obtained before the working class can engage in struggle. Their arid concept of the history of the working class is that only 'practical' goals can be achieved. But who decides what is practical? Historically, the proletariat, including the British working class, has advanced only by carving out from marble the steps of its advance.

Not for the first time, however, the sceptical leadership, together with the bourgeois, were to be confounded by the sheer scale, sweep and audacity of the movement in Liverpool and its repercussions throughout the country. Flushed with victory, the new Labour council began to implement its promises. The projected 1000 job losses were cancelled and the first steps were taken to create the *extra* 1000 jobs promised in Labour's manifesto. These measures engendered real enthusiasm and strengthened the bedrock of Labour support.

The announcement of 600 new jobs brought queues at the job-centres. The comments of those seeking jobs reflected both the corrosive despair of long-term unemployment and the new mood of hope and optimism engendered by the council. A third of those queuing at one job centre had been unemployed for three years. Many said it was the first time in a decade that anything had been done to create jobs in Liverpool. A correspondent to *Militant* gave an example of how the potential talents and skills of working-class people are wasted under capitalism: 'There was a Physics graduate, unemployed for three years, in the queue with his father.' In the same queue were four members of the local West Derby Labour Party Young Socialists—unemployed for a total of eight years between them.

Building Support for the Council's Case

The campaign to win money from the Tories began immediately. The council set up a Central Support Unit to co-ordinate the campaign and to produce propaganda. The youth, led by the Labour Party Young Socialists, together with the council workers, became the shock troops of this campaign. Its brief was to produce propaganda and to organise the campaign locally and nationally. Labour speakers like Tony Mulhearn and Derek Hatton, in a series of meetings, particularly those which led up to the momentous 19 November demonstration, explained that the council would introduce a deficit budget for 1984-5 and raise rates by no more than 9 per cent. This would pay for existing services plus Labour's new measures. In late September more than 500 shop stewards listened to council leaders John Hamilton, Derek Hatton, Tony Mulhearn and Terry Fields MP, pledging the council to go the whole way in its struggle.

This campaign, on a higher level and touching even more people than the local and general election campaigns, drove home the simple facts of the situation. Capitalism had failed the population of Liverpool. The private sector, upon which the Tories' strategy for rebuilding the inner cities rested, had failed. For the thousands of youngsters seeking work for the first time the only hope lay in the job opportunities generated by the council.

The great majority of the council workers understood that the struggle of the council was central to the employment prospects of the city. This was later demonstrated by the unprecedented support they gave in the 1984 local elections when 72 per cent of them were to vote Labour.

Meanwhile, Labour was also the target of a vicious demolition job, pursued in the council chamber by Labour's opponents and by the media both locally and nationally. A blanket of silence was drawn over Labour's achievements in employment and on rents. Not a word appeared about the imaginative Urban Regeneration Strategy. This inventive programme proposed to obliterate some of the city's worst slums and tower blocks and replace them with 6000 council houses. But even the figure of Mother Theresa, deep in the slums of Calcutta, was conjured up as an alleged opponent of Labour. The *Echo* accused the council of wanting to close down a hostel for the homeless. Labour had not made any such threat, they had merely indicated that the standard of provision in the hostel did not meet the council's criteria and for this reason, the council refused to refer any more homeless people to them. It was made clear however, that if those who ran the hostel wished it to continue operating, they had every right to do so. The decision of the council was motivated by concern for homeless people, not by an indifference reminiscent of Charles Dickens' heartless Mr Gradgrind in *Hard Times*.

A mood of grim determination began to grip the working class of Liverpool in support of the council's campaign. Michael Parkinson comments in his book *Liverpool on the Brink*:

> Labour's campaign successfully politicised the budget crisis, turning a complicated, financial argument into a simple choice between the government's version of the story and their own. It tied together the interest of the council workers, the consumers of local services, and of the domestic and commercial ratepayers. And it won the propaganda battle for Labour. The campaign persuaded enough people that the Labour council was right and that the major cuts in services and jobs or large rate rises were the only options.

Unbelievably, Labour was to be indicted later on by its opponents both inside and outside the movement for being 'conspiratorial' and 'secretive' over the details of its finances. Yet no council in Britain had driven home with such thoroughness and in such a simple and clear fashion the economics of the council. Moreover, pressure was exerted from below on the council to implement its programme.

The poorer parts of the city expected immediate results, some believed in miracles. Croxteth, with over 70 per cent youth unemployment, and an infant mortality rate 40 per cent above the national average, was demanding immediate action to alleviate the quite horrendous social and housing conditions in their area. Residents demanded immediate improvements in housing, including the demolition or conversion of flats. This pressure from below directly contributed to Croxteth being one of the priority areas for the Urban Regeneration Programme. The landscape and housing conditions of Croxteth were to be completely transformed within three years. Even the most bitter opponents of Labour could not deny the real change in the lives and conditions of working people that this programme was to bring.

The feeble basis for Tory reaction was illustrated in a 'revolt' of ratepayers in early August 1983. Three hundred and fifty 'besieged' the council, at one stage locking councillors in the council chamber, in protest at plans to build council houses near their homes!

The bold measures taken by the council set alarm bells ringing in Whitehall. This was reinforced with the election of *Militant* supporter Derek Hatton as Deputy Leader of the Council in August. This event merely confirmed what the bourgeois knew and feared: the Marxists provided the spinal column of the Liverpool labour movement in the looming confrontation with the government.

John Hamilton remained Leader. He typified the old reformist Left within the party who not so much 'led' as were dragged along by the mass movement. This was not without many sighs and regrets on their part and much wringing of hands.

Derek Hatton and Tony Mulhearn, on the other hand, personified the youthful, dynamic, working class forces who were determined to go to the end in the struggle against the government.

It was not just the fighting spirit of the working class which the Liverpool struggle so magnificently displayed but also the clear perspectives, strategy and tactics of the Marxists. Of course they did not have a monopoly of leadership, which also encompassed non-Militant supporters like Jimmy Parry, Tony Byrne, Dave Lloyd, Dominic Brady, Frank Mills and others. Nevertheless the Marxists played an important and sometimes critical role in the battle with the government. Derek Hatton's replacement of

Eddie Loyden, who had resigned when he was re-elected to Parliament, was noted by the bourgeois. It signified the seriousness with which the Liverpool labour movement viewed its struggle to rescue the city from the cycle of deprivation.

As early as July, the *Guardian* reported: 'Jenkin ready to take over Liverpool'. Seeking to mobilise opposition to the council, Patrick Jenkin had declared in a visit to Liverpool that he 'could seek special powers through Parliament to bring in a Commissioner'. This was not the last time that a threat to sweep aside a democratically elected council would be made and yet it evoked not the slightest protest from the Labour Party's front bench. Secretly many of them sympathised with Jenkin, although they would have to wait for a far more favourable moment to declare their intentions openly.

At the same time as securing Labour's base in Liverpool the campaign was taken onto the national plane. A letter was sent from the Liverpool Labour Group to all Labour MPs throughout the country. The Labour Party Conference in Brighton in September, which had seen the *Militant* Editorial Board expelled earlier in the week, listened to the leaders of the Liverpool labour movement explain how they had won their remarkable victory earlier in the year.

Tony Mulhearn contrasted the performance of Labour in Liverpool to the rest of the country. He asked the conference: 'Why did Labour's national vote slump to 27 per cent despite the massive unemployment under Thatcher's government?' He pointed towards the divisions within the Party, 'Fleet Street have been able to make much of the divisions in the Party due to witch-hunts and the attacks by leading comrades in the Labour Party.' Derek Hatton's speech was warmly greeted by the delegates. He explained how Liverpool had already moved to implement its promises. He then called for all Labour authorities to support Liverpool because they would be in the same boat in the following year and asked for a massive presence on the forthcoming 19 November demonstration. However, despite cutbacks which had already meant the disappearance of 100,000 local government jobs, 18,000 of them teachers, the NEC opposed a resolution, moved by West Derby, which supported the stand of Liverpool City Council.

The buoyant mood in Liverpool could not have been in greater contrast to the morbid scepticism and demoralisation which existed within the Labour Party in other areas of the country. Party membership nationally declined following the defeat of June 1983 while in Liverpool the membership, due to the active campaigning approach of the party, increased dramatically. In Broadgreen it doubled with the Young Socialists branch reaching 100 members, thereby gaining entitlement to a Labour Party Conference delegate in 1984.

The campaign also turned to the workers in the private sector. The recent spate of redundancies had reinforced the support for Labour amongst workers in private industry. Labour pointed out that the loss of 2000 jobs in United Biscuits saved the company nearly £11 million. But lost taxes, national insurance and rates, plus unemployment benefit and social security would amount to a cost of about £20 million (according to a social audit by the Merseyside County Council and Liverpool City Council). The council used this to explain that if the government was successful in forcing the council to sack 5000 workers, the cost of redundancy and lost taxes would have easily exceeded the £30 million demanded by Labour to pay for their programme.

Preparing for 19 November

The Tory and Liberal propaganda onslaught could not cut across the mood of support for the campaign which was shown in Autumn 1983. In early November 150 trade-union activists from factories, depots and offices throughout Merseyside met to give support to the campaign. This had followed an earlier meeting of 700 local authority stewards. Those who were opponents of *Militant,* and who were to express this opposition in the sharpest fashion at a later stage, were compelled at first to give support to the campaign. Peter Cresswell, leader of NALGO and secretary at that stage of the Joint Shop Stewards Committee, wrote a letter to the *New Statesman* (6 January 1984) in reply to an attack on Derek Hatton and *Militant.* He stated:

> I am far from being a Militant supporter and the trade-union members whom the committee represents range from Tories to Trotskyists—we encompass teachers, binmen, clerks and electricians. Yet among all these employees of Liverpool City Council, there is a growing realisation that the confrontation

towards which the council is heading is unavoidable...We know that we are going to have to fight for our lives in 1984—and, whether we have to fight the council, the government or commissioners, fight we will.

Unfortunately, this resolve was not shown by Cresswell when the going got rough in 1985. In the same issue of the *New Statesman* Paul Thompson, a leader of the minuscule Labour Co-ordinating Committee group on Merseyside declared:

> Whatever the other political divisions in the party, we are all united behind the current strategy of confronting the government. This is not a position of 'principled bankruptcy', but a product of our condition after a decade of disastrous Liberal-Tory rule in the city.

The only section of the Liverpool labour movement to express opposition at this stage was the rapidly declining Communist Party. Although claiming to be 'Communist' and 'Marxist' it had effectively abandoned Marxism. The 'Euro-Communists' led by Gordon McLennan and given theoretical expression by Professor Eric Hobsbawn were to the right of the Labour leadership on many issues. They have, for instance, come out in favour of an electoral alliance with the SDP traitors! The adherents to the *Morning Star* on the other hand, are a dwindling band of aged, unreconstructed Stalinists. Both wings of the CP had increasingly lost their base in the factories and workplaces. Its support within the unions was more and more located within the trade union officialdom, invariably acting as a 'left' cover for the most conservative stratum. Over decades they had become accustomed to wielding the conductor's baton whenever action was called for from the labour movement. But their support had declined in Liverpool as it had done nationally. They were being supplanted by *Militant* supporters in one union after another and they were virtually without influence in the District Labour Party, the main focus of working-class activity in the city. Incapable of expressing open political disagreement they were compelled to niggle over the details and the character of this or that demonstration.

Back in June the *Morning Star* had carried a headline 'Chaos Hits Mersey Dole Demo Plans'. At the end of September they wrote:

> We have already stated that whilst we support the demonstration in November and the campaign against unemployment, we feel that

the attitude of some *Militant* elements in the council tends to limit the scope of the campaign. It could be the same with this fight on the city's finances and services...Militants must also learn that they do not have a monopoly of answers and should stop acting like some pied piper expecting everyone to follow them. (*Morning Star*, 9 September.)

But pied pipers can only attract followers if they happen to be playing the right tune, i.e. if the programme, policy, and perspectives correspond to the mood of working people at a certain stage. The Communist Party were being pushed to the sideline and they did not like it one little bit. Their opposition to *Militant*'s influence in the struggle pushed them into becoming at a later stage the political attorneys of the most right-wing trade-union and labour leaders.

The leadership of the Labour Party meanwhile were taking fright at the scenario unfolding in Liverpool. They could comfortably coexist with Labour councils that were carrying out Tory cuts. No Labour leader condemned Newcastle City Council, which announced in November 1983 that 1300 jobs were to be cut from the workforce of 18,000. Jeremy Beecham, leader of that council, declared:

There will be painful and damaging reductions and the loss of many jobs among professional, administrative, clerical, manual staff and teachers. The quality of life in the city is bound to suffer although we shall make every effort to preserve services for the most vulnerable.

In contrast to 'extreme' Liverpool, even Sheffield and its Labour leader, David Blunkett, was praised by none other than *The Economist* for its 'socialist experiment'. The bourgeois, as subsequent events would demonstrate, could live with David Blunkett or Ken Livingstone and the trendy policies of the Greater London Council. They recognised that Livingstone and Blunkett would not go all the way, but in Liverpool they understood that something entirely different was taking shape.

If there *were* any doubts about the mood that was developing in Liverpool these were soon dispelled by the turn-out on 19 November. In bitterly cold weather, in a carnival-like atmosphere, more than 20,000 workers marched through the city's streets. It was a solid working-class demonstration. The council had circulated 210,000 bulletins and the District Labour Party had distributed 180,000 copies of their paper, *Not the Liverpool Echo*. There had been a colossal exertion of energy at factory gate meetings, street meetings and in the canvassing and work carried out by local Labour Parties and trade union branches. Labour Party workers—particularly the youth who flocked to Liverpool from all over the country—were rewarded with a magnificent demonstration.

Not just council workers but delegations from Fords, Cammell Lairds and all the major Transport and General Workers' Union branches participated in the demonstration. A big section of the march was composed of working-class women, particularly those who were affected by cuts in the National Health Service. Students joined in alongside a massive contingent of council workers and ordinary working people who had been drawn into the campaign and turned up on the day. A local housewife on a radio phone-in prior to the demonstration said:

> I am glad to have got a leaflet through the door about the march. I wouldn't have known any more about it otherwise. I am not in any political party. But I will be there. I'll just turn up myself and make my own demonstration. It's important you know to help your council.

Another worker declared:

> I started last week for the council, I'd been on the dole for a year. I'm a fan of the council. I couldn't repeat what I'd think. I'd be effing and blinding all over your tape.

Another stated:

> I was with my mates last night in the pub and one of them said, and he's a priest, 'It was the best thing that could happen because Liverpool has got to show the way in defeating Mrs Thatcher'.

The speeches from the platform were all greeted enthusiastically. Eric Heffer's demand for extra-parliamentary action was backed up by Derek Hatton's call for a city-wide general strike in the event of Tory Minister Jenkin moving to put commissioners into the city. President of the District Labour Party, Tony Mulhearn, declared that the demonstration was the biggest local demonstration since the struggle against Ted Heath's Industrial Relations Act—probably the biggest since the war. He declared:

This is a clear indication to the Tory government, to the establishment and to the ruling class that it would be a mistake to take Liverpool on...Make no mistake about it, the Tories can be beaten. The miners forced them back in 1981. Even within her own ranks, there is opposition to this seemingly impregnable iron government. They will not be defeated through rational argument. We have to believe we can win this struggle.

Neil Kinnock was invited to the rally but sent a message instead, in which he stressed, 'the Party is committed to a full-scale fight against the government's proposals to restrict local government'. The classical role of the Labour leadership towards any decisive struggle is like the man who is found following a crowd. When a by-stander asks him who he is, he replies, 'Oh, I'm their leader.' In the Liverpool struggle, however, the Labour leadership would shift from following to hurling rocks at the crowd! 1983 ended against a backdrop of growing radicalisation and combativity in the city but also with consternation on the part of the ruling class and the leadership of the labour movement about how to deal with the situation.

Towards a Deficit Budget

The demonstration of 19 November was seen merely as a springboard for an even wider and greater mobilisation of the working-class population of Liverpool behind their council. In early January 1984 a special Liverpool City Council campaign working party was set up to promote public, trade-union and political support for the policies of the council. More than 70 local leaders of trade unions in the private sector, tenants' associations, local authority workers and other local councils attended the inaugural meeting. In a unique development chief officers of each council department were also instructed to attend in order to ensure that the resources of their department were put behind the campaign.

The campaign working party agreed to organise 18 public meetings throughout the city in February, a series of factory gate meetings, and the production of regular briefing notes for circulation throughout the city. A 'democracy week' in defence of local authorities was planned by the TUC for late March. This subsequently proved to be a very tame affair in most of the country. But in Liverpool the call was made for a 24-hour stoppage and a mass demonstration on 29 March, which had been designated as the crucial council 'budget day'.

The choices facing not just the council but the working class of the city were explained in that tumultuous three-month period leading up to 29 March. The council was carrying out its programme and the working class understood this. The only promise with which Labour had found some difficulty was the implementation of a rent reduction of £2 per week. It discovered on coming to power that to implement this measure would have meant that, since more than 50 per cent of rent payers were on social security, the £2 would be deducted by the DHSS: £1.5 million would therefore go straight back into the coffers of the government. To avoid this the council implemented a £40 decoration grant for every council tenant.

Labour councillors did not contemplate illegality lightly. Derek Hatton explained the situation in early February:

> Obviously we do worry about the prospect of surcharge and bankruptcy. If we all stick together though, especially if we have a national campaign, the Tories will be powerless to act. This is not just a fight conducted by and on behalf of 51 councillors—it is a fight for a whole movement and must be conducted by the movement...Our programme to begin to tackle some of Liverpool's problems has been described as the work of 'mad Marxist loonies'. Our answer to that is—look at the disaster inflicted by the bosses, Tories and Liberals in Liverpool—who are the real loonies?

A rash of small strikes broke out throughout the Merseyside area. The most exploited and downtrodden sections of the working class were raised from their knees by the example of the militant stance of the city council. A bitter dispute broke out over the question of redundancies at Scotts Bakeries. John Wests faced their first strike for 100 years. There the management were forced to retreat, reinstating shop stewards sacked because they had refused to work hours imposed by the management. Crucial to victory was the decisive action of the city council which was about to boycott John West products.

Not a crumb of comfort however was forthcoming for Liverpool at the Labour Party's local government conference at Nottingham in February. GLC Leader Ken Livingstone received a rapturous reception from the 1000 councillors when, striking a defiant tone, he said: 'If it puts us outside the law, it is the laws which are wrong. We have the right and duty to defend our people.' But he was not able to live up to these fine words when put to the decisive test 12 months later.

Eric Heffer demanded that 'a future Labour government would indemnify Labour councillors defending their authorities'. The *Daily Telegraph* commented that this was a call for, 'an effective pledge that councillors who broke the law could not be put in the same position by a Labour government as the Clay Cross Councillors'. But Neil Kinnock, haunted by the coming confrontation in Liverpool, urged Labour councils to obey the law and remain in office to 'minimise the effects of any cuts'.

John Cunningham, Labour's local government spokesman, also showed his own preoccupation with Liverpool when urging the conference not to be 'obsessed with Liverpool'. He stated that, 'confrontation is not the way forward. We will not give Liverpool a blank cheque for what they want to do without telling all their financial details first.' But when they *did* receive 'all the financial details', this did not affect their approach to Liverpool one iota. They demanded that the council should carry out the dictates of the Tory government and in effect combine a massive rate increase with sackings.

Even David Blunkett, at this stage the darling of the left, declared 'We are not going to stab them [Liverpool] in the back...but we'll have to tell them that if they can stick with us then they should.' The suggestion that Liverpool should 'stick with us' was tantamount to urging Liverpool to carry out cuts in the forthcoming budget. Blunkett's statement was an anticipation of precisely how he, along with Livingstone and other alleged left-wing council leaders, would be prepared to act when put to the test in 1985.

The supine position of the Labour and trade-union leadership had encouraged the Tories in their attacks on local government. Their rate-capping legislation had centralised control over local authority spending in the hands of Patrick Jenkin, the Environment Minister. As many commentators, even those in the Tory Party, had hinted, this legislation effectively reduced local government to a sham.

Since the Tories had been in power the expenditure on building and housing repairs had been cut by more than 40 per cent and 83,000 council jobs had disappeared since 1979. Rate Support Grant (money given by government to local authorities) accounted for 66.5 per cent of local authority spending in 1975. But the Tory axe cut it to just over 50 per cent in 1984. Rates, as a whole, had increased by 94.8 per cent since 1979, compared to a 57 per cent increase in prices generally. Thus a massive £10,000 million had been added to the rates bill in the four years in which the Tories had been in power. The burden of this had naturally been carried by working-class families.

The scale of the Tories' attack had produced a mood amongst councillors and council workers that 'enough was enough'. The opportunity for a united fightback had never been greater and there were splits within the government on this issue. The 'wet' wing of the Tory Party were alarmed that the proposed cuts would result in a social explosion. The centralisation of power by the government contradicted the previous policy of the ruling class and was an indication of the desperate straits of British capitalism. In the period of the boom local government was relatively 'non-partisan'. In general it did not represent an arena of great conflict. The majority of councils were dominated by right-wing reformists who were quite happy to play a game of 'Ins and Outs' with the Tories and Liberals. It was also the time when a section of the right wing did not hesitate to fill their own pockets, resulting in the corruption and scandals typified by T Dan Smith in the North-East who was jailed for his involvement in the extensive corruption surrounding corrupt architect, John Poulson. After conviction Smith was expelled from the Labour Party, but following his release from prison was re-admitted back into party membership in 1987. This took place soon after *Militant* supporter Bill Hopwood had been expelled from the Labour Party.

One of those convicted in the Poulson scandal was Andy Cunningham, whose son John was the right-wing Labour spokesman on the environment. Marxists do not believe that the 'sins of the father are visited on the son'. But John Cunningham's gaining of the parliamentary nomination in Whitehaven was undoubtedly assisted by Andy Cunningham's strong influence in what was then the General and Municipal Workers' Union (now GMBATU), which was a powerful force in the local Labour Party. Moreover John Cunningham subsequently became a fervent advocate of nuclear power, and was thereby christened 'Plutonium Jack'. Opponents of nuclear power cruelly claimed that 'he glowed in the dark.' However it is no laughing matter for those who, as it has subsequently been shown, have contracted cancer from the nuclear waste emitted from the Windscale plant located in his constituency. Notwithstanding this, John Cunningham did not hesitate to associate himself with the dirty, unfounded allegations made by Roy Hattersley of 'corruption, literal corruption' against Liverpool councillors in 1985.

But the measures of the Tories, while centralising power in the hands of the government, also ran the risk of centralising the opposition. A unique opportunity for a national campaign embracing councils and their entire labour force in the major metropolitan areas, was presented by the measures of the government. However, once more, the Labour leadership bent all their efforts to keeping any 'opposition' within safe parliamentary bounds. John Cunningham even went so far as moving an amendment in the House of Commons to the Rates Bill which limited its measures to 'a particular number of authorities in any one year' thereby endorsing the overall provisions of the bill.

Incapable of appealing to the mass of the working class, the so-called 'left' as well as the 'right' substituted gimmicks for class action. The Greater London Council, for instance, planned to bombard Patrick Jenkin with Valentine cards, bearing the inscription, 'We Love London'. Livingstone's philosophy was 'Never mind the weather, all pals together.' George Tremlett, dissident Tory councillor and Anne Sofer, who deserted Labour for the SDP were happily recruited by Ken Livingstone to 'fight the government' over the abolition of the GLC! Without any real faith in the mass of working people the GLC later on centred all its hopes on the exhumed House of Lords! Giant banners extolling the 'opposition of the House of Lords' festooned County Hall.

In February, Kinnock had sent one of his acolytes, Jack Straw, to Liverpool to discover 'the real situation'. An inveterate witch-hunter, Straw was one of the worst candidates for such a role. The open hostility and contempt with which he was viewed by all strata of opinion on the left in Liverpool did not seem to daunt him. Like the Greek king Agesilaus, his motto seemed to be 'I seem to thee an ant, but one day I shall be a lion' but for his, ignominious role in Liverpool Jack Straw will forever remain an ant! Yet even Straw was to be taken aback initially at the scale of the problem confronting Liverpool. He was shown the books and given a detailed explanation of the financial position. He then declared to the press:

> The problems facing the city council are not of their own making but have been inherited from the irresponsible penny-pinching former Liberal-Tory administration. They need more money, not government penalties...The picture that I was given of the inheritance left to Labour last May by the previous Liberal-Tory administration was worse than I had anticipated...it appears that the Liberals had under-budgeted by some millions, so that the city council was already well into government penalty areas regardless of any of the policies on which it was elected last May. This is compounded by central government penalties which mean that for a modest increase in expenditure ratepayers could face rate rises of more than 100 per cent. (*Guardian*, 21 February.)

But while the Labour leadership, in the words of Neil Kinnock, were prepared to give 'sympathy by the trainload', they were not prepared to come behind Liverpool in facing up to the Tory government. Kinnock even refused to visit the city. Only when the relationship of forces had moved in favour of the right, did he deign to pay a visit.

Meeting with Jenkin

On the day following Jack Straw's visit to Liverpool, the Labour group travelled to London to meet Jenkin. In the days leading up to the meeting, through carefully leaked statements in the bourgeois press in what the *Guardian* called a 'political poker game', Jenkin had threatened to suspend the council and impose commissioners. When the Labour group came face to face with him, they were met with a blank wall of opposition which bordered on indifference.

Cocooned in his ministerial chair and in Parliament, he was ignorant of the scale of the problems which faced the city and the grinding poverty left him cold. As the council spokespersons outlined their case, they met with stony-faced opposition from Jenkin and his advisers. Unaccustomed to the language of the street, they were shaken by an interjection from Derek Hatton who said, 'Everyone is being too polite. I want to tell you mate, that you are for it if you don't give us our £30 million.' Derek Hatton also pointed out that demonstrations outside Mr Jenkin's house in London could not be ruled out. Labour councillors were facing the threat of surcharge, fines and the possible confiscation of their houses, for the 'crime' of defending the working class of their city.

Jenkin chose to interpret this as a threat of 'violence' and 'riots'. Yet Derek Hatton had stated no more than the obvious; the measures of the Tory government were preparing the soil upon which violence could take root. Others, like John Hamilton, had expressed the same views many times before. Even Alfred Stocks, the generally moderate Chief Executive 'was concerned that revolt was in the air in the city'. Jenkin's advice to the councillors was to increase rates by 70 per cent and to make drastic cuts in services and jobs.

The next day the press gave a relatively low key account of the talks. However a few days later Derek Hatton's alleged remarks were blown up by the right-wing tabloids. The *Sunday Express* (26 February) in a banner headline declared: '*Militant*'s Threat to Tory Minister'. It claimed to reveal 'one of the most chilling insights ever into the violent nature of left-wing extremism'. Patrick Jenkin was quoted as describing the Liverpool councillors as 'a very nasty lot'. Tony Byrne, who Jenkin incorrectly described as a 'hard Trot', countered by describing Jenkin as 'a very bad man'.

The reaction of Patrick Jenkin and Fleet Street had little to do with what actually happened at the meeting, but everything to do with the fact that the Chesterfield by-election in which Tony Benn was the Labour candidate was taking place. The miners' strike had also just begun and a number of violent confrontations were taking place on the picket line. The press tried to create an amalgam of students pelting Cecil Parkinson with eggs and tomatoes at Essex University, a picket organised against Mrs Thatcher in Warwickshire, the rather theatrical knocking over of the Coal Board boss MacGregor by demonstrating miners and of course the threats of 'riots' in Liverpool.

This approach may go down well in the Tory shires but had little or no effect on the working class of Liverpool. Derek

Hatton described Jenkin's account of the meeting as 'blatant lies'. He declared:

> The only violence we know about is the violence being shown by Patrick Jenkin and the rest of the Tory government against the people of Liverpool. It is the violence against those on the dole, those without houses and hopes for the future. None of us spoke to him in threatening terms. What we said was that if the government continued along the lines they are going now, there will obviously come a time when young people will react.

Preparing for Budget Day

A head of steam began to build up in the city in preparation for a city-wide strike on the council budget day, 29 March. Enormous enthusiasm was displayed at the series of public meetings organised by the council and the council received unprecedented support from most of the unions. NALGO ran courses for 180 shop stewards on the theme of 'Our City, Our Fight'. The 5800 members of NALGO were expected to come out solidly in favour of the strike alongside the 8000 GMBATU members and other manual workers. The only opposition to the strike came from the teachers' union, the NUT, and the National Union of Public Employees (NUPE) which had only 2000 members. At a mass meeting the NUT had turned down the strike by a narrow majority of 100. There was much bitterness in the labour movement at the ambivalent role played by the NUT leaders. While officially supporting the strike call, in practice their lukewarm attitude led to the majority voting against strike action. Incredibly, particularly in view of their own later strike action, Jim Ferguson, the NUT Branch Secretary and member of the Communist Party, declared: 'If we were seen to withdraw their services in March which means the loss of the full day's education, that would not be the best way to gain support from the parents'!

NUPE's attitude towards the strike was conditioned by the political opposition to *Militant* of NUPE leader Jane Kennedy. In most local authorities, there is one union which tends to act as a refuge for those workers who are not prepared to engage in struggle. In other areas this role had been sometimes fulfilled by the GMBATU. In Liverpool the roles were reversed. Nevertheless, had Labour leaders been allowed to address the rank and file of NUPE, they would undoubtedly have convinced them of the need to take strike action. However, the great 'democrat' Jane Kennedy was not prepared to sanction such a move nor was she or the other leaders prepared to give the members the right to vote on the issue of strike action. But the decisions of these two unions failed to cut across the expectant mood that began to develop within the ranks of the working class on Merseyside.

Layers of the population and organisations not traditionally associated with the struggles of the labour movement were drawn behind the council's campaign. The church, with 2000 years of experience behind it, has learned to bend with the prevailing social mood. It accommodated itself successfully to feudalism and then adapted to the variegated types of capitalist regimes over the last 300 years. Latterly it has even established a *modus vivendi* with Stalinism, the Catholic Church helping to dampen down the movement of the Polish workers in the last few years. As was discussed in Chapter 1 religion also played an important role in the past in the development of Liverpool and in the shaping of its politics. However, with a loosening of their grip on the working class, both Catholic and Protestant churches have leaned on one another to shore up their narrowing base in the city. At the same time the good shepherds of the church were bound to reflect the pressures on their flock.

In 1983, and to some extent in 1984, the Catholic Archbishop Derek Worlock and Anglican Bishop David Sheppard took a generally sympathetic approach towards Labour, although Sheppard was less 'sheepish' than Worlock, who was anything but 'warlike' in support of the council! At all times they attempted to persuade the council to abandon any idea of breaking the 'rule of law'. Nevertheless David Sheppard in particular did not hesitate to attack the government: 'We are wasting the God-given resources of the nation by leaving three million people on the dole and we are breeding a dangerously bitter spirit.'

At the same time secret communications and negotiations with the government were conducted by the church leaders. In reality they were as terrified of the movement that was developing in Liverpool as the ruling class itself. But they also had to wait for a more propitious moment, before they could openly form a common front with the government.

Shopkeepers began to display Labour stickers in support of the 29 March Day of Action. Even some policemen were reported by Labour workers to have indicated support for the stand of the council. Reformists have argued that Labour must take a 'middle-of-the-road position' in order to win the middle layers of society but, as Aneurin Bevan once said: 'If you stand in the middle of the road, you're likely to get knocked over.' *Militant* pointed out that if the labour movement acts decisively the ranks of the working class would fuse together in one unified movement, and this in turn would draw to its side the middle layers of society. Liverpool bore out what the Marxists have always argued. The outline of such a process began to develop in Liverpool in the early months of 1984. A similar phenomenon was witnessed when small shopkeepers, professional and managerial groups were drawn behind the miners: they clearly saw the closure of the mines as representing the death knell in their communities. Not just the miners would suffer if the government won, but whole communities including sections of the middle class.

The Labour council, as the 1984 May elections were to brilliantly underline, was the real champion of the needs of the city. Every corner of Liverpool life was affected by the struggle that was looming. The Milk Cup Football Final on 25 March was between Everton and Liverpool. Labour produced red and blue stickers for the different supporters with the slogan 'Liverpool/Everton supporters back our Labour council'. On the morning of the match, Labour workers who stood outside Lime Street Station and bus depots to hand out leaflets and collect money for the battle were warmly received. The mood of 'us against the world' was heightened by the Cup Final. One observer noted that on the tube from Baker Street in London to Wembley groups of Liverpool and Everton supporters travelling together were chanting 'Liverpool, Everton, Maggie Maggie Maggie, Out Out Out!'

The strategists of capital and their press began again to express their worry at the situation. *The Times* (21 February) gnashing its teeth, demanded that the Liverpool 'rebels' be shown no mercy: 'If martyrdom is unavoidable, the martyr could be given an ignominious obscure end.' But at the same time it expressed the growing consternation at the repercussions on the money markets of an 'illegal deficit budget' in Liverpool:

'Noises from Liverpool politicians have, without doubt, sent unpleasant shivers through the market for local government loans.'

The *Guardian* declared hysterically, 'The air is thick with talk of rebellion, even revolution.' Of course, ever mindful of the need for 'correct revolutionary tactics', the same journal proffered the advice:

> If Liverpool goes bankrupt, however, the ensuing chaos will discredit not the government but the Labour council. It will also occur a year before local authorities join battle properly with the government over rate-capping, thus risking spoiling that possible tactic with the memory of 'revolutionary defeatism'. Illegal rebellion on rate-capping would be difficult and dubious enough; for Liverpool to pull out the plugs now, while it still enjoys the doomed luxury of local accountability, seems pure folly. (*Guardian*, 21 February.)

Shades of Kinnock and Blunkett in these lines! Despite this, one year later when many authorities were in Liverpool's position, the *Guardian* advised them precisely 'not to join battle' but to accept the will of Parliament!

But the leadership of the council remained implacable in its determination to defend all the jobs and services. In reply to those who urged the council not to defy the law, Derek Hatton declared, 'If our predecessors in the movement hadn't broken the law, 12 year olds would still work down the mines and 14 year olds up the chimney. If we don't fight in 1984 we would either have to sack one in six of our workforce or to treble the rates. We are not prepared to do either of these, we will fight for jobs and services.'

The five Liverpool Labour MPs were no less intransigent. Terry Fields declared, 'All I can say, and I speak for the other MPs, is that we will be there on the picket lines and occupying the yards if it comes to that.' Eddie Loyden, Labour MP for Garston, was still a city councillor and if he was to be surcharged, it would probably mean his removal as an MP. He declared that there was 'no acceptable alternative to the course which the council is following. The course is set.' He fully accepted the danger to his personal position, but Liverpool was in 'a desperate position' with the possibility, according to the *Sunday Times* (19 February), 'that it will lead to civil disorder'.

This determination at the top was more than matched by the resolve from below. At a mass meeting of NALGO in early March, 3500 turned up to the Liverpool Boxing Stadium, although 1000 were locked out when the management of the stadium cited fire regulations. Those present at the meeting supported the strike call with not one contribution against.

The high degree of involvement and the politicisation that had taken place amongst the manual workers was best reflected in the mass meeting of the GMBATU City Council Cleansing Department. Out of an attendance of 1000 at the meeting, only one worker abstained! Deputy Convenor Bernie Hogan in attacking the previous Liberal-Tory council pointed out that when they were in control so many trees were planted in Liverpool in place of houses that 'If we are not careful Liverpool will end up like Sherwood Forest with us poor robbing the rich barons.'

The Liberals' Budget Proposals

The Tories were now of such little significance, and had lost so much of their base amongst workers in Liverpool, that they supported swingeing cuts rather than rate increases. The Liberals on the other hand, sensing the mood, were unwilling to be cast any longer as the party of cuts. They therefore demagogically proposed an 'alternative budget' with a 'cast iron guarantee' of no redundancies. Their figures were plucked out of the air with no real basis in fact. Tony Byrne declared:

> A Liberal budget of £220 million could only be achieved by compulsory redundancies. It also proposed that permanent council jobs be replaced with 5000 temporary MSC jobs. No mention was made of how these MSC jobs are to be funded by the council. The council's contribution would be nearer £8 million to top up wages and pay for other costs...nothing is said about the £6 million of cuts agreed in the previous Liberal budget which the Labour Party refused to implement...It would mean cutting around £50 million of jobs and services. A single figure rate increase for 1984-5 would mean a total spending of around £220 million. Even the Tory Party has admitted that the council would need to spend at least £245 million next year–equivalent to a 70 per cent rate increase for the city services.
>
> Council workers who think it offers a 'lifeline' should think again. Members of the public who think there is a painless way out of the

city's financial crisis should think again. The Liberal figures are an illusion. There are no easy options—if there were, we would have taken them.

The sheer lack of credibility of the Liberals' 'alternative budget' served to divide them from the Tories and was a factor in the split between both parties in the crucial 29 March budget debate.

Meanwhile, Liverpool's campaign had found a big echo nationally. A *Militant* public meeting held in Bermondsey, London, in early March was addressed by Liverpool councillor Paul Astbury. After the meeting an enthusiastic worker approached him to declare 'If they take your home you can come and live in mine. If they take your car, you can have mine.' This was typical of the reaction of workers in the city and throughout the country.

Despite the hysterical press campaign and the personal vilification of the leaders the bourgeois were incapable of breaking the will of the working class on Merseyside. The Liverpool drama was unfolding against a background of heightened class struggle. The miners' strike had begun and the democratic right to belong to a union had just been denied to the workers at the GCHQ communications headquarters by government dictat.

Merseyside was the area of greatest solidarity with the GCHQ workers when a total of 100,000 workers responded on 28 February to the call for action by the TUC. All the major workplaces Shell, Cammell Laird, Vauxhall, British Aerospace, Pilkingtons came out on a one-day strike. In Liverpool itself the council workforce was solid and the only large-scale industry which failed to respond, by a very narrow majority, was Fords. The strike of the bus crews had kept attendance at a demonstration through the city to 5000, but the combativity of the Merseyside workers was unmistakable.

This mood was fuelled by the callous indifference of the government towards the avalanche of redundancies in the area. Thatcher's response to a request to intervene to prevent the redundancies of British-American Tobacco was to reply: 'The government would not wish to intervene in matters concerning a company's commercial judgement.' While refusing to act to prevent job losses, the Tories were quick enough to back up bosses like Eddie Shah. Millions of pounds were spent mobilising the police to defend his strike bound Warrington printworks.

Right-Wing Split in Labour Group

By now, Thatcher, Jenkin and the strategists of capital were grimly looking for points of support within Liverpool upon which they could base their opposition. Given the composition of the Labour group, with only a minority of *Militant* supporters and with the presence of a number of open right wingers, it had remained remarkably cohesive. But the capitalists, together with the leadership of the labour movement, were exerting enormous pressure on the small right-wing rump to publicly break with the left and thereby sabotage any possibility of an 'illegal budget'.

The long-predicted split was delayed until early March. Without ever once expressing their opposition either within the council or in the Labour Party, seven councillors declared in the press that they were not prepared to support an 'illegal budget'. They were led by longstanding right wingers, Eddie Roderick (who had in the past supplanted John Hamilton as Labour group leader in a short-lived right-wing coup in 1978), Bill Snell an USDAW official and Paul Orr from Vauxhall ward. Roderick had already been deselected by his ward for the forthcoming election in May, and therefore calculated that he had nothing to lose. Gilmoss Labour Party, which embraced the ward represented by councillors Roderick, Murphy and Snell, three of the seven, immediately dissociated the Party from their actions. It called upon them to make an immediate retraction. Tony Mulhearn declared that any councillors that broke the mandate upon which they were elected in the May 1983 elections and voted for cuts in jobs and services would be seen as 'political lepers' by the mass of the working class on Merseyside.

One of the councillors who declared her intention to vote against the budget was Margaret Delaney who said: 'We should put the city through what the government is telling us to do and let the wounds bleed. It is not until the people of the city have been put through mass redundancies and forced to pay high rates that they will realise what the government is doing.'

It is the Marxists in the past who have been accused, quite falsely, of propounding this 'theory' of 'increasing misery' but in fact, Marxism teaches that it is *not* necessarily a big drop in the conditions of the working class which radicalises them. It is more often the change from one epoch to another. This can come from an upswing following on from a period of stagnation as much as from a decline in production after a period of prosperity.

The views of Delaney, who soon after resigned from the council, with her contempt towards the working class and a cynical disregard for the suffering of working people, were the same as the rest of the 'scabby seven'. At a lobby of the Labour group on 23 February, Roderick, one of the seven, passed lobbying stewards and spat out at them, 'There's no way I'm going to vote for an illegal budget. Do you think that I want to end up on the dole like you lot? I'm not that bloody stupid.' The rebels were hailed as the 'sensible seven' by John Cunningham and the rest of the Labour leadership.

A delegation of councillors and labour movement representatives from Liverpool met Neil Kinnock in the House of Commons on 19 March. The full details of Liverpool's position were once more outlined by the council's main spokespersons. Tony Mulhearn said that the press had played up the meeting as an attempt at a compromise: 'It was nothing of the sort. Liverpool had come to ask the national leadership for full and unequivocal support. They were prepared to listen to anyone who could show an alternative that did not include massive rate or rent increases or job losses.'

Kinnock agreed that it was not a meeting to call for compromises. He enquired however what Liverpool could achieve with the powers that it had: 'Whatever course of action, you will be deprived of achieving your aim.' He then propounded his theory of the 'dented shield': 'It would be better to stay in office to mitigate the damage of the Tory government...we will make representations to the government to secure additional finances if the situation makes it possible' (i.e. if Liverpool kept 'within the law'). John Hamilton replied to Kinnock saying that the consequences of big cuts would be catastrophic in Liverpool. He pointed out that the breakdown of social order was just below the surface.

Kinnock was asking the Liverpool councillors to remain within the framework of the law, although the Labour leadership had backed the trade unions in calling for the defiance of Tory laws on the issue of GCHQ. He was saying that Liverpool could not win. After the 1981 riots the government had coughed up £20 million—why, therefore, could not the government be persuaded to find the money in this case, asked John Hamilton. They also questioned why the Parliamentary Labour Party had not had a much fuller debate in Parliament on the issue. Why was it left to David Alton to initiate a debate on Liverpool in Parliament?

Kinnock's silence was eloquent testimony to the fact that the Labour leadership did not want the issue to be aired in Parliament at all for fear of revealing what their real programme for Liverpool was. Peter Lennard, then Chairman of the Liverpool GMBATU local authority convenors, pointed out how his members had actively supported the election of a Labour council. They would, he said, totally oppose all cuts. If Labour betrayed its policies it would not be returned in the 1984 elections.

Tony Mulhearn further pointed out that the stand of the Upper Clyde Shipbuilding workers in 1971 had forced the Tory government into a U-turn, eventually paying out £25 million 'to avert social disorder'. A mass movement in Liverpool, particularly if it was backed by the full might of the labour and trade-union movement nationally, was a parallel situation. Kinnock for his part denied that there were any parallels with Upper Clyde, Clay Cross or the struggle of the Poplar councillors in the early 1920s.

When pressed by Terry Harrison as to whether the Labour leadership were telling Liverpool to make cuts, Neil Kinnock replied that he was not saying that workers should be sacked, nor was he washing his hands of Liverpool. But when he was asked if he would come to Liverpool to examine the problems he declined, saying that this would be 'pointless'. The attitude of the national Labour leadership was quite clear: like the government, they were hoping for a split in the council which would avert the acceptance of an 'illegal deficit budget'. Kinnock was just not telling the whole truth when he said that he was not in favour of cuts. Following Jack Straw's visit to the city in February, his office had produced an alternative budget which suggested a 60 per cent rise in rates. Later Kinnock was to deny that such a proposal was ever made, but local government spokesmen, John Cunningham and Jack Straw, had mentioned this figure from a number of platforms.

Quite apart from the effect on home-owners, the majority of whom are working class in Liverpool, the effect of a 60 per cent increase would have been devastating for local businesses. Replying to speculation about such an increase, one of the biggest stores in Liverpool, Lewis's, issued a statement: 'Inevitably we would be forced to do the very thing the council is trying to avoid and shed labour.'

The net result of a 60 per cent increase, even when moderated by the county council structure to a 50 per cent rate rise for householders and a 45 per cent rate increase for local businesses, would have wiped out the jobs of shopworkers employed in the private sector. Ironically, one of the 'sensible seven' was Bill Snell, a full-time official of the shopworkers' union!

The national Labour leadership were being ground between the millstones of an intransigent government and an implacable working class in Liverpool. Success in the class war is not guaranteed by a correct programme or perspectives, although this of course is decisive. But without the will to see the programme through, success will never be achieved. The perspectives of the Marxists have been vindicated on many occasions. In Liverpool their will was also being tested as they led a mass movement, seeking to compel the government with its panoply of powers to retreat. What is more, they were without the support of the leaders of the Labour Party.

7.
A Trial of Strength

THE RESOLVE of the leadership of the Liverpool labour movement, particularly of the Marxists, was clear and communicated itself to the working class of the city. In the early part of 1984 another round of mass meetings took place. On 27 February a huge rally of 1700 trade-union representatives and activists was held in St George's Hall and speakers included Ron Todd of the Transport and General Workers' Union. Local authority workers were represented alongside those from private industry, from Fords, Vauxhall, etc. 'We won't budge' was the mood of the meeting. John Hamilton and Tony Benn received standing ovations for their speeches. Tony Benn declared at a further meeting on 24 March: 'no gains for working-class people have ever been made without people taking risks and going outside the law'.

These meetings set the scene for the magnificent strike and demonstration on 29 March. On that day Liverpool witnessed one of the largest city-wide general strikes in British history. 50,000 marched to a rally at the Town Hall in a crushing demonstration of the power and organisation of the Merseyside working class. This great demonstration of solidarity with the council drew in all sections of the labour movement and of the working class. Roars of approval followed the speeches from the balcony of the Town Hall. A representative from the Yorkshire miners, visibly moved by the demonstration declared: 'The miners are in the same position as Liverpool council, and in both cases if we stay united we can't be defeated.'

Terry Fields MP got a great reception from the crowd when he declared, 'In 1921 in Poplar, 30 councillors were jailed for standing up for local workers. Like Liverpool it was a high unemployment docks area. Like some present day leaders, Herbert Morrison then told Poplar to stay inside the law.' Terry Fields told the rally that they should join the Labour Party Young Socialists and the Labour Party. Bill Jones, speaking as the Chairperson of the Joint Shop Stewards Committee stated: 'council workers helped return this socialist council. We are now fighting to save all jobs, and we've got the most magnificent demo ever in this city.' In its fervour and enthusiasm, the crowd exceeded that at a derby between Everton and Liverpool and it sang in football style: 'Labour council, Labour council, we'll support you ever more'.

Postal workers, firefighters, water workers, printers, car workers, builders, seafarers, dockers, hospital staff, civil servants, office workers, miners, ferryworkers, shopworkers, railway workers, transport workers, shipbuilders and many other groups of workers joined the masses of council workers on the demonstration. Another impressive feature of the demonstration was the large participation of youth, including large contingents from the Further Education colleges. One woman on the march expressed the feelings of many that day: 'We brought our kids along because it's their future we're fighting for. I think Kinnock should have been here today showing his support.' Another worker said: 'I am a steward in the Speke area and I'm out here in support of these people who are fighting for jobs, not just that, but for education and jobs for our children.' Another: 'I am an unemployed heavy goods driver and I am 120 per cent for what the council is doing. We've got to have a go at this, otherwise we'll really be on the floor.'

Knowsley NALGO came out on strike in support of their Liverpool brothers and sisters, and one worker commented: 'There is no other option to supporting the council unless you want to go back to Victorian values—pay for this and pay for that. You can't have Cruise [missiles] and have social services, it's as simple as that.' Teachers were also evident on the demonstration with a particularly striking banner being carried by members of the college lecturers' union, NATFHE. They taught prisoners at Walton jail and their banner read, 'Today we teach the real robbers.' The 'scabby seven' needed a police escort into the Town Hall—so much for their claim of popular support.

'The Sting!'

The debate in the council chamber reflected all the passion and commitment of irreconcilable opponents who are confronting each other across a class divide. The debate was conducted against the background of the roars and chants of the crowd outside as well as the active participation of the workers in the packed public gallery. The Liberals in moving their budget pitched their appeal at one and the same time to the Tory government and Labour's right wing. The figure of Neil Kinnock was invoked many times by the Liberals in the course of their contributions. At one stage their spokesman Paul Clark thought he had made a telling point: 'The Labour Party we see here in Liverpool is the Labour Party nationally in ten years' time.' He was somewhat nonplussed when the public gallery greeted this with a prolonged outburst of applause!

The Labour councillors rose to the occasion and acted as real tribunes of the Liverpool working class. The Liberals had talked about 'natural wastage'. Pauline Dunlop in a forceful speech declared: 'There is nothing natural about it...It is not us that creates chaos but capitalism. There are people dying unnecessarily whilst firms such as GEC announce record profits and lay off 1000 workers. We want an alternative, a planned socialist society where people can fully develop.' The effect of such speeches was heightened by the fact that there was a continuous local radio transmission which was attentively followed by the majority of the population throughout the day. She went on to declare: 'Listen to the people inside and outside the council chamber. They are saying *no* to a policy of despair.'

When Derek Hatton rose to speak he was greeted by cheers from the public gallery and applause punctuated his speech. The Liberals were staggered when he revealed that in the ward next to that of Liberal spokesman Paul Clark, the Liberal candidate for the forthcoming council elections, Beryl Molyneux, had just resigned and was applying to join the Labour Party. He then made an indictment of capitalism as it was manifested in Liverpool. He referred to the television programme *Brass Tacks*. This had shown that a man living in Netherley, the ward he represented went to the DHSS to ask for money for a car to take his daughter's body to the funeral.

However he was told to take the coffin on his knee in the car he was travelling in!

The Labour council's argument, explained Derek Hatton, centred around their demand for the £30 million shortfall, which was owing to Liverpool anyway, to be paid out of the government's contingency funds. In the recent budget the Tories had given £35 million in tax handouts to 650,000 people already earning over £15,000 a year. He received an enormous cheer when he sat down after his onslaught on the Tories and Liberals. The Tories were not able to climb out of the gutter. Their leader Chris Hallows made a racist comment that Neil Kinnock had no backbone, 'because he had a nigger in the woodpile, Tony Benn'. He refused to withdraw these remarks.

The sentiments of Labour's opponents was that Labour could shout as much as they liked but as far as the government, the Labour leadership, not to say the Liberals and Tories were concerned everything was set up for a Labour defeat. By refusing to sanction a deficit budget the 'rebel seven' Labour councillors were going to swing the vote and save civilisation as we know it.

But all the best plans of mice and men go astray! Colossal pressure was being exerted by the people of Liverpool through the partial general strike and demonstration outside the Town Hall. Labour's opponents did not wish to be seen as the willing accomplices of the Tory government and the six rebel Labour councillors (one was not at the meeting) were not yet ready to associate themselves with the savage cuts foreshadowed in both the Liberal and Tory alternative budgets. The 'rebels' voted with the Labour group against these budgets, but then a motion to adjourn the meeting until 11 April to allow a deal to be cobbled up between the six, the Liberals and the Tories was passed.

Labour proposed as an emergency measure that a small, all-Labour committee be established to allow essential services to be funded up to the 11 April meeting. The Liberals and Tories waxed indignant. They declared that they were the masters now, as Labour's budget had been defeated. But even the six found this hard to swallow and voted with Labour to establish the all-Labour emergency committee.

The motion now consisted of two parts: For a recalled council meeting on 11 April and for an interim all-Labour emergency committee until then. The Tories and Labour's right wing decided to vote in favour as they wanted a recall meeting to try to force through a budget before the May local elections. Trying to be clever, the Liberals thought that since Labour would vote in favour, they would decide to vote against. If their plans had worked, they could then have gone to the May elections speaking about a Labour-Tory coalition and how radical they, the Liberals, were. But Labour abstained, completely out-manoeuvring the Liberals. The 30 Liberal votes defeated the 24 combined votes of the Tories and Labour's right wing.

The whole motion was therefore defeated leaving Labour without a budget but still holding effective control of the council through the chairs of committees, and there would be no recalled council meeting on 11 April. John Hamilton added to the discomfort of the Liberals when he announced, to wild applause from the public gallery, that by voting against the Liberals had made themselves liable to surcharge. It would now be the electorate in the May elections who would be the judge of the budget suggested by Labour. To jubilant chants of 'Here we go!' and cries of 'How about a whip round for the Liberals?' the Labour councillors and members of the public triumphantly left the meeting. Thus came to an end eight and a half hours of debate.

The government was absolutely stunned by this development. The calculations of a coalition of the Liberals, Tories and Labour traitors had come unstuck. Environment Minister Patrick Jenkin now desperately attempted to patch up a deal that would result in the downfall of the Labour council and the isolation of the 'Militants'. According to Michael Parkinson in *Liverpool on the Brink* (pp55-6), he secretly approached Paul Orr, the leader of the 'rebels', with an offer of 'more money than the city has ever seen from the Manpower Services Commission, the Sports Council and the Urban Programme, if you get the show on the road with a legal budget'. The right wing are the people who have consistently accused the Marxists of 'underhand tactics' and 'conspiratorial methods'. Yet here was the right wing secretly conspiring with the hated Tory government to defeat Labour's plans.

Unfortunately for Jenkin, although the right wing voted against an 'illegal budget', they had not yet been brought to the position where they could openly form a block with the Liberals and Tories. 'If you sup with the devil, make sure you use a long spoon'—it was one thing to discuss behind the scenes, but quite another to publicly embrace the Tories and Liberals in a coalition to attack the working class. Such a step would have completely shattered the myth they had fostered that it was they, the seven, and not the *Militant* who were 'the real Labour Party'.

Meanwhile, the movement in Liverpool, buoyed up by the 29 March events, began to prepare for the local elections. The crucial role of *Militant* and its supporters was reflected in the rally organised by *Militant* in St George's Hall with a record attendance of 500 people. The clear programme, perspectives, strategy and tactics of the Marxists had led to a spectacular growth in the support for *Militant*, particularly amongst the youth and the council workforce.

At the same time, the Local Government Subcommittee of the Labour Party National Executive backed the stand of Liverpool City Council. Some right wingers were absent but the only vote against was from Charlie Turnock of the NUR, an anticipation of the hatchet job he was to do later in dismantling the District Labour Party in Liverpool.

Who Will Run the City?

Following the dramatic 29 March meeting and the thwarting of all the attempts to unseat the Labour council, the press unleashed another round of attacks against Labour councillors. The spectre of commissioners and even troops being sent into the city was raised once more. The *Sunday Times* (1 April) declared that the Tories had prepared an emergency bill to send in commissioners in view of the fact that 'they expect Labour gains in the city's May elections may yet produce a majority for the proposed Labour budget'.

Thus the great Tory democrats were considering suspending elections, sending in troops, and in a semi-Bonapartist dictatorial fashion were even threatening to run the city through commissioners. If in tiny Clay Cross the use of commissioners foundered on the opposition of the unions and the working class, then what prospects for success were there in using them in Britain's fifth largest and most militant city?

The Times claimed that 'municipal services could be run or rates levied by appointees of central government...The ranks of uniformed Merseyside constables guarding the Town Hall the other day would turn out again if need be.' The *Sunday Times* was more sober: 'The caretakers have to unlock the doors, the computer has to be set up. There are twenty-five things that have to happen before you can sit in your grand office and pretend to run the city.'

Jenkin and the ruling class did not see things going smoothly in the event of the use of commissioners. The movement in Liverpool was still on the upswing as the forthcoming local elections would demonstrate. Moreover, the more serious sections of the ruling class were still haunted by the relatively recent 1981 Toxteth riots. Napoleon once said of his unsuccessful occupation of Spain: 'You can do anything with bayonets, but you cannot sit on them.'

The resistance of the council workforce could have triggered off a movement in the private sector and in the charged atmosphere that existed on Merseyside could have fused together into a city-wide revolt. Such a movement, particularly against the background of the miners' strike was entirely possible. In February, *The Times* had urged: 'It is a moment for Mr Jenkin to show his famous phlegm.' But Jenkin was reported at this stage to be lying awake at night, haunted by the consequences of a false move in Liverpool. His advisers were strongly urging him not to use commissioners at that stage.

With local elections approaching, the Liberals were eager to avoid giving any impression that they favoured draconian cuts in jobs and services, but at a special council meeting on 25 April the deficit budget was once again voted down because the six Labour traitors voted with the opposition. In the decade up to 1983 the Tories and Liberals had found no difficulty in collaborating with one another, but now they were incapable of agreeing on a common budget. Like an estranged couple, with Jenkin and his advisers desperately playing the role of the marriage guidance counsellor in the background, these parties could not be brought together to 'save the city'. It was the mass pressure and the fear of what would happen to them in the election that stayed the hands of the Liberals.

In the run up to the local elections, the two capitalist parties once more resorted to their scare tactics. They played the 'commissioners' card for all that it was worth. But press reports had indicated that those who had been approached to take on the job of commissioner in Liverpool were not at all keen. Press speculation indicated that the Governor of the Falklands had been approached; he preferred taking on 'The Argies' any day rather than Liverpool! In the 25 April council debate Derek Hatton stated:

> It was reported to us by the national leaders of our Party, that even Patrick Jenkin himself put his hands in the air when approached by John Cunningham and said, 'Who on earth could I put into Liverpool as a commissioner anyway? Even MacGregor [head of the Coal Board which had just provoked the national miners' strike] wouldn't take that!'

The May 1984 Local Elections

Canvassers during the May 1984 election campaign discovered that the mood had consolidated behind Labour. Even opponents of Labour were drawn behind the stand of the city council. A voter commented to a Liberal canvasser: 'I can't stand the *Militant* but at least someone is standing up to the bitch in London.' An opinion poll had also revealed that a majority of Liberals, 53 per cent, and a substantial minority of Tories, 28 per cent, believed Labour's claim that the government had not given a fair deal to Liverpool.

Another blow was suffered by the Liberals when Beryl Molyneux, the former Liberal candidate, revealed why she had left them to join Walton Labour Party. Although the *Echo* did not comment, her statement received wide circulation through publications of the labour movement:

> I nearly made the biggest mistake of my life. I was the selected candidate for Melrose Ward in Walton. It was a rushed decision to stand, but as time went by and I attended Liberal meetings and met so-called 'top' Liberal people, I began to ask myself had I made the right choice.
> I asked questions and the answers were not the ones that should have been given. How and why were government cuts allowed to happen? Why was no fight put up to prevent these cuts? I'll tell you why, I honestly didn't believe that the Liberals care enough about the city or its people. I attended the Labour Party 'Liverpool in

Crisis' public meeting and got answers that I could relate to. Why should the people of Liverpool have second best? Why should we stand still and let our city die?

Much has been said about Labour's illegal budget. But what is illegal about saving jobs, defending services which have deteriorated over the last ten years of the Liberal-Tory alliance. I believe only the Labour Party can help the city. Liverpool needs now, more than ever, strong leadership.

The result of the elections in May 1984 was a stunning victory for Labour. The *Post* (4 May) declared:

> Voters in Liverpool took a huge step to the left in yesterday's local elections giving Labour a clear 17 seat majority on the city council. It is seen as a massive vote of confidence in Labour's confrontation over spending on local services...Opposition members were astonished at the size of the support. They had hoped that a year which saw the abolition of the Lord Mayor, a growth of the Militant Tendency on the city council, unpopular education reorganisation proposals and the introduction of a budget which could be £190 million outside the government target, could have helped their case. The size of the triumph was a major boost to Labour Party confidence and an enormous 'thumbs up' from the electorate over the fight with Thatcher and the government.

The turn-out of 50 per cent was astonishingly high for local elections—10 per cent higher than in 1983, indicating the increased political consciousness that had developed in the city. Yet predictably the national press attempted to underplay the success: 'Even Labour's *Militant* triumph in Liverpool is not quite as impressive as it seems.' (*Sunday Times* 6 May). This was not the first or the last time that the electoral success of Labour, and the influence of *Militant* in this success was to be consciously diminished. But the facts, stubborn facts, spoke against the critics of Liverpool. In 1982 Labour got 54,000 votes in the city, in 1983 77,000 votes, and in 1984 this soared to over 90,000. In 33 of the 34 contested seats Labour's vote increased. Labour held all 14 seats it was defending and seven seats were won from the Liberals and the Tories.

The Liberals claimed 'the best ever Liberal vote'. But their 'house journal', the *Echo*, pointed out that they must have been severely embarrassed because they gained four seats from the Tories but lost six to Labour. The SDP, fighting seven seats as the SDP-Liberal Alliance, was completely wiped out.

For the Tories the results were an absolute disaster. For most of the previous 20 years they had shared control of the council with the Liberals. Now their vote had collapsed to 19 per cent.

An even more ignominious fate had befallen the Communist Party which, to the irritation of Labour activists, had stood against well-known left wingers. These worthies had consistently accused the *Militant* of being 'sectarian'! Their share of the vote dwindled from 0.28 per cent in 1983 to 0.13 per cent. In one ward they gained just 30 votes. *Militant* supporters on the other hand, despite the press poison, did spectacularly well. Tony Mulhearn, President of the District Labour Party, received the highest vote for Labour for many years in St Mary's Ward. Felicity Dowling, Secretary of the District Labour Party, increased the Labour vote in Speke by over 1000. Seven additional *Militant* supporters were elected to the council.

Looking for any crumb of comfort the press incredibly attempted to use the results in Liverpool to predict Labour defeats in any future general election: 'Our analysis showed that a Liberal would now defeat *Militant* Labour MP Terry Fields in Broadgreen, where Liberals won three out of the five wards.' (*Sunday Times*, 6 May). But in 1984 Labour had got 38 per cent of the vote in Broadgreen—exactly the same as in 1983. Undoubtedly the class polarisation had resulted in a high turnout in Broadgreen; 50 per cent voted, which exceeded the turnout in some constituencies in other parts of the country in the general election.

No matter how much Fleet Street scribes attempted to cover over the lessons of the Liverpool election results, the major parties in Liverpool were under no illusions. Appearing on television on the night of the election a dejected Trevor Jones, leader of the Liverpool Liberals, in a rare moment of honesty stated: 'the Labour Party in Liverpool has raised the political consciousness of the people...that's why we had such a high turn-out.' Michael Parkinson correctly states:

> As many as 51 per cent of the electorate turned out to vote—an extraordinarily high figure for a local election. And the confrontation appeared to touch everyone in the city and involved them equally. Women voted as often as men. The social classes behaved similarly, with working-class people voting only a little less frequently than middle- and upper-class groups. The highest

turnout came from housewives and old age pensioners. But the unemployed, for example, voted almost as heavily as the employed. Nor did housing tenure affect turnout. Identical proportions of home owners, council tenants and private renters voted. Whatever the views about the causes of the problem, people in Liverpool were obviously affected and mobilised by it. (*Liverpool on the Brink.*)

The higher than average turn-out among council workers, 72 per cent supporting Labour, was an indication of the support the council was building. The contrast between the result in Liverpool, as well as other areas in the country controlled by the left, and the performance of the right, was almost as striking as the year before. In nearby Blackburn for instance, 'power base' of Jack Straw (witch-hunter and arch opponent of Liverpool council), the turn-out was under 40 per cent. Labour won one seat but lost another! In Hyndburn, Labour lost control of the council to the Tories. The area shared the same local paper as Blackburn and therefore carried the details of the internecine warfare in the Blackburn Labour Party which resulted in the expulsion of *Militant* supporters. Moreover, the majority for Labour on the Blackburn council was put in jeopardy by the defection of the witch-hunting councillor Michael Gregory, whose 'evidence' had furnished the basis for the expulsion of *Militant* supporters.

Nor was the success of *Militant* supporters restricted to Liverpool. In Glasgow, for example, five supporters of *Militant* were elected, including two in seats previously held by the Tories. The campaign had been fought around a policy of no rent or rate rises and no cuts.

In neighbouring Manchester, Labour also made gains fighting on a platform of no rent or rate rises, with the left faring much better than the right in the elections. Graham Stringer, leader of Manchester City Council later stated: 'In fact, Liverpool council leaders John Hamilton and Derek Hatton had helped Manchester elect a Labour council because the media, Tories and Liberals, had kept saying Manchester would become another Liverpool if you voted Labour.'

For months the fainthearts and sceptics led by the national leadership of the labour movement had intoned that the 'adventurist' stand of the Liverpool City Council would not be supported by the mass of the population. *Militant* supporters, on the contrary, had argued consistently that such were the conditions in Liverpool that Labour's stand would evoke a great response from the working class. This position was completely confirmed by the local elections of May 1984.

Reactions to the Results

In the wake of the election victory a mood of grim determination to face the Tory government affected not just the council leaders but perhaps the majority of the population of Liverpool. In a city-wide survey, voters were asked what action they thought could be taken to oppose a Tory government takeover: 62 per cent of Labour voters supported demonstrations; 68 per cent occupation by redundant council workers; 59 per cent a strike by council workers; 48 per cent a rent and rates strike; 56 per cent supported a refusal by council workers to cooperate with commissioners; and an incredible 55 per cent in favour of a city wide general strike. Moreover 28 per cent of Liberal voters favoured occupation of council premises by redundant council workers. Even 8 per cent of Tories favoured similar measures. Liverpool was like a tinderbox: one false move from the government and it would explode.

The government was playing for time, and despite Labour's success in the elections, was hoping that the war of nerves would result in a split in the Labour group. But only one councillor resigned and left Liverpool looking for a safer haven. The government, through the medium of the Labour leadership, were compelled to go once more into negotiations.

In late May, a decision was taken to set up a joint investigation into the finances of the Liverpool City Council by Patrick Jenkin's officials and Liverpool local government officials. The capitalist media mischievously suggested that this was a sign that the council was about to capitulate to the government. But Tony Mulhearn stated: 'The bottom line as far as the Liverpool Labour Group are concerned remains the same—that there must be no job losses, no cuts or massive rent or rate increases. There will be no secret deals with the Tory government.' He gave a promise that the organisations of the Liverpool labour movement would decide on any settlement.

Meanwhile, it was not just the government or the national Labour leadership who were uncomfortable at the success of the tactics of the city council. Just after the splendid March demonstration and strike the *Morning Star*, then the national organ of the Communist Party, stated:

> The criticism of the [Liverpool] Labour group has been their unwillingness to find a point of unity...the direction of a council leadership faced with an apparent no-win scenario has also provided bitter resentment for many people in the city who have hoped for a fundamental breach with past practices of 'rule from the top' and who have been looking for a period of involvement and consultation.

This statement would have graced any of the bourgeois journals which have habitually attacked Liverpool City Council. The author was John Blevin, who once worked alongside Ian Lowes as Deputy Convenor in the Cleansing Department but left to take up a full-time position with the Communist Party. The article continued: 'Despite warnings of a Clay Cross development, despite the national Labour Party advice, despite the lack of a broad-based mass appeal, the council has chosen to create anti-Tory struggle virtually in isolation.' Thus the Communist Party was at one with the extreme right wing of the Labour Party.

Just precisely what the 'broad approach' meant was revealed in the manoeuvres of Communist Party officials when the Confederation of Shipbuilding and Engineering Unions (the Confed) convened a meeting of trade unions, community representatives, churches and other 'interested groups'. Representation from the Labour group on the city council was specifically excluded at the first meeting of this group because it took place on 25 April, the day of the second budget meeting.

A further meeting was called by the Confed for 4 May, the day after Labour's victory. At this meeting Tony Mulhearn moved a resolution calling for support for the city council, but the chairman, Barry Williams, a member of the Stalinist wing of the Communist Party, refused to accept it on the basis that 'a broad, consensus' was sought from the meeting. Just precisely what this meant had been indicated in the Communist Party's literature which had been circulating in the city, calling for the inclusion of 'sections of the Tory Party' in a 'broad alliance'. Imagine Chris Hallows and those Tories-in-disguise like Trevor Jones, in a common delegation to see Patrick Jenkin! Perhaps the

Communist Party was thinking more of people like Paul Orr and the 'scabby seven' who had stabbed Labour in the back.

The same cynical opportunism was to be displayed by the Communist Party on a number of subsequent issues, from the appointment of Sam Bond as Principal Race Relations Adviser, to the strike in September 1985 and the whole question of the witch-hunt. Thus Communist Party member Jim Ferguson suggested in the council Joint Shop Stewards Committee that rate rises should be used to avoid redundancies. He subsequently denied, as did his allies, that he had suggested a 70 per cent rate rise. Yet even Neil Kinnock and Jack Straw had admitted that it would require a 60-70 per cent rate rise in order to avoid redundancies.

Just what this advice meant was revealed in the performance of other, predominantly right-wing councils in Britain at that stage. In Birmingham a Labour council was facing £17 million of 'savings', that is cuts in services, together with a massive 30-50 per cent rate rise in order to keep within the government's budget guidelines.

Neil Kinnock was soon to have first hand experience of the indignation of workers when faced with Labour councils carrying through Tory cuts. At the Labour women's conference in Swansea he was to witness what the 'dented shield' means for working people. Two hundred angry parents were protesting against West Glamorgan Labour Council's decision to cut school buses, thus leaving their children with long walks to school on roads with no pavements. Yet there were to be no ringing denunciations of this Labour council at the Labour Party Conference in 1985 where he made his infamous attack on Liverpool City Council. The Labour leadership nationally, while constantly undermining Liverpool and shamefully vilifying the council later on, passed over in silence the cuts of right-wing Labour councils, which were crimes against their own supporters. The Labour leadership were at pains to present the image of 'honest brokers' between Liverpool and the government. But as subsequent events in 1985 and 1986 were to demonstrate, they had a clearly worked out purpose in undermining Liverpool City Council. At this stage, however, given the explosive mood in the city and its support on a national scale, all of those who opposed Liverpool's stance had to tread very carefully.

Alongside the threat of commissioners in the period leading up to 29 March, the District Auditor, Leslie Stanford, warned of the consequences of 'wilful misconduct'. The council's rejoinder was to remove him from their offices. They did not see why their future jailer should be comfortably ensconced in municipal property.

Their Morals or Ours?

The Labour councillors were blackened through the media as 'immoral' and 'lawbreakers' but at a *Militant* public meeting in the city at this stage this charge was fully answered by Peter Taaffe:

> Marxism does have a 'moral' code. But it does not approach morality in the fashion of Neil Kinnock who has consistently indicted Thatcher for not representing 'the moral majority'. By her own lights Thatcher was acting in accordance with a moral code. Her morality was that of the ruling class itself; all measures, no matter what the suffering, are justified so long as it defends the capitalist system.
>
> Conversely, Marxism justifies all those measures which strengthen the working class, increase its cohesiveness and confidence and above all raise its level of understanding, both of the nature of capitalism and the need for the socialist reorganisation of society. In no way does Marxism subscribe to the Jesuitical moral precept 'the end justifies the means.' Not all means can be justified, no matter how well meant, in the struggle for socialism. The Stalinists have not hesitated to conspire behind the backs of the working class, to engage in ballot rigging, in order to maintain their positions in the labour movement. Measures which lower the estimation of the working class of its own historic role—into which category fall those attempts at manoeuvre, intrigue and the imposition of decisions on the working class—directly hinder the struggle for socialism.

It was this 'moral code', a class approach to morality and to law, which motivated the Marxists in Liverpool and elsewhere. Marxism is prepared to break the hypocritical class morality and the laws of capitalism. There is no shortage of legal weapons in the hands of the ruling class (and its local acolytes, if it comes to that). Under the 1967 General Rate Act 'any aggrieved person' (including obviously, any ratepayer or creditor to the council) could have challenged Labour in the High Court, or the government could undoubtedly have initiated legal action, through the Attorney General, for example, to *make* the city set a legal rate. The fact that they chose not to do so speaks volumes of the situation that existed in Liverpool at this stage and the impotence of the ruling class to decisively affect events. The Liberals were warning of chaos and hysterically denouncing Labour every day. The Tories likewise. Yet neither Trevor Jones nor Chris Hallows despite hints in the press, resorted to the High Court in order to insist on a 'legal budget'. This reflected two things: the fear of the odium that would be attached to any political party in Liverpool that took the step of removing a democratically elected body, and the enormous increase in support for Labour as reflected in the 1984 elections.

Like seals passing a ball from one to another, the Liberals and Tories appealed to Jenkin, Jenkin appealed to them, Jones and Hallows looked to the District Auditor, and all appealed to God to do something to 'rescue our unhappy city'. In this situation the government was compelled once more to go into negotiations in the hope of buying some time. In the words of Michael Parkinson: 'It could no longer be argued that the council had hijacked the city. It had popular support.' Under enormous pressure, Jenkin agreed to visit the city in June.

Support for Miners

The Liverpool struggle was coalescing and being identified in the minds of the mass of the working class with the heroic struggle of the miners which was then at its height. Under a huge banner 'Victory to the Miners, Support Liverpool Council', 2000 delegates gathered at a 'Fightback Conference' on 23 June. Derek Hatton declared: 'Either the government gives us the money we need, or we'll go back in the council chamber on 11 July with the same budget we put forward on 29 March.'

Like other councils, Liverpool City Council was heavily involved in support for the miners. All firms who scabbed during the miners' strike were declared blacked by the Personnel Committee, which was chaired by Derek Hatton. The city council provided facilities for collecting cash to buy food which was delivered to the mining areas by the lorry-load. The Labour Party Young Socialists organised an extremely effective rock concert in Walton Park where thousands of youth gathered to hail the struggle of the miners and of Liverpool.

A Tory cabinet committee, involving Thatcher, Jenkin, Heseltine, Tebbit and an array of top officials, was monitoring the situation weekly. It was with some trepidation that Jenkin had agreed to visit Liverpool. After his much publicised meeting with Derek Hatton in February he had confessed on the radio that it was 'the most frightening' confrontation he had ever experienced. But it was as nothing to the real horrors, rather than the imaginary ones concocted by the press in February, which faced him when he actually visited Liverpool.

Labour took him on a short bus tour which showed the appalling conditions which thousands of working-class families lived in, particularly in the Vauxhall and Everton districts. By the end of his tour he was visibly shaken. According to Tony Mulhearn 'he was like a criminal returning to the scene of his crimes'. The local tenants did not pull any punches and three demonstrations stopped the bus he was travelling in and demanded action. With local Labour Party Young Socialist branches and *Militant* supporters out in force, Jenkin was compelled to walk around one estate with over 100 local tenants behind him, demanding that they be transferred out of the terrible housing conditions. Two small children pointed out dead rats which was a normal, everyday occurrence in the area. Workers carried placards declaring: 'We want out—the worst slum in Europe', 'We have more leaks than the Tory Cabinet' and 'If the Iron Lady lived here, she would rust'.

At the end of the tour, in a much publicised statement, Jenkin declared, 'I've seen some awful housing conditions today— I've seen with my own eyes some deplorable conditions which have got to be tackled as a matter of urgency.' Some commentators were subsequently to claim that Jenkin's statement was a 'tactical error'. For a capitalist spokesman to be touched by the conditions which his system creates, and for once to admit to being shocked by them, is considered to be 'a tactical error'!

When he returned to the Town Hall, Patrick Jenkin was subjected to a barrage of questions and demands, not just from the Labour councillors but from top council officials. One pointed out that the government had been prepared to pour money into Liverpool for a Garden Festival and reclamation on the dockland, but would not give money for a democratically elected council to deal with the terrible social conditions of people in the area.

The only reason why Patrick Jenkin agreed to visit Liverpool was because of the pressure exerted by the population of Liverpool. Notwithstanding this, the District Auditor sent out a letter in early June, threatening every Labour councillor with a £2000 fine unless a budget was set by 20 June. When a legal budget had not been set by 20 June however, the District Auditor did not proceed to enforce this threat because his masters in London were about to climb down. His successor would only be given the green light to proceed once the government were on firmer ground.

8.
Jenkin's Retreat

EVERY VICTORY of Liverpool City Council, whether in elections or in negotiations with the government, has been disputed and denigrated by the ruling class and by the right-wing leadership of the labour movement. But no victory has been more attacked than the eventual settlement with the government in July 1984. So terrified were the ruling class of the contagious example of Liverpool that any pretence of 'objectivity' was abandoned.

A balanced account of these events conclusively demonstrates that it was the mass movement in Liverpool that compelled the Tory government to beat a retreat. Liverpool gained major concessions, although not all that was demanded. It was only the second time since Thatcher came to power that she had been forced to beat a retreat.

The Liverpool council, the council workforce in particular, and the mass of the working class of Liverpool proclaimed the 1984 settlement as a great victory, although Patrick Jenkin, the Environment Minister angrily disputed this claim. While the capitalist press at first leaned towards Liverpool's interpretation of the agreement, they subsequently did everything they could to back up Jenkin's account. There is no shortage of analyses, academic papers, and even books (such as Michael Parkinson's *Liverpool On the Brink*), which provide a searing indictment of the government's approach to the terrible social problems in Liverpool. Yet no academic, no matter how 'unbiased', has unequivocally sided with Liverpool.

What then are the facts pertaining to the agreement? Since coming to power in 1979 the Tories consistently used the block grant system of government financial support to local authorities to cut spending. The government claimed that its method was being used to:

equalise the financial position of local authorities and to make sure that local authorities with very different financial resources can provide a similar level of local service which their different populations need, for a similar rate level.

Any pretence of 'equalising' the position of all local authorities, however, has been undermined precisely by the crude method of penalising authorities who 'exceed' the government's prescribed limits.

The government succeeded in slashing back local authority spending: the percentage of local expenditure financed by central government fell drastically from 61 per cent in 1979-80 to 48 per cent in 1985-6. Moreover, the total block grant fell in real terms by 16 per cent between 1981-2 and 1985-6. This meant (as has been outlined in Chapter 7) that, in order to balance the books, a local authority would either have to increase the rates, sometimes by a massive amount, or savagely cut back on jobs and services.

In the case of Liverpool, the government acted in a particularly arbitrary and unfair fashion. Once explained in simple propaganda terms by Labour, these facts helped to fuel the colossal local resentment felt throughout Merseyside against the Tory government. The calculation of how much the government gave in grant to a city was based on past expenditure levels of the local authority. The benchmark was the expenditure of local authorities in the year 1978-9. In Liverpool's case, the Liberal-Tory coalitions had deliberately underspent throughout the 1970s. If Liverpool's expenditure had increased at the same rate as other authorities and even within government guidelines throughout the 1970s, then the city's target set by the government for 1984-5 would have been much higher. Liverpool's subsequent difficulties in meeting targets and balancing budgets would have been far smaller if the city hadn't been penalised because of the penny-pinching role of the previous Liberal-Tory coalitions.

Robbed of £30 Million

In 1984-5 the total target figure in real terms for all English authorities was only 6 per cent lower than their expenditure in 1980-1, but Liverpool's target was 11 per cent lower than their spending in 1980-1. Liverpool's officials estimated that between

1978-9 and 1983-4, the city had lost between £26 million and £34 million in government grant as a direct result of penalties being imposed for spending over target. This was the £30 million that the council claimed the government had stolen.

Other cities in a roughly similar position to Liverpool were treated better. Manchester, under Labour control, had spent much more than Liverpool throughout the 1970s, and in the long run this worked to their benefit. Liverpool was given a target for 1984-5 of £216 million while Manchester was given a target of £240 million. This was despite the fact that the government itself had actually estimated Manchester's 'need' to be £4 million *less* than Liverpool.' If Manchester and Liverpool had been treated equitably, which was the stated intention of the government, Liverpool's target for spending should have been £244 million, and there would have been no budget deficit in 1984-5.

In its 'assessment of need' the Tory government rubbed salt into Liverpool's wounds. In one of the most deprived cities in Britain, the government estimated in 1981-2 that Liverpool's expenditure should be increased by only 8.5 per cent while the average increase for all metropolitan districts should be 14 per cent, and for all local authorities was 17 per cent. Michael Parkinson comments:

> Overall, officials calculated that since the Conservatives had taken office in 1979, Liverpool had lost grants in four different ways. Liverpool had had to pay heavy penalties for spending over its targets. It had also suffered because the way the grant was distributed between different kinds of local authorities had moved money away from the cities. On top of that, the government had failed to increase its grant in line with the level of inflation. And it had also reduced the overall percentage of local spending it would fund. Local officials calculated the combined effect of all these upon the city was that it had lost £116 million in 1983 figures.

At the same time, despite having a significant black population, the city was denied the grants given to other local authorities with 'racial disadvantage' and ethnic populations. Because the black population of Liverpool had been longstanding, it did not qualify for 'ethnic deprivation'. This, merely three years after the Toxteth riots!

The 'Joint Report'

At the end of June 1984, officials of the council and of the Department of the Environment produced a 'joint report'. Predictably, government-appointed civil servants demanded that Liverpool adopt an austerity regime. All Labour's plans for new spending on housing, education, etc, should immediately be cut. It suggested 'capitalising' housing repairs in 1983-4 and 1984-5. This meant transferring housing repairs from the revenue (day to day spending) account to the capital account. This would have meant that fewer resources would be available to finance the housebuilding programme. It would also have meant that in seven years the extra interest charges payable on the capital account could have added up to the original cost of repairs. The money needed to pay off the additional interest charges would then have incurred even greater government penalties for higher spending. The government hatchet men also suggested raising rents, selling off municipal property, and a freeze on employment. All of these demands were rejected by the Liverpool City Council.

Moreover, even with the most 'creative' of government creative accountancy, the national civil servants could only come up with a budget that would entail a rate rise of between 37 per cent and 71 per cent. Michael Parkinson correctly states: 'Liverpool surely won the larger argument that it was facing major financial problems which were aggravating its even larger economic and social problems and that government policies, especially the target system, were making that bad situation worse.' In Labour's eyes, the 'joint report' completely vindicated its stand. Liverpool was impervious to all attempts of the government to bring it to heel and continued to insist that it would set a deficit budget. In this situation, negotiations behind the scenes recommenced.

Undoubtedly, one of the factors which compelled the government finally to come to an agreement was the nervousness within the money markets. On 13 May the *Observer* reported: 'If Liverpool carries out its threat to set an illegal rate and the government fails to bail out the city council, local authorities throughout the country may be unable to raise loans on the money markets.' The same article quoted a director of a municipal brokers: 'If the government puts Liverpool into that situation, it could have a devastating effect on the status of borrowing requirements of other local authorities.'.

The Agreement with Jenkin

Patrick Jenkin, undoubtedly with the support of Thatcher, wanted a quiet and behind-the-scenes deal which would cover up the extent of the government's retreat. But the Liverpool labour movement was having none of that. They wanted to trumpet their victory to the labour movement nationally—and not without justification. When all the details were revealed, it clearly demonstrated the extent of the government's climbdown.

Labour estimated that the deal would be worth something like £60 million. It involved £3.2 million from the Urban Programme to cover for 'time expired schemes' (landscaping for instance) which the council had expected to pay for and which would otherwise have been carried on the rates. There was £0.5 million (capital) for environmental works on the housing action and general improvement areas. £1.5 million of new Urban Programme funds were also provided to cover schemes otherwise borne by the rates. In total it came to just under a £7 million net increase in aid to Liverpool. However, under the penalty rules imposed by the government, for every £1 of the rate 'saved', the council got back another £2 in rate support grant which would otherwise have been withheld by the government. The cost to the Exchequer of the concessions, therefore, was in fact about £20 million. The deal provided another £40 million as a result of capitalising the £13.6 million from housing repairs. These would now be paid from borrowed money on the basis of an undertaking from Jenkin of around £130 million a year from the government but this would not affect the house building programme.

The programme included some concessions by Labour to the government. Labour had promised a £2 reduction in rents, although as explained earlier, 70 per cent of council tenants were in receipt of supplementary benefit rebates. If the rents had been reduced, the government, through the DHSS, would automatically have taken the amount of the reduction out of the benefit rebates. Labour attempted to overcome this by introducing a decoration allowance and two such payments were distributed. The government then introduced legislation to block this and Labour pledged to find other ways of benefiting council tenants. Eventually the council were forced to retreat on this but rents did remain frozen from this point.

Another concession was made in setting a 17 per cent rate increase which was 8 per cent above that which the District Labour Party outlined in its manifesto. A 17 per cent rate increase added 45p a week to most tenants' costs, although again many got much of this back in benefits. To have refused to set a budget and to have entered into a mass struggle on the basis of saving ratepayers 45-50p per week would have been seen as unreasonable by the mass of working people in Liverpool. Given the prospect which previously loomed—massive rate increases and job losses—the settlement wrung from the government was correctly seen as a tremendous victory. The council had got 95 per cent of what it was claiming.

No matter how much the opponents of the Liverpool City Council and of Marxism whined, once the details were outlined to the active workers in the labour movement, there was enthusiastic support for the agreement. The Labour group unanimously accepted the package. A meeting was then held of over 400 District Labour Party members who also gave full support to the deal. This was followed by a meeting of 500 local authority stewards where John Hamilton and Derek Hatton were cheered to the echo even before they spoke. Mass meetings were held the day before and on the morning of the budget meeting to explain the offer. One of the most ecstatic reactions to the deal was at a meeting of the 1000 new workers who had been taken on by the council since they had come into office.

Not so enthusiastic were the bourgeois. In the days that followed, they poured out their rage in the press and in Parliament. The august *Times* (11 July) thundered: 'Danegeld in Liverpool'. *Danegeld* comes from the tribute paid by English kings in the Tenth century to buy off Danish invaders. Beside themselves with fury, they went on:

> Today in Liverpool, municipal militancy is vindicated...a third rate provincial politician, a self-publicising revolutionary...Mr Derek Hatton has made the government give way...Mr Hatton and his colleagues threatened a course of disruptive action. The reward is the abrogation of financial targets which 400 other local authorities have been told are immutable...in order to buy off *Militant*.

The *Daily Mail* (11 July), under a headline 'Two Unlovely Black Eyes', declared:

> If a week in politics is a long time, then the past fortnight for Environment Secretary Patrick Jenkin must have been a pulverising eternity. He is now sporting not one but two far from lovely black eyes. Biff! their lordships in the Upper House forced him into embarrassing retreat over his plans for dismantling the Greater London Council.
>
> Bang!—the Trotskyites and others of the hard left who run Liverpool have had the best of the fight with him in their threat to defy the law on that city's overspending...No doubt the decision was not just his (Jenkin's) but was taken by the whole Cabinet. No doubt, the calculation was that the confrontation should be avoided in Liverpool at a time when the government has enough on its hands with the pit strike. Even so, the impression must be that militancy pays. What Liverpool got away with in 1984, a gaggle of left-wing councils will be queueing up to try on in 1985.

The Daily Express (10 July), not to be outdone by the other tabloids, carried under its own headline, 'A cowardly deal', the statement:

> Environment Secretary Patrick Jenkin seems to have bought himself some peace from the *Militant*-led Liverpool City Council. This is a shoddy and cowardly deal...Mr Jenkin has shown that defiance pays (and that the hapless taxpayer will do the paying).

Even the usually urbane and sober *Economist* (13 July) declared:

> After all its huffing and puffing, the government this week capitulated to Liverpool City Council's threats of an illegal budget—and set the scene for a full scale rebellion next year by Labour councils threatened with ratecapping. Both Mr Jenkin and Mrs Thatcher have made brave efforts at damage limitation. There was no concession, they insisted.

The threadbare protestations of 'no concessions' from Thatcher and Jenkin could not hold water. This did not prevent the Labour leadership (and the ultra-left sects on the outskirts of the labour movement) from echoing Thatcher's claims. Squirming in embarrassment, the Labour leadership paradoxically claimed to have orchestrated the Liverpool settlement while at the same time disputing any claims of 'victory'. John Cunningham declared: 'The settlement is far closer to what Neil Kinnock has wanted, from day one, than anything the Militant Tendency has ever said.' *(Sunday Times*, 15 July)

Incredibly, Jack Straw in his local paper, the *Lancashire Evening Telegraph* (10 July), was quoted as claiming responsibility for the Liverpool deal:

> A delighted Mr Jack Straw was today able to claim victory in his fight to prevent a major clash between the government and Liverpool City Council...It was widely believed today that without Mr Straw's intervention there would have been a confrontation between the council and Mr Jenkin leading to commissioners being sent in to run the city.

Derek Hatton, in a letter to the same paper, disabused its readers of Jack Straw's claims:

> I am sure he [Jack Straw] has not sought to claim that our victory in Liverpool was due to him. I recall that in March 1984 Jack was telling us to raise the rates by 60 per cent, an option which would still have meant job losses and cuts in services. We rejected that advice and continued our campaign, which was successful in securing the extra resources we needed. The Tory government only gave in because they knew that we had massive active support of the majority of the working class in Liverpool...The biggest contribution that Jack and others can make in the fight against the Tories is to stop expelling young people from the Labour Party and get on with the job of building a national campaign against the Tories.

Predictably, the press played up the criticisms of the ultra-left sects: 'By contrast, the Trotskyist newspaper *Socialist Worker* has dubbed the deal a sell-out. Under a headline "The No Surrender council gives in", the paper asserts that Liverpool was happy to settle for a "few measly concessions".' The *Sunday Times* (15 July), which gleefully carried this statement, also reported that 'Kinnock takes a very similar view'.

Thatcher and Jenkin joined hands with Kinnock and the ultra-lefts in decrying Liverpool's claim to victory. But not so the Liverpool working class, nor the miners who were given an enormous boost by Liverpool's success. William Wordsworth was to declare of the French Revolution, 'Bliss was it in that dawn to be alive, but to be young was very heaven.' Liverpool in early July 1984 had not yet quite reached the stage of the French Revolution. But a working class which had experienced more than its fair share of disappointments and defeats was determined to enjoy its moment of victory.

Victory

Joyous scenes, more reminiscent of Anfield or Goodison football grounds after a famous cup victory, were enacted inside and outside the Town Hall at the council budget meeting. The lobby of the council saw local authority workers, miners, young workers, unemployed and housewives with their young children all listening to the victory speeches. All Labour speakers were greeted rapturously, while over the benches of the Liberals and Tories, hung a mood of dejection and demoralisation.

Trevor Jones, the Liberal leader, poured out the class venom and spite of the Liberals and Tories in personal vituperation unleashed against Derek Hatton. He claimed that Labour had fooled the public, fooled the media(!) and had even fooled the clergy. He declared that a 17 per cent rate increase would mean a mass exodus from Liverpool, and the answer from the public gallery was a loud 'When are you moving?' In his desperate search for allies, he even quoted from *Socialist Worker*. This was probably the only support which the Socialist Workers Party could find on that day, since their members were virtually chased from the Town Hall by angry local authority workers.

Tony Mulhearn for the Labour Party warned the Tories that the Liverpool labour movement would never be bought off. Liverpool still faced appalling problems and would not be satisfied until the Tory government was removed from office. When Derek Hatton closed the debate he got a tremendous reception. He outlined in detail the extent of the gains for the working class which the Liverpool council had achieved. He also went on to warn the working class: 'The Tory government has backed down from the organised and mobilised city of Liverpool. But just as the Tories regrouped and tried again after the U-turn over the miners in 1981, so the Liverpool labour movement must be prepared for future battles.' This has been the theme of Marxism throughout the Liverpool saga.

All victories, no matter how great, are temporary so long as capitalism continues to exist. Jenkin had complained that *Militant* and Derek Hatton personally were attempting to dance on his political grave. Derek Hatton replied in the council chamber, 'We won't be satisfied until every Tory Minister has lost his seat and we see the return of a Labour government with socialist policies.'

The vote for Labour's budget was carried by 57 votes to 38 and concluded in scenes of wild celebration, with a standing ovation for the councillors from the public gallery. In appreciation of the role played by *Militant* in the struggle, the Labour councillors placed a large advert in the paper shortly after the victory: 'Fraternal greetings and thanks to the *Militant* newspaper and its supporters for the outstanding help and assistance given to our campaign to defend jobs in Liverpool.' Amoung those signing this declaration were not only well-known *Militant* supporters but John Hamilton, Roy Gladden (who was later to stand against Derek Hatton for the deputy leadership) Mike Black and other future opponents of *Militant*. *Militant* itself celebrated with a rally which attracted over 500 people and marked a further increase in its support and influence in the city.

No matter what attempts were made to muddy the waters, the more sober journals of capitalism were forced to concede that Liverpool had won substantial concessions. Like Shakespeare they replied to Jenkin's claims: Methinks he doth protest too much. Thus Robin Pawley, *Financial Times* local government expert, boldly declared, 'The fact is that Liverpool's muscle won...Mr Jenkin has been wrong-footed by Liverpool almost daily for three months.' (17 July). Even Michael Parkinson, who disputes the scale of Liverpool's claims of victory wrote:

> In fact, the government gave four pieces of aid and a promise of future help in the crucial area of housing...'This would reduce its grant penalties...The government tried to suggest that it could all have been achieved through the normal process of consultation, without the bankruptcy campaign.

He further comments, in a masterly understatement, 'This seems doubtful.'

The concessions which Liverpool had extracted from the government were immediately seized upon by other local authorities who were preparing to do battle in 1985. John Austin-Walker, leader of Greenwich Borough Council, declared, 'I believe that many authorities may refuse to levy a Tory rate ... The government is quite frightened at the prospect of Liverpool City Council not being able to meet its loan debt and I believe that it is a powerful weapon in the council's hands'. *(The Times*, 25 June) Even the arch right-wing leader of Birmingham City Council, Dick Knowles, agreed in a letter to *Labour Weekly* (3 August) that 'They [Liverpool] succeeded in getting from the government enough money to save about £20 million.'

Of course, the major reason why the government, with the acquiescence of the ruling class had conceded, was because of the miners' strike, which was the powerful backdrop to the Liverpool drama. Teddy Taylor, Tory MP for Southend and severe critic of Jenkin for his capitulation over Liverpool, was to admit as much in a private discussion with Derek Hatton before a television programme. He declared: 'We were amazed how much Patrick was prepared to give', and went on, 'However, in 1984 we were determined to "get Scargill" and not to fight on two fronts.' In other words, the Tories wanted to deal with the major 'enemy within', the miners, before concentrating attention on crushing Liverpool. In the miners' strike and in Liverpool the seeds were planted for the future mass conflicts which will convulse Britain on a national scale in the next decade. In 1984 the Tories were already frightened by the prospect of a mass movement unfolding in Liverpool under a Marxist leadership. There can be no other explanation for the vile and unprecedented campaign of slander and personal vilification against the leaders of the city council and the District Labour Party. In 1985 in particular, the ruling class would construct a veritable Tower of Babel of misinformation, and half-truths and lies.

9.
A Record to be Proud of

By the mid-1980s, the Conservatives saw Liverpool as the power-base of the Militant Tendency. And they wanted to defeat it. The scene was set for a political confrontation...the government recognised that it had lost the propaganda battle in 1984 and had failed to get its arguments across to the electorate. The government now decided to shift the ground of the argument and attack the Labour council directly in future, portraying the conflict not as a technical dispute about money and grant systems, but as a Militant plot against the government. (Michael Parkinson, *Liverpool on the Brink.*)

THATCHER PLACED Kenneth Baker, the mailed fist in the velvet glove, into the Department of the Environment to stiffen up the hapless Patrick Jenkin. The ruling class were preparing to take revenge on Liverpool for the defeat they had suffered in July. First, however, the miners' strike had to be 'seen off' and this was not to take place until March 1985. In the meantime, they did not hesitate to renege on the agreements, particularly on housing, made in July 1984. This came as no surprise to Marxists. Agreements between bosses and workers, between unions and management, between antagonistic states do, of course, take place. But once the relationship of forces which led to an agreement is superseded by a new balance of forces, the stronger force will not hesitate to break it. In the period leading up to the agreement in July, Jenkin had written to John Hamilton:

I can give you an assurance that I will do my very best to ensure that allocations to Liverpool next year under the Housing Investment Programme and the Urban Programme, taken together, will enable the council to make positive progress in dealing with the city's severe needs, having regard to the scale of your capital commitments and the resources (including possible proceeds of sale of council dwellings and freeholds) available to you.

Jenkin had clearly offered to give substantial financial aid to Liverpool to continue its housebuilding programme. The Liverpool council had estimated that Jenkin's promises on housing aid amounted to £130 million. Hardly was the ink dry on this agreement when the government slashed Liverpool's housing funds for 1985-6 by almost 20 per cent. Despite this the Labour council pushed forward with implementing the programme on which it had been elected.

It is one of the ironies of the 1980s that, in general, those councils dominated by reformists do the dirty work of the Tories in carrying through 'counter-reforms'. Yet they have never hesitated to lecture Marxists on 'practical' politics, on the need to do things for people now rather than in the misty future. Yet it was precisely the one council where Marxism held a decisive sway which carried through substantial and imaginative reforms. These reforms were only possible on the basis of the mass movement which the council campaigns generated.

Real improvements were recorded in Liverpool in three key fields in particular: housing, education, and the relationship between the council and the unions.

Architects, under the baton of right-wing Labour councils, and the Tory-Liberal coalition of the 1970s and early 1980s, had created a housing nightmare in Liverpool. In 1952 the *Architect's Journal* published a feature suggesting a two-mile ring of 20-storey tower blocks surrounding the city centre. Three years earlier, Bessie Braddock had argued against the construction of 'barrack-like' buildings for working-class people. This did not prevent her husband and councillors influenced by her ideas from proceeding to build barrack-like tower blocks.

In the early 1950s a newspaper survey, not surprisingly, found that 96 per cent of those on the council's waiting list preferred houses rather than flats. Nevertheless, encouraged by successive national governments who gave greater subsidies for flats than for the building of houses, the nightmares of Cantril Farm and Kirkby were thrown up in this period. Thus in the early 1980s on one estate in a tower block built by the unit Camus method, an inspection found that of 272 external panels on each block and 90 balcony frames, there was something wrong with every unit. It became cheaper to knock down these tower blocks and start again rather than repair them.

The Urban Regeneration Strategy

Liverpool's Urban Regeneration Strategy (URS), which was launched in 1984, represented a complete rupture with all previous housing schemes in Liverpool. Fourteen inner city areas and three on the outer estates were designated as priority areas, with 40,000 people living in over 400 hectares of densely populated land. In an area once full of derelict land and some of the worst housing in the city, a new park, Everton Park, was created. More than 5000 houses were built in the period 1983-7. The achievements were hailed by housing experts, several of whom disagreed with the *political* position of the council. The *Post* (12 September 1985) carried a headline: 'House-proud city has got it right.' It went on to state, 'The city's 3800 new homes, all with front and back gardens, earn praise from author Alice Coleman..."Liverpool", she told council chiefs and local builders, has "got it right".' Ms Coleman, a housing expert and author of a book, *Utopia on Trial,* had carried out detailed research into housing conditions. She completely concurred with the main thrust of the URS and of the council's conviction that the majority of people preferred to live in traditional houses. She went on record saying that she regarded the Liverpool efforts in urban housing as an example of the way the problem should be tackled.

Real enthusiasm was generated once the population began to see the effects of the slum clearance and housebuilding programme. In the first 18 months, more than 1000 houses were built in the largest building programme in the country. Tenement blocks, like Tommy White's Gardens where hundreds of families lived in squalor, were demolished and the residents moved to houses.

Moreover, the spin-off effect of the city's housing programme on employment had been publicly recognised by building companies, who are not usually friends of Labour. In the three years from May 1983 to April 1986 it was estimated by one study that 6489 jobs in the private sector had been generated by council housing programme contracts. Wimpeys, the big building monopoly, declared:

> The contracts have had the effect of stabilising our workforce and giving us the opportunity to offer more permanent appointments.

> We have been steadily increasing our level of staff over the last 18 months, the first time in many years, and also have been able to increase our intake of apprentices. It is therefore essential, having reached the level of staff and apprentices, that work is still released to enable us to carry this forward (quoted in Liverpool City Council's *Success Against the Odds*).

Of course, the achievements of the city council were not given unqualified support by the media either. After all, this would have justified the political strategy and tactics of the 'Marxist-dominated city council.' The local press, the *Post* and *Echo*, carefully created the impression that it was the wicked Marxists who were responsible in the first place for the catastrophe in the conditions of existing housing and in housing repairs. They refused to explain that these problems were inherited from the past. Only occasionally did they balance their coverage with an article which showed what the city was achieving.

On 19 February the *Echo* ran an article with the headline: 'Flats riddled with damp and rot.' A week later another headline on a similar article was: 'unforgivable...Life of misery in the home where water pours in, bedrooms can't be used and a bath is two bus rides away.' It also reported: 'Judge orders action and asks: if people suffer, doesn't the council feel a duty to help them?' Eighteen months later another judge will condemn and fine Liverpool city councillors precisely *for* attempting to help people kept in such housing conditions.

The scale of the national housing problem was indicated by an editorial in the *Echo* on the same day:

> It is estimated that it will cost about £30 billion to carry out the necessary repairs and would take 900 years at the present work rate. Despite the recession, housing deserves a far higher priority, not only as a human need but because living conditions have social implications outside the home.

The same newspaper mercilessly attacked the council and its Urban Regeneration Strategy precisely *for* attempting to change the lives and housing conditions of people.

The programme provoked some controversy and opposition from alleged 'specialists'. The Communist Party paper, the *Morning Star* (30 January 1985), eagerly picked up the verdict of Shelter on Liverpool's housing programme, 'A recipe for

Disaster'. The article complained that there would be no tenants' control, no housing co-operatives, and no role for the voluntary sector. The real objection was that the programme was firmly based in the public sector. But the URS did allow for improvements by home-owners, whether owner-occupiers or landlords, with the support of improvement grants. It also allowed for partnership with housing corporations and local housing associations to ensure co-ordinated use of resources.

Any opponents of the Urban Regeneration Strategy were championed by the press. Thus, the proponents of housing co-ops found their cause being supported not only by the *Echo* and the *Post*, but even the *Daily Mail* and the *Daily Express*. The council's refusal to give extensive aid to some of these co-ops was not at all based on any 'doctrinaire' approach, but flowed from the understanding that, with very limited resources, the first task was the designated priority areas and to house people in the greatest need. To have given housing co-ops the £6.5 million being demanded would have meant severely cutting the council's housebuilding programme.

Councillor Tony Hood, Chairman of the Development and Building Control Subcommittee, referring to one local case, declared in March 1985: 'The government was using the people of Vauxhall to get at Labour's housing policies in the city.' The Vauxhall co-op organisation had asked for £6.5 million from the city council to finance the community group's housing co-op scheme. When it was turned down, the government stepped in to provide the necessary finance. On the principle of 'the enemy of my enemy is my friend', the Tories were prepared to use *any* opponent of the city council, no matter how ideologically opposed to themselves.

The Urban Regeneration Strategy provoked much discussion and not a little opposition when it was first launched. But once the visible effects of the programme were evident, much of the opposition was dissipated. A letter to the *Echo* from a Speke resident in March replying to opponents of the council declared, 'Never before have I seen so much new development in Liverpool as I have over the last year or so...Don't drag the council down, it is fighting on our behalf against huge rate increases, cuts in services and cuts in jobs.'

The Council's Relationship with the Trade Unions

The campaign against the URS was as nothing compared to the
ferocity with which the local media attacked the council's
relationship with the unions and its own workforce. Under the
Liberal-Tory coalition the trade unions had had no
representation on council committees and disputes invariably
broke out because of delays in hearing grievances. The
Liberal-Tory coalition was a vicious anti-union employer. The
council's unions which had been a major lever in bringing
Labour to power, now quite correctly demanded an extension of
trade union and democratic rights.

What attitude do Marxists adopt towards the relationship
between the unions and a local council? This thorny question
was to arise again and again between 1983 and 1986. Adherents
of *Militant* were influential both in the Personnel Committee and
in leading the council workforce. They were subject to intense
and sometimes different pressures—how to reconcile the
demands of the council workforce for substantial improvements
in their rights and conditions and the council's responsibility to
the working class as a whole. The white-collar union leaders,
locally and nationally, and the national leadership of some of the
manual unions sought to present the relationship between the
council and local authority unions as the normal boss-worker
relationship. In a Tory council, or one controlled by right-wing
reformists, this would undoubtedly be the case. But Liverpool
aspired to be a socialist council.

As we shall see later, no other council accorded greater power
or influence to the local authority unions than Liverpool, or
tried to involve them more. The council was committed to
defending the services and conditions of all Liverpool workers.
Undoubtedly, the town hall unions were a crucial force behind
this struggle. Nevertheless, *Militant* supporters recognised that
while the unions were the council's main supporters, they still
had a vital role to play in defending the workers against
arbitrary actions, particularly from the pro-capitalist officers
who had served the previous Tory-Liberal regime.

Comparisons were drawn with the positions of trade unions in
a democratic workers' state, where in some respects an
analagous position would exist. In a healthy workers' state in
contrast to the bureaucratic dictatorships which currently rule

The Docks—Once Busy.

Tate and Lyle's sugar refinery—1983.

New housing in the shadow of the infamous *Piggeries* (now
demolished).

Moving in. Vauxhall 1985.

Our new home, Toxteth 1985.

Children on the Radcliffe Estate. Redevelopment began May 1986.

Park Road Sports Centre.

Rathbone nursery—one of six new units opened by the council.

over the planned economies of Russia and Eastern Europe, the trade unions would still be independent, with the right to strike . They would defend the working-class against bureaucratic excesses of the state—even of 'their state', as Lenin put it. At the same time, they would be the main props of a democratic workers' state. Indeed, the management of the state would be drawn from the trade unions. Marxists draw on the experiences of Lenin and Trotsky. They learn from the past, but do not live in the past.

A local council restricted to one city, however is far from being in the position of a healthy, democratic workers' state. Its actions are still dominated by the capitalist economy generally, and by constraints imposed by the government. It is still subject to the laws of capitalism. Even under the most radical leadership, therefore, the actions of the council can at best ameliorate the conditions of the working-class.

Moreover, the powers which the Bolsheviks had in Russia in the early, healthy period of the revolution, to put more and more executive administrative control into the hands of democratically elected workers' committees—soviets—obviously did not exist in Liverpool. Unlike the Bolsheviks, the council did not have the power of removing recalcitrant officials.

In fact any attempt to remove recalcitrant union officials could have led to strike action from the Town Hall unions which would have bedevilled the work of the council and prevented the carrying through of its programme.

Nevertheless, Liverpool showed that it was possible to cement a relationship between the majority of the unions and the council.The system of 'nomination rights' whereby the council allowed the trade unions to nominate 50 per cent of candidates for new jobs was ferociously attacked because the consultation and involvement of the council workforce in 'management prerogatives' was absolutely repugnant to the bourgeois and their press. On 22 January 1985 the *Echo*, in its 'investigative' series 'Cause for Concern', described Derek Hatton, the Deputy Leader and Chair of the Personnel Committee, as 'Mr Fixit'. They declared: *'Militant* for Jobs ... how the left wing has the last word on who does what.' 'Blatant use of power over democracy', it thundered. The *Echo* was scandalised by the words of Derek Hatton which it quoted: 'It would be no good us employing a Director of Education who believed in private schools. It would be no good us employing a Director of Housing who did not believe in building council houses.'

The Liberals, pursuing the 'jobs for the boys' theme, even tried to rouse the unemployed. Spokesman Richard Pine, declared that the measures were 'a slap in the face for the city's unemployed who would find 50 per cent of the jobs reserved for friends of the unions and those sympathetic to the Labour Party'. But this was answered by Pauline Dunlop, Deputy Chair of the Personnel Committee, who declared: 'We are not saying that you have to be a member of a union to get a job—how could we, when so many young people have never had a job and therefore have never had a chance to join a union.' She went on, 'The Joint Shop Stewards who represent 30,000 workers will be invited to selection meetings to give technical advice at the invitation of the Chair of the (Personnel) Committee, Derek Hatton, just as the council officers attempt to give advice when asked. There will be no involvement in personalities.' From a Marxist standpoint, the major criticism of this policy is that it did not go far enough. Too many of the council officials, particularly the top echelons, were inherited from previous Liberal and Tory administrations. They were no friends of this Labour council and on many occasions secretly resorted to sabotaging major policy decisions. Three years before Labour came to power, Derek Hatton declared that he would like to see 'socialist managers' in the top positions, but the council was hemmed in by union agreements, and national factors such as the unpreparedness of the trade unions or Labour leaders to support such a policy. This was one of the limitations which Labour was compelled to accept within the confines of a struggle limited to one city. It was to complicate and partly undermine Labour's plans in the next three years. However, one worker wrote to the *Echo*:

> I am an employee of Liverpool City Council, appointed since Labour came to power. My interview was very fair and all questions asked were to do with my motivation, ability and qualifications to do my job. I was not asked anything about my political views. I wish I could say the same for interviews I have had with some other local authorities.

Tearing at the heartstrings of its readers, the *Echo* (23 January) detailed the case of a team of 12 gardeners who had allegedly been persecuted by Ian Lowes and Branch 5 of the GMBATU. They had been banned to a so-called parkland 'leper colony' for allegedly upsetting a *Militant* controlled council union. These twelve tagged the 'Dirty Dozen' by their workmates, had a record of refusing to abide by union decisions to come out on strike in the past although they had never, of course, refused to accept any wage increase that had been gained through union action! Naturally, other council workers were reluctant to work with them. They were moved to the parkland site in order to avoid industrial action from the majority of their workmates. The attitude of the workers was: 'why should scabs benefit from the power of the unions, in particular the bonus system, which had been fought for and gained by union activity?' The ruling class and its organs naturally see such action as 'intimidation', whereas workers see it as a natural expression of class solidarity.

While tall headlines in bold type detailed the 'jobs for the boys' theme of the local press, tucked away usually on the inside pages were the real achievements of the council. Thus a one-paragraph report in the *Post* on 18 January 1985 stated: 'Liverpool's Labour administration is to take 100 young people off the dole queue and find them staff positions on the council workforce. The youngsters, mainly 16-year-old school leavers, are likely to be recruited from among this Easter's school leavers.'

If the Liberals and Tories had taken such measures they would have warranted front page banner headlines. Labour also immediately proceeded to introduce a £100 minimum wage. This benefited 4000 of the lowest paid workers. The council also began to implement a reduction of the working week from 39 hours to 35 hours.

Of course the bourgeois press finds it entirely permissible for the Tory government to put its own stooges in charge of the nationalised industries and even the BBC. The *Echo* (22 January 1985) emphasised the need for a 'proven track record of professional success'. What 'professional success' did Ian MacGregor have when Thatcher appointed him to butcher the coal industry? He had come from the steel industry where he had carried through a similar operation, but he knew very little about the details and the overall position of the coal industry in Britain as subsequent events were to prove. Nevertheless

Thatcher needed him as a club with which to beat the miners.

Not only did the council actively involve the trade unions in its decision making but it also required councillors to play an active role in trade-union activities. Councillors were organised to participate on a rota of Lancashire picket lines. Haulage contractors who were known to be crossing picket lines were deleted from contract lists. This was part of a little-known but important aspect of council policy, contract compliance. The council insisted that all firms with which it did business complied with health and safety legislation, conformed to equal opportunities, granted at least the minimum wage determined by appropriate national or district negotiations, and recognised the appropriate trade unions for the workers which it employed. In this way, the council was used as an instrument to enhance and develop the power of the workers in private industry as well as in the council sector.

The Static Security Force

The capitalists are completely hostile to any attempt to undermine their grip on the state machine, either at national or at local level. They have always guarded jealously their control of all aspects of 'security' and have made political appointments as and when they felt it necessary. Ex-police inspectors, many of them already with pensions, were preferred for key security positions by the Tories and Liberals. Previous Labour administrations also went along with this procedure. But this time Labour broke with 'tradition' and appointed an unemployed Labour sympathiser as Chief Security Officer, responsible for the 'Static Security Force'—workers who watched over and maintained security on council premises. The press set up a hue and cry denouncing the Static Security Force as 'Derek Hatton's private army' *(Echo*, 21 January). The workers reacted angrily, and shop steward John Dunbell protested to the *Echo* (24 January): 'There is no way we would become a political force for anyone.' Another worker commented in the same article that 'when the Liberals were in power, they tried to get rid of the static force, and brought in more and more private firms to do the work'. He pointed out that under the Liberals 'security men were working 100-120 hours a week for 50 pence an hour. I think Derek Hatton should be praised not attacked...He has given us dignity and self respect by changing our name to static security and giving us uniforms, giving us a 39-hour week and doubling the labour force.'

Ian Lowes, Convenor of the Branch 5 GMBATU and well-known *Militant* supporter, was bracketed with Derek Hatton and councillor Pauline Dunlop as the villain of the piece. Trevor Jones declared *(Post,* 22 January 1985): 'It is almost a blueprint of the way Lenin and Stalin gained power in Russia, by taking over their own army and propaganda machine.' Derek Hatton hit back: 'It is not unusual for a particular department to have 100 per cent nomination rights. In the printing industry throughout the city, trade unions have 100 per cent nomination rights. We felt there was nothing untoward about them [GMBATU] having the control of the nomination rights.'

Ian Lowes in a letter to the *Echo* (30 January) answered all the charges levelled against him:

> The GMBATU operates an unemployed register. Unlike most other unions, however, we do not confine acceptance to our register to GMBATU members only. Unemployed people from other unions have been accepted, unemployed people not in a union due to them being unemployed have been accepted, and unemployed people who have never been in a union have been accepted. There are three main criteria: people who apply must be unemployed; they must not have sold a previous job through voluntary redundancy; and they must be willing to join the union if they secure employment with the council.

Completely answering the charges of the *Echo* that he, one person on a committee of eleven, decided who should get the jobs, he declared:

> Application forms are sent out and the completed application form is considered by a committee of eleven people. All those applications which are successful are placed on an unemployed register. When vacancies arise, nominations are taken from that register. All trade-union nominees are interviewed by management, the decisions as to who is ultimately appointed lies with management, and not with the union.

This did not prevent the *Echo* from continuing with their smear campaign. It declared (30 January):

> Junior Environment Minister William Waldegrave was today handed a copy of last week's three page Special Report...he was

given the *Echo* article by Mossley Hill Liberal MP David Alton, who accused the city council of being 'sinister and corrupt' and labelled Deputy Leader Derek Hatton the 'Mr Fixit' on staff appointments and promotions.

However, the *Echo* itself was forced to record the substantial support which existed for the council's stand both on jobs and on the security force. One correspondent, not a *Militant* supporter, wrote:

> Correct me if I'm wrong, but is it not an obvious fact that ... the static security has become stronger in number, younger and more able to combat the ever increasing crime and wanton vandalism of public property, thus cutting the cost of replacement and repair.

'We Will Never Forget You'

Throughout the miners' strike, permits were issued for collections throughout the city. Between £2000 and £3000 was collected each week, and in all council offices there were collection boxes for the miners. Food lorries were organised to assist the workers in North and South Wales. Leading South Wales miners spoke at Liverpool events and participated in solidarity action. A leader of the South Wales miners, Terry Thomas, was given warm hospitality and solidarity in Liverpool. Unfortunately he later repaid this by supporting the expulsion of *Militant* supporters in his own area and nationally.

Any group of workers on strike in the Merseyside area could count on support from the Labour council. The ruling class never forgave the Liverpool City Council for granting the freedom of the city to the Cammell Laird shipyard strikers. It was a bitter and protracted struggle, which led to an occupation by a section of the workers with 37 of them eventually jailed. Scandalously, Frank Field, the Labour MP for Birkenhead, came out on the side of the management, supporting those workers who wished to have a 'sweetheart' relationship with the employers as a means of 'getting work for Merseyside'. Virtually all the other Labour MPs on Merseyside gave unqualified support to the occupation and the strike.

A group of Ghanaian seamen who struck in Birkenhead in October 1984 also received support from the council. They occupied the vessel, *MV Maiseni*, because the Dutch owners had not paid them for nine months. Owed about £45,000 in back wages, they were desperate for money to buy food and medicine because their families in Ghana had been forced into poverty. One crew member had even received a letter from his wife saying that their marriage had ended. Labour Party Young Socialists and *Militant* supporters were to the fore in raising cash to sustain the occupation of the ship. The ship was actually 'arrested' by the Admiralty who considered having it scrapped in order to pay the crew. Their morale was especially boosted with the news that Liverpool City Council and Terry Fields MP had taken up their case. Eventually the owners of the ship were forced to pay the seamen at least part of their wages. They considered it as a great victory and stated that it would have been impossible without the help of 'the LPYS and *Militant*'. Thanking Terry Fields they said: "We will never forget you.'

The youth of course were among the main beneficiaries of the policies of the council. In taking on an initial 16 of an expected 81 apprentices, the council declared that not one of them would be sacked when they completed their training. This policy was adhered to despite all the later financial difficulties and problems created by the refusal of the trade-union leaders to support the council's struggle.

'Crisis on the Bins'

Thwarted in its attempt to blacken the council on the issue of 'jobs for the boys', the *Echo* (6 February) turned to 'The crisis on the bins'. This was featured one month after the previous campaign. Labour conceded that the state of the refuse service was extremely bad but pointed out that the problem had been inherited from the Liberals and Tories. Even the *Echo* had to comment that (6 February): 'It is true—as Liverpool's Labour rulers never tire of pointing out—that we are now paying the price for years during which the Cleansing Department's refuse collection fleet was allowed to degenerate through age.' It went on: 'In spite of the urgency of the situation, in 1983-4 the Liberal budget included only £800,000 earmarked for its vehicle replacement programme—even though Mr Cucksey [the City Engineer] told the council in 1983 that at least £3.6 million was needed immediately.' It graciously quoted Bill Jones, Transport and General Workers Union convenor at Breckside Park and then Chair of the city council Joint Shop Stewards Committee, 'We could have stopped all this if they had listened to us in the past. Everybody warned the Liberals that if we did not invest in plant, vehicles and machinery we would have this situation.'

Nevertheless, the main blame for the bin service was placed on the Labour council. No ringing headlines appeared in the _Echo_ denouncing the Tory government for cutting back on the programme which would have allowed Liverpool to have spent the necessary cash on acquiring new vehicles and the latest machinery in order to do the job properly. Nor did the _Echo_ hail the colossal efforts made by the council to correct the situation, buying 28 new vehicles from 1983-6, and moving towards a weekly collection of the bins, which for Liverpool was a colossal achievement! But the efforts of the council did not go unrecognised:

> I'm fed up with reading in your paper comments about refuse collection and street cleansing. Can't these people see that if Labour rulers were to go out and buy a fleet of new bin wagons and equipment the ratepayers would complain. If it wasn't for the past Liberal council not keeping up with new spare parts and failing to buy at least a couple of new wagons each year to keep the refuse fleet up to scratch, we wouldn't be in this mess. The Conservatives and Liberals make me sick. All they think of is privatisation. For once we, the Liverpool people, are getting jobs created instead of redundancies. (_Echo_, 28 February.)

Another letter to the _Echo_ (13 February) stated:

> I was dismayed but not surprised to see the January [1985] unemployment figures relegated to an apparently insignificant position on page 16 (31 January). Yet another example of the _Echo's_ 'unbiased' interpretation of what is or isn't newsworthy. With one in five on the dole and no end in sight, when will the _Echo_—the self-styled voice of Merseyside—speak with a Scouse accent and attack this government's policies. Reserve your venom for Maggie not Derek.

Another declared (_Echo_, 12 February):

> It's a pity that our Members of Parliament have not got the fight of Derek Hatton ... even if you don't agree with their policies and views you have to admire their spirit. It's about time that people who made their wealth here put some of it back.

The council also sought to exert control over the council grants to numerous firms throughout the city. In the past they took handouts without any attempt to explain or account for their actions to the council or the people of the city. When Labour proposed in 1983 that they should take some equity share in local companies to which it gave grant aid, the directors of these firms were outraged. However, the *Guardian* (3 October 1983) was forced to comment:

> The reaction of some of Liverpool's businesses to the new Labour council's industrial policy seems a trifle overwrought...considering Merseyside's sad experience of firms which have taken various forms of public subsidy only to up and out when it suited them, the Labour council's objective seems eminently sensible. Its means are more debatable.

The Education Programme

The educational achievements of the city councils are perhaps the greatest of any comparable local authority in the country. In 1982, when the Liberal-Tory coalition dominated the city, the *Echo* declared in October 1982: 'Will no-one sort out the festering scandal of Liverpool's schools reorganisation?' Almost as soon as Labour came to power they proposed a complete reorganisation which had been dodged by the Liberals and Tories. The schools had experienced falling rolls over the whole decade of the 1970s. By 1984 the number of pupils entering the schools was only one third of what it had been ten years earlier. There were 9000 empty secondary school desks. Some schools were half empty, while others were full. An imbalance existed in different parts of the city, restricting the choice of subjects available. Only a complete reorganisation could solve this. The problems arose from the failure in the 1960s and 1970s to develop education on a comprehensive basis. Attempts at re-organisation in the past were class-based closures and they were resisted by the working-class people who were most affected by them. This was the background to the closure of Croxteth Comprehensive which would have deprived one of the poorest areas of the city of its only public amenity.

Labour's plan was to completely reorganise the secondary sector into 17 community comprehensives. The plan received massive support from the teachers' unions, the manual and auxiliary workers, and from educationalists in general. Naturally, the schools reorganisation provoked tremendous controversy since parents are deeply concerned about the education of their children. There were massive turn-outs at the public meetings, sometimes of 500 or 600 parents. At these meetings, a dialogue took place between parents, teachers and councillors. The Liberals whipped up tremendous unfounded opposition to the reorganisation, especially in the better-off areas, presenting it as school closures and cuts. The butchers of Croxteth Comprehensive now posed as the champions of parents! But once the scheme was established and parents, particularly working-class parents, saw the advantages of the new scheme, with a teacher-pupil ratio that was one of the best in Britain and a wider choice of subjects etc, this opposition completely evaporated.

The most outstanding feature of the reorganisation was the building of six new nursery school units, something that had been completely neglected for decades. The council attempted to provide nursery facilities in every area of the city. Unfortunately, Tory education ministers stepped in and prevented Liverpool from building a further six nursery classes.

In a visit to the city in February 1985, Caroline Benn, an educationalist, considered that, according to the *Post* (2 February 1985): 'toddlers in Liverpool are the envy of the country, thanks to the city council'. She was in the city to open one of the new nursery units which were then being set up and she commented: 'I've looked round and I cannot tell you how impressed I am with what I've seen. Many districts would give anything to have what you have here.' She went on to say that her studies had convinced her that children between three and four years old take on ideas which stay with them all their lives and that this sort of provision was therefore particularly important.

In stark contrast, in Wakefield the right-wing Labour council had sent in police and bailiffs to successfully break up an occupation of a nursery threatened with closure in February 1984. The leader of Wakefield council, Sir Jack Smart, was one of those who had consistently supported the expulsion of Marxists from the Labour Party. There was to be no attempt on the part of the national leaders of the Labour Party to discipline or attack this worthy.

Another important area of the council's education programme was in improving conditions in the Further Education colleges. By 1985 students in Liverpool had won a number of measures that would not even be dreamed of in other education authorities. This included: Funding for three full-time student union officials; increased funding for student unions; time off lessons for student union meetings and for YTS trainees to meet with trade-union representatives during college hours; free meals, books, paper and travel tokens for the unemployed and those under 18; increases in grants and free nursery facilities in every college.

Not the least of the achievements of the council was the increase in numbers *employed* in education: from 16,317 in June 1982 to 16,836 in June 1986—an increase of 519! Liverpool has consistently exceeded the statutory limits laid down by Tory education ministers for the numbers employed in education. This, one would imagine, would have evinced tremendous support from the teaching unions. But the leaders of the NUT, like Jim Ferguson, well-known Communist Party member, were completely impervious to these achievements and to the long-term interests of their own members. Despite the sacrifices the councillors were prepared to make on behalf of the educational needs of working people as a whole, and in defence of teachers' jobs, the NUT leadership acted for their own political ends in the most spiteful fashion at critical periods in the campaign, seizing any opportunity to undermine the council campaign.

Great achievements have been recorded in Liverpool in all aspects of education. But as Felicity Dowling, former teacher, and then Secretary of the Liverpool District Labour Party declared in *Militant* in March 1984:

> When Labour was first elected there was a period of euphoria in the schools. It was felt that most of the problems could be solved. I think it has now become clear to all that although important changes are being made, the underlying problems of poverty and lack of resources remain. They cannot be tackled without a major government intervention in terms of money. And only fundamental socialist change will make education genuinely accessible to all.

Thus even while energetically pursuing reforms, no matter

how limited, *Militant* and its supporters on the council continually linked the struggle for reforms with the idea of the socialist reorganisation of society.

The achievements of Liverpool City Council in other fields, together with those mentioned above are a monument to the heroic struggle conducted between 1983-7. They are a glimpse of what could be achieved on the basis of a planned socialist economy. Much of the initial opposition to Labour, and particularly to the Marxists, evaporated once the real achievements and possibilities of Labour rule began to be recognised by the working people in the city. By the same token, the capitalists and those who support their system within the labour movement, were mortally afraid that the example of Liverpool would prove contagious in the explosive social situation that had opened up in Britain during the 1980s.

10.
The Battle Against Ratecapping

A SHORT INTERREGNUM followed the July 1984 settlement
between Patrick Jenkin and Liverpool City Council. However,
the government was soon preparing its next round of measures
against local councils. 'Rate-capping' was imposed on a number
of councils, most of them Labour. Ostensibly to limit rate rises,
the effect of setting a limit on rate rises (which if exceeded would
result in councils losing government grant under a penalty
system) in the context of cuts in the central government grant,
was that the spending of councils was being ruthlessly slashed.
Rate-capping was to force a whole number of councils into the
'front-line' of opposition to the Tories.

What were the lessons of Liverpool? Did it serve as a platform
for other councils who would now find themselves in the same
position? Would it be possible to forge an alliance between
councils and those trade unions also singled out for attack by the
Tory government? Would other councils take the Liverpool
road and compel the government to beat a retreat?

Any criticism of Liverpool seemed to evaporate as other
councils attempted to use the city's experience as justification for
their resistance to the government. Even the ultra-lefts who had
condemned the agreement in July now switched tack. 'Sold
Down the Mersey!' *Socialist Worker* had declared but now they
argued: 'The other side of the Labour left's local government
upturn is Liverpool. It is a very different story from the GLC...it
involved a considerable degree of trade union mobilisation as a
central part of its strategy. Liverpool has achieved what most
people consider to be a notable victory.' (*Socialist Worker Review*,
November 1984)

Even the National Executive Committee of the Labour Party
was carried along by the growing conviction that the

government could be defeated. In August a meeting between the Executive's Local Government Committee and representatives of local authorities on the government rate-capping hit-list took place. The Labour leadership proposed 'a long-term strategy' which involved a series of so-called 'bush wars' stretching over a period of three years. Its purpose was to avoid a battle in 1984-5. But the Local Government Committee decisively rejected this proposal, accepting a motion moved by Steve Morgan (Labour Party Young Socialists' representative on the Executive) that a series of national demonstrations be organised in the period up to March 1985. It also suggested the calling of a one-day national local authority workers' strike on 'Democracy Day' which was set for 7 March 1985. Anticipating his future role, David Blunkett opposed the idea of a one-day strike. He argued that this would play into the hands of the Tories!

Such was the pressure from below that many councils were compelled to pose the question of open 'illegal defiance' of the government's proposals. This was reflected at the Labour Party Conference at the end of September, with 32 resolutions and 14 amendments on local government, the biggest number on any one subject. Thirteen resolutions expressed total support for Liverpool City Council. A resolution moved by Derek Hatton, supporting the stand of Liverpool City Council and calling for defiance of the Tory government, was carried despite the opposition of the National Executive Committee. Neil Kinnock, in his sniping at Liverpool and other 'hard-left' councils, was later to repeatedly pass over this decision of the Labour Party Conference.

The savage cuts demanded by the Tory measures were compelling even formerly 'moderate' councils to take up a militant posture. In Leicester, a meeting of the District Labour Party was attended by 200 people at which leaders of the council declared their intention to fight government cuts that could have meant 500 job losses. Tony Byrne, Finance Chairman of Liverpool City Council was given an enthusiastic reception by the meeting. Even Tory councils, such as the London Borough of Hillingdon which loyally prostrated itself before the government, found that its services were to be slashed to the bone because of penalties of £8 million imposed by its own government. Left-wing councils like Hackney and Southwark joined with Sheffield, the GLC, the Inner London Education Authority and more than 20 other councils in opposing the government's measures. These councils had the choice of acting either as rate and rent collectors and hatchet men of the government, or of following the example of Liverpool.

There could not have been a greater contrast, however, between the approach of Liverpool and that of the other councils which had joined in an uneasy alliance against the government. A number had already come into head-on collision with their own workforce because of previous attempts to implement cuts. Thus, a bitter strike of white-collar workers had developed in David Blunkett's Sheffield. The council had decided to tear up an agreement on new technology which had been in operation for two and a half years. A 'left-wing' councillor declared that NALGO members were 'overpaid, underworked and should think themselves lucky to have a job'. Thirteen NALGO members were suspended after refusing to implement a new agreement which had not been agreed by their union. The dispute was bitter, with a 24-hour strike of all Sheffield NALGO members on 24 October. If such a development had taken place in Liverpool, it would have received enormous publicity on a local and a national scale. In another example in Sheffield, when striking workers in a building firm called Gleesons asked the council to take the firm off their official tender list, the council—with the open support of David Blunkett—refused. As explained in Chapter 8, such a development would have been impossible in Liverpool with its policies of contract compliance and support for workers in struggle.

Despite the difficulties a united front, at some cost to the principled position of Liverpool (as explained further below), *was* forged in late 1984 between Liverpool and other authorities which had been rate-capped. Undoubtedly, a key element in the stand that David Blunkett, Ken Livingstone, Lambeth's Ted Knight, etc, were taking, was the colossal pressure that had developed from below, largely as a result of the stand that Liverpool had taken earlier. An organisation which brought the shop stewards together in London, the London Bridge Committee, now called for a one-day strike on 17 November.

In the past, local government had been, to some extent, a

refuge for workers from the demands of 'private industry'. This was particularly the case during the post-war boom. But it had now been brought home to the workers in this field that, given the threat that the government had made, unless they put up a determined struggle many of them would be forced onto the dole. This led to an increasing militancy within the unions and the beginning of the transformation of the shop stewards' organisations. The older, less energetic, more right-wing layer were being elbowed aside by young workers who were prepared to fight. The process was most marked in Liverpool, but it was mirrored in many other council workforces throughout the country.

A Deficit Budget or 'No Rate'?

A debate opened up amongst the leaders of the rate-capped councils as to which tactic for fixing the annual rate, due to be set in March 1985, could best mobilise the undoubted opposition which existed to the government's policies. Liverpool's method of setting a rate that left a deficit in the budget, presenting a clear demand on the government to give more resources to the council to make up the difference, had shown in practice that it was an excellent means of mobilising the mass of the working class for battle. The 'trendy left' typified by Ken Livingstone, David Blunkett and Margaret Hodge, Leader of Islington council, counterposed to this a so-called 'no-rate' policy—a strategy which called on rate-capped authorities to refuse to set budgets until the government made concessions. As subsequent events demonstrated, this was an attempt to *avoid* (or, at best, postpone) giving battle to the Tory government in a clear and unambiguous fashion. An argument in favour of the 'no-rate' policy was that it would bring all authorities fighting the Tories into confrontation with the government at the same time. But, as *Militant* supporters pointed out, some councils such as Camden and Islington who had received no rate support grant, would run out of money before others. The position of each council was different, making it virtually impossible to harmonise the precise date when all councils were to face bankruptcy. More-over, the 'no-rate' policy was a negative one, leaving the initiative in the government's hands.

There was a further fundamental difference between

Liverpool's proposal and that of the other councils. Liverpool completely opposed the idea of off-setting government grant cuts by massively increasing rates. But the advocates of the 'no-rate' policy were in favour of precisely such steps. Despite many misgivings and the frankly stated opinion of the Marxists that many of the 'trendy lefts' would back away from a confrontation when the chips were down, Liverpool councillors went along with the 'no-rate' policy. This was done in the interests of a common stand by the 25 councils against the government. In the 1983-4 battle Liverpool, despite having no choice, had been accused by Blunkett, Livingstone and others, of 'jumping the gun'. To have stood out now on the issue of the 'deficit budget' would have given an excuse for these worthies to abandon their own stand against the government.

Confused as the tactic undoubtedly was, it evoked tremendous support and spurred local authority workers into action. Thus in November 1984 100,000 London workers came out on strike in boroughs threatened by rate-capping and the abolition of the Greater London Council. 30,000 marched in the capital. The example of Liverpool was evoked more than once that day. Greenwich council leader John Austin-Walker declared: 'The time for fudging is over. We should learn the lesson from Liverpool—we can win!' Ken Livingstone, referring to the £6 billion owed by the rate-capped boroughs to the banks, roused the meeting with his statement, 'I am afraid we will have to say to them, "sorry but you'll have to wait until the struggle is over".' Dennis Skinner declared: 'the lesson has to be learned, stand by your class'. Unfortunately, Austin-Walker and Livingstone were not to match their fine words with deeds.

Once more, the unions and the working class rallied enthusiastically to the side of the Liverpool council in the looming battle with the government. A mass meeting of 2500 trade unionists assembled in the Philharmonic Hall on 11 January 1985 to hear Liverpool's Labour leaders outline the stark alternatives. The council faced an invidious choice of 6000 job losses or a 220 per cent rate increase, unless a struggle was mounted to force the government to give concessions. This would involve a 1.5 per cent cut in education, spending on school meals being cut by 29 per cent, housing services cut by 17 per cent and employment cut by a minimum of seven per cent. David Blunkett declared in the *Post:* 'No local authority will be acting independently, and none will make individual agreements.'

The intention of the rate-capped authorities was to synchronise their budget meetings for 7 and 8 March which coincided with the TUC's proposed 'Democracy Day' demonstrations. The *Echo* gloomily declared on 17 January: 'It now seems we are in for another year in which Liverpool will be in the forefront of a clash with the government.' Nor was the opposition to rate-capping restricted just to Labour authorities. Bradford, a hung council but with the Tories as the largest party, had been given the target budget of £174 million. The city estimated this was £4 million short of what it required and went to court in order to get back the money 'stolen from it' by its 'own' government.

The rate-capped councils, unified into one body, decided to approach the government for negotiations in the middle of January 1985. David Blunkett declared:

> Our authorities and the trade unions are totally united behind the stand taken of non-compliance...today we made it clear that, whatever the government says, we are not going to be divided. No authority will try and get itself off the hook by accepting deals from the government individually.

But the government had taken stock of the 'trendy left' who were leading the struggle. This was an entirely different beast to that which they had confronted on Merseyside. *The Times* (18 January) declared:

> The time is for resolution. A start should be made at once by a government announcement that it will not pay rate support grant to councils which by the end of March have not made a valid rate. That threat by striking the Labour Party where it hurts—in the pockets of the municipal unions—will at once distinguish the Town Hall posturers from the genuine revolutionaries.

The attitude of the government towards Liverpool had always been different. One Whitehall mandarin confided to Tony Mulhearn that 'London was pure theatre, Liverpool is serious.'

The potential for a unified struggle against the government had never been greater. Splits had opened up with Tory MPs voting against the government's regulations to curb council spending on housing in February 1985. However the timidity of the 'official' leaders of the struggle was indicated by the visit of Hodge and Blunkett to the Bank of England. They attempted to 'allay concern in the city about loans to local authorities on the government's hit list'. Even while ostensibly leading an all-out struggle against the government they hinted to *The Times* that: 'The visit to the city was intended to counter the image of fiscal irresponsibility raised by Mr Ted Knight, Leader of Lambeth.' Patrick Jenkin was quite happy to meet such 'irreconcilables', making no concessions but playing them along, confident in the knowledge that they would run for cover when faced with 'illegality' in March or shortly afterwards.

'Let them Stew'

In Liverpool the whole tone and mood of the government and its local satraps was entirely different. To begin with, Jenkin even refused to negotiate with a delegation which included Derek Hatton. Nevertheless, the government was extremely sensitive to the social situation in Liverpool. Thus *The Times* reported: 'The background is the threat of civil disturbance in the city, which was torn by riots in 1981. Special Branch and Home Office reports continuously monitor events in Toxteth and specifically, the activity of extremist politicians in fomenting discontent.' The 'extremist politicians' were those such as Derek Hatton, Tony Mulhearn as well as non-'Militants' who had been democratically voted into office by the population of Liverpool.

Sensing the impending battle, the opposition in Liverpool launched increasingly hysterical attacks on the council. The Tories, a pathetic and dwindling force in Liverpool, attempted to launch a petition against 'massive rate rises'. They of course failed to mention, as did the local press, that Liverpool was pledged not to increase rates to compensate for cuts. Liberal MP David Alton, from the safety of Parliament, described the methods of the 'Militant Labour leaders' in the city as the 'tactics of the jackboot'. This was the prelude to the vicious campaign of personal slander which Alton was to launch and which was eagerly seized upon by the *Echo* and the *Post*. Backed by all the local media, the counter-campaign of the Liberals moved into overdrive. Trevor Jones demanded 'an enquiry into the running of Liverpool City Council'.

On the same day that Jones launched this attack, Jenkin sent a sharp rebuff to the city council. He declared, 'I can see no basis for a meeting with you on the terms you propose...you appear determined on a rerun of the disruptive and damaging campaign you mounted last year'. Jenkin was further quoted in the *Post* (28 January): 'We let them stew in their own juice. We are prepared to sit it out.' Three days later, Jenkin conceded the necessity of a meeting which involved Derek Hatton. By hints and 'lobby briefings', Jenkin indicated: 'Ministers believe nearly all rebel councils will cave in when the crunch comes. But they admit that a handful of hardline Labour leaders—probably in Liverpool, Manchester and a couple of London boroughs—could take their authorities to the brink.'

In the meantime, the workers in Liverpool prepared once more for a stoppage, on 7 March. When Neil Kinnock met a delegation at the House of Commons he advised them to make a gesture of defiance on that day and then 'accept reality'. *Tribune*, the journal of the soft left, reported: 'Labour local government leaders and trade unionists emerged from meeting Neil Kinnock on Monday cautiously optimistic that the party leadership will back their campaign against rate-capping.' (25 January). Yet, a few lines later, the same journal commented: 'There was a clash between Mr Kinnock and Lambeth's Ted Knight and Liverpool's Deputy Leader Derek Hatton, when Mr Kinnock warned that it would be impossible to turn back Tory allegations of illegality if councillors call for defiance of the law for its own sake. There will be no pledge of indemnity for surcharged councillors.'

Defeat in Vauxhall Ward

Desperate to seek a point of support within the labour movement the slightest opposition, no matter how tiny, was magnified in the capitalist press. The *Post* and *Echo* were supplemented by Maxwell's *Daily Mirror* which became the main tabloid to attack Liverpool in the two years which followed. On 3 December it screamed about 'The saving of Liverpool', highlighting the opposition which had developed in just one ward, Vauxhall, led by renegade councillor Paul Orr. The *Daily Mail* in its advocacy of 'co-ops' proclaimed: 'Tenants rout left in fight for their own homes.' The *Echo* went further—a giant

Militant logo led into a headline which said, 'How they got the boot'.

Perhaps this indicated the defeat of *Militant* in the Liverpool labour movement? If one reads the article by Peter Phelps, who was soon to join the *Daily Mail*, it certainly seemed that way: 'Now is the time for all good men—and women—to come to the aid of the party. That is the heart of the message coming like a clarion call out of Vauxhall in Liverpool's dockland, where traditional socialists are spearheading a fightback against Militant Tendency's iron grip on the city Labour Party.' (*Echo*, 21 January). One of Orr's lieutenants, reported to Phelps: 'If anyone disagrees, there is the kind of intimidatory behaviour which happened in the beer cellars of Germany during the 1930s.' The same individual who made this statement physically attacked Liverpool city councillors two years later when acting as a very ineffective praetorian guard for Larry Whitty outside a Labour group meeting. Yet this deluge of support for *Militant's* opponents was provoked by their victory in just one ward out of the 33 in the city. At just one particular meeting the left, including supporters of *Militant*, were temporarily defeated. But when proposals from Vauxhall ward for the expulsion of *Militant* were put to the Riverside constituency party, it was defeated by 45 votes to five! Tony Hood, Chair of the constituency, characterised the 'moderates' as 'an unrepresentative clique... there is no way we are going to expel people because of alleged membership of the Militant Tendency or because they distribute certain newspapers.'

Occasionally a letter would appear in the *Echo* which would reflect the real views of the rank and file of the party:

> Firstly he [Peter Phelps] described this group of opponents of the Militant Tendency as 'good men and women and traditional socialists'. This may well be correct. However, I would contend that members and supporters of *Militant* are as well.
>
> It was also mentioned that last month the Vauxhall ward tried to have certain *Militant* supporters expelled for 'bringing the party into disrepute'. As a non-*Militant* delegate to the Riverside constituency that rejected that proposal, I object to the claims that the vote was rigged...Vauxhall's carping now is based purely on the fact that democracy prevailed and their silly divisive proposals were hugely rejected by the party...in three years' active membership of the Labour Party, I have yet to see any of their alleged intimidation.

When the right-wing dominated National Executive Committee of the Labour Party was to conduct its infamous inquiry into the Liverpool District Labour Party (DLP) and the activities of *Militant* supporters on Merseyside, it was the baseless allegations of Vauxhall ward and not the genuine voice of the rank and file that they listened to. The *Echo* a few days later boasted: '*Militant* loses out in bid for key post.' *Militant* supporter Phil Rowe had been defeated when he stood for the Chair of West Derby Labour Party, but this was not an uncommon occurrence in that constituency up to that stage.

Meanwhile, plans were made for mobilising the workforce for the battle to come. Five hundred local authority stewards representing the 30,000 strong workforce were called to a special meeting to launch the campaign. Leaders of the council addressed the meeting with many stewards supporting them from the floor. At the outset of the meeting one prominent Communist Party member argued for 'trade-union independence', saying that the shop stewards should not discuss the campaign until every trade union had discussed it separately. Ian Lowes replied on behalf of the majority of the workforce: 'If we went into battle this year with two separate campaigns, one by the council and one by the local authority unions, we would be doomed to failure. If we don't stand together we will have to face up to the fact that 6000 redundancies will occur.' Out of 500 stewards, only two voted against supporting the council's campaign, including Communist Party member Jack Kaye.

The Communist Party's opposition was matched by that of Neil Kinnock at national level. Opening the Labour Party Local Government Conference in Birmingham early in 1985, he once more appealed for councils to remain 'within the law'. Derek Hatton responded: 'What we did not hear was an absolutely unequivocal commitment on the part of the parliamentary leadership to say "Yes, we support those groups to fight for no loss of jobs and no cuts in services".' Even David Blunkett, forced at this stage to take up a 'left' position declared that he expected the leader's support for the council's line of defiance, 'right or wrong'.

As was to be expected, the government and the capitalist press took great heart from Kinnock's statement. Jenkin turned down the pleas of the 25 Labour council leaders who met him in early February. Moreover, the *Post*, which had consistently argued that a more conciliatory and negotiating posture would get better results than the 'confrontational approach' of the city council supported Jenkin to the hilt: 'Quite rightly, this year he is firm, resolute, and yesterday's delegation was told its proposals were absurd.'

The Asda Affair and Other Smears

Fearing the impending struggle, the *Echo* and the *Post* launched a smear campaign, unequalled in the recent history of the city. This was particularly aimed against Derek Hatton. Every insubstantial smear and dirty innuendo of the Liberals and Tories was blown up into huge feature articles. One of the biggest smears was on the issue of whether or not to grant planning permission for the superstore Asda to build a complex in the Speke enterprise zone. Leading Labour councillors like Derek Hatton and a majority of the District Labour Party leaned towards granting Asda's application because of the jobs which would be provided. Shopworkers' union chief Bill Snell, well-known right winger, used this issue to attack the left-dominated DLP. The *Echo* (6 February) declared in a deliberately slanted headline: 'I'm in the clear, says Hatton.' The implication was that Derek Hatton stood to receive some 'financial gain' from granting the application, but had cleverly covered his tracks. David Alton, in a typical example of his cowardly approach, used parliamentary privilege to make the most vicious character assassination on Derek Hatton. Alton complained about Labour's 'jobs for the boys' policy, while the Tory MP for Wirral South, Barry Porter, in the same debate (in an aside) declared: 'Some of them are crooks.' Alton would not take up the challenge of Merseyside Labour MPs to repeat his allegations in Liverpool.

A similar broadside was launched against councillor Jimmy Hackett implying that he had used his personal position to get his ex-wife a council house. The complete rejection of this charge by Tony Byrne received only minimal coverage. The same criteria applied to the reply to the attacks on the Asda affair by the District Labour Party who condemned

> the campaign being conducted against the council and the party and particularly the McCarthyite campaign of character assassination

against Derek Hatton, instigated by Alton and other Liberals and Tories, aided and abetted by the *Liverpool Daily Post* and *Echo* and the national press...the real objectives of which are to discredit the party and undermine support in the forthcoming campaign to defend jobs and services from the attacks of the Tories.

The Liberals demanded a 'police investigation' into implied 'corruption'. Enquiries that were conducted found no evidence to sustain the smear campaign and the same was true of enquiries into alleged misuse of council expenses by Labour councillors. Nevertheless all this would serve to undermine and weaken, as the capitalists calculated, the resolve of Liverpool workers to take on the Tory government. Ironically, two years later the Asda project was approved by Patrick Jenkin himself as a means of bringing jobs to the city! (The real facts of the Asda affair were set out fully in *Militant*, 15 February 1985 and 17 January 1986).

Such was the indignation in Labour's ranks, however, that a special delegation was organised to see the editors of the *Echo* about their conduct in relation to the council. Tony Mulhearn declared after this meeting:

> The power of the press is an extra obstacle to overcome, but I believe our campaign will succeed. Workers are conscious of what is taking place. The press campaign has hardened their resolve. It is in the wider population that the job of counteracting these press lies has to be done...The local press has always been anti-Labour, castigating the so-called extreme leadership of the Labour Party in the city. But in the last three months there has been a far more concerted and escalating attack on Labour.

Seizing on what he undoubtedly considered was the disarray that existed in Labour's ranks over the Asda affair, Jenkin was threatening special legal measures against the council. At a press conference in the city, he gave a two-week deadline after which he threatened to take control of the council's capital spending. He declared:

> Such a direction would oblige the city council to seek my consent for new contracts or work undertaken by direct labour above a given value and to the making of any capital payments above the legal ceiling. I very much regret having to carry out this step but, given the facts we know, I would be failing in my duty if I didn't act and I would be open to challenge in the courts by any ratepayer.

Jenkin was clearly threatening to cripple the housebuilding programme. There was an angry reaction from Labour councillors, with Tony Byrne saying: 'He is trying to stop us spending the resources we have every right to spend. As far as we are concerned, the right thing is dealing with people's housing conditions, conditions which should have disappeared 100 years ago.'

The ruling class undoubtedly felt as though they had Liverpool in a vice between Jenkin on the one side, and the local Liberals and Tories, together with their mouthpieces, the *Echo* and the *Post,* on the other. However, the press campaign was proving, to some extent, counter-productive. Even businessmen such as Alec Langsham BA, Director of Britannia Hotels Ltd, wrote to the *Echo* (12 February) complaining of the effects of the campaign:

> Depicting caring and hard working city leaders like Derek Hatton as irresponsible crooked playboys, is not only incorrect but causes permanent irreversible damage to Merseyside's image...it is far more important that the media sensationalised the good things which are happening to Merseyside than carry out a character assassination of an industrious political leader whose virtues should perhaps be extolled.

Having successfully answered the Liberal smears in relation to Asda, Labour was compelled a few days later to answer the *Echo's* charge of an 'Overtime Bonanza'. This journal even attempted to make political capital out of the use of council cars by councillors on council business. The fact that Labour had abolished the Rolls Royces and all the trappings of the Mayor etc was conveniently forgotten by the capitalist press. With the miners' strike coming to an end, the government displayed a much greater resolve than in the previous year to confront the local authorities. As the issues became more sharply posed and a class polarisation began to take place, all those who had earlier supported the council in a lukewarm fashion one by one began to peel away. The Church leaders began to separate themselves from the council's stance. The Anglican Bishop of Liverpool, David Sheppard proposed to confront the government by organising 'a civic mass against abolition' of the Merseyside County Council and in support of Liverpool's claims. But in the age old spirit of the Church, render unto Caesar what is Caesar's', Derek Warlock, the Catholic Archbishop, 'last night appealed to the city's Labour leaders not to defy the law and to hold emergency budget talks with the government Ministers.' (*Post* 12 February)

Preparing for Battle

Labour concentrated its energies between July 1984 and March 1985 on a series of mass meetings to explain the choice facing Liverpool. At the same time, changes took place within the Joint Shop Stewards Committee (JSSC) to bring it more into line with the demands of the council workforce in the looming battle with the government. Extensive participation of stewards took place in the JSSC, although the representatives did not always reflect the balance of forces within the workforce. NALGO, with its 5000 members, had more representatives on the JSSC than the GMBATU with its 9000 members. A new system was introduced weighting representation according to union membership, which was obviously more democratic. Ian Lowes, a well-known *Militant* supporter, was elected Chair of the JSSC, but Peter Cresswell of NALGO, a committed opponent of *Militant*, was reelected unopposed as secretary of the committee.

Incredibly the *Morning Star* reported (18 February 1985): '*Militant* splits council shop stewards' body.' Yet as Peter Lennard, Education GMBATU representative, said 'Some people are only happy with democracy when it's them doing the "democking".' Shamefully, the same individual two years later was to display precisely the same tendencies when challenged in his own section of the GMBATU. He was to move into the camp of those he had criticised in February 1985 when the Communist Party and its supporters were instrumental in splitting the JSSC. Their policy was one of 'rule or ruin'; either they were to control the joint body or it was to be shattered. The need for a common front with the government was secondary to their purpose of maintaining what they considered to be their 'traditional' position amongst the unions and the workforce of Liverpool.

Their splitting tactics did not, however, prevent the mobilisation of the workers in Liverpool, or nationally, in the period up to 7 March. What was at stake was not the 'prestige' of a few trade-union officials, but all the past gains in terms of jobs, services and conditions. Nationally, at least 75,000 jobs would be lost. Housebuliding programmes and services would be decimated and the old, sick and disabled would be severely hit if the Tories' attacks were allowed to go ahead unchallenged.

The consciousness of local government workers in the course of the battles up to February-March 1985 was quite remarkable. Their determination was in sharp contrast to the prevarication of the largely middle-class Labour council leaders. This was the case even in those boroughs which were not faced with immediate cuts, and where the local council leadership was able to argue that they were going to have a 'growth budget' for the following year. The best of the leading stewards understood that it was better to have a combined national struggle immediately and to fight together rather than to go down separately in the following years. Moreover, the battles in local government in 1985 were seen to be a prelude to the ferocious struggles that would undoubtedly take place over 'privatisation'.

The movement amongst local government workers outside Liverpool was a harbinger of the coming transformation of the unions and the Labour Party. In Southwark an outline of what will take place in the future in all of the London Labour Parties, and many other parties presently dominated by the middle-class trendy left, was evident. The unions moved into the Labour Party and began to transform the wards and constituency Labour Parties in a way which Marxists had always anticipated would happen. This process of renewal is a beginning of the movement of the working class, taking the labour movement back to its roots.

In Liverpool on 23 February an historic conference of local authority workers took place. Shop stewards from rate-capped and threatened authorities met in Liverpool to plan co-ordinated action and to organise a national conference of local authority trade unions. The conference was the joint initiative of the London Bridge stewards' organisation and the Liverpool Joint Shop Stewards Committee. Out of this and subsequent events came, for the first time amongst local authority workers, the formation of a national shop stewards' organisation. This development was undoubtedly one of the factors which increased the hostility of national trade-union officials towards the struggle of Liverpool and the struggles of many other local authorities. The initiative for battle was being taken out of the hands of officials by shop stewards who were closer to the workers. Had the rate-capped councils remained firm, as had Liverpool, then this body would have been the vehicle for calling supportive national industrial action.

As the 7 March budget day approached, the war of nerves between Liverpool City Council and the government continued. Junior Environment Minister William Waldegrave declared that Liverpool was 'famous for municipal irresponsibility...a city delighting in the prospect of conflict'. Jenkin was using every opportunity to paint a lurid and dismal picture of Liverpool's prospects in the event of a failure to set a rate! He said that it would be 'the poor and the sick' who would suffer; not of course adding that the responsibility for any suffering would lie at the door of himself and his government.

A Deal with French Banks

Liverpool council were to have a further surprise in store for the Secretary of State. On 22 February, Finance Committee Chair, Tony Byrne announced that Liverpool City Council had, earlier that month, finalised a deal which would evade Jenkin's attempt to control capital spending and allow the housebuilding programme to continue. The city had arranged a deal with a banking syndicate headed by Banque Paribas, one of the largest French banks which had been nationalised by the French Socialist government of Mitterand. Under Tory directives, Liverpool had sold 7000 council houses and was receiving monthly mortgage payments from them on a long-term mortgage basis. The city's interest in those mortgages was sold to the banking syndicate and in return the council was to receive a lump sum of £30 million immediately. The *Echo* commented: 'It is a nice irony that the Conservative government's encouragement of council house sales created this pool of mortgages which the council has realised to raise instant cash.' (22 February)

Gnashing his teeth, and after much hesitation, Jenkin announced at the end of March that the deal was legal. Other councils eagerly sought to go through the breach which Liverpool had created by attempting to fix up deals of a similar character. But in July Jenkin stepped in with a new law that prevented any similar deals from taking place. The Liberals, who had seen Labour once more evade the noose which had been tightened around its neck, furiously denounced both Labour and the banks: 'We did not run and put the city in hock to the bandits of Lombard Street who you now embrace', complained Trevor Jones. The deal effectively allowed Liverpool to continue with its housebuilding programme and made some contribution to narrowing Liverpool's budget deficit. But the basic problems still remained and would only be overcome by compelling the government to give concessions to Liverpool and the other rate-capped authorities.

The District Labour Party, at its annual conference, met to approve the strategy and tactics for the impending battle. Tony Mulhearn declared after the meeting:

> They [the delegates] recognise that this year we are faced with the position of either making 6000 workers redundant or increasing rates by 220 per cent. Both those options were unanimously rejected. The Party recognised they have a big battle to get extra resources from the government to make ends meet, but we have decided we are not going to increase rates to compensate for Tory cuts. If, in the fullness of time we do increase rates, it will be on the basis of inflation and extra spending.

Other authorities and local government leaders appeared to be in a similarly determined mood. Ken Livingstone declared on 3 March that the London Labour Party Annual Conference's decision to refuse to operate the government's rate-capping proposals ranked second only to the miners' decision to go on strike. He confidently predicted to the Greater London Labour Party members 'that the struggle would involve not only Labour councillors and the unions, but whole communities'.

At a mass meeting in the Philharmonic Hall, David Blunkett spoke as a guest speaker of the Liverpool Labour Party. He said: 'Unity is the strength that will see us through...We will lift and sustain each other. We must motivate, educate and organise.' According to the *Echo* (15 March), 'he paid tribute to the battle fought alone for the last 12 months by Liverpool City Council and said that this year other Labour-run authorities were joining in that war, saying enough is enough.' Unfortunately, Blunkett was subsequently to eat his words. Liverpool remained true to Blunkett's declaration, only to be rewarded later on by his support for the expulsion from the Labour Party of the leaders of the struggle.

The ruling class had already taken the full measure of Livingstone, Blunkett etc. On the eve of the crucial budget meeting, Jenkin declared: 'Labour's budget revolt is crumbling.' *The Times* declared on 7 March: 'Final act for fun revolutionaries.' They commented: 'Labour's left-wing councillors value power more than a place of glory in the Socialist Pantheon...they will cling to office and make the shifts required, shifts which in most cases are perfectly manageable.'

Jenkin's approach towards Liverpool was entirely different to that adopted towards other councils. Once more on 5 March he declared that 'the government could face a decision on putting in Commissioners to run Liverpool in weeks rather than months if the city council refuses to make a legal budget for 1986'. The *Echo* on the same day carried the headline: 'I'll go to law, warns Jenkin.' The *Echo* interpreted his warning as meaning: 'The government today threatened to take legal action to force Liverpool City Council to fix a rate. Attorney General Sir Michael Havers could intervene in the budget crisis by seeking a High Court writ for *mandamus*. If the council refuse to obey the court order, it would then be in contempt of court.' Unbelievably, the *Daily Star* invoked the Liverpool example as an indication of what can be achieved by remaining *within* the law: 'As Liverpool showed last summer, councils with special problems and public support can win major concessions by their arguments. Breaking the law makes everyone a loser.'

Budget Day

As budget day dawned, the local press reflected the mood which had developed in the city. The *Post* proclaimed: 'Thousands get ready to fight Jenkin's law.' The *Post* was not to be disappointed. The demonstration which marched to the Town Hall, according to Tony Mulhearn, was 'one of the biggest in 100 years in Liverpool'. More than 50,000 were on the march and the response was even more solid than in the previous year. Every section of the council workforce was represented under their different banners. Even NUPE had sections of their membership participating in the demonstration despite the open opposition of the NUPE leadership to the council campaign. Big numbers of uniformed firefighters marched alongside busworkers although the busworkers were not technically on strike because they had made an agreement with the campaign organisers to provide transport for the demonstration.

After all the calumnies directed against the council in the previous six months, the demonstration and the meeting was a huge triumph for Labour. So taken aback was the *Echo* that it spent two issues disputing the organisers' estimate of 50,000 participating in the demonstration. The *Echo* reckoned that a mere 8000 took part and it went to the lengths of carrying a photograph, especially lined to indicate, so it claimed, the numbers attending. Yet the photograph it printed shows people crowding from the Town Hall right through Castle Street and down into Lord Street. One thing is sure; there have been few demonstrations to the Town Hall which required such massive numbers to gather in Castle Street. Derek Hatton captured the mood of the workers in declaring: 'This city is going to go to the end of the road in defence of the working class of Merseyside.'

The determination of the demonstration was carried into the council chamber where Labour councillors refused to set a rate. Unfortunately this resolution was not to be matched by other councils.

GLC and ILEA Abandon the Field

Local authority workers responded in a series of demonstrations throughout the country in defence of the 'no-rate' tactic and against cuts in jobs and services. But all their hopes were to be cruelly dashed. At the Inner London Education Authority (ILEA) meeting some Labour members joined with the Tories and the SDP to force through 'a legal rate' after eight hours of debate. Then the Greater London Council, headed by Ken Livingstone, led the retreat of other councils. Despite all his heroic words and gestures, he led the majority of London Labour councillors into a position of remaining 'within the law' and setting a rate and budget which would mean cuts. This represented a turning point in the struggle of Labour authorities against the government.

Livingstone sought to justify his retreat on the spurious basis that a number of councillors had only agreed to support the 'no

-rate' policy because they were banking on enough right wingers voting with the Tories to enable a rate to be set! In other words, the GLC's opposition was merely verbal, and was a repetition of its climbdown in 1982 when the Law Lords ruled against its 'Fares Fair' cheap transport policy. Livingstone also took refuge in the fact that, unlike London boroughs, the GLC had to legally set a rate by 10 March. He said that it was unreasonable to expect GLC members to break the law alone and to refuse to fix a rate while borough councillors were not yet in a similar position. This of course ignored the fact that Liverpool had consciously taken an 'illegal' step in the previous year and that Hackney Council had also 'gone illegal' by refusing to set a rate in defiance of a court order to do so.

Livingstone typified the 'fun revolutionaries' who, when the chips are down, prefer their parliamentary careers to going down the road of 'illegality' in defence of workers' rights and conditions. In effect he wanted a guarantee of complete support before taking a step outside the limits of bourgeois legality. *Ipso facto* he adopted the arguments of Neil Kinnock-the policy policy of the 'dented shield'.

Livingstone argued that the GLC was following the 'deficit budget' strategy of Liverpool. But as subsequent events demonstrated, having sold the pass on 7 March, the GLC were not prepared to follow through in defying the government as Liverpool had done in the previous year. The £55 million gap in their budget resulted in cuts in services.

In the wake of the GLC's collapse, Kenneth Baker jeered: 'The united front of the *Militant* left has crumbled before our eyes. Instead of opening a second front with the miners some of their troops have fled the battlefield.' Neil Kinnock joined the fray describing councillors who continued to defy the government as 'the fingernail of the labour movement.' Derek Hatton replied for Liverpool councillors:

> Is he therefore saying that Labour councillors should put their hands up for cuts and redundancies, because that would be the position if Liverpool and other councils obeyed the Tory law over local government cuts. Neil Kinnock should remember that it is official national Labour Party policy for the leadership to give a lead and to defend those local authorities who break the law in order to protect jobs and services. What he has said will have no effect at all on Labour councillors in Liverpool.

Despite the united front of Baker and Kinnock, there were still rate-capped councils who were holding out against the government. On 12 March the representatives of 25 local authorities met and decided to step up the fight against the government. Derek Hatton declared: 'We all regret the way the GLC leadership behaved in the last few days.'

In the midst of this battle, a significant incident, largely unreported in the national press, developed around Kieran Devaney, anchor man for Liverpool Radio City's controversial chat show *Devaney*. The Independent Broadcasting Authority demanded that the programme be closed on the grounds that it was 'guilty of contravening the Broadcasting Charter by its political content and comment'. The programme was unceremoniously scrapped within 24 hours of receiving a warning letter from the IBA. Unbelievably, Devaney had been accused of 'showing political bias towards city council leader Derek Hatton who has appeared on the show more than anyone else' (*Echo* 13 March). The pressure from the IBA had come from the intervention of Rosemary Cooper, Liberal city councillor, who had been described by Devaney as 'a boring old gossip'. This programme, perhaps slightly and inadequately, compensated for the anti-Labour, anti-Hatton, anti-Mulhearn and anti-*Militant* propaganda which had poured down like a deluge from the pages of the *Echo*, the *Post* and the local radio in general. The axing of the *Devaney* show was a conscious and blatant example of political censorship. Subsequently Devaney displayed antagonism and hostility to the city council. He had learned that it was not wise to offend his IBA masters!

Meanwhile, despite the threats of Jenkin, and the hostility of the national trade-union leadership, the labour movement in the city swung even further to the left. Months before, the *Echo* and the *Post* had confidently looked for a groundswell of opposition to *Militant* in the District Labour Party. Now the Echo was compelled to report (15 March): '*Militant* tighten grip'. It went on: 'In last night's DLP Executive elections, *Militant* supporters boosted their seats in the 33 member Executive Committee from 10 to around 17.' It also had an interview with Tony Mulhearn in the same issue. In a comment which said as much about the *Echo* and capitalist politicians as it did about Tony Mulhearn, it said: 'Unswerving loyalty to the hard left ideals of Militant Tendency have produced a low key politician who appears to believe what he says'! Tony Mulhearn declared:

I do not believe there has been any other Labour council in the
history of this city which has received such a lambasting from its
political opponents and from the press both nationally and
locally...the party has withstood all that and has emerged in the
phase of the campaign in fine fettle. It is a party filled with vitality.

Towards a National Combine Committee

During this period the unions in other local authorities were
gearing up for industrial action in support of their councils'
refusal to carry through the dictates of the government. On 19
March, 500 London council shop stewards met, with
representatives of the Liverpool JSSC present. Liverpool
stewards were arguing for national industrial action, a call which
evoked the comment of the *Echo* about an alleged 'master plan
on strikes'. A decision was taken to organise a national local
authorities' combine committee (NLACC) on 30 March. This
underlined *Militant's* contention that a firm stand by those
councils which remained 'in the frame' would result in
enormous support from workers on a national scale. Naturally,
Labour's opponents and their press mouthpieces, attempted to
play up any opposition they could find within the workforce.
Early on, the press had lighted on the teachers, led by
Communist Party members, who had opposed strike action on 7
March. However, the attempt to present the teachers as one
reactionary bloc was contradicted by a letter in the *Echo*:

> Teachers of whatever political persuasion should acknowledge that
> the Liverpool City Council with all its faults, has always shown great
> sympathy for the teachers' case. Again they are being put under
> unbearable financial pressure by Mr Jenkin and his monetarist
> cabinet ideology. It is their [the government's] policy which is
> worsening the 'social and economic climate'.

The end of March and the beginning of April saw the
conclusion of a period in which a number of local authorities
were united against the government. One by one, they would
crumble and leave Liverpool alone. This in turn would allow the
ruling class and the labour and trade-union leaders to marshal
all the forces at their command in an attempt to crush the
example of Liverpool. Liverpool was the one council which was
to remain defiant until the end. They presented as much a

danger to the national labour and trade-union leadership as to the Tory government. If they were to succeed again in their struggle against the government, this would vindicate '*Militant* methods'. All efforts were therefore bent on isolating Liverpool City Council and particularly *Militant* supporters.

11.
Moving into Illegality

> SINCE LIVERPOOL was *Militant's* 'jewel in the crown', it was also
> important for them to be seen to be running the city efficiently and
> scoring propaganda victories over Thatcher. In this way, they could
> present Liverpool as 'the model working-class state, a kind of
> socialism in one city'. (Michael Parkinson *Liverpool on the Brink.*)

In fact, *Militant* supporters approached the Liverpool council
struggle in an entirely opposite fashion to that described by
Parkinson. The slightest acquaintance with the ideas of
Trotskyism would have shown him the philosophy of 'socialism
in one city', or one country for that matter, was completely
foreign to the outlook of *Militant* supporters. But the charge of
Liverpool's 'isolationism' was a convenient smokescreen behind
which ever Labour faint-heart, afraid of taking on the
government, could cringe.

There were frequent charges that Liverpool wanted to 'go it
alone' or that *Militant* supporters were only willing to build
support for Liverpool. Yet nothing was further from the truth.
The council had already accepted unfavourable tactics, the 'no-
rate' stance, in the interests of unity with the other councils.
Likewise, the efforts of *Militant* supporters were directed
towards gaining support for Liverpool in a common struggle
with other councils throughout the country. Quite heroic efforts
were made by councillors and local government workers to
establish links through a joint strategy with their counterparts in
other authorities. Indeed, between April and June 1985 the
unswerving determination of council workers to compel their
councils to put up a resistance to the onslaught of the
government demanded such cooperation.

Liverpool did become 'isolated' in the course of the decisive
year of 1985. But this had nothing to do with the tactics of the

Liverpool council leadership. It had much more to do with the fact that many Labour councillors in other authorities who had pledged to resist the Tory government, ran for cover at the first whiff of grapeshot. The main attribute displayed by these 'principled lefts' was the suppleness of their spines. When the GLC and ILEA threw in the towel, most of the other rate-capped councils initially indicated their willingness to maintain the 'no-rate' policy. When most of them retreated in the following weeks and months, they were often met with the open resistance of their workforce, which in some cases were prepared to take industrial action.

The Liverpool labour movement in the previous period had become accustomed to being the main hate object of the media, particularly since the end of the miners' strike. However, the previous slanders, the diatribes and personal vituperation were as nothing compared to the mud which would be thrown in the period of April to December 1985.

In the wake of the Heysel Stadium tragedy in April when Italian football fans were killed in clashes with Liverpool supporters at a European Cup Final, the whole of the population of Liverpool were collectively condemned as 'barbarians' and 'lumpens'. The press seized on horrifying examples of drug addiction, not the preserve of Liverpool alone, to dub the area as 'Smack City'. Its purpose was to reinforce the isolation resulting from the desertion of other councils, in preparation for the downfall of the council. The government confidently expected that this isolation would evoke a 'more responsible' attitude by the labour movement. A chastened Labour council, they predicted, would carry out the same kind of 'compromises'—outright retreats—as other Labour councils had done.

The government, not to say the national Labour leadership, were relishing the prospect of rubbing Liverpool Labour's nose in the dirt. Yet in the months of April, May and June, the grim determination of the Liverpool working class was to shine through. This in turn was to confound the government's expectations and catch them completely off balance when Labour decided in June to make an illegal budget.

April had opened with a meeting of the National Local Authority Co-ordinating Committee (NLACC) at which 250 delegates were present, representing half a million workers in

60 councils. Ian Lowes declared; 'We have said clearly, we expect Labour councils to stand firm and we will support them. But if any Labour council opts out and attempts to make cuts we will oppose them and take whatever action is necessary, including industrial action.' The formation of NLACC was undoubtedly a factor which strengthened the resolve of local government workers in Liverpool to prevent any action which would lead to cuts in local government.

The spirit of resistance reached all layers of the labour movement. In no other area of Britain were the Labour Party, the council, the council workforce and the MPs united in one campaign. Liverpool's Labour MPs in the House of Commons, reflecting the determination of the Liverpool working class, showed unflinching support for the stand of the council. At the beginning of April, Eric Heffer, in a lecture dedicated to the memory of a 19-year-old trade-union pioneer who had been hanged in 1803, said that the law had always been used to repress the labour movement. According to the *Echo*:

> He quoted with approval the words of miners' leader, Arthur Scargill, last October, when he said he was prepared to go to jail rather than betray his class or his union. That should be the view of all trade unionists.
>
> He claimed that first the train drivers, then the printworkers in the NGA at Warrington, and staff at the government GCHQ had been left stranded in disputes 'which should have led to a threatened general strike'.

Mersey Militancy—A Strange Disease

Many capitalist commentators were to ponder on the explanation for 'Mersey Militancy'—a strange disease which seemed to infect even 'responsible' Labour MPs. But there was nothing mystical in the mood and outlook of the population of the area. It was grounded in the long and bitter experience of Liverpool as a deprived and underfunded city.

Merseyside experienced in early 1985 a further plethora of job losses. Guinness axed 300 workers, Cammell Lairds a further 420. 'Merseyside has crashed through the 100,000 barrier of jobs lost since the government came to power' reported the *Echo* on 14 February 1985. Derek Hatton declared: 'This is a milestone of misery and deprivation. Since we came to power on the city council, we have saved 1000 jobs and created another 1000. Those 100,000 jobs lost are 100,000 reasons why people should never again vote Tory or Liberal.' A total of 449 factories closed on Merseyside between 1979 and 1985. Even the Merseyside Young Tories, a very rare breed, were reported as 'spearheading a national call for more government action over unemployment'. But the government steadfastly refused a special debate on the matter in the House of Commons which Merseyside MPs demanded.

The desperation of the unemployed was highlighted by an unemployed 29-year-old Kirkby man parading regularly in the city centre with a placard which read 'please give me a job'. Others, and not the most militant, took more decisive action. Thus a group of clerks who perceived that they would be made redundant with the ending of the Manx Ferry decided to occupy one of their vessels. This was typical of the general militancy that permeated the area and which was undoubtedly influenced and inspired by the stand of the city council.

Later in 1985 a devastating report entitled, *Liverpool's Economy* by Chief Planning Officer Michael Hayes, added to the gloomy prospects for the city on the basis of capitalism. The report showed that a possible 32,000 further job losses could be experienced in the city by 1991. This would result in an unemployment rate approaching 30 per cent. Between 1978 and 1985 40,000 manufacturing jobs had been lost, 46 per cent of the 1978 number. The decline in the area's fortunes was underlined by the growth in the rate of the long-term unemployed. Seven years previously, the percentage of unemployed out of work for more than a year was 34 per cent. In 1985 it was 53 per cent. Since 1981 an average of 12,000 Merseysiders have lost their jobs every year. In the first seven months of 1985 a further 3500 had been thrown out of work through large-scale redundancies.

The city's manufacturing industry was dominated by the so-called 'Magnificent Seven'. These seven companies—Fords, Plesseys, Dunlop, United Biscuits, General Electric Company, Eric Bemrose (Printers) and Glaxo—employed between them almost 23,000 people. Plesseys announced 720 'shedding of staff' at its Huyton plant. Dunlop announced 130 redundancies. GEC announced further cutbacks. A question mark had hung over Eric Bemrose, now owned by press mogul, Rupert

Murdoch. United Biscuits had already carried through redundancies.

Peter Phelps, *Echo* correspondent, pointed out: 'To achieve even 5 per cent unemployment by the end of the decade would require the creation of 70,000 new jobs—and the protection of every existing job.' Little wonder that Tony Mulhearn, President of the District Labour Party, could declare at a city council meeting: 'The report shows the failure of private enterprise. We have in Britain the most corrupt, effete, degenerate capitalist class in the history of the world. If the trends continue there will be no manufacturing jobs left in Liverpool by 1990. The only alternative is a socialist alternative.' There was no possibility of a lifeline for the city or the area on the basis of capitalism. Even the poodle-like *Echo* was constrained to denounce Thatcher. It plaintively declared on 9 July: 'By 1990 we may have no industrial base at all in an area which was once the main port of the empire and a great commercial and manufacturing centre.'

Tory Employment Minister, Tom King, on a visit to the city, blithely declared: 'I am optimistic that we shall see a real improvement in employment in the country. But I am concerned as to whether Liverpool will get its proportional share.' Predictably; 'Mr King admitted things were grim, but slammed Liverpool's Labour council for its continuing rates battle, (*Echo*, 12 July 1985).

Patrick Jenkin and the rest of the government set their face implacably against the claims of Liverpool, confident in the belief that once their unstable allies had deserted them, the council would be compelled to retreat. Meanwhile the government did not miss any opportunity to impose further suffering on the poorest sections of Liverpool. In April, thousands of low income council tenants were faced with a cut of up to £5.75 per week in the cash aid they received towards rent. This arose because the government no longer regarded Liverpool as a 'high rent area' following the changes in the Tories' Housing Benefit scheme. These subsidies would only be reinstated if the council increased rents! This only stiffened the resolve of the Liverpool working class to defeat the government. In all their schemes however they did not take into account the importance of the fact that behind the council were tens of thousands of workers determined that this time a stand would be made.

The letters column of the *Echo* was full of the most heart-rending letters outlining the misery and suffering of working people without a job in the area. One declared: 'As a young unemployed...it is not a case of getting on your bike and finding work; you usually have to hop on a plane.' Another working-class woman from Kirkby wrote: 'My 17-year-old son "got on his bike", but after having a metaphoric 98 punctures to his bike, that is two replies from 100 letters, his hopes were fading.'

Undaunted, the *Echo* pumped out its poison against the council as the source of the major ills of the area, backed up in April by the Liberal MP David Alton who suggested that *Militant* thrived on misery. But occasionally a letter would appear which indicated the rage and disdain which many felt for the local press:

> How is it that David Alton gets more attention by the media than all the other Liverpool MPs put together. With his anti-Labour rantings, he has developed his own Tory type 'fanatical policies'.

Another replied to Alton:

> In reply to *'Militants* prey on jobless', I think Mr David Alton has a cheek. It is because of people like him that we still have 'young people on the dole living in depressing and ugly conditions'. Mr Alton seems to think socialists are glad we have social conditions the way they are today, but it is because of the broken down, rotten system of capitalism which he and his counterparts, the Tories, try to run, that we still have drug pushers in society. I am a young worker who is fed up with people like him avoiding the real issues. (*Echo* 10 April)

A poll by the *Liverpool Star* (11 April) revealed that 90 per cent of Liverpudlians thought that the government didn't care about the people of Merseyside.

'Left' Councils Crumble

Meanwhile a ferocious struggle was taking place within many of the councils which had pledged themselves to the so-called 'no-rate' policy. One by one the right wing Labour councillors within these authorities voted with Tory and Liberal opposition to introduce a 'legal rate'. But this was not without tremendous opposition from workers, tenants and other groups who would be affected by the cuts.

In Manchester, the right wing supported a Tory motion on 31 March and followed the GLC into 'legality'. In the middle of the night of 3-4 April Lewisham introduced a 'Tory rate'—that is, set a rate while Labour councillors were out of the council chamber. The Lewisham Federation of Tenants immediately threatened a possible rent strike if there was a rent rise. Hackney unions were demanding that the council stand firm in the teeth of a High Court Order to fix a rate by 16 April. In mid-May Hackney council workers occupied the council chamber after right wingers defied the decision of the Hackney Labour Party Borough Conference and voted left wingers off all the committees in preparation to push through a cuts budget. Meanwhile, the *Sunday Telegraph* (7 April 1985) revealed that Tory MP Sir Hugh Rossi passed a document to Kenneth Baker for him to decide whether a police investigation and charges of 'criminal conspiracy' were possible over the plans to fight rate-capping organised by the shop stewards in the London Bridge organisation.

In most local authorities the 'firm stand' on the 'no-rates' policy was by now fraying at the edges. Apparently, some 'left-wing' Labour leaders were secretly inviting right-wing councillors to break the whip and vote for 'a legal rate'. For example, Sheffield City Council set a legal rate on 12 May when some Labour councillors voted with the opposition. This, despite the fact that the Sheffield District Labour Party had voted only one week earlier—by two to one—*not* to set a rate and to step up the local and national action against the Tories.

Ten Labour councillors in North Tyneside went as far as voting with the Tories to remove the Labour leader and Labour members from committee chairs!

Meanwhile, Tory dignatories, no matter which distant part of the globe they were visiting, were not allowed to forget the spectre of Liverpool. In mid April, Thatcher visited Indonesia. According to the *Post* (12 April):

> Dissident students taunted Mrs Thatcher with a defiant cry when she visited Bandung University...'Liverpool, Liverpool', they chanted in unison, adding the only sour note to an otherwise rapturous welcome for the British Prime Minister. No one quite knew whether

the chant had a football connection, or if news of Liverpool City Council's defiant stand against Mrs Thatcher's government really had travelled half way round the world to dog her footsteps.

Why should 'dissident', politically inspired students, chant the name of one of Britain's most successful football teams as a means of irritating a politician they oppose? The struggle of Liverpool City Council, which had been commented on widely in the foreign press, had found an echo even in this distant outpost of the former Dutch empire. Little wonder that Thatcher, according to Michael Parkinson, 'personally and politically...detested the *Militant* Liverpool leaders'.

Liverpool remained firm in the teeth of government intransigence and the collapse of other 'left' councils. All the main council spokespersons in Liverpool made declarations expressing their refusal to carry through cuts. Dominic Brady, Chair of education, stated on 12 April:

> Labour would continue its policy of retaining 200 teachers over the 'establishment' [government guidelines for job levels in education]. We give notice that this council intends to make no cuts in the education service, no redundancies amongst teachers and ancillary staff. Unfortunately it means we are in conflict with central government.

But this stand was not supported in any way by the leaders of the NUT who had previously refused to organise their members for strike action on 7 March. Moreover, they had gone to the court to demand the payment of wages for their members for that day, and had even subsequently organised their own one-day strike to reinforce their demands on this narrow, selfish issue.

Notwithstanding the pressure of the government and the growing isolation of Liverpool, the council still attempted to offer a hand to out of work youngsters. Even the *Post* (3 May 1985) reported:

> Liverpool City Council today offered 100 jobs [to unemployed youth]. Deputy Leader, Derek Hatton, threw out a challenge to the city's industry chiefs to follow their lead. Clerical jobs are on offer through the government's Youth Training Scheme (YTS). But instead of the jobs lasting just 12 months, all successful applicants will be offered permanent employment with the council.

Unlike YTS schemes elsewhere, the council 'topped up' the allowance to the 'rate for the job'. Derek Hatton went on to state: 'We have often said that Liverpool City Council, as the largest employer on Merseyside, needs to lead by example. We challenge private industry to follow us.' GEC responded by announcing the axing of 100 more jobs at its East Lancs Road factory.

National School Students' Strike

The identification of the council with the aspirations of the youth of the city was reciprocated in the support that was forthcoming from young people. The combative mood of the youth was shown in the movement of the school students in April. At the beginning of the year, Tory Employment Minister, Tom King, had announced that the government was considering 'conscripting' all young people without a job onto the YTS schemes. These schemes were widely perceived by young people and their parents as slave labour because they lacked elementary trade-union rights, were without proper health and safety cover and usually led not to 'real jobs' but, after the short period of the schemes, back onto the dole. The government threatened that youth would be forced to accept these schemes, with the penalty for refusal being the withdrawal of social security benefits. This produced widespread revulsion.

The Labour Party Young Socialists (LPYS) conducted an energetic and militant campaign in the earlier part of the year. In Glasgow, a highly successful one day strike of school students had taken place in March. This brought down on the heads of the organisers of the demonstration, the Glasgow LPYS, not just the condemnation of the media and the capitalist parties, but also Labour spokespersons. It was all very well for the students in South Africa to campaign and strike for their rights, but not the youth of Britain! But the Glasgow strike indicated the mood of the youth and reinforced the determination of the national leadership of the LPYS to support a proposal for national strike action against the proposals of the government, organised under the banner of the Youth Trade Union Rights Campaign (YTURC). The national strike was planned for 25 April and was intended to demonstrate the opposition to the Tories' YTS schemes and against education cuts.

The ruling class and their echoes within the labour movement were terrified by the prospect of a school students' strike which would overwhelmingly involve students from a working-class background. The mood amongst students, including school students, is a weather vane of developments in society. The movement amongst the students in France in 1968 was a harbinger and, to some extent, a trigger for the far more serious movement of the French working class in the magnificent 10 million strong general strike. The school and college students strikes in France and Spain in 1986-7 were directly influenced and inspired by the movements that had taken place in Britain.

The *Post* in early April 1985 had benignly supported: 'gymslip protesters [who]...marched on Liverpool's education offices. The girls staged their lunchtime protest last week in support of teachers they claim are being demoted or transferred as part of Liverpool's schools reorganisation.' However, the tone of the press changed abruptly when working- class students entered on the scene, demanding their rights.

A national School Students Union (SSU) had previously been formed by LPYS members, with branches in every city in Britain and with Labour MPs Terry Fields and Dave Nellist supporting the union. Yet the *Echo* front page declared on 13 April: 'Kids all out call by Militants'. Predictably: 'The new strike threat brought swift condemnation from the city's Liberal leader, Sir Trevor Jones, who claimed it was an attempt to brainwash children.' David Alton, in the House of Commons, demanded that Thatcher should ban the forthcoming strike. Thatcher duly 'condemned the plan in the Commons yesterday' (*Echo*, 17 April 1985).

A few days ahead of the rest of the city and the country, the school students of Kirkby marched out on strike. They were met by police and harassed by the media and 14 school students were arrested. The Liverpool City Education spokesperson Dominic Brady immediately came out in support of the school students union. This in turn prompted the headline in the *Echo* (23 April): 'Power to striking pupils . City schools chief in move for "free pardon".' All that Dominic Brady had said was that students fighting against industrial conscription should not be punished by the education authorities. Trevor Jones declared: 'Councillor Brady is not fit to hold office.'

In the House of Commons Terry Fields attacked Thatcher for condemning the action by school students. He told her: 'You had to travel 7000 miles to Indonesia to get the acclaim of some school children. Thursday [the day for the strike] will show what the children of her own country think of her.' The denunciations of the proposed action by Liberal and Tory spokespersons evoked equally ferocious comments from school students:

> The strike on 25 April is the only means that the school students can vent their anger and mobilise themselves into opposition against the proposals of YTS conscription being imposed by the Tory government. As for David Alton condemning the proposed strike, what has he done to help the youth fight against YTS conscription? (*Echo*, 23 April.)

In simple language, they were drawing on the example of the stand of Liverpool City Council. Only *action* would force the government to bend, they were completely impervious to words and speeches. The same letter to the *Echo* declared: 'Today's youth understand that YTS is just a means of cutting the dole figures and making a profit for the bosses. The school students have a crucial role in this struggle as it is they who are being condemned into an era of slave labour in the form of YTS.'

So intense was the feeling amongst school students that there were premature walk-outs before 25 April, not just on Merseyside but in Portsmouth, Southampton, Havant and Arbroath. Even the Liberal spokesperson had to make 'sympathetic' noises about the plight of youth, declaring in the *Guardian* (24 April) that in his area of Knowsley:

> Only 4 per cent of 4,000 16 year-olds who left school last year had a permanent job. In some areas of the city youth unemployment was as high as 90 per cent. To sit back and do nothing would be totally wrong, but I object to a trade-union campaign by a collection of Young Socialists, run by *Militant*, who are not really concerned about unemployment but are seizing the chance to make rich pickings among young and fertile minds.

As with all strikes, the charge of 'intimidation' was made in relation to the school students' strike. Thus the Tory education chief on Wirral council, Kate Wood, reported that one mother had told her that 'he (her son) and his pals feared that they might be "done over" unless they joined in'. The *Echo* reported that an unnamed woman at Highfield Comprehensive, Queens Drive, had declared: 'older pupils from other schools, around 17 and 18 years old, have been approaching some children and warning them that if they did not join the marches they would be "got at".' Liberal councillor Neville Chinn claimed that he had received reports of bullying at school gates. Tucked away at the bottom of the article, the *Echo* remarked: 'A senior member of staff at Highfield School denied that there had been any bullying of children at the school gates.' This did not prevent the editorial of the *Echo* being headline 'The Way of the Yobbo'. It declared that any support for the strike would be 'inviting children to play truant so they can demonstrate against the Tory government'.

The strike on 25 April was a huge triumph for the organisers. An estimated 250,000 school students marched out of their classrooms in demonstrations in most of the major cities of Britain. In Liverpool 25,000 struck. A boisterous demonstration of 10,000 marched to St George's Plateau to be addressed by school students' leaders and Terry Fields who received a tumultuous reception. Even the *Echo* was to declare:

> School's Out—for all but three. Only three children reported for lessons in one school, whereas at Croxteth Comprehensive, the headmaster said that no disciplinary action would be taken, and was reported as saying: 'I am not in support of the action but I agree with the protest because I think they are right. I am very much against the YTS schemes'...Mr Blair said the pickets had been polite and well-behaved, but denied that teachers had incited the pupils.

Most of the schools were out in Kirkby. Some head teachers claimed that they closed the schools for fear 'of intimidation'. But the strikers were extremely disciplined and well organised. The only complaint of the police was the speed at which the school students marched and the liveliness of their demonstration. They complained however, without foundation, that 'It could have been very serious indeed.'

School students found ingenious ways of participating in the strike. Thus in one Liverpool school, Campion High, pupils climbed out of a first floor window after the head teacher had locked the gates. Chanting, 'Maggie! Maggie! Maggie! Out! Out! Out!' and 'Here We Go!', the demonstrators were determined to force the government to retreat. Predictably, the youth and the organisers of the demonstration were compared by some correspondents in the *Echo* to 'Hitler's Youth'.

Dafties?

In his usual flippant fashion, Kinnock characterised the 250,000 who had marched out of schools as 'dafties'. Hattersley condemned what he called the 'exploitation of youngsters which was squalid and cynical'. Eddie Loyden, Garston MP replied: 'This sort of constructive, peaceful and organised protest is far better than the way young people displayed their anger in the Toxteth riots.' Moreover, the parents of the school students showed tremendous support for the demonstration and strike. Liverpool Labour Party Women's Council had canvassed support amongst the parents in the weeks leading up to the strike. Leaflets were distributed to explain what the strike was about and to counteract attempts by the press and others to claim that the strike was irresponsibly exploiting the fears of young people. One parent declared to a member of Broadgreen Labour Party: 'I will be marching with my daughter after what happened to my son after a year of demoralisation on a YTS scheme. He was no longer the same character.'

The youth on this demonstration showed that, faced with a far more difficult and bleak future than previous generations, they were more determined to fight. Roger Bannister, Secretary of the Broadgreen Labour Party, gave some of the reasons for this in a letter to the *Echo* (3 May):

When I left a Manchester Comprehensive School in 1970 not one of my fellow pupils had to sign on the dole. Some of us went to college or university, others obtained jobs in the Post Office, insurance and engineering. Three years later I left university with only a temporary summer job as a brewery labourer to go to. But within three months I had obtained employment suitable to my qualifications. Today the alternatives for school leavers are mass unemployment, exploitation on a YTS scheme or deferring the dole for three years by going to further education again, with little chance of a job at the end. Britain's young people are not stupid, neither are they prepared to be used as a pool of cheap labour by the Tory government. They have made it clear by their actions that they will fight for a future.

The Labour leadership denounced the strike, but they were also aware that one of the keys to the future success of Labour would be the mobilisation of the youth vote. The strike had convinced them of the enormous discontent that existed amongst all layers of the youth. So at one and the same time they rushed out a 'Youth Charter' whilst evicting YTURC from Labour Party national headquarters. The printing trade union, SOGAT, immediately stepped in and offered alternative premises to YTURC.

The government also learned from the events of 25 April. The British bourgeois, unlike their French and Spanish counterparts recently, have learned to recognise early on when unfavourable winds begin to develop. The French government of Chirac was forced in late 1986 to withdraw its Education Bill only after mass strikes and demonstrations of students and moreover when the mass of the working class were threatening to join in the students' action. Similar protracted struggles were necessary in Spain before the government was forced to give some concessions.

In Britain, on two occasions in recent years, the Tory government quickly withdrew measures that could have provoked a mass movement of the youth. In 1981 the Labour Party Young Socialists had organised a massive campaign on the issue of rights, training, conditions and wages on the forerunner of YTS, the Youth Opportunities Programme. As soon as they saw this movement developing, the government increased the YOP allowance. Similarly, with the mood developing amongst school students in 1985, demonstrated most particularly in the strike of 25 April, Tom King and other Tory spokespersons unceremoniously abandoned any idea of conscripting youth by withdrawing unemployment or social security pay for those who refused to go onto YTS schemes.

The school students' strike was undoubtedly a landmark in the development of the labour movement in Britain and in Liverpool. Its success indicated the enormous impact which the struggles of the miners and Liverpool City Council had on the generation which will play a key role in the struggles of the working class over the next decade.

Taken aback by the firmness of the city council, the ruling class decided to step up its propaganda offensive. On the prompting of the Liberals the police were called in to investigate the council expenses of Derek Hatton. The flimsy basis for their investigation was the complaint of Liberal councillor Rosemary Cooper that a council car had been 'misused'. Immediately, headlines appeared in the press suggesting that the case was virtually proved: 'Police check Hatton's expenses'. When approached by the *Sunday Times* to confirm this, Derek Hatton's rejoinder was apt: 'the *Sunday Times* is getting like an upmarket *Sun* these days'.

The Pressure Mounts

Patrick Jenkin, buoyed up by the press, was exerting enormous pressure on the council to abandon its stand. A combination of factors, including creative accounting, low interest rates and falling inflation, plus extra housing subsidy from the government itself, seemed temporarily to ease Liverpool's financial difficulties. But the council was still holding out for the concessions on housing finance which Jenkin had promised in the previous year.

Liverpool's demands for more finance were reinforced by facts which emerged on the cost of maintaining 'Fortress Falklands' for the government. The initial cost of building the Falklands Airport was £1 million for each of the 1800 islanders. The island was also being subsidised by an additional £1 million *per day* which meant that something like £5 billion of taxpayers' cash had been spent in the previous three years. Thus the Tories were prepared to squander the wealth of the British people in maintaining this tiny imperial outpost with a population of less than 2000, while the demands of a city of half a million for the return of £30 million out of the £500 million the government had taken from it, were completely rejected.

Tony Mulhearn, on behalf of the District Labour Party, stated in mid-April: 'The position of Liverpool City Council is still firm. There will be no cuts in services, no redundancies, no rate increases to compensate for Tory cuts.' Labour suffered a blow in a council by-election in Dingle ward on 18 April but on the same day, in Speke ward, Labour romped home with a 2000 majority. The Liberal leadership, together with their mouthpiece the *Echo* used Dingle to write premature political obituaries for Labour. Trevor Jones declared: 'It is a step in the

Sam Bond on a demonstration in defence of Asian youth.

Budget Day, 29 March 1984.

Budget Day, 29 March 1984. 50,000 march to the Town Hall. No budget is set.

Terry Fields canvassing in Broadgreen.

Support for the council came from all quarters.

On the march.

19 November, 1983—25,000 march in support of the council.

right direction. It gives us a much better launching pad for when we regain control in 1986.' Labour honestly faced up to its defeat in Dingle. Tony Mulhearn explained soberly the reasons for Labour's defeat: "This is a clear indication that the cleansing services in the area are totally inadequate and the Liverpool labour and trade-union movement must get to grips with this problem. We see the result as a hiccup in our campaign and, once this problem is resolved, we can go on with the job of building mass support.' In Speke, on the other hand, the population were beginning to see the fruits of Labour rule in the new houses which were being built.

Nevertheless, the by-election setback in Dingle undoubtedly gave a fillip to Jenkin and the government, as well as their local cohorts. In a series of carefully timed pronouncements Jenkin attempted to break the councillors' resistance. On a visit to the city he 'predicted that the nationwide rate revolt by Labour authorities would fizzle out and Liverpool could be left isolated. They will find themselves on their own, with no support from Labour's front bench, and the law snapping at their heels.' (*Echo*, 23 April 1985).

This indicated that private assurances and backing had probably been given by Labour's front bench to Tory spokespersons in their offensive against the remaining defiant rate-capped councils. Anthony Bevins, then correspondent for *The Times* and personal friend of the then Labour MP Robert Kilroy-Silk who in turn was close to Kinnock, confidently anticipated 'Labour set for clash with Left'. Kinnock and Labour's Environment Spokesperson John (Jack) Cunningham, seeing the crumbling of the GLC, ILEA and other authorities, were prepared to be more open in their opposition to those councillors who remained defiant.

The government appointed a new 'tough guy', Mr Thomas McMahon, as the District Auditor for Merseyside. His predecessor, Stanford, was no less 'tough' but he had been constrained by the mass support for the council in the city and the fear of national repercussions if action was to be taken against the councillors. With the capitulation of other councils, the government and its local representatives, such as the District Auditor, felt the wind in their sails. John Banham, the £60,000 a year boss of the 13 District Auditors around the country, weighed in with a broadside against Liverpool at the beginning of May. He once more threatened the council leaders with dire 'legal' consequences if they maintained their defiance of the government. In an interview with the *Echo* (2 May 1985) he also warned:

> ...that Liverpool's local watchdog would step in before the middle of next month—the deadline for giving ratepayers their legal right to pay their bills in ten instalments...If the Labour councillors still refuse to set a rate they would face personal fines and could be banned from office for five years.

Despite these threats the council pushed ahead with its promised reforms for the council workforce, introducing a 35-hour week and £100 minimum wage at the May council meeting.

With tensions mounting, the slanders against the councillors became cruder. Norman Tebbit, then Secretary of State for Trade and Industry, exercising his personal brand of political subtlety, attempted to link left-wing councillors like those in Liverpool with 'Hitler's National Socialists'. Eric Heffer denounced Tebbit and 'demanded an apology for democratic socialists who fought arms in hand, against the Nazis, and laid down their lives'.

Despite the propaganda barrage, and the threats of Patrick Jenkin and the District Auditor, the government did *not* choke off Liverpool's financial lifeline. While it received little rate income in April, May or June, the council did receive government grants, despite the fact that the government and the District Auditor were later to claim that Liverpool was acting 'illegally'.

Every dirty slander in the locker of capitalism was marshalled against Liverpool at this time. Thus the satirical magazine *Private Eye* published the most outrageous lies about Derek Hatton. It suggested that he had moved from his house to a mansion and switched his children to 'private schools'. Derek Hatton threatened to sue *Private Eye*, declaring at the same time: 'I have lived in the same house for the past ten years. It has never been on the market...my children go to local primary schools—they will go to the local comprehensive.' Features began to appear in the press about the drug problems on some of the working-class estates in Liverpool. A picture of Liverpool working people as 'work-shy, drug-addicted and incorrigible scroungers' was presented by the national media.

The Heysel Stadium Tragedy

The incident which most clearly highlighted the conscious policy of denigrating Liverpool because of its political stance was the Heysel Stadium tragedy on 28 April. At the European Cup Final in Brussels a clash between Liverpool and Juventus fans resulted in the collapse of a wall and the death of 38 Juventus fans. The horrific scenes witnessed on television appalled all workers, not least those in Liverpool. But it later became quite clear that a combination of inadequate facilities at the Heysel Stadium, lack of proper policing and chaos in the allocation of tickets and seats for the different fans had all contributed to this tragedy.

Unconcerned with the terrible suffering of families in Italy who had lost sons and fathers, Thatcher and the gutter press in this country unleashed all the pent-up hatred of the ruling class at what the city represented. They used the incident to conduct a ferocious, collective character assassination of Liverpool people. Entirely ignored were the social conditions which breed mindless hooliganism and soccer violence.

Moreover, evidence clearly pointing to fascist groups both in Britain and in Italy seeking to exploit the football spectacle for their own ends, was airily dismissed by many capitalist commentators. Robert Maxwell, publisher and owner of the *Daily Mirror*, revealed on television shortly after the tragedy his deep loathing of *Militant* and Liverpool city councillors: 'Why have the Liverpool fans turned nasty? The answer is the Militant Tendency, as an example in Liverpool, that has taken over; they have shown elected councillors and MPs they don't care for society, or civilised behaviour. This is the kind of thing that encourages hooliganism.' (*Breakfast Time*, 30 May.) Shortly after the Liverpool council's architect had conclusively proved that the stadium was unsafe. This enabled the *Daily Mirror* to completely exonerate the Belgian football authorities and the Thatcher government from any blame in the affair. Many fans, quite independently, commented that the fascist British National Party were handing out leaflets on the ferry taking fans to the match. The Socialist group in the European Parliament in *Against Racism and Fascism in Europe*, published in October 1986, also commented: 'On the Italian side, it was discovered that young fascist militants had also travelled to Belgium with the intention of having a confrontation with the Liverpool "reds".

They had been told that Liverpool was run by a Communist-dominated administration.'

While the capitalist press and television commentators were demanding every conceivable repressive measure against 'football hooligans—the birch, imprisonment, the reintroduction of national service, banning alcohol, etc—the council moved to repair the damage. Labour councillors took the initiative and suggested that a delegation be sent from Liverpool to Turin to offer condolences and to discuss with the authorities what could be done to get to the root of the social conditions which breed violence. This proposal was immediately denounced by the Tory leader, Chris Hallows, as 'insensitive and too early'. Nevertheless the proposal received enthusiastic support from the mass of the population. Church dignitaries and representatives of Everton and Liverpool football clubs were included in the delegation. The *Echo* pleaded: 'Let us for once forget politics and act in a manner worthy of this moment.' This at a time when the entire media was attempting to make the maximum political capital out of the carnage in Brussels! Eric Heffer wrote in the *Echo:* 'The awful talk about Liverpool, animals, murderers, the blood bath etc, has really sickened me...the events have more in common with the Glasgow tragedy [when a stampede at an exit at Ibrox killed dozens of fans] than the Luton football riots [where visiting fans clashed violently with police on the pitch].' The pressure for the visit was so great that the Tories were compelled to change their mind and reluctantly dragged at the heels of Labour.

The idea of the visit was a courageous act. Some English tourists had been beaten up in Italy in the wake of the Brussels tragedy and a postcard had been sent to a Liverpool newspaper warning 'We will exterminate you red animals.' But Derek Hatton and Tony Mulhearn, while making it clear that they were visiting the city to offer condolences to the relatives of those killed, at the same time stated unequivocally that the origins of mindless soccer hooliganism was rooted in the terrible social conditions which affected both Merseyside and Turin. Derek Hatton declared:

> We will also be going to establish links with the socialist parties and trade unionists in Turin, collectively to fight the root causes of the hopelessness felt by many young people. They think there is no future for them whatsoever in society and that they have nothing at

all to lose...unemployment among young people in Turin is currently running at 33 per cent. Unemployment in parts of this city is running at more than 90 per cent. Jointly we will be looking towards resolving the problems that brutalise sections of our young people. We will be exchanging views with the Turin authorities about how we should jointly tackle the social conditions which lead to much of the violence happening in society.

Furious that the Liverpool mission was not approaching the Turin visit in the necessary spirit of 'humility and contriteness', the press began to denounce the Labour councillors again. The *Daily Mail* declared: 'Liverpool Militants leading Liverpool's peace mission over the Brussels disaster turned it into a political football yesterday as they flew to Italy.' Derek Hatton was furiously denounced for publicising the statement of the Liverpool investigator into the Heysel Stadium which showed that it was UEFA, the European football association, which arranged and condoned the holding of the match in this stadium, and which therefore bore the prime responsibility for the tragedy.

The visit was very successful in cementing relations between the working people of Italy and their organisations and the Liverpool working class. The delegation spent a large part of their time speaking to the socialist Mayor of Turin and city councillors, but also in visiting the factories in this, one of Italy's most important industrial areas. On his way back to Britain Derek Hatton commented: 'The reception in Italy showed that in real terms Italian working people have far more of an affinity with Liverpool working people than our own Prime Minister has.' This drove Maxwell's *Daily Mirror* to paroxysms of fury. It declared:

> The Militant Tendency boss of Liverpool council, Mr Derek Hatton, accuses Mrs Thatcher of creating the conditions which led to the riot...the stadium in Brussels may be old. It may not be built to the security specifications of Walton jail, but it served the Belgians well−until Liverpool played there. Let us face the facts. What happened in Brussels was wholly the fault of English football fans and English football clubs, not only last month but over a long period of years.

But Derek Hatton's statement continued to receive support from the population of Liverpool who were sick of the relentless campaign against the city and its population. Undoubtedly the visit to Turin by the delegation from Liverpool enormously raised the standing of the city council in the eyes of local people Further links were forged when Juventus fans visited Liverpool a month later. As a consequence of the Turin visit,Terry Harrison also visited Milan later in the year and spoke at a very successful meeting organised by the Italian Communist Party in which he outlined the stand of Liverpool City Council and its link to the struggle for socialism in Europe.

The attempts by the capitalists to use the tragedy as a means of crushing the spirit of the Liverpool working class completely failed because of the speedy reaction and initiatives of the Liverpool Labour movement and in particular of *Militant* supporters. Even the capitalist press was compelled to comment as early as September that: 'Liverpool is shrugging off its soccer shame.' (*Observer*, 1 September 1985). This mood was not just because of the successful Turin visit but of the sharpening of the battle with the government and the expectation of a coming clash.

12.
Nine Per Cent and No More

UP UNTIL the day that the council was to set an 'illegal' rate, the government had been confident that Liverpool would come to heel in the wake of the capitulation of other councils. On 13 May, Patrick Jenkin repeated his earlier refusal to talk to the council. John Hamilton angrily declared: 'If he came to Liverpool to try and explain his policies, then his ideas would be slaughtered.'

But Jenkin was by now receiving open support from elements within the labour movement. George Wright, right-wing contender in the re-run ballot for the position of General Secretary of the Transport and General Workers Union, used a foray to the outskirts of the city ot launch an attack on 'Liverpool's *Militant* Labour left'. '*Militant* must go,' he said, and attacked in particular '*Militant* official Richard Venton, city councillor Pauline Dunlop, European MP Les Huckfield, and MPs Eddie Loyden, Bob Parry, and Alan Roberts'. Liverpool *Militant* supporters replied:

> We are surprised that George Wright should attack Liverpool council during the critical period in our struggle against the Tory government. If this struggle is lost, 6000 jobs will go. Liverpool council has a proud record of building houses and creating jobs. The Transport and General Workers Union (TGWU) locally have consistently supported us in implementing these policies. In fact, at a time when the TGWU membership in local authorities are on the decline because other councils are carrying out Tory government cuts, Liverpool membership has increased because of the new job opportunities brought about by Liverpool council...

Wright declared that he would be interrupting his campaign to 'go on to Llandudno where today he would be urging the Welsh Labour Party to continue the battle to oust *Militant*'.

Wright's venom towards *Militant* was not at all accidental. Militant supporters had consistently provided Ron Todd (the candidate of the left) with a platform in Merseyside. Tony Mulhearn and Derek Hatton had many times spoken with him at mass meetings. In the re-run ballot *Militant* TGWU members had been most energetic in support of Todd but they were rewarded later with the TGWU supporting their expulsions, with Ron Todd playing a decisive and shameful role in this. 'There is no gratitude in politics': this was applied with zeal by even the most 'left' national trade-union leaders when it was to come to the expulsion of Marxists from the Labour Party. Any feelings of 'gratitude' were more than cancelled out by the 'danger' to them and their privileged position.

The National Union of Public Employees (NUPE), at its national conference in May, joined the witch-hunters. Jane Kennedy, secretary of the Liverpool City General branch, moved a resolution calling for the expulsion of *Militant* supporters. This was taken as the first item on the agenda and bulldozed through by the Chair. NUPE, from being a left-wing bulwark within the Labour Party had moved over to become one of the chief opponents of the *Militant* and others on the left.

Approaching the Crunch

By the end of May four councils were holding out on the 'no-rate' policy—Southwark, Camden, Liverpool and Lambeth. On 22 May the District Auditor threatened the Liverpool councillors with heavy fines and banishment from office unless they set a rate within nine days. Finance Chairman Tony Byrne declared, 'There is absolutely no possibility that this authority will have set a rate by the end of the month.' Nevertheless, the government confidently expected that the Labour group would capitulate given its isolation. What they totally underestimated was the extent to which the relentless decline of the area and the frightening deterioration in the social conditions reinforced the resistance of the council. Even the *Echo* felt it necessary to detail the absolutely dismal prospects for Merseyside's youth. It reported on 7 June: 'Almost 32,000 Merseyside youngsters will be chasing just 112 careers' office jobs this summer.' The statistics showed that in the region as a whole there were an average of 280 candidates chasing every full-time job on offer.

In Knowsley, the picture was far worse, with just three jobs available and 3900 young people about to leave school in August. The *Echo* published a map of despair, indicating the total number of jobs available throughout the area—45 in Wirral, 24 in Liverpool, nine in St Helens, three in Knowsley and 31 in Sefton.

Nevertheless, the capitalist press urged Patrick Jenkin not to give in. The *Daily Telegraph* declared, 'Liverpool's ultra-left leadership must be pressurised'. After Southwark and Camden capitulated in early June, the District Auditor weighed in with final demand letters to Liverpool and Lambeth. He warned that there was now enough evidence to pursue action over the councillors' failure to set a rate. The *Sunday Times* reported that '300 may face council ban'. In other words, even those councillors who had delayed setting a rate beyond the March deadline, but who had eventually capitulated, were now being threatened with surcharge and banning from office.

As the crunch time approached, both the government and the *Echo* still expected Liverpool to capitulate. They were not the only ones. Obviously encouraged by headlines in the press which predicted that Liverpool would set a budget and a 20 per cent increase in rates, the tiny ultra-left sect, the Workers' Revolutionary Party in its paper *Newsline*, in the rather delicate language for which this paper was renowned, declared (12 June):

> Lambeth stands firm: Liverpool capitulates. The Militant Tendency's bluff was called by the capitalist state in Liverpool this week—and it produced abject capitulation from the right-wing [ie the left leaders fo the council] reformist group. But there is Lambeth standing firm, ready for a joint struggle.

The very next day *Newsline*'s prediction was to be turned upside down when some Labour members in Lambeth voted with the Tories to pass a cuts budget. The WRP's pessimism for Liverpool found a strange bedfellow in the *Daily Telegraph* which declared; 'Liverpool U-turn on rate likely' and the *Daily Mirror*: 'Liverpool, the only other council still holding out against rate-capping is about to climb down.' But contrary to all the speculation in the capitalist press, as well as those on the ultra-left fringe, there was no prospect of Liverpool abandoning the struggle and carrying through massive rate increases or cuts.

Commenting on this development Michael Parkinson in *Liverpool on the Brink* wrote: 'the national and local *Militant* leadership could not have controlled their rank and file, even if they wanted to do anything else.' Parkinson's hunt for these 'differences' is entirely false. *Militant's* 'national and local leadership' were as determined as the 'rank and file' not to squander the political capital which the Liverpool struggle had built up over the previous two years. Of course, had there been a principled compromise available that kept the gains of the city council intact, then that line would have been taken. No Marxist worthy of the name would deliberately and consciously inflict suffering on working people.

In the battle in the previous year, despite the shrill denunciations of the ultra-left, *Militant* supporters had easily justified the agreement with the Tory government. Sometimes after a battle such as a prolonged strike, it is necessary to beat a retreat. But Liverpool still had not yet experienced a serious confrontation with the Tory government. Worse than defeat after struggle, is to give way without giving battle. In the previous two years the Liverpool struggle had been more in the way of preparatory manoeuvres before an inevitable collision. A 20 per cent rate increase, which in any case would not bring in sufficient income to cover expenditure for the year, would represent a real cut for thousands of working-class households in the city. Moreover, it would have had to have been combined with quite savage cuts in social services, in order to make the budget 'legal'.

A Deficit Budget

There were lengthy debates amongst *Militant* supporters at local and national level and within the local labour movement as to what course of action should be pursued. At the end of these debates, with the collapse of the 'no-rate' front, it was concluded that the only course of action open was to confront the government.

At the eleventh hour, on 11 June, the city council once more appealed for discussions with Jenkin. He refused, hoping to see Labour eat dirt and relishing the prospect this time round of 'dancing on Derek Hatton's grave'. But the temper of Labour was indicated by Tony Byrne who said: 'I can give this categorical assurance to the people of the city. This Labour Party will not cut a single job, will not reduce its housing programme. There will be no threat of privatisation and no rent or rate increases to compensate for cuts in grant.' In an editorial *Militant* urged Liverpool to stand firm. Its advice was matched by the mood of the majority of the working population of Liverpool. One back bench councillor explained: 'I am not a Marxist, I don't even believe in all this political stuff. I just don't think it's fair and I wouldn't vote for anything (beyond) a 9 per cent increase.'

At an historic meeting on 13 June, the District Labour Party unanimously agreed to set a 9 per cent rate—no higher than the real rate of inflation and with no cuts. Nearly all the Labour councillors were there, and there was *not one* dissenting voice at the meeting when this policy was put forward. Moreover, any last minute hesitations were dispelled the next day when Thomas McMahon, the District Auditor, sent a letter saying that a 'crime' had already been committed and he was going to act against them for losses they had incurred between 1 April and June. Thus any potential defectors were dissuaded from such a course by the fact that even if they betrayed Labour, they could still be surcharged.

Rarely had the Liverpool labour movement been so united (apart from the 'scabby five'—two of the original seven were no longer on the council—who had opposed the council's strategy all along). The District Labour Party and the Labour group were virtually unanimous in validating the council's stand. At two days' notice, 1000 council workers lobbied the council meeting which adopted the deficit budget. The mood was enthusiastic, but unlike the previous year, sombre. There were very few interruptions to the Liberal and Tory speeches which were now considered to be an irrelevance. Labour speakers were rapturously applauded, of course, but there was an unmistakable eagerness to proceed to the vote in order that the workforce could be prepared for the coming battle with the government.

With a 9 per cent rate, and with government refusal to give further grants, it was quite clear that the city would run out of money at a certain stage. Labour were not setting out deliberately to bankrupt the city, but intended to use the time available to mobilise the population of Liverpool and to appeal nationally to local authority workers to exert pressure on the government.

After only two hours' debate at the council, this budget was adopted. In *Liverpool on the Brink*, Michael Parkinson gives an insight to the atmosphere in Whitehall. The government was absolutely stunned: 'The council's senior officers were shattered by the decision...the civil servants who were sending memos down to London could scarcely believe their contents.' The government met the following week to decide what to do. A senior civil servant said: 'We can either sit on our hands or dust off the Commissioner file from last year. The Commissioner option looks as unattractive this year as it did last. It's just too uncertain.'

Another option considered by the government was to use the Attorney-General to quash the rate and to set a 'new legal rate'. It is a striking fact that in this whole period not one of the main opposition forces to Labour was prepared to go to the court to quash Labour's rate and budget:

> The Liverpool Chamber of Commerce thought about it, but decided against it. The leaders of the opposition parties considered it but, quite apart from the expense involved in legal action, there were political imperatives not to do so. They might be accused of bringing the house down. More important, they would have to suggest a higher rate to be set and, given the mood in the city, that could only damage them with the electorate. Everybody was waiting and wondering about the next move...Ministers sat round the table gradually realising the position that their policies on local government finance had finally led them to. They were drifting towards the confrontation they never really wanted with no apparent way of avoiding it. (*Liverpool on the Brink*).

But the actions of the city council immediately found a response in the council workforce and in the labour movement, with tremendous sympathy amongst the wider population of Liverpool. The National Local Authorities Coordinating Committee, still representing the workforces of 26 councils, had indicated that they would come to the assistance of Liverpool in the event of an all-out clash with the government. A campaign was set in motion in Liverpool to mobilise all sections of the council workforce for industrial action if necessary in the event of a collision with the government. The only union to oppose strike action in early June, was once again the teachers.

The press again began to take up the theme of the Commissioners in Liverpool. The Daily Express declared on 20 June: 'Maggie set to send in own man to run rate rebel city.' But even NALGO shop steward and convenor Peter Cresswell declared: 'We pledge ourselves to call for massive industrial action if a Commissioner is sent in.' The government became so worried of the scenario opening up in Liverpool that suggestions began to be floated that in the event of a serious confrontation the Commons would have to be recalled during the summer recess.

At the same time reports began to appear which recognised the great progress in the field of housing. CHAR (the campaign for single homeless people), after examining the facilities of 302 local authorities declared: 'The city [Liverpool]...is the only authority to rehouse all homeless, single women.'

Acknowledging this and other measures (outlined in Chapter 9) support from the labour movement was forthcoming with the National Labour Women's Conference coming out four-square with the council. Militant declared: 'After two years of shadow-boxing, the Tories are squaring up to take on Liverpool council for its defence of jobs and services. The gloves are now off...the Tories will be made to understand that they are not taking on a council, but hundreds of thousands of working people in the city'.

The national Labour leadership were as stunned as the government by the stand of the council. In June Kinnock had written to Lambeth saying: 'I do not accept that chaos in local government brings benefits, either to the people of a borough or the Labour Party.' This could have been culled from any of the speeches of Tory ministers in their attack on 'left-wing councils which create chaos'. Moreover, it was in complete violation of the decision of the Labour Party Conference which in 1984 voted to support the councils that defied the government and refused to implement cuts. It was also in complete contrast to the enormous support that existed for this position. At the very moment when Liverpool had adopted its 'stand' NALGO, the 766,000 strong local government workers' union, 'threatened widespread industrial action and non-cooperation in an attempt to thwart the government' over cuts in local authority jobs.

The National Executive Committee of the Labour Party decided to 'support councils defending and promoting services and jobs and calls upon all sections of the Party to offer maximum support to those councillors in Liverpool, Lambeth, Edinburgh and other authorities in seeking to prevent the threatened disqualification and surcharge'. But Kinnock immediately went on television in an attempt to water down the effect of the resolution and true to form, the *Echo* preferred to feature his statement rather than the decision of the NEC. The campaign amongst the private sector workers, always considered as a vital part of the council's strategy, was having a big effect. In early July, a solidarity rally of 500 private sector workers throughout the Merseyside area was organised in support of the campaign of the city council. Ian Lowes declared, 'This is a fight for every working class man, woman and child in the city.' Forming themselves into the 'A-Team', a group of council workers volunteered their time to visit depots and build support for the campaign. Despite the opposition of management they received enthusiastic support in their visits to factories, both in Liverpool and on a national level. The work of the A-Team crushed the myth disseminated by some 'lefts' that the campaign was the preserve of the 'employers'—the council—without an independent voice for trade unionists.

Wilful Misconduct

Undoubtedly, the action of the District Auditor on 14 June in surcharging 49 Labour councillors £106,000 for 'wilful misconduct', galvanised support behind the Labour council. It also laid bare the dictatorial powers exercised by the District Auditor.

The Liverpool and Lambeth cases demonstrated this in a very graphic fashion. Under the auspices of the National Audit Commission a network of District Auditors has the function of rolling back the boundaries of the welfare state. In 1982, a new Local Government Finance Act gave the Auditors extensive new powers. The District Auditors can investigate local councils and then act as judge, jury and executioner in serving certificates of surcharge and disqualification.

Contrary to all the other principles of the British legal system, or any other for that matter, the prosecutor, in this case the District Auditor, does not have to prove a case against the accused in a properly constituted court of law. Their dictatorial powers allow them to surcharge and disqualify without any of the other legal safeguards that are normal in a court of law. Councillors are allowed to appeal to the courts, but the onus is on them to prove their innocence.

In the Liverpool case the councillors were threatened with surcharge and wilful misconduct because of an alleged 'loss' to the council arising from the delay in receiving government housing benefit and payments 'in lieu of rates' on Crown property between April and June when the council had not set a rate. He argued that if Liverpool had received this money, it would have been banked and would have been receiving interest. But the interest on these payments was being made, the only difference being that it was accumulating to the benefit of the national exchequer which had this cash lodged in the bank. Therefore no real 'loss' resulted from the delay in receiving housing benefit.

Yet on this flimsy basis, 49 working men and women were to be dragged before the courts, threatened with bankruptcy, seizure of their houses, and banning from office. This could mean terrible suffering for ordinary councillors such as Harry Smith. He told *Militant*:

> At the moment my wife is in full-time employment. I've got three children, aged 9, 11 and 16. What little we've got has been brought in by my wife. They are just small luxuries which have been saved up for and scrimped for. I've been out of work on and off now for five years. The sacrifice is going to be great for us, but we are determined that we are going to win.

Notwithstanding these threats, the 49 socialist councillors declared that they were prepared to fight to the finish. Derek Hatton, speaking at a magnificent 10,000 strong Youth Trade Union Rights Campaign demonstration in the city in late June, warned that the Liberals would not be allowed to take office because of council workers' resistance if Labour was barred from office. He also said: 'Every time the leadership of the Labour Party nationally say, "Isn't there a better way of doing it? Why are you breaking the law?", we say to them, "show us the 6000 people we should make redundant." '

The national press predictably foamed at the mouth at the scenario that was beginning to take shape in Liverpool. They were driven to fits of rage when the council decided to evict the District Auditor from council premises. Two senior council officials were suspended for allegedly cooperating with him. The *Post* declared, 'Anyone who believed that *Militant's* left council had gone as far as it would in defiance of the government by setting a rate which was patently inadequate, has now been proved wrong.' The *Daily Express* thundered: 'The mantle of Arthur Scargill has fallen on Derek Hatton, *Militant* deputy leader of Liverpool council...to the left of the left there is always the left—and anarchy' (21 June). The mood of approaching battle was reflected in the decision of the council's security guards to physically repel any attempt by commissioners to take over council property.

The support of ordinary workers throughout the city was evident in the days that followed the threat of surcharging the councillors. In Norris Green people flocked to sign a petition in support of the council. When renegade Labour councillor Bill Snell appeared amid cries of 'scab' from people gathered around, he accused activists of being 'communists'. He then said that the councillors should try and convince the Tories that Liverpool needed more money. He received the reply, 'We've been doing that for two years. What's your alternative?' Labour punched home the fact that the Tory-Liberal alternative budget would have involved a cut of between £25 million and £37 million which in turn would have meant an immediate cut of 3000 jobs in order to balance the books.

The increasing militancy of the council workforce, particularly of the manual workers, raised expectations of a serious clash with the government once the cash ran out. Even as early as June, the *Echo* began to rehearse the theme that it was to take up with gusto in the September events: 'council security men have pledged to put a stranglehold on Town Hall services in support of Labour's rebel budget stand. The 136 staff who control all council buildings have voted unanimously to take indefinite strike action if legal steps are taken against city leaders.' Derek Hatton declared that any Commissioner would not be let off the M62 motorway, never mind take control of the city. These were no idle boasts, given the heightened mood of expectation that began to grip the council workforce and the population in general. At the same time, an occasional letter would appear in the *Echo* indicating just what progress had been made by the city council:

> As a visitor from Portsmouth to your city, I have been most impressed by the housebuilding programme of your city council. In Portsmouth, with a Conservative council, no houses are to be built in the next five years, yet Hampshire faces an extra 250,000 people needing accommodation in the same period. Does it really matter if the *Militant* is behind the city council if they are the only people in the country standing up against the mad policy of turning Britain's major cities into slums? I would support the 'Man from Mars' if he built 2000 houses in our city'.

Yet once again Patrick Jenkin refused to talk, but instead announced that the city was to be rate-capped in the next year. In the House of Commons, Terry Fields MP, in a prophetic warning to Jenkin, declared that the council would be, 'dancing on his political grave' if he continued with his policy. There was fury at the further attacks on Liverpool workers which the rate-capping proposals represented. It fuelled the mood of opposition which led to Eric Heffer warning that 'Liverpool could face serious problems of unrest this summer without a settlement of the city's budget crisis.' More than 50 Labour MPs signed a Commons motion supporting the councillors and calling for lost Rate Support Grant to be restored to Liverpool.

Piling on the agony, the Public Works Loan Board threatened on 31 July that loans would be withdrawn unless a 'legal budget' was set by the council. Anticipating that a huge electoral bonus could be seized by them, the SDP-Liberal Alliance poured in 'Party funds in an attempt to seize control of the city council' (*Echo*, 15 July 1985). In a vicious 66-page report called *How Labour sacked the city* the Liberals detailed an alleged 'reign of terror against senior staff at the council'.

Time and again, however, the enemies of Labour were to ignore and underestimate the colossal reservoir of support which the council had built up in the period during which it had been in power. The perception of the population of the city that their council was being persecuted for standing up for ordinary working people was underlined by the splendid campaign organised by the Labour Party involving the families of the threatened councillors. In late July, over 50 members of the Liverpool Labour Council Families Support Group, along with their children travelled to London to lobby for the council. They challenged Thatcher to come to Liverpool to meet the elected councillors and their families. Their challenge was repeated on the floor of the House of Commons by Labour MP, Dave Nellist.

Wherever council spokepersons went ordinary working people were astonished to learn about the rights and conditions enjoyed by the council workforce in Liverpool. Thus when Tony Mulhearn addressed a packed public meeting of Chesterfield Labour Party, one local authority worker declared: 'If only all Labour councils were like that.' A NUPE member, discovering that Liverpool took on all workers full time, commented bitterly that one third of Chesterfield's refuse department were on six-month, three-month or six-week contracts. He asked, 'In Liverpool, do you ever get Labour councillors on such committees telling the workforce they are lucky to have a job?' Tony Mulhearn replied, 'All hell would break loose.' He also commented that the local officers of the building workers' union UCATT had no unemployed joiners on the books, thanks largely to the council's stimulus to the local building industry. Indeed, he quipped that so successful had Labour's campaign on housing and building been that 'most people in Liverpool believe that Trotsky was a bricklayer'.

It became clear to the ruling class that the support which was consolidated behind the council had to be broken quickly. The horrifying case of 14-year-old Jason Fitzsimmons, a heroin addict who came from the Croxteth Estate, who had overdosed and was on a life support unit, was eagerly seized on by the national press. The *Daily Mirror* in particular viciously attacked the council for allegedly not doing enough. Yet it was Labour activists like Phil Knibb and the LPYS who were to the fore in a serious campaign in the Croxteth area to mobilise local people against the drug pushers. Moreover the Liverpool Council Drugs Unit, established in January 1985, is one of the most effective in the country, carrying out training for teachers and developing health education programmes to be incorporated within secondary school curriculums.

The increasing polarisation in the city also compelled the Church dignitaries to choose sides. Inevitably, the tops of the

Church gravitated towards the opponents of Labour. This was not an unusual occurrence in the history of Liverpool. Largely hidden from public view, the Churches had been conducting a systematic campaign of denigration of the city council. Obscure fossils of the past history of the labour movement were dragged up as representing 'moderate' opinion.

The Church Finally Takes Sides

Former right-wing secretary of the TGWU Transport Group, Bob Robinson, was interviewed in the *Catholic Pictorial*, denouncing the Liverpool labour movement. This worthy was fulsome in his praise of the electricians union, the EETPU, but with horror he pointed to the growth of the left in the Liverpool labour movement: 'Yes, the Marxists and Trots—particularly the Militant Tendency, and speaking parochially about Liverpool...they have an influence that I have never seen in all my years as a trade union officer, and for the many years I have spent in the Labour Party.'

This was followed with a statement in the *Catholic Pictorial* on 28 July: 'Liverpool Rates Crisis'. After detailing the terrible decline of the city, there is an implied criticism of the stand of the council. This paper merely called for people to pray for 'deliverance' from the catastrophe that loomed! However, they appealed to trade unions not to respond to calls for widespread strikes, to the council not to use 'the language of revolution' and for the government to recognise the need locally for jobs and services.

The Church was attempting to straddle an increasing chasm between the deprived population of Liverpool and a determined and vicious class-based government. It even admitted: 'It would have seemed part of our customary role of reconciliation to call for further talks between the government and the city council. But the government has made it plain it will not discuss the city's finances with the councillors.' Despite this, the Church leaders unmistakably came out against the city council when they appealed: 'We understand that it is possible for an interested person or body to go to court to secure the setting aside of an inadequate rate and requiring the council to set an adequate rate for a legal budget.'

Those good shepherds, the Bishops, were impervious to the fact that it would be their flock, ordinary working-class house-holders, who would pay the price of massive rate increases. But nobody was prepared to seize the nettle, to attach to themselves the odium of being the instigators of higher rates. The paralysis of Labour's enemies was itself an indication of the head of steam which had been built up behind the council's campaign.

Labour's campaign of counter-propaganda over the years had gone deep amongst the working people. These points were now repeated in letters to the *Echo*. One, on 9 July, quoted former Tory leader, Reg Flude: 'We're not interested in winning seats if the Liberals are carrying out Tory policy better than the Tories themselves.' But the local press began to whip up a feeling of impending doom: 'Compromise is nowhere near on the horizon.' (*Echo* 8 July) On the same day, this same paper reported, 'Jenkin lines up Governor of Liverpool'. It went on:

> An urgent head hunt has been ordered by the government to find the man who would be sent in to run Liverpool if the city council's cash crisis deepens...it would be an unprecedented act to send in what Whitehall describes as a 'Roman Governor' with sweeping powers...it is clear that the government is finding it difficult to get the right man...

Nevertheless, Labour spokespersons made it quite clear that unless the government could be compelled to give extra resources, the cash would dry up at a certain stage: 'We are only in a position to guarantee wages until the end of July' commented Dominic Brady, Education Spokesman. Appearing whiter than white, and completely out of touch with reality, Trevor Jones hypocritically declared in July: 'If Labour rate rebels are surcharged and banished from office, we [the Liberals] pledge no compulsory redundancies.'

Labour spokespersons and MPs in the House of Commons continued to harry the government to come to the assistance of Liverpool. Eric Heffer furiously denounced Thatcher for characterising Liverpool as a city 'where there had been violence for a very long time'. This theme of violence and of the old and sick suffering allegedly through Labour's 'uncaring attitude' would reach fever pitch in the period from September to December.

Although August is a 'holiday' month, in Liverpool hardly a day went by without the city's cash crisis featuring heavily in the local press and nationally. There were to be no holidays that August for leading activists in the labour movement. Decisions that were taken by the city council at that time were to have a dramatic effect and represented the turning point in the development of the struggle in Liverpool.

13.
The Sam Bond Affair

IN THE saga of Liverpool no figure, apart from Tony Mulhearn and Derek Hatton, was to become as well known both inside and outside the city as Sam Bond. His appointment as Principal Race Relations Officer in October 1984 triggered off a ferocious and sometimes violent campaign against the council and against *Militant* supporters in particular. The opponents of the city council gathered together like one big boil. With one voice, the self appointed 'leaders' of the black population of Liverpool 8 (the so-called Black Caucus), the Liberals, the Tories, the soft left of the Labour Party and the Church, denounced the appointment of Sam Bond. In the next three years, hundreds of thousands of words, and 14 violent assaults by the Black Caucus and its supporters were carried out in an attempt to reverse Sam Bond's appointment. Why such ferocity over one individual?

The issues raised by the Sam Bond affair were rooted in the long history of the black population of Liverpool. More than any other city in Britain, Liverpool was built on the slave trade. Before the slave trade, Liverpool was 'an insignificant seaport, a small port of little consequence...a few streets some little distance from the creek – or pool – which served as a harbour'. The slave trade was 'the pride of Liverpool' which flooded the town with wealth:

> which invigorated every industry, provided the capital for docks, enriched and employed the mills of Lancashire and afforded the means for opening out ever new lines of trade. Beyond a doubt it was the slave trade which raised Liverpool from a struggling port to be one of the richest and most prosperous trading centres in the world. (Peter Fryer: *Staying Power – The History of Black People in Britain*)

Liverpool's population grew five times as fast as its nearest sea-port rival, Bristol. Of the 19 British firms that transported the most slaves to Jamaica after 1781 all but three were located in Liverpool. By the 1790s one quarter of Liverpool's total shipping was employed in the slave trade, accounting for 60 per cent of the British slave trade and 40 per cent of that of Europe as a whole. Without the slave trade, as Marx pointed out, there would have been no world market, and without the world market capitalism would not have developed. The rise of capitalism was directly 'and frankly regarded as resting on slavery'. As Peter Fryer has pointed out: 'Rising British capitalism had a magic money machine, an endless chain with three links: sugar cultivation; manufacturing industry; and the slave trade. And the slave trade was the essential link.'

Liverpool merchants were infamous for their cruelty and for cutting their expenses to the bone, maltreating both slaves and sailors. Peter Fryer also comments: 'The clergy was scarcely less eager than the grocers, barbers and tailors.' Indeed, the clergy of the day sanctified, and even glorified the slave trade with all its inhumanity and degradation. Such is the guilt of the present Church dignitaries that their atonement for the past crimes of the Church is achieved by adopting a supine, not to say cringing, attitude to the black middle-class gathered together in the 'race relations industry'.

The slave trade in turn promoted the shipbuilding industry, which was to remain a dominant industry in Liverpool right up to the present time. Moreover, the slave merchants were to play a key role in the local government of the city. At least 26 of Liverpool's Mayors, holding office between 1700 and 1820 were, or had been, slave merchants or close relatives. All the 'grand old Liverpool families' were more or less steeped in slavery, including that of the famous William Gladstone who became a Liberal Prime Minister. In his first speech in the House of Commons he defended slavery on the family estates in British Guyana. When the slave trade was abolished in 1807, the Liverpool merchants had already begun to diversify their interests. They switched from transporting slaves to another profitable commodity—cotton—which just happened to be produced by slave labour. The symbolic heads of African elephants and African slaves engraved on the facade of the town hall, built 1749-54, symbolise the role of the slave trade in the building of the city.

Race Riots

Liverpool 8 is probably the most ghettoised area of Britain. Unlike most of the 'black areas' in other parts of Britain, the population of this area is in the main long-established with most families having lived there for generations. Yet it is the black community of Liverpool 8 which has faced racism in a more searing fashion and over a longer timespan than any other section of the black population of Britain. Apart from the 1981 uprising the most serious incidences of racial attack took place in 1919 and 1948.

The demobilisation of troops in 1918-19 had enormously increased the competition for jobs. The capitalists encouraged the fear that blacks were taking 'white workers' jobs'. The police then, as now, inflamed the situation by picking on and beating up blacks. An attack in 1919 on a black seamen's boarding house resulted in a clash with the police in which one policeman was shot in the mouth, another in the neck, and a third was slashed on the face and neck.

At one of the houses raided in Upper Pitt Street lived Charles Wootton, a young ship's firefighter, variously described as a Bermudan or a Trinidadian. Wootton had been discharged from the Navy in the previous March. He ran from the house when the police raided, but was pursued by two policemen and a large crowd of between 200 and 300 people hurling missiles. The police caught hold of him at the edge of the Queen's Dock but the lynch mob tore him from the policemen's hands and threw him into the water. He was pelted with stones as he swam around, and soon died. No arrests were made of those who led the mob.

In the next few days, an anti-black reign of terror raged in Liverpool. Gangs of between 2000 and 10,000 roamed the streets, 'savagely attacking, beating and stabbing every negro they could find'. The local press poured oil on the fires. The *Liverpool Courier*, the predecessor of the *Liverpool Echo*, declared:

> One of the chief reasons of popular anger behind the present disturbances lies in the fact that the average negro is nearer the animal than is the average white man, and that there are women in Liverpool who have no self respect. The white man...regards [the black man] as part child, part animal and part savage. It is quite true

that many of the blacks in Liverpool are of a low type, that they insult and threaten respectable women in the streets, and that they are invariably unpleasant and provocative. (*Liverpool Courier,* 11 June 1919.)

Following the 1981 riots Kenneth Oxford, the local police chief, described the inhabitants of Liverpool 8 as 'the product of liaisons between white prostitutes and African sailors'! The attitude of the summits of society has hardly changed since 1919!

Clashes took place, although on a smaller scale, in 1948. The causes were very similar to those in 1919. By 1948 about 8000 black people were based in Liverpool, most of whom had come to Britain to help the 'war effort'. The competition for jobs prompted the National Union of Seamen (NUS), under firm right-wing domination, to organise a drive to keep black seamen off British ships. About 30 per cent of black adults were seamen, and another 10 per cent had shore jobs. Sixty per cent of the black population were therefore unemployed as a result of this 'colour bar'. The attacks of the NUS leadership added to the general discrimination and hostility to blacks in the city. When clashes took place the police invariably took the part of the whites.

In August 1948, a 300-strong mob gathered outside an Indian restaurant. They attacked a West African and this led in turn to clashes between whites and blacks throughout the South End of the city. The next day, 2000 whites attacked a hostel for black seamen. The blacks barricaded themselves in, but when the police came they arrested the defenders! On the third day, the black community received details of an attack on a club, Wilkies, in Upper Parliament Street. They prepared to defend the premises.

The police then attacked the club, inflicting serious damage on many of the defenders. A white woman, who saw police beating up black men 'unmercifully' protested to the police and was arrested for her pains. The police then went on the rampage, beating up and attacking blacks throughout the area.

In 1972 a racial clash took place between whites and blacks over the allocation of new council housing to black or racially mixed families in the Fulton Estate in Liverpool 8. These clashes were a prelude to the far more widespread and serious upheavals in the 1980s.

The Boom—Racism Continues

The economic upswing of 1950-75 had resulted in an appreciable rise in the living standards of the working class in Britain, with minimal unemployment, a rise in home ownership, paid holidays, a shorter working week, etc. However, throughout this whole period the population of Liverpool 8 was largely denied the benefits of the upswing. With endemic and mass unemployment well over 50 per cent, the black worker was denied opportunities to work in industry and in the council. Thus in 1975, there were only 75 black workers amongst the 10,000 employees in 19 Liverpool shops. Even as late as 1983, after millions of words and dozens of reports detailing the situation, a mere 12 black staff out of a sample of 3000 employees in the city centre were found.

A report on the Liverpool Area Health Authority in 1983 found three black training nurses out of a total of 306. None of the 136 staff nurses in Liverpool were blacks. Out of 16,000 staff, the Liverpool Area Health Authority employed a mere 110 black people.

Black people in Liverpool, to a much greater extent than elsewhere, were pushed out of the mainstream of society. More than 50 per cent of the black population were born in Liverpool. Many have a white parent or grandparent, but their confinement to the ghetto area served to reinforce the prejudices which existed, and still exist, amongst sections of the white working class. Undoubtedly, racial hostility to black newcomers in the 1950s and 1960s was open in its initial phases in most parts of Britain. But living alongside of, and struggling and working together with blacks, undermined many of the prejudices of white workers and softened this racial animosity, although without completely burning it out of the consciousness of big sections of the working class. However, in Liverpool where the black population has been far more isolated, racial prejudices, even in a latent form, have continued for much longer than in the more racially mixed areas of Birmingham, Bradford and London.

This racial animosity, born out of a false sense of superiority, was and is particularly prevalent amongst the Liverpool police force. If the situation was bad for blacks during the boom, it became catastrophic by the early 1980s. Unemployment in

Liverpool between 1974 and 1981 rose by 120 per cent, but in the same period black unemployment in Liverpool 8 increased by 350 per cent.

The clash over the appointment of Sam Bond was not at all accidental, nor did it involve merely the fate of one man. Two entirely different philosophies, reflecting diametrically opposed class forces, clashed on the issue of his appointment as Principal Race Relations Officer to the Liverpool City Council. On the one side stood the class conscious approach of the labour movement. On the other side stood the race relations industry, feeling threatened to the very marrow of their being by the appointment of just one Marxist to such a potentially important position. Standing behind them were all the forces of 'official society' (ie capitalism) determined to purge discussion on racism and how to combat it, of any trace of a class analysis.

This opposition was orchestrated by the Black Caucus, a body which originated in 1980, when the then Liberal-controlled city council invited the local Community Relations Council to appoint representatives to sit on a new race relations committee. These 'representatives' subsequently called themselves the Black Caucus. This body consisted of just 12 members who first came to prominence in 1983 when they organised a coup which resulted in the removal of some of the original liaison committee members.

Attempting to answer the charge of the Marxists in the labour movement that this clique was 'unrepresentative' of the black population of the area, the Black Caucus claimed to represent 70 black organisations throughout the city. They have never named these 70 organisations, and indeed have been repudiated many times by a number of black organisations as in no way being representative of the black community of Liverpool 8. The close-knit character of the black area was such that the role of these self-appointed leaders was to be exposed very quickly and clearly. Amongst the great majority of the black population of Liverpool 8 they were looked on with contempt.

The Black Caucus is however representative of and has a base among the 'race relations industry', the sects on the fringes of the labour movement, the Churches and latterly all those bourgeois elements who have come into opposition to the council.

The Race Relations Industry

The ruling class were alarmed at the emergence of black militancy in the late 1960s and 1970s in the wake of the movement of the American blacks. The generation of blacks born in this country, unlike their parents, became more and more alienated from capitalist society and naturally gravitated towards a philosophy which criticised the system. Elements of black nationalism fused with a searching for a class analysis. This fear of the ruling class was reinforced by the riots in Bristol, Brixton and Toxteth in 1981.

The spectre of an alienated and combative black youth linking up with an equally determined and increasingly radicalised white working-class youth terrified the ruling class. The elements of such an alliance were present in the riots of 1981, and again in the uprising on the Broadwater Farm Estate, Tottenham, in 1985. The ruling class were determined to create points of support within the black community as a means of staving off such a development.

This philosophy was given perhaps its most finished form in the statements of Employment Minister, Kenneth Clarke. A speech of his was greeted with the headline, 'Jobs Programme to create black middle class'. The *Daily Telegraph* (23 June 1986) stated:

> The Employment Minister said the eventual aim of this programme for the inner cities was the formation of a black middle class which he believed could provide a role for young members of ethnic minorities.

The soil upon which such a class, in reality a privileged caste, could grow has been nourished by the £80 million per year being ploughed into the inner cities in grants and other aid by 1986. This sum is channelled through the vast array of race relations agencies and advisers which now litter the inner city ghettos. Lord Scarman, in an article in *New Society* in February 1986, reinforced the strategy of the more far-sighted representatives of the ruling class:

> Our underlying social strategy should be to create ethnic minority opportunities in the universities, the professions, the civil service, the police, politics and public life, in business activities and in industrial management. In other words, we must create a black British middle

class. If we can create a black middle class then we will also be creating *a group that can exercise responsible and creative leadership in their own community and in the nation—to the benefit of all of us in Britain.*(Our emphasis)

The establishment of the 'race relations industry' was an attempt on the part of the British bourgeois to replicate in Britain the measures of 'affirmative' or 'positive' action developed by the American ruling class in the wake of the civil rights movements and the riots of the late 1960s and early 1970s. In cities like Detroit they poured in millions of dollars to refurbish those areas affected by the riots. A whole series of laws enforcing quotas for the employment of blacks were introduced.

The aim was to blunt the teeth of the movement of black militancy which had become evident in the 1960s and 1970s. Given the enormous resources of American capitalism and the continuation of the economic upswing the American possessing classes were partially successful in this exercise. Most of those militants who participated in the struggles of the 1960s and 1970s were skilfully drawn back into the 'system'. Big openings were created for black policemen, civil servants, lawyers, mayors, members of Congress, etc.

The illusion was created that the average black could 'make it to the top'. However, this did not substantially alter the desperate plight of the overwhelming majority of the blacks, who were working class. Moreover, the measures of 'positive or affirmative action' are now being deliberately undermined by the Reagan administration, and in a period of slump and mass unemployment will either be discarded or become the source of endless friction between black and white. The attempt to create a stable point of support amongst the black working class of America will, in the long run, prove to have failed. In Britain this failure will be even more apparent than in America.

In the mid-1960s the Wilson Labour government introduced a series of racist immigration laws. The Race Relations Board and the Community Relations Commission (later amalgamated into the Commission for Racial Equality) were set up, in effect to check and defuse the rise of black militancy. From its inception, the race industry has come under fire from the most radicalised sections of the black movement.

In his book *A Different Hunger: Writings on Black Resistance,* the veteran anti-racist campaigner, A Sivanandan, comments:

> It [the Community Relations Commission] has successfully taken politics out of the black struggle...It has, together with the Race Relations Board, created a black bourgeoisie to which the state can now hand over control of black dissidents in general and black youth in particular. (p 121)

His statements about a black bourgeoisie are not accurate, but he hits the nail on the head when he says: 'They had to be allowed to move upwards within the existing system so that they would not threaten to transform it into a different system.'

Those who constitute the leadership of the Liverpool Black Caucus are drawn precisely from such a social milieu. Their philosophy is a peculiar mixture of crude black nationalism and right-wing reformism. They have a consensus approach to race which ingratiates them with all those forces and parties which rest on capitalism.

In *Black Linx,* the organ of the Merseyside Community Relations Council (December 1984), they attacked Sam Bond for stating:

> I view racism not as a natural process, but as a phenomenon that specifically arises out of the prevailing economic and social framework and which has been developed and used as a tool to further the specific political and economic interests of a certain section of society.

They comment:

> Particularly disturbing here is the assertion that racism is 'used as a tool' by sectional interests within society. This view is no more than a crude conspiracy theory. It suggests that racism is propagated by the conscious will of those with a vested interest in maintaining inter-racial conflict. If this were true, the task of anti-racists would be very simple. However, reality is much more complex than a dogmatic, uninformed *Militant* position.

Thus a class analysis is airily dismissed as 'a crude conspiracy theory'. This is music to the ears of the spokespersons of British capitalism. The guiding principle of the British ruling class in carving out its empire was the policy of divide and rule tested in Ireland, developed in India, and reinforced in its conquest of its African colonies. *Black Linx* goes on to argue:

> It is clear that racism is embedded in the language, traditions, legal structures, education systems and communications media—and that such instances of racism have not always developed out of the conscious intent of any sectional interest group. Conspiracy theories of this sort invariably over-simplify the problem. They obscure the interaction of social institutions and structures in the historical context of British imperialism, colonial exploitation, slave trading etc. Racism is an intensely complex phenomenon. Entirely unconvincing 'analyses' such as those offered by Mr Bond merely confuse the subject, and render the task of genuine anti-racists much more difficult.

Thus only the 'experts' of the race relations industry can understand the 'complex issues' of race. The average 'uneducated' black worker must leave it to these experts to hand down their highly 'complex' analyses of racism in Britain. *Militant* and the broad labour movement have always approached the question from a diametrically opposite point of view.

Black workers are doubly oppressed. They are exploited as workers and also face persecution and discrimination because of the colour of their skin. *Militant* does not dodge the issue of racism amongst sections of the white population. But the 'race relations industry' approaches this question in a one sided and therefore erroneous fashion.

British imperialism as part of its domination of its colonies deliberately fostered superior racist attitudes which have left their imprint on the outlook of significant layers of the British working class. But as Leon Trotsky pointed out, within the breast of the British working class beats two souls. One betrays a political backwardness, tinged with prejudice against black workers. The other reveals a heroic tradition of combating the ruling class and making sacrifices in the interests of workers of other countries.

The Labour Movement Combating Racism

Karl Marx underlined the colossal sacrifices which the Lancashire cotton workers were prepared to make in opposition to the slave states in the American civil war. By refusing to handle the cotton from the southern plantations, hundreds of thousands of cotton workers were either thrown out of work or reduced to short time and thereby to penury. Nor should we ever forget the internationalism of the London dockers who refused to load the *Jolly George* which was taking arms to suppress the Russian Revolution. The way to combat racism is not, as the Black Caucus and the race relations industry imagine, by lecturing workers on the evils of racist attitudes.

Militant has been to the forefront of the struggle to defend the interests of black workers, against police harassment, racial attacks, deportations and for equal rights in employment and housing. But it is only by uniting the struggles of all workers in combating their day to day problems and linking this to the establishment of a socialist society, that the antagonism of black and white workers will be dissolved.

In all the scribblings of the race relations industry, the backwardness, prejudice, and so-called ingrained racism of white workers is emphasised. There have been examples where right-wing leaders of unions have taken measures against the employment of black workers, attempted to introduce quotas etc, as was the case with the National Union of Seamen in 1948. However, the majority of the labour movement have always been implacably opposed to such a policy. Also, strikes of black and white workers have taken place where racist management or supervisors have attempted to victimise black or Asian workers. Trevor Carter, in his book *Shattering Illusions,* gives the example of the railway workers in Camden:

> Shunting is a dangerous job and it is impossible to work in fog. One such foggy night we were in our guards' and shunters' cabin, waiting for a heavy mist to lift, when in burst a man we didn't know. He ignored the white shunters and railed at the black ones, 'Where do you think you are, in the jungle? Get out there and do your job.' I represented the guards and shunters and asked, 'Who are you?' 'An outside inspector', he replied, 'to report on some of the nonsense that goes on here.' 'Is that so?' he was told, 'in that case, you can report that there will be no more work done here tonight, tomorrow and perhaps for quite a while, unless there is an apology for your behaviour which is acceptable to all of us.' He stormed out. There was a great cheer from all of us and we prepared to brew a jug of tea for what might be a long stay. It wasn't too long. Euston [headquarters of British Rail] called me to the telephone for our

version. In a short while, back crawled the 'outside inspector' with an abject apology. We worked joyfully for the rest of the night shift. It's a great feeling when workers together declare 'No racism here'.

The Camden railwayworkers took the struggle outside the workplace. They smashed the colour bar in the pubs surrounding the station. They organised protests, challenged breweries and took on the licensing authorities. It was slow, hard work, but they drew on their strength as organised workers as well as individuals.

The basis for such united class action had been laid by a long, stubborn struggle of union activists in the Camden railway unions. To begin with, there had been a downing of tools and even threats of strikes when the first black workers appeared on the railways. Only a policy of educating black and white workers in the need for class solidarity was to lay the basis for the magnificent stand of the Camden railwayworkers. Moreover, the black workers themselves, by their solid support for strike action which followed these events and for the unions, shattered the overt racism that undoubtedly existed in the initial phase of black involvement.

Throughout the last three decades, there have been many similar examples of strikes in defence of black and Asian workers: at Fords, British Leyland, Longbridge and Cowley for example. Of course, this does not mean that latent racial antagonisms and prejudices can be burned out of the consciousness of workers in a single industrial struggle or by a single action. Only through the constant example and efforts of the labour movement and through ideological and political education will racism be combated successfully.

One thing is certain, the methods of the race relations industry in the form of the Black Caucus, had they been allowed to flourish in Merseyside, would have had catastrophic consequences for the local labour movement. The appointment of one of *their* members as Principal Race Relations Officer, in preference to Sam Bond, would have enormously complicated the struggle against racism.

Militant has been asked many times whether the decision to support Sam Bond, particularly in the face of such relentless and ruthless opposition, was not a tactical mistake. Peter Taaffe, editor of *Militant*, in a statement at the time answered this question:

There is not a shadow of regret among *Militant* supporters for the continual support that was given to Sam Bond. Firstly, an exceptional and honourable record in beginning to cement relations between black and white workers in Liverpool was undertaken by Sam Bond and the Liverpool City Council. Secondly, any supporter of the Black Caucus [in the position of Principal Race Relations Officer] would have divided and set workers against one another.

We only have to look towards the example of some of the trendy left councils in London on the issue of racism. They create an atmosphere of fear and suspicion amongst white workers. Yet the aim should be to bring black and white together, to overcome differences and prejudices. This is the traditional method of the labour movement and is central to the approach of *Militant*. It is not a question of pandering to the backwardness or prejudice of whites, but of seeking to overcome such prejudices in the course of struggle, political discussion and education. *Militant* supports several of the concrete measures which were taken by left councils such as the introduction of equal opportunity advisers, who encourage sensitivity to the diversity of cultures within schools. *Militant* and the general labour movement wholeheartedly support such measures.

Not only is it a question of what is done, but of who does it, why they do it and how it is done. The black petit-bourgeois who dominate the race relations industry jealously guard what they consider is their constituency. They wish to maintain the illusion of a non-class black community and any independent movement of black workers threatens to undermine their position. In the Labour Party they wish to separate out and divide black workers from the rest of the labour movement. Thus, when Linda Bellos (leader of Lambeth Council) in 1987 outline a cuts package, she berated her critics on the left, saying that they opposed her only because they were a 'white-left split'.

In contrast, the whole history of the labour movement internationally has been to overcome race, religious and ethnic differences by fusing workers together into one organisation. *Militant* advocates special commissions within the Labour Party and trade unions composed primarily of black and Asian workers to highlight and campaign, to involve and solve the problems of black and Asian workers. But this is entirely different from building separate organisations which is what the Black Sections movement attempts to do. Moreover the logic of the position of the Black Caucus, and the race relations industry, is that only these 'experts' will be able to teach black and Asian children—a thoroughly reactionary position.

In Hackney an attempt was made to demand that only black workers should be employed in certain departments of the council. Both black and white workers should strenuously oppose such a development. Black workers, as opposed to the so-called race relations experts, instinctively understand that such measures in the long run would undermine the position of the black population in Britain. It would fuel the policies of the fascists and racists by further dividing black from white.

The actual size of Liverpool's black population is uncertain. The 1981 Census reported the section of the ethnic minority population of Merseyside falling under the 'New Commonwealth and Pakistan' (NCWP) heading to be 15,000. This clearly under-estimated the real figures for the black population. According to the 1981 *Labour Force Survey* (LFS), a big proportion (about 40 per cent) of those of NCWP ethnic origin lived in households headed by someone born in the UK, a much higher proportion than in other cities. These Liverpool-born blacks did not show up in figures for minority groups given in the Census, which classifies the population according to the national origin of heads of households. As a result, the city council was for years denied additional government funding freely given to other cities to provide resources for their black communities. There were not even resources for thorough research to determine the real figures, a prerequisite for an assessment of the needs of minorities.

The Merseyside Community Relations Council (MCRC), which is dominated by the Black Caucus, correctly argues that the Census, the Labour Force Survey, and other surveys, for various reasons, under-estimate the black population. In 1983 the MCRC put forward their own estimate for Liverpool's non—white population: between 20-30,000, with about 37 per cent of them being black British. This figure was widely accepted, including by the Manpower Services Commission (MSC), which was carrying out research into unemployment among blacks in the area. Alex Bennett, a prominent member of the Black Caucus, was a member of the Ethnic Sub Group of the MSC's Area Board, which positively endorsed the MSC report.

In 1985, however, the MCRC put forward a new estimate of

between 40-50,000, though without producing new data or explaining the reasons for this revision. According to the MCRC the non-white population of 40,000 is made up of 20,000 Liverpool-born blacks, 8000 Chinese, 4000 from India and Pakistan, 3000 Africans, 3000 from the Caribbean, and 2000 Somali and Arab people. There is no dispute that over half the black population live in the five inner-city wards of Liverpool 8, in the case of Granby ward making up over 20 per cent of the residents.

The Black Caucus in Control

The hysteria with which the appointment of Sam Bond was greeted by the Black Caucus indicated a well-founded fear that once the labour movement in Merseyside seriously took up the issues confronting black people, the virtual monopoly exercised by this petit-bourgeois clique would be broken. An elaborate smokescreen, denouncing as a 'racist' anybody who challenged them was established to prevent a close examination of how they disposed of the considerable funds that had flooded into the area from government and other agencies. There is much evidence to show that funds were continually mismanaged. A year before Sam Bond's appointment Mr Zach Williams resigned as Director of the Charles Wootton Centre. He wrote to the Chair of the Management Committee:

> Another area of serious disagreement with you (and may I also add, the Administrator) pertains to your attitude towards public funds. It seems clear to me that you and the Administrator believe that the Centre could accept public funds and projects without any adequate accounting system.

Williams pointed out that the Charles Wootton Centre should constitute 'the collective frame of reference for all Liverpool 8 black people, and not just a small clique of self-interested individuals'. In a four-page letter dated 2 November 1984 the Manpower Services Commission (MSC) indicated an astonishing series of financial irregularities in the running of the Charles Wootton Centre, an institution dominated by the Black Caucus. The letter was written to Liz Drysdale, who was running the Charles Wootton Centre and was a prominent member of the

Black Caucus. The MSC complained:

> The standard of entries remains poor. There is still quite a lot of over-writing and many figures are difficult to read...National Insurance. The paying-in book shows the latest payments to be on 21 August 1984. The cash book shows a payment of £865.14 on 18 October. Why is this so?...August pay sheets for w/e 10 August and 3 August are still missing. Why is this? We need access to these to complete our checks...M. Julienne was paid £86.70 w/e 16 August 1984 and £86.70 w/e 23 August 1984. This is the full-time participant rate; but there is no provision within the agreement for a full-time post in the Video Workshop. Please explain what happened here. We note that he was promoted to supervisor beginning 27 August 1984.

The attempt of the Liberals when they were in power to question the financial arrangements and administration of Charles Wootton House had produced a clash between them and the Black Caucus. But now not a whisper of criticism appeared about the past or current methods of the Black Caucus, who they saw as potential allies against the council.

Sam Bond's Appointment

The opposition to Sam Bond had nothing to do with the fact that Sam Bond was not a 'Liverpool-born black' and it was not primarily of an ideological character. It had everything to do, however, with the fact that the material interests of this petit-bourgeois clique were threatened by the appointment of someone who would forcefully present the city council's socialist policies to fight racism. Up to his appointment, every single race relations job in the city was held by a supporter of the Black Caucus. From 1984 right up to Sam Bond's dismissal by the Liberal-Tory coalition in April 1987, the Black Caucus fostered the legend that Sam Bond was a *Militant* 'plant'. They have spilt not a little ink attempting to prove that the interviewing panel that chose Sam Bond was rigged. Yet even the Caucus were to admit subsequently that the majority of those on the interviewing panel were not *Militant* supporters. Moreover, the council had agreed to three Caucus supporters being on the interview panel.

The candidates recommended for shortlisting by the Caucus

were largely their own members. One of the leading members of the Black Caucus, Alex Bennett, was himself one of the candidates for the job. Moreover, some Caucus members on the panel were also referees for those they were interviewing, a highly irregular procedure. There was no objection to Sam Bond being on the shortlist at that stage. The Caucus were absolutely confident that one of their candidates would walk the interview and get the job. But on the day, Sam Bond proved to be by far and away the most outstanding candidate. This was a view unanimously endorsed by all the Labour councillors. It was only then that the Caucus cried foul, criticising the interviewing procedure and even claiming that Sam Bond did not have the support of his union, NALGO. In fact, the whole interviewing process had been ratified by NALGO's National Emergency Committee.

What then were the objections to Sam Bond's appointment by the main representatives of the Black Caucus? Steve French arrogantly declared:

> For us, Sampson Bond wasn't a candidate. Mr Bond possesses the same qualities and background in race relations as most of the black people out on the street. He hasn't any great expertise in management or in all the other areas such as education, housing and employment.

What academic qualifications did Martin Luther King, Malcolm X, Hughie Newton, Bobby Seal and George Jackson possess in the 1960s and 1970s for fighting the racism which was endemic in the USA? The 'race experts' in the Urban League and other such 'coloured' organisations had the same haughty contempt for Martin Luther King and Malcolm X that the professionals in the race relations industry have today to the ordinary black worker who understands and is prepared to combat racism.

Sam Bond's credentials were far superior to those of his critics. He had been involved in the battle against racism at street level in Lewisham and in the formation of the biggest black youth organisation which Britain has seen, the PNP Youth in the early 1980s, and first-hand experience of combating the effect of racism within the trade-union movement. Moreover, because of his work in Liverpool, the Newham 7 Campaign, a group fighting against police harassment and victimisation of Asian youth in East London, subsequently appointed him as their spokesperson in Liverpool.

No amount of professional qualifications, without a serious grounding in the socialist policies of the labour movement, is capable of mobilising the black working class, together with the labour movement, to combat racism. Moreover, the objection that Sam Bond was not a Liverpool-born black was answered many times by pointing to the many Liverpool-born blacks holding similar positions in Manchester and various boroughs in London.

But the Caucus were not to restrict their opposition to the appointment to words alone. On 10 October, when Sam Bond was about to take up his job, a group of Black Caucus members, leavened by a number of people well-known for their criminal record, occupied and imprisoned Derek Hatton in his office. Some press reports attempted to give the impression that this was just a friendly occupation and that as a result of negotiations and 'dialogue' Derek Hatton and other councillors agreed to reconsider Sam Bond's appointment and re-advertise the post The reality is that Derek Hatton, Tony Mulhearn and other councillors were taken hostage, threatened with physical violence and had no option but to sign the 'agreement' which was put in front of them by the Black Caucus.

The leadership of Liverpool NALGO, under the control of members and supporters of the Communist Party and petit bourgeois Labour ex-'lefts', dismissed any suggestion that violence was employed against councillors in the siege of the municipal buildings. Yet members of their own union in the City Solicitor's Department issued a statement in which they commented:

> People associated with or members of the Black Caucus who took part in the outrageous activity, are a group of self-appointed leaders elected by nobody and whose views are unrepresentative of the black community. They stormed into an office occupied by two NALGO members and then held hostage, under threat of physical violence, several city councillors and Sampson Bond, a black NALGO member from Brent. They were told in no uncertain terms that if they attempted to leave the office they would be subjected to physical violence. Extremely obscene and offensive language was used. A black member working in the Campaign Unit was told, amongst other things, 'You're a traitor; go away and paint your face white.'

The priorities of the Caucus were shown in the seige. A GMBATU member, who appealed for the release of the councillors in order that they could go to the council meeting to vote on important issues affecting all the workers of Liverpool, including the jailing of Cammell Laird workers, was told: 'Go away, or you'll get it.'

NALGO was joined in its opposition to the appointment of Sam Bond by NUPE and the NUT, both unions which had opposed the strike action on 29 March organised in support of the council's stand. Moreover, at the Joint Shop Stewards Committee the previous week, they had opposed a call for a 24-hour strike in protest against the jailing of Cammell Laird's workers. The NALGO leaders refused to put this or their opposition to Sam Bond to a vote of their members. A bloc of NALGO, NUPE and the NUT pushed through a resolution on the Executive Committee of the Joint Shop Stewards Committee, deploring the decision of the District Labour Party to uphold Bond's appointment and calling for a boycott of the post.

The District Labour Party met the evening following the siege of the municipal buildings. They completely rejected the statement which had been signed under duress and reaffirmed the appointment of Sam Bond. After a full debate, the DLP, attended by about 150 delegates, voted overwhelmingly for this decision. When the issues were explained clearly to the unions, there was overwhelming support for Sam Bond. GMBATU Branch 5 took the lead, together with other unions in supporting the decision of the District Labour Party.

The Caucus claimed the right to disseminate their lies and distortions throughout the labour movement. But the council's attempt to counter this by letters to the workforce explaining the background to the appointment of Sam Bond was denounced as 'MacGregor style' tactics. Thus the action of a socialist city council was put on the same plane as those actions of the vicious anti-union chief of the National Coal Board who had just defeated the miners. It is a question not just of what is done, but who does it, why they do it, and how.

The aim of the Liverpool City Council was to defend and to raise up the conditions of life of the working people of Liverpool. It was on the opposite side of the barricades to MacGregor and all those capitalist managements who have attempted to use anti-union propaganda in the form of letters to their workforce. The Marxists completely rejected the idea that the city council did not have the right to inform the council workforce of its position, particularly as on the Sam Bond issue the leaders of NALGO were systematically lying to their own members. The attempt to equate the Liverpool City Council with MacGregor was to forget one little detail, that they proceeded from opposite class standpoints. The very fact that NALGO and the Black Caucus could squeal about 'MacGregor-type tactics' was an indication of their fear of the likely reaction of ordinary workers once they were informed about the facts.

The Liberals, incapable of attacking Labour on the issues of jobs, homes and education quickly moved to join with NALGO and the Black Caucus in exploiting the Sam Bond issue. Adept at political amnesia, the Liberals dropped all opposition to the Black Caucus. Trevor Jones came out as a champion of the black population of Liverpool 8—yet he had called on the government to use troops in the 1981 riots! The National Steering Committee of the Labour Party Black Sections weighed in: '*Militant's* vision for tackling inner city poverty ignores black people by reducing everything merely to *class.*' This reflected the increasingly non-class position of the trendy left within the Labour Party and the 'Euro-communist' leadership of the Communist Party.

Militant had never presented the issue of race or the struggle against racism in the crude fashion portrayed by its opponents. *Militant* argues there is a special oppression of black people, as with women, in capitalist society. But in the final analysis these problems are rooted in the class nature of society—a conclusion which the Black Caucus, Communist Party 'theoretician' Eric Hobsbawm, and the trendy lefts within the Labour Party criticised as 'class reductionism'. They were, in reality, criticising the analysis of society which is the basis of Marxism and the labour movement.

By simply posing as a solution to the problems of black people the redistribution of the existing limited number of jobs from white to black, the trendy left and their allies were advancing a formula for fratricidal strife within the working class. Liverpool City Council, on the other hand, pursued a policy of increasing jobs, of expanding services and, in the process, of creating the basis for increased opportunities in employment, housing, social services, etc, for the black people of Liverpool 8. Moreover, in the teeth of every conceivable obstacle the council's record was remarkably successful between 1983-7.

Combating Racism

In their campaign of vilification, the Black Caucus found some unusual bedfellows. They denounced Derek Hatton as a racist. The British National Party, on the other hand, wrote in their journal *British Nationalist* in December 1984: 'Hatton is one of the biggest negrophiles on Merseyside, having spent his political career championing black causes.' This did not prevent the BNP and the National Front, in their subsequent feeble and unsuccessful attempts to penetrate Merseyside, from chanting support for the Black Caucus on their demonstrations. They worked on the principle that 'the enemy of my enemy is my friend' and at the same time recognised that the Black Caucus were never a threat to them.

The fascist thugs themselves gave recognition of who was combating their poisonous attempts to gain a toehold in Liverpool. In an act of undisguised intimidation, they sent letters to the home addresses of a hundred *Militant* supporters and sympathisers.

The job of clearing the fascists out of Liverpool was undertaken by the labour movement under the leadership of *Militant* supporters and the Labour Party Young Socialists. The LPYS had been canvassing and leafleting the area around the Liverpool football ground where the National Front had a tenuous foothold. Clashes developed and the fascists began counter-leafleting throwing racist muck against the Liverpool City Council.

The LPYS replied by organising a public meeting in opposition to the activities of the National Front. Black youth from the LPYS and Derek Hatton spoke at the meeting. He explained the differences between the District Labour Party and members of the Black Caucus on how to fight racism. He explained the council's policies: trade-union representation on all interview panels for jobs; monitoring of all jobs to ensure no discrimination; a council award of £150,000 to the Liverpool 8 Law Centre; black trainee housing manager schemes to ensure that black housing problems were dealt with; racial awareness courses for all council employees; and a Chinese Unit was proposed for the Social Services Department. The fascists dared not show their heads at this meeting and for a period open National Front activity was stamped out.

The Black Caucus and their supporters were at pains to paint Sam Bond as some kind of tame Uncle Tom. There were perhaps even some in the Liverpool Labour Group who supported his nomination as a 'soft option' thinking he might excuse the labour movement for its lack of commitment in combating racism in the city in the past. In a speech to the Labour group on 17 December, Sam Bond crushingly answered his critics. He declared:

> Some of you, I know, have had to face a tirade of insults and abuse over my appointment, and I thank you for holding to your principles and standing firm. I was attracted to apply for my present post by the principled stand taken by the city council in its defence of jobs and services. Since my appointment, I have had to face a barrage of personal attacks. Both my family and I have received threatening phone calls. I have been pushed around, my car has been followed, I have been spat at, and subjected to a torrent of abuse.
>
> Even though I have never broken a single rule of NALGO, it appears that even officials of my union are prepared to condone the threats of violence against me. Nonetheless, I want to make it absolutely clear that I have no intention of bowing to threats of intimidation of any kind. I have been appointed to do a job, and I have every intention of carrying it out...This city was built on the backs of black people. The basis of its wealth was derived from black slavery. The historians may attempt to cover up the true history of Liverpool, but it is up to you to face it squarely, because racism continues to scar this city as much now as it did in the past.
>
> Black people continue to be treated with contempt. They are still condemned to the greatest misery and deprivation. And let us be frank, the labour movement must accept its share of responsibility in allowing the cancer of racism to spread and develop in this society. The record of Labour governments on the issue of race has been appalling. The labour movement in Liverpool has failed in the past to seriously address itself to the plight of blacks and other minorities. But now you must seize the opportunity to seriously take up the issue. You must declare war on racism.
>
> Much has been said about adopting a strategy of positive action and ethnic monitoring. I do not wish to dwell on these issues tonight,

but for the record I want to make it clear that I've never been opposed to these measures. But it would be a mistake to think that such action alone can solve the problems of racism. Many Labour councillors in London, and even some Conservative councils, already make extensive use of positive action and monitoring. While these policies may have benefited a handful of blacks, they have made very little impact in improving the conditions of the majority of unemployed blacks. Positive action has been in operation for nearly ten years, yet in that time unemployment amongst black people has risen by over 400 per cent.

Therefore, while I am not opposed to positive action and monitoring, it is clear in Liverpool that we need to go much further. Finally, may I say that it seems to me that I am being used as a scapegoat for what is, in reality, a more general attack on the stand taken by the city council. There are many who would like to see this council go down. But I am sure that you will continue to stand firm. You have declared a commitment to fighting against racism, and you must see that fight through to the very end.

This bold statement, which was repeated at many management committees of the Labour Party in the city, did much to cement the support and affection for Sam Bond in the labour movement. Pushed back, the Black Caucus sought allies outside of Liverpool in its attempt to break the will of the council.

In early December Russell Profitt was drafted in to boost their campaign. He gave perhaps the most finished expression to the haughty contempt of the race relations industry for ordinary blacks when he declared that, as race relations adviser for Brent Council in West London, 'he would not have short-listed Mr Bond for a race relations job in Liverpool, Lewisham or Brent because of his lack of experience'.(*Morning Star*, 15 December 1984) The real motives of those opposing the appointment of Bond was indicated in a statement by Peter Cresswell, NALGO Branch Secretary: 'I think that the council will have to back down. It's the first time for years that *Militant* have come across strong opposition in the labour movement locally. Everyone's been in awe of them, but we're not.' The *Morning Star* (12 December) declared: 'The Liberals in Liverpool are now looking forward to more support from the Tory government in their campaign to eventually win back control of the council from Labour.' In other words, once having gained a victory on the Bond issue, all the opponents of Liverpool council in the labour movement would seek to reverse the fighting stand of the District Labour Party and the council.

Over the next period, a series of escalating attacks, both on the city council and on Sam Bond was organised by the Black Caucus and their new-found friends in the Liberal Party. The Black Caucus produced a book, *The Racial Politics of Militant in Liverpool*, in which the central theme was that the labour movement on Merseyside and in particular *Militant* are 'colour blind'. Mild criticism is made of the Liberals when they were in power, but the book consists in the main of a diatribe against Labour's record.

At the council meeting in early February 1985 Sam Bond was confirmed as Principal Race Relations Officer. The Liberals promised in the debate that if they won control of the council, they would sack anyone from any post they considered 'political'. Steve French, principal spokesperson for the Black Caucus, did not turn up for the council meeting although he had been invited to speak. In his absence, the Chair allowed a resident of Liverpool 8 from the public gallery to address the council. A young, unemployed single parent, she fully supported the council in its struggle to combat racism, welcomed the establishment of a Race Relations Unit, and wished Sam Bond every success: 'Sam Bond has been given a job, let him have a chance to get on with the job, and let us get on and fight the Tories.'

14.
Rebuilding Liverpool 8

DESPITE ALL the obstacles enormous progress was made in alleviating the conditions of the black population of Liverpool 8. Just as important, an avenue was opened up through the council committees and the trade unions for the advancement of black workers.

Between 1984 and the end of 1985, the council had taken the following measures in Liverpool 8:

* Spent £48 million on housing—more than any other local authority's local housing budget.

* Rehoused 1730 families.

* Built 978 dwellings.

* Carried out large-scale improvements to 1782 dwellings.

* Demolished 2100 empty slums.

* Carried out major landscape work.

* Rebuilt 150 shops.

Facts, stubborn facts, speak louder than all the millions of words which the Black Caucus and its supporters have hurled against the council. After ten years of Liberal and Tory rule, Labour inherited the situation where less than one per cent of the council's workforce were black. The council housing allocation system operated by the Liberals was blatantly racist, contributing to a process which condemned most black families to ghetto conditions. Desperately seeking to exploit any issue, the Community Relations Council 'branded the city housing chiefs as racists' in early February 1985. Yet shortly before this, the Black Caucus had forcibly prevented Sam Bond from meeting and discussing with the Housing Director, Jim Burns, to discuss the issues of the housing conditions of the black population of Liverpool 8.

Of the 3000 meals-on-wheels provided daily by the previous Liberal-Tory council, only nine went to black families. While Labour was in power, the number of black people in receipt of home-helps and meals-on-wheels rose from 0.3 per cent to 13 per cent. Wherever the council was not obstructed by the NALGO boycott of Sam Bond, between 20 per cent and 30 per cent of new workers taken on were black. The NALGO leadership loudly proclaimed their support of 'positive action' to secure a better deal on jobs. Yet this same NALGO leadership with more concern for their own career prospects, stubbornly and viciously opposed any attempt to 'externally advertise' jobs in the middle and higher grades, a policy which would have secured the opportunity to advance the position of black workers.

While criticising most private sector employers, the Black Caucus have extolled the virtues of the Littlewoods empire. Following the 1981 riots, the Littlewoods Chair John Moores began a 'five per cent black' policy. This was hailed by the Black Caucus as 'an excellent example of a good employer'. This, of course, had nothing to do with the fact that the company employed a specialist 'race adviser' (a Caucus supporter) and moreover was prepared to dole out grants to favoured black groups, such as those in the Caucus. But the real record of Littlewoods goes no further than mere tokenism. Only 42 (or 0.5 per cent) of Littlewoods' 8000 strong workforce in Liverpool are black!

Physical Attacks

As was mentioned above in relation to the threats of violence on Derek Hatton and other councillors besieged in the Town Hall, the Black Caucus were prepared to go a lot further than mere words of denunciation of the council. On 8 February 1985, Sam Bond was physically attacked by two Black Caucus supporters who went to the municipal offices. When a friend of Sam's went to his assistance, the attackers loudly protested that they were being assaulted. Ever eager to maintain an even hand, Peter Cresswell, NALGO leader said, 'Obviously, the incident and the allegations of violence from both sides will be investigated. We always deplore violence in any form'!

When direct physical attacks failed to break Sam Bond, the Caucus threatened riots unless he was removed. Moving phantom armies in Liverpool 8, they declared on 12 February 1985: 'Solve the dispute over Sam Bond or we bring the city to a halt.' Shortly afterwards, a leading Caucus supporter, Liz Drysdale, was at the receiving end of threats at her workplace. According to the *Echo* (5 March 1985):

> She decided discretion was the better part of valour, when she was confronted by chain-wielding Richard Agailowura, an industrial tribunal heard. Drysdale stated: I couldn't get out of the room—there was only one way out. He [the potential assailant] backed off when she gave in and told staff to pay his wages—realising it was no good trying to discuss matters with him, she said. But then an emergency committee meeting voted to sack him after he refused to apologise about the incident.

In other words, faced with an actual physical assault Drysdale, like Derek Hatton in October, first of all agreed to the demands of the assailant, but quite correctly at a later stage withdrew from any 'agreement'.

Yet the attacks on labour movement figures like Derek Hatton, Tony Mulhearn and Sam Bond, were considered by the Caucus as the 'legitimate violence of the black community'. But when Black Caucus supporters were on the receiving end, then violence or threats of violence were condemned out of hand.

In March, April and May, the Black Caucus moved heaven and earth to have Sam Bond removed from his position. They denounced *Militant* for allegedly wishing to 'brainwash' Liverpool blacks. This was merely because Sam Bond began to group around him young blacks who responded to the socialist measures taken to combat racism in the city. Attempts to put a different position to that of the Black Caucus were construed by Steve French as 'going out and causing friction in the black community'.

Moves to channel attempts to combat racism through the Principal Race Relations Officer, Sam Bond, were immediately met with the charge that the council was 'attempting to financially strangle opposition to Sam Bond'. This lie was to be repeated many times in the next two years, and was regurgitated in the Black Caucus's book. The truth is that Liverpool 8 grant-aid projects and organisations received far more funding from the council than other organisations in any other area in

Merseyside. The funds to these organisations were upgraded to
£2 million per year, despite the feelings of many in the labour
movement that the financial running of these organisations was
never properly investigated and where there was considerable
cause for concern, as with the Charles Wootton Centre. This
investigation, regrettably, was never done by the Labour council
or Labour group for fear that the Caucus would use any action
to muddy the waters on the Sam Bond issue.

The myth that the black community were united behind the
Black Caucus in their opposition to Sam Bond was shattered in
early March 1985 when the Afro-Asian Caribbean Standing
Committee declared that Sam Bond should be given a chance to
show whether he could do the job as Principal Race Relations
Officer. Subsequently 21 black organisations publicly dissociated
themselves from the Black Caucus. To the chagrin of the
Caucus, the Commission for Racial Equality also met Sam Bond
in London in a follow-up meeting to a critical report of
Liverpool council's race policies. 'We have been betrayed,'
declared the Caucus in a statement printed in the *Post.*

Any attempt by black or labour movement organisations to
solve the dispute over Sam Bond and move forward to tackle the
terrible social conditions facing the black population in
Liverpool 8 was sabotaged by the Caucus. But Sam Bond's
message and that of the council was having an effect on the
more discerning sections of the black population. In early May
Sam Bond declared: 'I am fed up at seeing the Black Caucus
putting itself forward as the representative of the black
community, because it is not.' This brought the response from
the Chair of the Black Caucus: 'We don't claim to represent the
entire black community. We are a caucus group, unconnected
with other organisations, trying to improve life for black people
in this city.' This flew in the face of everything that they had said
before and which they would say in the future.

Clinging to the coat-tails of the Caucus, the Liberals, in a
hypocritical *volte-face* on their previous attitude towards the
population of Liverpool 8, attacked the council: 'Liberal Richard
Pine accused Labour's deputy leader, Derek Hatton, of ensuring
"only tame blacks" got jobs.' (*Post* 8 May). He was cheered on by
Caucus members who shouted down Labour spokespersons at a
meeting to organise a new Equal Opportunities Committee. The
actions of the Caucus delayed the establishment of a Chinese

Unit composed of three social workers and headed by a Chinese senior social worker. This decision had an enormously deleterious effect on the position of the 7000 Chinese-speaking population of Liverpool, the second biggest Chinese community in the country, after London.

Thug Violence Against Labour

Even 'non-political' semi-social events organised by the city council were disrupted by the Caucus. Thus the tribute to Liverpool and Everton Football teams by Derek Hatton at an event organised by the council was greeted with jeers and catcalls from 30 supporters of the Caucus.

It was precisely at this moment that Neil Kinnock decided to intervene in Liverpool, not to support the stand of the council against the Tory government, but to give succour to its enemies in the Black Caucus. He agreed to visit the city to discuss with Caucus supporters. This enraged not only the labour movement, but also 17 black groups who signed a letter of protest. But it emboldened the Caucus supporters to engage on an even more disruptive campaign. This culminated with the Caucus hurling eggs at Labour spokesperson, Derek Hatton, and others during the council meeting on 22 May.

Predictably, the *Echo* sanctimoniously declared: 'A plague on all your houses.' Once again it reworked the theme of '*Militant* violence' even though *Militant* was on the receiving end:

> Protest, demo and yah-boo tactics like shouting down your opponent, are the life-blood of the Militant Tendency approach to politics. Yesterday the *Militant* leaders of the Liverpool City Council were given some of their own medicine. No one can condone the riot staged in the council chamber by leaders of the city's Black Caucus... It is, however, understandable that there is bitter frustration among the black community. Mr Sam Bond was brought here from London and foisted upon them as chief race relations officer in what they see as a blatant political appointment. (*Echo* 22 May.)

Labour anger boiled over at this, just the latest of the *Echo's* lying attacks. The District Labour Party's statement, for once, was printed in the *Echo*:

> Liverpool Labour leaders were totally united today in the condemnation of the Editor of the *Liverpool Echo*, Mr Christopher

Oakley, for what councillor Derek Hatton described as 'the most disgraceful editorial that's been published by the *Echo*—and given their consistent hate campaign against Liverpool council, that has taken some doing'.

It is not, never has been, and never will be the policy of Liverpool Labour Council or *Militant* supporters to shout down opponents or engage in blatant physical intimidation and violence as was alleged in Wednesday's *Echo* editorial (*Echo* 24 March).

The council leaders and District Labour Party also attacked the *Echo* for: 'giving tacit support for violence directed against the councillors by the Black Caucus, a group of 25 people which is totally unrepresentative of the black community as a whole. This is a new low in the *Echo's* history of gutter journalism, and they are using the Black Caucus to discredit the council.' Meanwhile, confidence in Sam Bond was growing, with over 240 people from the Toxteth area visiting him by the end of May.

It was the council and Sam Bond who were to the fore in highlighting and campaigning against racism. In July 1985 he warned about the increasing race attacks, including petrol bombings, which had been taking place in the city particularly against Liverpool's Asian community. As explained previously, it was the Liverpool labour movement and the LPYS in particular who combated the fascist National Front's attempt to organise demonstrations and conferences in Liverpool.

Meanwhile Caucus leader Steve French declared: 'The consequences for the Labour Party are dire indeed, if, as the May 1986 local elections approach, this dispute [the Sam Bond affair] is not resolved.' (*Echo*, 17 July 1985) Together with the Liberals, the Black Caucus wished (although not openly) for the defeat of Labour in the May 1986 elections. They were to be bitterly disappointed, along with all the other enemies of the council.

The hysteria and the attacks, including physical attacks, on Labour spokespersons increased in inverse proportion to the narrowing of the base of the Black Caucus. Steve French gave succour to the government with the statement: 'Liverpool Black Caucus members have warned the city's Labour leadership not to look for their support in the rates fight with the government.' (*Post*, 30 July). This threat was backed up with a vicious attack at a Labour Party meeting on 30 July in Toxteth. Even the *Daily*

Mail commented: 'Reporters were threatened as they tried to enter the building, and left-wing leaflets and newspapers were ripped up by the activists and strewn across the street.' The Black Caucus thugs shouted down Labour spokesperson Tony Byrne, while a black female LPYS member was assaulted and one of the speakers, Councillor Felicity Dowling, was spat at continuously by Black Caucus supporters.

Two days later, Labour organised a meeting in Shorefields Comprehensive School, Dingle Vale, close to the Toxteth area, to underline Labour's right to organise democratic public meetings. Tony Byrne told the meeting of 150: 'This is a show of solidarity from the people who were there last night. I would like to compliment our members of the Party for their bravery under the most outrageous threats of violence.'

When the council took on 100 school leavers in permanent jobs, Derek Hatton declared: 'We have often been criticised for having only about one per cent of our 31,000 workforce from the ethnic minorities. The Black Caucus says we should have seven per cent. The fact that 20 of today's 100 are black is a clear indication that our policies are working and the Black Caucus is out of touch.' One of those taken on, a young working-class girl, declared to the *Post*: 'If it was not for this, we would all have gone on to the dole.'

Undaunted by the outrage felt by the Liverpool labour movement, the Black Caucus continued their campaign of intimidation and violence. At a meeting organised in early August by the Community Relations Council, Derek Hatton was invited to speak. On his way into the meeting, he was viciously punched by a well-known Black Caucus supporter. He was knocked to the ground with a wound over an ear. Nevertheless, he still went into the meeting and despite repeated heckling attempted to speak to the people who had assembled there.

This attack was the last straw for the Liverpool labour movement. Breaking off all further contact with the Black Caucus, the city council declared: 'The city council is determined that any group of people in Liverpool has a right to listen to and debate the council's case without undemocratic interference from a group of thugs who are prepared to break meetings up.' When Labour organised proper stewarding and defence of meetings, this was denounced by the *Echo* as 'heavy-weight guards'.

One Year Contract Retreat

As a means of countering the inevitable propaganda barrage of
the Black Caucus and its supporters, the city council outlined in
a special letter, the background to the dispute. It detailed the
discussions and negotiations which had taken place behind the
scenes and indicated that the council leadership were prepared
to make substantial concessions in order to meet the objections
of the Black Caucus:

> The issue of Mr Sam Bond's qualifications was subsequently the
> subject of further discussions with Black Caucus representatives, in
> the presence of the Liverpool bishops. In an attempt to make a
> positive response, the council took the unprecedented step of
> agreeing to put Mr Bond on a temporary, one-year contract and
> monitor his work, on the understanding that the contract would not
> be renewed if either the council, the trade unions or the black
> groups were not satisfied with his performance.
> At this time it was overwhelmingly accepted that Mr Bond must at
> least be given the chance to prove whether the council's policy could
> successfully begin to tackle racism. It was recognised that it would
> have been totally unjust to terminate Mr Bond's contract before his
> commitment and experience could be tried and tested.

The Black Caucus remained unsatisfied and refused to accept
this arrangement. Many others, including *Militant* supporters,
were totally opposed to it because it was seen as unjust to Sam
Bond. However, although Sam Bond could easily have
established in a year's work his suitability for the post, the
philosophy of the Caucus remained 'rule or ruin'. They were
determined to have their own nominee in the job at all
costs.

What is more, despite the council's concession, the Black
Caucus now moved into increasing opposition to the socialist
policies of the council. They became open supporters of the
right wing within the Labour Party, declaring that *Militant* was
'the enemy within the labour movement'. They were using the
language of Thatcher's diatribes against the miners. However,
in their book *The Racial Politics of Militant*, they were forced to
concede the overwhelming support for the city council within
the labour movement: '*Militant's* formal demise has largely come
about through external pressure and intervention from the
Labour Party leadership and from the court case brought by the

District Auditor.' They also had a strange ally in Kenneth Oxford, unelected Chief Constable of Merseyside, who slandered *Militant* supporters by suggesting that street clashes in September 1985 were a direct product of 'outside political influences'. He said that a *Militant* leaflet distributed in the area may have created the situation! This leaflet was outlining the programme of the city council to combat racism.

The increasing stridency of the Black Caucus and their supporters was shown in September when Caucus supporters completely disrupted a rally against unemployment at the Pier Head, shouting down Eric Heffer when he attempted to speak on the problems confronting the population of the city.

'We want Sam Bond!'

Early in September, the Black Caucus called a meeting which was attended by over 600 members of the Liverpool 8 black community. The intention of the Caucus was to denounce Sam Bond and berate the city council, but this plan failed dismally during the course of the meeting. Several people in the audience insisted that the Caucus had no right to put themselves forward as community representatives. By the time Sam Bond arrived at the meeting, the majority of the audience were chanting 'We want Sam Bond.' At this point the organisers dismantled the microphones and told people to leave. Following the meeting the Merseyside Action Group was formed. This comprised a group of black organisations who opposed the Black Caucus and supported the stand of the city council on the issue of Sam Bond.

It was against this background that Neil Kinnock launched his vicious attack on Liverpool City Council at the 1985 Labour Party Conference on 1 October. On the morning of his speech an open letter from the Liverpool bishops in *The Times* specifically attacked the appointment of Sam Bond. The bishops were, in turn, answered by the Merseyside Action Group who denounced the attempts by the Church hierarchy to link *Militant* supporters to the clashes which had occurred in Toxteth. In the wake of his Labour Party Conference speech, Kinnock refused to speak to the Merseyside Action Group, preferring to maintain links with the Black Caucus.

Nevertheless, on 1 November, Sam Bond and the Liverpool labour movement were able to mark the first anniversary of his appointment as race relations officer. The vile abuse and intimidation had not succeeded in breaking the will of either Sam Bond or the city council.

While proceeding with the practical measures of improving and ameliorating the conditions of the working people of Liverpool 8, the city council organised a propaganda counter-offensive against the Black Caucus. This, in turn, drove the Black Caucus to more out-and-out abuse and lies. In December 1985 they accused 'the *Militant* dominated city council' of 'racism, bribery, intimidation, misappropriation of funds and appointment for political reasons of unqualified race relations staff'. These lies were carried in every journal which opposed *Militant*.

The Merseyside Anti-Apartheid group, dominated by sympathisers of the Caucus, organised a demonstration in February 1986 and issued threats against *Militant*:

> We regret to have to inform you that owing to the strong feelings expressed by the Liverpool 8 community, we feel that we will not be able to offer any protection to individuals who attend the demonstration...selling *Militant* papers or other material associated with *Militant*, or who display the *Militant* banner.

Needless to say, *Militant* supporters refused to accept this intimidation and marched and sold their material on the demonstration.

Throughout 1986 and 1987, a series of reports was produced, attempting to create the impression that Liverpool City Council and the District Labour Party were 'racist'. Thus the Caucus found new bedfellows in Murdoch's *Sunday Times* which declared in June 1986: 'Liverpool Council to face race enquiry.' In November, the *Daily Telegraph* declared: 'Black leaders accuse Mersey left of racism.' Later that month, the *Observer* declared: 'Blacks accuse *Militant* city hall of racism.' The *Caribbean Times* in the same month declared, 'Militant Tendency is racist'. Not to be outdone, the *Echo* declared in February 1987: 'City's appalling racism record'. It went on: 'Racist...that is the accusation made against Liverpool City Council by a Commons Select Committee of MPs. The council's record in employing members of black and other racial groups is described as abysmal.' All of these reports stemmed from a House of Commons Committee Report on racial discrimination and from the Black Caucus's own book. Not one paper, apart from *Militant*, mentioned that one of the six members of the House of Commons Committee which condemned Liverpool City Council was Tory MP John Gorst, who had made his mark by leading the attacks on the Asian women strikers at Grunwick's in 1977! At no stage did the Caucus seem to wonder why papers out of Murdoch's stable which also prints the blatantly racist *Sun*, or the likes of John Gorst, were echoing their arguments.

Epitaph

One would think that after such an avalanche of criticism against the city council that the Black Caucus supporters would find some echo within the black community of Liverpool 8. Yet when they stood against Labour in the Granby ward (home of most of Liverpool's black community) in the May 1986 council elections, they were decisively beaten. Their candidate, along with the Liberals, made the Sam Bond issue a central feature of the campaign, but Labour secured its biggest ever vote in the ward. The Black Caucus candidate received 477 votes to Labour's 2287.

Despite the torrent of filth and criticism, the record of Liverpool City Council, with Sam Bond playing a key role, stands as a monument to what the labour movement can do in beginning to combat racism. Apart from the measures in Liverpool 8 mentioned above, the council introduced throughout the city radical reforming measures in a whole number of fields. Thus it appointed race advisers to all the community schools. It introduced the first ever anti-racist code of practice for schools in Liverpool and co-ordinated parent support groups for primary schools in Liverpool 8. It introduced further childcare facilities for Liverpool 8 families, and also mother-tongue facilities in nurseries. It built a fully equipped modern sports centre in Liverpool 8 and upgraded youth facilities so that now the majority of such facilities in the city are situated in Liverpool 8. It massively improved the funding of the youth projects within the area and it funded at least 32 voluntary organisations in Liverpool 8. It also campaigned for further government funding in an attempt to set up an ethnic library service, a Chinese social work unit, a multi-cultural support centre and a language centre.

The Liverpool City Council spent more per head on the black population of Liverpool 8 than any other council in the country. This is the real epitaph of the three years of the Liverpool City Council and of Sam Bond in combating the long, historical legacy of racism which has scarred Liverpool. The opponents of Labour were not able to defeat them in open, honest and democratic debate. They had to wait for the dismissal by the courts of the heroic 47 councillors in March 1987, after which the Liberals, who had never been elected to office, dismissed Sam Bond from his position. But this is merely the end of one chapter in the continuing struggle to raise up the black population of Liverpool 8. That task cannot be undertaken by self-appointed petit-bourgeois black 'leaders'. Only the labour movement can mobilise behind its banner the black workers of Liverpool 8, particularly the youth, and weld them together with the white working class in one movement to benefit the working people of the city as a whole.

15.
On the Brink

THE MONTH of September 1985 proved to be a decisive turning point in the Liverpool struggle. Isolated by the capitulation of other councils, the Liverpool labour movement was thrown back on to its own resources. While the National Local Authority shop stewards Combine Committee had indicated that they were still prepared to support Liverpool in the event of a confrontation, any decisions had to take into account the retreat of the other councils. Moreover, Kenneth Baker and Patrick Jenkin continued their refusal to help Liverpool. This, together with the setting of the 9 per cent rate, meant that money to pay wages and provide services would run out at a certain stage.

At this decisive juncture, Thomas McMahon, the new, 'tough' District Auditor, stepped in. He demanded that the council either cut its services or spending, and go to the High Court to get the original rate quashed in order to set a new one that would in effect pay the bills, or start preparing redundancy notices for its 30,000 employees. Thus the idea of issuing 'redundancy notices', which was to have such a baleful effect on the course of the struggle, had originated with the District Auditor and been echoed by Treasury and council officials.

Capitalisation

The opponents of the council, both at national and local level, including the white-collar union leaders, argued for 'capitalisation' in order to temporarily 'dig the council out of a hole'. This meant spending money available for capital projects (eg new building) instead of certain areas of revenue (day to day) spending. The City Treasurer had identified £27 million of housing repairs and maintenance for the two years 1984-5 and 1985-6, which, though normally revenue spending, could be classified as capital work. As long as it was paid from existing capital receipts (eg income from council house sales) and not from borrowing, it would avoid the limit the government placed on the city's capital spending. If enough capital receipts could be found, this could reduce the revenue budget by £27 million, reducing the overall expenditure of £255 million, which in turn, would mean that government grants would begin to flow back, enabling the council to reach the end of the financial year before the money ran out. This, the preferred solution of the national labour and trade-union leaders, could have solved the immediate financial crisis, but at the cost of the housebuilding programme and of the jobs that it created both in the public and private sector, something the council was determined to resist.

Prison to Paradise

Increasingly, even the perjured local press and media had to reflect the delight of those who had benefited from the housing programme. On 12 September the *Echo* expressed the genuine appreciation of many towards the improvements introduced by the council:

> Margaret Dolphin has just moved home. It was a short move, but it took her from prison to paradise. Prison was a grotty tenement building targeted by mindless vandals; paradise is a spanking new, two-bedroomed house with its own garden. 'It is marvellous. It is like a million dollars to me', said Margaret, 62, as she proudly showed off her new home in Leason Street, just off Scotland Road.

The article was a complete vindication of the Urban Regeneration Strategy and the concept which lay behind it. Even the *Echo* was constrained to comment:

> More than 3000 families have been rehoused, and work is continuing on another 3000 properties in the urban regeneration strategy which is designed to provide houses with gardens, straightforward street layouts, improved street lighting, landscaped areas and parks and better community facilities. [Tony Byrne said] It is the most important programme which has happened in Liverpool since the war. We are creating environments where people can live happy lives and bring up their families, and by doing this we are creating work in the private sector.

The *Echo* commented:

> The figures back up the proud claims; a £3.5 million road improvement scheme, in conjunction with Merseyside County Council, 100 community shops improved, £140 million worth of building contracts which have generated 12,000 jobs.

How could the *Echo* comment otherwise, given the delight of ordinary workers:

> 'It is just like the old days', added Margaret, whose old school friend Annie Devine has moved in two doors down, 'I think they are gorgeous, especially after living in a flat for 30 years', said Annie (60)...'I lived in the Great Mersey Street flats and they were terrible. We had awful damp coming up from two empty flats below, and we only had a little verandah. It is a lot quieter here. It is marvellous having a garden, and I would not be without one now. I do not think that those other flats we lived in should have ever been built.'

The *Echo* painted an almost idyllic scene: 'Neighbours lean over garden walls and fences for a chat as the community spirit flows again.'

But there was no such 'community spirit' displayed by the *Echo*, and *Post* and the national media towards those who had rescued workers from the slums. Capitalisation, if adopted, would have maintained a situation in which thousands of working-class families were condemned to years of damp and sometimes vermin-infested hovels which passed for homes in parts of the city. Many of the white-collar union leaders in particular were to put what they falsely considered were the short-term interests of their own members and their jobs before those of the wider working-class. The councillors sought to defend all jobs, those in the private sector building programme as well as council jobs and services. In the period leading up to September, the leadership of NUPE and the NUT consistently opposed any action in support of the council, and yet the councillors risked surcharge, with a fine of £106,000 hanging over their heads, bankruptcy and possible imprisonment to defend the jobs of teachers and NUPE workers, amongst others. In the face of the implacable refusal of the government to give further assistance, the councillors decided to approach the government for a £25 million loan, which would allow it to balance the books. At the same time, they made contingency plans for when the money ran out. The council's legal and financial experts had advised them that under the 1978 Employment Protection Act, once the money ran out, they would be forced to terminate the contracts of all council employees. Failure to do so could have left the councillors personally liable for the £23 million 'redundancy pay' which the 30,000 local authority workers were entitled to. Under local government law, a council cannot lay off workers but has to terminate their contracts, which in effect is redundancy. Moreover, the City Treasurer advised that failure to act 'legally' by issuing the redundancy notices would have resulted in the Public Works Loans Board refusing permission for Liverpool to raise loans on the money markets to pay for day to day expenditure. This in turn would have meant that the council would have run out of money within a few weeks. Therefore workers would receive no wages after this period. The 'legal' device of redundancy notices would at least allow wages to be paid until the end of 1985. This would have allowed time to build the campaign to force the government to pay back the cash stolen from the city.

The ruling class has deliberately framed local government law in order to entangle councils in such legal niceties. Perhaps if the Liverpool City Council had been entirely made up of *Militant* supporters there would have been no argument as the Marxists would have gone the whole way. But the councillors had felt let down, particularly by the refusal of the white-collar union leaders to fully back them. The Labour group decided on the 'tactic' of issuing 90-day redundancy notices to the 30,000 strong workforce to gain that period as a breathing space in order to build the campaign. It was absurd to suggest, as the press and to their shame the national trade-union leaders subsequently did, that 30,000 workers were to be sacked. The *raison d'être* of the struggle was precisely to *defend* jobs.

However, the issuing of 'redundancy notices' turned out to be a major tactical error. The great military strategist Clausewitz once said that 'military warfare needs the kind of mathematics of a Euclid or a Newton'. More simply, political algebra is necessary. For anybody leading a major political struggle, it is necessary to visualize, not just how the active workers will view the problem, but how your enemies can exploit your statements, strategy and tactics.

When the tactic was explained to those workers who could be reached, there was support and understanding. In particular there was widespread support from among the manual workers. For the wider population of Liverpool, for people nationally, and even for the majority of the 30,000 local authority workforce, however, political understanding is gleaned primarily from the fragments of news which are snatched from the television or the press.

As soon as the issue of 'redundancy notices' was raised, a hue and cry which dwarfed all other campaigns, was set up by the national press. On 6 September, the *Daily Express* screamed: 'Threat to sack 30,000 workers.' *The Times* waded in: 'Liverpool to lay off 30,000 staff.' The *Sun* reported the 'redundancies' as an accomplished fact: '30,000 workers sacked by rebel city council'. The predictable headline in the *Echo* was: 'Happy Christmas—Get your Cards'. Even the ultra-left *Newsline*, journal of the tiny Workers Revolutionary Party stated: 'Liverpool workers face sack'. Kenneth Baker, Environment Minister, while making ritualistic statements about the council's 'irresponsibility' nevertheless said that he would reconsider the request by the council to borrow £25 million. This however was subsequently turned down as the Tories decided to put the screws on Liverpool.

The 'redundancy notices' issue split the leaders of the council workforce. Many white-collar workers were genuinely concerned that if their contracts were terminated, and in the meantime the threat of surcharge brought a Liberal-Tory coalition to power, many would not be re-employed. These fears were well-founded, as the *Echo* pointed out that: 'the Liberal Sir Trevor has already warned that the "Jobs for the Boys" tactics have been noted and that known Militants would be sacked if his party took control'. However, the white-collar union leaders did not advance a viable alternative to the scheme of the council. Nothing was proposed which could offer a way out to councillors who were faced with a £23 million surcharge for defending their members' jobs and conditions.

The issue came to a head at a meeting of the Joint Shop Stewards Committee on 7 September. After a long and bitter debate, the white-collar unions won the day. The acceptance of the redundancy plan was narrowly beaten by 51 votes to 48. Now instead of the money running out in December, it would run out in a matter of weeks. However, unless the Labour councillors at least appeared to be 'issuing redundancy notices', they would still be financially liable. In order to prevent this and to safeguard the councillors, the council workforce decided to surround the Town Hall and to prevent the council meeting from taking place.

At the Labour Party's Local Government Committee, the Chair, David Blunkett, promised that the next Labour government would introduce legislation to lift any penalties which fell on the 81 councillors involved (in Liverpool and Lambeth). He said:

> This action confirms a long-held view that the audit service is being used as a political tool by the Tory government...I want to give notice now that any penalties imposed on the councillors will be lifted by the next Labour government (*Labour Weekly*, 13 September 1985).

The *Daily Telegraph* screamed: 'No case to indemnify.' Ever sensitive to the democratic workings of the Labour Party, it declared:

> It has only now, following the District Auditor's decision to surcharge Lambeth and Liverpool Labour councillors, become clear that it is Labour Party policy to indemnify councillors against these surcharges. It slipped through [at the 1984 Labour Party Conference] without even a vote, no doubt while everyone was concentrating on the miners.

On 13 September, the controller of the Audit Commission, John Banham, attacked the 'lawlessness and wilful misconduct of councillors at Labour- controlled Liverpool and Lambeth.' (*Guardian*, 14 September 1985). Banham at the time, and since, has been at pains to declare that the Audit Commission was 'non-political'. But this body was set up under Thatcher's government in 1983 to coordinate the auditing of local government. It claimed to have set itself the goal of weeding out 'overspending' and inefficiency in local government. However in 1984-5 it employed 596 people at a cost of £17.5 million. In 1985-6 it employed 600 and cost taxpayers almost £22 million. This worked out at almost £30,000 per worker in 1984-5 and almost £37,000 per worker in the year 1985-6, an increase of 21 per cent–about seven times the rate of inflation. After doing the dirty work for Thatcher in local government, Banham in 1987 went off to become director-general of the CBI.

His replacement was David Cooksey, who had been associated with three Scottish manufacturing companies in 1983 in which he had the majority of shares and which went into receivership, owing £500,000 and making 85 people lose their jobs. Not a hint of 'surcharge' against this worthy, and yet the people who were saving jobs and defending working people were being hounded by the agency which he presided over.

Again the *Echo*, in the midst of the 'redundancy notices' crisis, reported the delight of working people at the change which had resulted from the measures of the city council. On 13 September, they carried a photograph of Tony Mulhearn and council chair Hugh Dalton being toasted by council tenants who had been rehoused in the Garston area. It declared: 'For decades, the people of Shakespeare, Otway and Byron Streets in Garston, have lived in some of the worst slums in the city.' Working people have very modest aims, as the statement of one pensioner showed: 'This area is my home, and I wouldn't want to leave. But our old houses were disgusting. Now I've got everything I want in life—my friends around me and a beautiful new home.' A young mother of two said, 'We are one, big, happy family here, and I wanted Peter and Stephen to be part of that. We could never have been happy in the old slums, but now everything is perfect.'

The *Echo* carried this under the headline 'The happiest stories are in your *Echo*.' There would have been fewer happy stories if capitalisation, which the *Echo* supported, had been implemented. The imaginative scheme of Liverpool City Council gave just a glimpse of what would have been possible on the basis of a national housing plan which involved the complete eradication of the slums.

All-out Strike?

The Liverpool City Council Joint Shop Stewards Committee (JSSC) met and vetoed capitalisation. Instead, they proposed an all-out strike to force the government to aid the council. NALGO attempted to drag its heels, insisting on the withdrawal of the 'redundancy notices'. Meanwhile, a ferocious campaign was launched by the media to break the spirit of council workers. The *Daily Mail*, once more in the vanguard, in an editorial (16 September) declared: 'Playing Trot Poker with the city's fate.' They were urging the government to prepare for war:

The government is quite right to be ready to mobilise all its resources for whatever might happen...Nobody should underestimate the risks of such an unprecedented modern confrontation between the British state and the socialist revolutionaries entrenched in the crumbling structures of one of its once great and now stricken cities.

Reflecting on the changed conditions in which the battle was taking place that year, it commented: 'Last year, Tory ministers had Arthur Scargill and the striking miners to contend with and they weren't anxious to fight on two fronts.' However, the ruling class were still not entirely confident of the outcome of such a struggle despite the end of the miners' strike. This was indicated by the comments of the *Daily Mail*: 'There is this year all too recently the horror of Handsworth [an area of Birmingham where savage riots had recently taken place] to brand in the political consciousness the ease with which mob criminality can engulf a decaying urban landscape.' Its front page (16 September) declared: 'Plans for troops in crisis city'. On the basis of inside information it went on:

'An evacuation programme to transfer people under the council's direct control to the Isle of Man. This would cover those in detention centres, approved schools and council care. An empty hospital on the island is among buildings already requisitioned.

Kenneth Baker denied reports of the possible use of troops in the event of council services collapsing, but admitted: 'The government has general contingency plans for the maintenance of essential services throughout the country. It's up to the council to put things right.' The *Daily Express* once more characterised Liverpool as a 'City in a shambles'. But reflecting the fear that things could get out of hand it stated: 'There are many battles ahead. But few can now underestimate the potential seriousness of the ruling left's strategy in Liverpool.' The press were at one in declaring that Baker must remain 'firm'. The *Daily Telegraph* commented:

He must ensure that Liverpool fully realises the consequences of voting in *Militant* and that central government is not prepared to pay for the consequence of the council's policies. Yet he cannot allow the administration of the city to collapse completely. For the time being Liverpool should be left to sweat it out. Commissioners, if they are needed, should be sent in later rather than sooner.

Threats of Commissioners, of legal action, of action by the government and the District Auditor, were all hurled at the councillors. *The Times* reported: 'Asked if it was legal to call a strike this way, Mr Lowes (Chair of the JSSC) said: "I don't know, and I don't particularly care".'

The Liberals and their partners once more had the whiff of power. They were looking for an early demise of the council, and the sharing of power with the Tories. They even offered to collaborate with the Labour 'moderates' in a 'grand coalition' to run the city. The *Sun*, in its usual sober fashion, had an 'exclusive' of a 'secret plot'. On 17 September, they had a headline: 'Red Wreckers in Secret Plot to Seize a City.' Labour were supposed to have had a plan which involved 'barricades in the streets, businesses paralysed, rubbish war on wealthy, schools and courts shut'.

Occasionally, behind the hysteria, the capitalist press would cast some light on the real intentions of the government and the background to the crisis: 'Certainly the fact that the two batches of certificates were issued to councillors in Lambeth and Liverpool on the same day last week seems to suggest that for the first time two Auditors had coordinated their actions rather than working as individuals,' (*Guardian* 17 September). This disposes of the claim that the Audit Commission was entirely neutral and not a political tool of the Thatcher government.

The decision of the JSSC to recommend all-out strike action initiated a period of unprecedented and widespread political debate that spread beyond the council workforce to all corners of the city. The pioneers of Trotskyism in the city in the 1930s had wistfully looked towards the day when mass meetings under their influence would take place in the Liverpool boxing stadium. Now the outline of this scenario was beginning to take shape. One section of the workforce after another trooped towards the stadium to discuss and debate the merits and demerits of an all-out strike. Local cafe owners and pubs ran out of food and beer as workers poured into and out of the stadium. At one stage it was even suggested that a mass meeting of the full 30,000 council workers would take place at Goodison Park, home of Everton Football Club. This plan, however, was vetoed by the white-collar leaders who insisted on separate meetings.

The first group of workers to take a decision were the teachers. A mass meeting at the Philharmonic Hall heard speeches from Derek Hatton and others calling for strike action. Labour speakers outlined Liverpool's programme for defending education. Unfortunately, the teachers, miseducated over a whole period by their leaders, who were opposing all-out strike action, voted narrowly not to come out on strike. This caused great bitterness amongst other workers and was a considerable boost to the government and the opponents of the council.

Unlike the manual workers, a significant section of teachers lived outside the city boundaries and were putting their own narrow interests before those of the workers of the city and particularly the youth whom they taught. Jim Ferguson, the Liverpool Branch Secretary of the NUT and member of the Communist Party, even declared that it would be 'unfair to deprive the city's school-children, many of whom had reached a crucial time in their education', by going on strike! This statement could have been lifted from any hostile capitalist newspaper during the teachers' strikes in the following year.

Sensing that the initiative was passing out of the hands of the council, Kenneth Baker piled on the pressure. He rejected out-of-hand permission for the council to borrow £25 million on the money markets but this rejection, rather than deterring the manual workers, only reinforced their determination. GMBATU members, at a series of mass meetings, voted by 4345 to 2934 in favour of all-out strike action. UCATT stewards voted by 54 to 4 to recommend strike action, which was upheld by mass meetings. The TGWU also voted by massive majorities in favour. A majority of the manual workers had now voted in favour of strike action and despite their public display of confidence, the ruling class in these crucial days were not at all convinced that they could control the situation.

David Steel, on behalf of the Liberals in Merseyside, launched another broadside on 22 September, threatening to take the council leaders to court. He also urged the government to take whatever 'legal action' was necessary to dismiss the council. His local acolyte, David Alton, called for a 'rainbow coalition' of Tories, Liberals, and Labour 'moderates' who would support massive job cuts. Included in this 'rainbow coalition' were the self-appointed 'leaders' of the black community, the infamous Black Caucus who had used violence against Labour representatives. But, even now, despite all the talk of 'chaos', the Liberals and the Tory government hesitated to use legal action against the council.

Every voice seemed to be raised against the council from the hysterical *Sun*, right through to *The Times* and embracing the trade-union and labour leaders. The *Sun* (21 September) quoted a neighbour of Derek Hatton: 'He is a hated man and known as the Thing of Thingwall Road'. Another, from the safety of Woolton declared: 'Militants—I could shoot the lot of them. My daughter Alison is about to sit her 'O' Levels. I am very very worried. Our children read newspapers. They feel they are in a hopeless situation already. Even if they pass exams, what work will there be for them?' *The Times* (21 September) however admitted that the problems of Liverpool were not created by the 'Militants': 'The city of Liverpool would have faced gross fiscal difficulties in this decade, regardless of who might rule in the municipal chambers.' But this rare admission was followed in the same article with the demand that Baker must punish the whole city for daring to vote for the 'Militants':

> Liverpool must undergo its trial...now, and perhaps for much of the Autumn, the city and the watching nation must be educated by the example it wants to make of itself. Mr Hatton and Labour made their decisions in their budgets for this year. The results are on their heads'.

The Times confirmed here what Leon Trotsky referred to as the 'cold cruelty' of the British ruling class in its dealings with its colonial slaves. It was now displaying the same feelings towards the population of the fifth largest city in Britain. The next few months were to show that the policies of the ruling class were to inflict the maximum suffering on the most vulnerable sections of the population of Liverpool, using this in turn as a weapon with which to attack the Liverpool Labour movement.

'Disown Them'

Pressure was stepped up on the Labour leaders to 'disown' *Militant* and the Liverpool labour movement. This phrase, first used in an editorial by the *Daily Mail* on 23 September, became

Kinnock's stock phrase during the ensuing crisis. The national union leaders exerted pressure on the regional officials, particularly those in the GMBATU. The 200 shop stewards representing GMBATU members working for Liverpool City Council were written to by the regional officials, urging them to oppose the all-out strike. Ian Lowes' rejoinder reflected the attitude of the majority of the GMBATU stewards: 'I will be advising members to ignore the region, which has an appalling record over saving jobs on Merseyside. All they will be doing is to lead us to sign on the dole.'

Maxwell's *Daily Mirror* outdid even the *Sun* in a typically 'balanced' editorial on 24 September headlined: *'Militant Madness'*. Bending the truth it declared:

> The roots of the call for a strike lie not so much in Tory cuts as in the purpose of the Militant Tendency-dominated council. Other cities in Britain have been as badly hurt by government policies. But all...compromised rather than cause chaos in the cities they rule. Why is Liverpool different? Because it is dominated by Militant Tendency...Despite what they proudly proclaim about their achievements since coming to power, policies they have pursued have hurt most the homeless, the poor, the unemployed and the children.

Thus, even the well-documented achievements of the council were completely denied by multi-millionaire 'socialist' Robert Maxwell, such was his hatred of what *Militant* and the city council represented. Derek Hatton was attacked as a 'Red Messiah, destined to bring on the revolution.' The Communist Party joined hands with the *Daily Mirror* when they stated on the eve of the proposed strike:

> Many union officials are concerned about being bounced into strike action, without adequate consultation with council leaders. They want to examine any alternatives that may avoid serious industrial chaos within the city. (*Morning Star*, 29 September)

In a statement which angered all the best militants in the GMBATU who had fought against the dead hand of bureaucratism over years they also commented: 'The dangerous ultra leftism within the struggle at Liverpool was again reflected yesterday in attacks on regional officials of the GMBATU by Deputy Council Leader Derek Hatton, and by the Joint Shop

Stewards Chairman, Ian Lowes, on the unions which are not supporting the strike call.' These union leaders had played a baleful role in the course of the struggle over the previous two years. They were now to play a decisive role in derailing the call for all-out strike action in the period leading up to 25 September.

All-out Strike Rejected

Fifty-eight per cent of GMBATU members voted for strike action. UCATT members voted by three to one and the TGWU also voted by a good majority to come out on strike. Of the manual unions, only the EETPU had voted against. The decision as to whether the council workforce would undertake an all-out struggle was lying in the balance pending the decision of leaders of NUPE and NALGO. But the NUPE leader, Jane Kennedy, who was later to attack the District Labour Party for its 'lack of democracy', refused even to sanction a vote on the issue amongst the 2700 NUPE members. This 'super-democrat' was prepared to support a one-day strike, but urged her members not to participate in the all-out stoppage. She did everything to whip up opposition towards *Militant* and the council leadership among NUPE members. Thus, in the same issue of NUPE's *Advice and Information News-sheet* which urged support for a one-day strike, it quoted in full the anti-*Militant* witch-hunting resolution that had been passed at the NUPE conference. This behaviour, however, was not lost on the low-paid NUPE members whose jobs were at stake in this battle. In the aftermath of the 25 September strike, these workers, many of them very low-paid women workers, almost mobbed Jane Kennedy at an unprecedented NUPE branch meeting. Hundreds turned out, blocking Dale Street and forcing the NUPE leadership to abandon the meeting.

The leadership of the college lecturers' union, NATFHE, who similarly opposed the militant stand of the council, also refused to allow their members to vote. The decision as to whether to go ahead with the strike rested then on the shoulders of NALGO.

NALGO leaders Graham Burgess and Peter Cresswell (the former a Communist Party member) were on record in support of the defence of their members' jobs by the city council.

However, this 'support' took a curious form. For months, NALGO campaign briefings had prominently featured articles which lampooned Derek Hatton, repeating all the slanders of the capitalist press about his 'expensive suits'. Moreover, many slanted articles were carried attacking the appointment of Sam Bond. While giving verbal, lukewarm support for an all-out strike, the actual material put out by NALGO implied the opposite. On the eve of the proposed all-out strike, a NALGO newsletter carried the following statement:

> Tuesday's *Echo* carried a story headed: 'Strike was our idea, says NALGO leader', quoting branch chairperson Graham Burgess as saying that the strike was 'all our idea'...it is not however the case that the strike on the 25th was 'NALGO's idea'; in fact, we initially suggested that no action be taken until the money ran out. But the majority of trade unions voted for a strike, and we have an obligation to put that before our members.

If this was support for strike action, what would opposition look like? At the mass meetings in the stadium, the NALGO leaders formally put the motion for strike action, but were heavily defeated by 3891 to 1445. Given the lack of a campaign, indeed given the anti-council standpoint of its leaders together with the vicious baiting in the press, it is incredible that almost 1500 NALGO members were still firmly in favour of all-out strike action.

The stewards of the manual unions, strongly influenced by *Militant* supporters, had to take a fateful decision on the early evening of 24 September. The question was posed: should the manual workers, despite being in a minority, unilaterally take strike action? The manual workers had voted solidly in favour of strike action, and would have been able to 'tie up' the city if they had come out. The caretakers alone could have closed all the schools in Liverpool but the only branch of the GMBATU which had voted against strike action was in the education department which was led by convenor Peter Lennard who was not a *Militant* supporter. Indeed he was later, for a mixture of personal and political reasons, to become an opponent of *Militant*. Amongst those sections of the workforce where *Militant* supporters were in strength or had a decisive influence, the case was put firmly and the majority of the workers, in a secret ballot, voted for strike action.

The ultra lefts urged the manual workers to strike. Reference to the minority voting for strike action was denounced as 'ballotitis' that is, an alleged fetish about achieving a majority before a strike could be called. Unbelievably, they invoked the example of the miners in 1984. Yet as *Militant* has consistently pointed out, one of the fundamental weaknesses of the miners' strike was the failure of the leadership to hold a ballot which would have resulted in an overwhelming majority confirming the strike action which was in progress. The idea that the actions of a 'determined minority' can bulldoze other workers to come out on strike without discussion and a democratic vote is absolutely false.

The total vote of all the workers was 7284 for strike action and 8152 against. In this situation, to have gone ahead with strike action would have courted a split between the trade unions, with the possibility of conflicts on the picket lines which would have been exploited by the press and all the opponents of the council. Therefore, while saluting the workers who voted in favour of strike action, particularly the manual workers, the stewards recommended that the strike be called off.

Acquiescence to this decision was achieved with some difficulty. Many council workers such as members of the security force and the cleansing workers who had most to lose if the council were defeated, congregated at the Town Hall to await the decision of the stewards. It also seemed as if the world's media were gathered outside the municipal annexe that evening. The press at one stage had to be protected from the anger of these workers, and only the intervention of *Militant* supporters from amongst the stewards, prevented a violent assault on the press corps.

Frustrated that their call for all-out strike action had failed, the stewards of the manual workers' unions decided to recommend that a one-day strike go ahead the following day, 25 September.

While this drama was unfolding, the *Guardian* (25 September) carried a letter which once more underlined the achievements of the council. This letter was all the more remarkable as the author, Lord Reg Underhill, was a long-standing opponent of the *Militant*. His hostility, however, could not prevent him from recording what he had seen with his own eyes:

As President of the Association of Metropolitan Authorities, I attended a conference at Southport and in the afternoon of 18 September, with a number of other delegates, I went to see the effects of Liverpool's regeneration strategy. After visiting an excellent exhibition in the City Hall, we toured the city and looked at many of the 17 priority areas already being developed.

The five year plan is to get rid of outdated and sub-standard housing, the crumbling tenements and soulless system-built tower flats. Already 3800 separate homes have been built, with their own private gardens and nearby off-street parking...improved street layouts, with tree-lined residential roads are planned. We saw the start of the 100 acre park at Everton and of the initial development of other local parks. There are to be seven support centres; three have just been opened. The scheme will provide work for 12,000 with side effects producing further thousands of jobs. Without commenting on the rating situation, how much is being saved to the Treasury by this employment?

Shamefully, this letter was buried amongst the gloating headlines which greeted the calling off of the strike. The *Daily Mirror* jeered, 'Militants forced to stop city strike.' In London the *Evening Standard*, notwithstanding the vote, declared 'Liverpool's strike ballot rigged', and '*Militant* rebellion left in tatters'.

But the most malevolent comments came from the political correspondent of *The Times*, Anthony Bevins, who wrote on 25 September:

> People of Liverpool wait for deliverance...The 540,000 people of Liverpool are caught between the *Militant* devils and the deep blue Conservative government in a clash which is not of their making...it is a measure of the *Militant* terror that there is not one Labour MP or union leader who will come out into the open and say publicly what they say in private about the Trotskyist takeover of the party and the unions in the city.

On the evening of 24 September, Bevins confided to a *Militant* supporter that Kinnock was planning a 'Bombshell' for *Militant* and its supporters. Bevins was confident that this would effectively eliminate the influence of Marxism in the city. Fifteen months later, after Kinnock had tried every measure to undermine support for *Militant* the same Bevins, having shifted his journalistic allegiance, was to write: 'He [Kinnock] had not broken the Trotskyists and never will'. (*Independent*, 7 January 1987)

The 25 September Strike

Kenneth Baker was naturally triumphant at the rejection of all-out strike action: 'The morale of the Militants must be very low this morning.' (*Echo*, 25 September). He declared: 'Derek Hatton had lost...it is a major setback for the revolutionary politics of the *Militant* councillors and the *Militant* shop stewards.' Yet the *Echo* on the same day, reporting the effect of the strike, declared 'Strike City...Liverpool was a city in chaos today as thousands of council workers downed tools in protest against the government. Services were cut, some schools were open, some were shut.'

Despite the defeat of the all-out strike motion, the demonstration in the city that day was extremely buoyant. Upwards of 50,000−nearly one in ten of the city's population− in a remarkable display of support of the working class for the council's fight against the government, marched to the Town Hall. Derek Hatton declared: 'This strike and demonstration is not a wake, but a springboard for further action.' Nevertheless, the councillors keenly felt the defeat of the all-out strike vote. The feeling that the white-collar union leaders had once more abandoned the councillors who had put everything on the line to defend jobs, was widespread.

The next week was to see a barrage of propaganda, orchestrated by Fleet Street, against the city council. This was the week before the Labour Party Conference and the press exerted colossal pressure on Kinnock to attack both Liverpool City Council and the miners. The miners were demanding indemnification for the vicious fines and financial attacks on the union and Liverpool was demanding the future reinstatement of any surcharged and debarred councillors.

National union leaders stepped in just before the Labour Party Conference to back up those who were opposing the 'redundancy notices' but they did not offer a viable alternative which would prevent the councillors from being surcharged. Yet the only other alternatives were an all-out strike, which they had already opposed; or massive cuts which would affect their own members, or huge rate increases which they would not dare to propose.

The councillors, to their eternal credit, despite being rebuffed in the all-out strike call, still stubbornly refused to carry out cuts.

The right-wing Labour opponents of *Militant* had no other policy than to hope that 'something would turn up'. The NALGO leaders, loftily declared that they were prepared to 'let the money run out'. This did not solve the dilemma confronting the councillors who each faced a £500,000 surcharge if the necessary arrangements to pay 'redundancy pay' were not made. In this situation, the redundancy notices that had been withdrawn when all-out strike action looked possible were now, incorrectly put back on the agenda.

Safe in the knowledge that the national and local trade-union leaders would not come to the assistance of the council, Baker, was 'intent on letting Liverpool stew' according to the *Guardian*. At the Tory Party Conference a few weeks later, he would boast that Liverpool had been allowed to 'twist in the wind'. Thus the sick, the old, the suffering of the disabled were used to bring the council to heel. The *Daily Mirror*, speaking of the forthcoming three months when the money would run out, warned of 'a winter of death' but firmly placed the responsibility on the shoulders of the city council and not on the Tory government, while the *Star* reported that 'Crisis city faces probe by police.'

Labour Party Conference

The issue of *Militant* was to dominate not only the Labour Party Conference, but also the Liberal, Tory and SDP Conferences. Just before the Labour Party Conference, David Alton, Liberal Chief Whip, demanded that Neil Kinnock 'Leader of the Labour Party...expel *Militant* leaders of the council.' Four Cabinet Ministers at the Conservative Party Conference, led by Tebbit and Thatcher, denounced *Militant* and Liverpool City Council, and also demanded that Neil Kinnock carry through the expulsion of *Militant* from the Labour Party. This call, long before the Labour leaders had decided on expulsions, showed where the real instigators of the witch-hunt were—in the Tory Cabinet.

In the run-up to the Labour Party Conference, many articles and almost every editorial in the capitalist press, numerous programmes and comments on the television, were all directed at securing a blow against the left, and particularly against *Militant* supporters and councillors in Merseyside. The *Sun*, striking its usual moderate tone, asked, on 28 September: 'Will

Kinnock keep his mad dogs at bay?' It said: 'If Tony Benn gets the chance, he will swing the conference behind *Militant* Derek Hatton's crazy bid to bankrupt Merseyside.' Woodrow Wyatt, incredibly once on the left of the Labour Party, in his *News of the World* column dismissed the 'Loony Left's way to lose jobs'. The *Sunday Express* predicted that Kinnock 'in a big set speech at the Party's Conference on Tuesday, will tell both the miners' leaders and the *Militant* councillors at Liverpool: grow up—or get out'.

The *Sunday Mirror* carried vicious attacks on Derek Hatton, with a probe into his private life. Yet in the midst of this tirade, an opinion poll carried in the *Sunday Times* (29 September) showed the roots which the council had sunk amongst the population of the city. When asked which way people would vote if an election were held, 55 per cent said they would vote Labour, 34 per cent SDP-Liberal Alliance and 11 per cent for the Tories. This represented an incredible 9 per cent increase of Labour's share of the vote since the 1984 elections, when 46 per cent had voted Labour. In what the *Sunday Times* called 'unprompted replies...55 per cent blamed either Mrs Thatcher or the government for the dispute'. A colossal 86 per cent of those questioned declared that the government did not care for the people of the area, which included 56 per cent of Tory supporters! At the same time, 88 per cent were in favour of Baker, Secretary of State for the Environment, agreeing to talks.

Thus, despite all the turmoil and inevitable confusion generated by the 'redundancy notices' issue, the bedrock of Labour support had increased. Unfortunately, the Labour leadership were completely impervious to this. Kinnock was determined, it subsequently became clear, to use the occasion of his Labour Party Conference speech to show that a Labour government led by him would be 'safe' for capitalism. The miners' leadership and Liverpool City Council were to be the whipping boys.

In the pre-conference round of interviews, Kinnock gave a none too subtle hint of the nature of the attack which he would make on *Militant*. On *TV-AM* on 29 September he criticised Liverpool City Council for provoking what he called a 'crisis of anxiety' amongst the authority's 30,000 employees by issuing redundancy notices. He came out in favour of a £27 million capitalisation of housing income, which he argued could solve the crisis. Pressed on the influence of *Militant* and particularly of Derek Hatton and Tony Mulhearn, Kinnock said that the presence of the Militant Tendency was exaggerated, but that he was 'interested in getting people like that out of the Labour Party. They could only be removed on the basis of firm proof that they were members of *Militant*, but when that proof comes—out they go.' (*Guardian*, 30 September). Tony Byrne, in a typically blunt fashion replied:

> It's about time he [Kinnock] stood up and represented ordinary working-class people instead of trying to persuade Labour councillors to comply with Thatcher cuts...Before he starts using fancy words like capitalisation, he should be brave enough to explain to ordinary working-class people just what it means. He should tell people living in tenements that they will have to go on living there, and tell old people living in unimproved houses and using outside toilets that they will have to go on using them.

Kinnock's anomalous position with respect to the councillors was shown when the NEC decided on the Sunday before the conference to support a motion which instructed a Labour government to compensate retrospectively Labour councillors in Lambeth and Liverpool if they were surcharged.

Hostility to the left in the media was nothing new in the run-up to the Labour Party Conference. But the unanimity, the similarity of language deployed against the left in general, and against Arthur Scargill and Derek Hatton in particular, was striking. The 'Labour' *Daily Mirror* ranted on the day the conference began:

> Scargill and Hatton are mob orators...Militant policies, reckless posturing and deliberate law-breaking offered nothing to the mass of working people whose plight created the Labour Party...What Labour's mad left won't understand is that any party pledged to those policies will never form a government...if it still wants to win, it has to reject Scargill and Hatton.

Kinnock's 'Grotesque' Speech

The campaign against *Militant* by Kinnock and others at the Labour Party Conference, was carefully prepared. On the morning on which Kinnock was to deliver his speech, *The Times* carried a vitriolic attack by the Liverpool church leaders: 'Stand up to Liverpool's Militants.' Meanwhile, the Bishops lamely argued the case for a 'consensus' approach:

> Faced with such difficulties, a great city needs to bring all the resources which people of good will can muster. Our Christian teaching is that we are members of one another. The dogmatic, divisive policies of the *Militant* leadership reject this...now the head-on clash has occurred, and a very dangerous moment in the life of our city is being reached.

The class gulf, which had now widened to a chasm, between the great majority of the working-class population of Liverpool and the Tory government with their capitalist backers could not be comprehended by these good shepherds. But in arguing their case, they did not hesitate to bend the truth: 'We deplore the confrontation that has, to a great extent, been manufactured by the *Militant* leadership of the city council.' Perhaps the *Militant* engineered the 'confrontation' in Toxteth in 1981? All the powers of dialogue, millions of words arguing the case for 'Christian' compassion and consensus had not touched the 'soul' of various Tory governments.

Only when the population of Liverpool, 'got up off its knees' and in their tens of thousands moved into action did a different tone emanate from the corridors of power. The Bishops had been unnerved, like many others with their roots in the middle class, by the determination of the working class to see the struggle through to a conclusion. It was precisely to avoid the incredible misery and suffering in the city that the struggle had been engaged in the first place. Yet the bishops piously declared:

> *Militant's* intransigence and unwillingness to engage in serious dialogue creates divisiveness and uncertainty in which the most vulnerable elements of the community suffer, usually school children and elderly people, unable to cope with a reduction of services.

At the same time, they gave their blessing to the arguments of the Black Caucus:

> The deliberate importation into the city of black members of the Militant Tendency from London brings a dangerous threat to the

fragile but growing emergence of local black organisations. The appointment of Sam Bond as Principal Race Relations Adviser was a needless affront to the black community.

Sam Bond's appointment was an affront to nobody but the self-appointed black leaders around the Black Caucus.

On the morning of Kinnock's speech at the Labour Party Conference, Liverpool displayed its remarkable ingenuity in managing its financial affairs, when, to the astonishment of the ruling class, the city council managed to negotiate a £30 million facility through the city stockbrokers, Phillips and Drew. This allowed the city to continue financing its capital projects *and* its housing programme. But all of this was of secondary importance to Kinnock, as he prepared to send a signal to the ruling class. Selected journalists were informed of its contents in advance, while most of the press did not receive a copy of his speech until after it had been delivered, something which up to then was quite unique for Labour Party conference.

Not one syllable of Kinnock's tirade will be accorded any importance by history, save for his venomous assault on the heroic Liverpool councillors which outdid even the Tories in its viciousness. Not a word of support was uttered for the struggles of Liverpool in defence of the workers of the city and yet not a word of criticism was made either about those Labour councils such as Rhondda, Newcastle or Wakefield, which had provoked strikes by privatisation, closure of nurseries and other cutbacks.

His infamous statements about the alleged 'grotesque chaos of a Labour council hiring taxis to scuttle around a city handing out redundancy notices to its own workers', produced pandemonium in the conference hall. Eric Heffer, National Executive Committee member, and MP for Liverpool Walton, stormed off the platform. Boos and cat-calls greeted Kinnock's statement. While the Liverpool councillors were in power, from 1983-7, no one was made redundant. Unfortunately, the same could not be said of Neil Kinnock in the autumn of 1987, when he pushed for 40 *real* redundancies among staff at the Labour Party's Walworth Road headquarters.

Kinnock's attack provoked widespread indignation throughout Liverpool; the council telephone exchange was jammed with calls of protest. It was interpreted by the great majority of Liverpudlians as yet another attack on the city. In the weeks and months leading up to the Labour Party Conference, the press had pilloried Liverpool as 'Smack City', inhabited mainly by 'mindless football hooligans, of the unemployed and unemployable, of layabouts', an attitude immortalised in the shameful phrase of the *Sunday Times*: 'A majority of lumpens'. Kinnock now seemed to be siding not just with opponents of *Militant* but with the enemies of Liverpool. The whole Labour group was united in its condemnation of Kinnock's attack. Even right wingers like Roy Gladden and Joe Devaney, Prospective Parliamentary Candidate for Mossley Hill, were at one with *Militant* supporters in repudiating Kinnock's speech. The Liverpool Labour MPs were unanimous in their condemnation. Bob Parry, the Riverside MP, denounced Kinnock as the 'biggest class traitor since Ramsay MacDonald'.

The capitalists greeted Kinnock's speech with Hosannahs. The *Mail on Sunday* gloated: 'A great speech Neil' and it went on: 'Everything that Mr Kinnock had to say about the miners and everything he has had to say about the *Militant* takeover of Liverpool are what the so-called right wing capitalist press have been saying—and roundly denounced for doing so—for ages.'

Kinnock's attack gave the opportunity for 'red baiting' which the press had been waiting for. The *Daily Mirror* gloated: 'Left in the Lurch'. The *Daily Express* went further and urged Kinnock to 'Give Bernie Grant, [the Labour candidate in Tottenham] the boot!' It went on: 'Either Bernie Grant will be expelled from the Labour Party, or Neil Kinnock will be exposed as a fake, and the prisoner of the extremists he denounces.' At the Tory conference later, Tebbit was to declare:

> Nothing could really have changed until extremists and the *Militant* were thrown out of the [Labour] party altogether...The Labour Party is not going to be able to hide Mr Scargill, Mr Hatton and Bernie Grant under the cloak of moderation. We must not let Mr Kinnock rest until he moves those people from positions of power in his party.

Echoing Thatcher's theme in the miners' strike, the *Daily Mail* denounced the 'enemies within...they are the latter-day disciples of Marxist revolutionary Leon Trotsky. They are the supporters of Militant Tendency.' Every opponent of the left, was to be encouraged to raise their head and declare their opposition. The *Sunday Telegraph* correctly forecast that the attack on *Militant* was the beginning of 'Kinnock's counter-revolution' against the gains on policy and programme which had been achieved by Labour's rank and file in the period of 1979-83.

Kinnock cynically intended his anti-*Militant* blast at the 1985 Labour Party Conference to be the means of riding to power on an anti-left 'moderate' surge. It was calculated to appeal to the so-called middle ground. The Labour right were of course in transports of delight at Kinnock's speech. Denis Healey declared that this one speech would result in a Labour victory at the next election. Yet at the beginning of 1985 Labour stood at 38 per cent in the opinion polls. Two years later, after the assault on *Militant* which went hand in hand with the jettisoning of left policies and the attack on reselection of MPs, Labour's popularity remained at the same level and subsequently sank down to 31 per cent in the June 1987 General Election.

Kinnock's assault on *Militant* and the left was immensely popular in the boardrooms of the monopoly companies and in the editorial chambers of Fleet Street. However, it alienated wide layers of the advanced workers in the Labour Party and trade unions and thereby helped prepare the way for the June 1987 General Election defeat.

Even the filtered *Guardian* letters columns echoed the widespread indignation and opposition of workers in the labour movement:

> As an ordinary branch member, my emotions changed during Mr Kinnock's Bournemouth oration from one of solidarity when he talked of 'values' and 'deceptions' and 'policies' encapsulated by the labour movement to one of disbelief during his attack on Liverpool comrades. I did not join the Labour Party to support a 'leader' who seems to be as equally corrupted by potential power as David Owen does. I did not join the Labour Party to 'play politics' with people's jobs, homes or services. Nor did I join the Labour Party to denounce councillors for carrying out socialist policies. (*Guardian* 7 October)

On the other hand, the character of Kinnock's support was perhaps indicated by another letter:

> The allegation is that the only real choice for the Labour Party today was between Stalinism and Trotskyism. Faced with such limited options I opt for Stalin every time. Stalin knew how to

conduct a good purge and remove the undesirables from the party.

Shades of a Labour 'gulag' to which *Militant* extremists could be banished! Another correspondent wrote:

> I am a member of the Liberal Party and I don't admire Derek Hatton and Arthur Scargill, or their comrades. I do think they are entitled to respect, for following their principles and the Labour Party's policies, and in the case of the Liverpool and Lambeth councillors being prepared to put themselves at risk. But it is difficult to respect a leader of the Labour Party, who offers principles and policies to the electors like lollipops, but abuses those in his own party who try to follow them. Why is it that Labour Party leaders are so much better at attacking those who should be their friends than they are at attacking the Tory Party?

In a bitter speech, which brought tears to the eyes of miners' wives present in the conference hall, he set his face against any indemnification of the fines incurred by the miners' union by a future Labour government. He adopted a similarly implacable position on the surcharge of the councillors of Liverpool and Lambeth. He claimed that no government had ever acted in this fashion, yet in 1975 the Labour government had passed the Housing Finance (Special Provisions) Act to indemnify councillors fined and disqualified for failing to obey a 1970 law obliging them to put up council rents. However, because of the rebellion by the Labour right in the Commons, this legislation did not protect the Clay Cross councillors who had taken a lead in the rent struggle that year.

Despite Kinnock's intervention, the conference passed a motion calling on a Labour government to recompense the miners and reinstate sacked miners. It also upheld the NEC's resolution which promised indemnification for councillors.

But above all the right wing and the capitalist press were eagerly looking for the defeat of the motion supporting Liverpool's struggle. The debate at the conference was one of the most rigged in the recent history of the labour movement. A series of right-wing speakers were lined up to lambaste the council and *Militant* supporters. Every delegate in the hall was required to occupy the seat allotted to them by the Standing Orders Committee but Jane Saren of NALGO, a confirmed opponent of *Militant,* and a delegate from the Riverside constituency, was seated for the debate alongside John Cunningham in the parliamentary section. From there she could easily be seen by the chair and, needless to say, she was duly called to launch her assault on the council. Jane Kennedy, a 'rank and file' NUPE delegate, was similarly spotted by the conference Chair. After the conference, Julia Langdon, a former correspondent of *Labour Weekly* and then a journalist with the *Daily Mirror* claimed that these 'two women trade unionists are living in fear after threats from left-wing extremists'. Not a shred of evidence was ever produced to justify this. The only supporters of Liverpool allowed to speak in the debate were Derek Hatton and Tony Mulhearn. The right wing couldn't prevent this since they were moving and seconding the motion.

At the end of the debate, David Blunkett, replying on behalf of the NEC, without consulting Kinnock, asked Liverpool to withdraw its motion in favour of the NEC's statement. Conference delegates felt an enormous urge for unity reflecting the widespread sentiment of the labour movement. Derek Hatton's gesture in withdrawing his resolution was therefore widely applauded. It contrasted very favourably with the vicious, divisive speech of Kinnock the day before.

The right wing were dismayed by Blunkett's tactics and they attacked him behind the scenes for his gesture. The capitalist press on the other hand hailed Blunkett's 'tactical adroitness' and skill. In fact, the initiative had not been his but was suggested to him by *Militant* supporters in a discussion with Tony Mulhearn and Derek Hatton. To have withdrawn the motion before the debate would have prevented Derek Hatton and Tony Mulhearn from speaking to the conference. To have allowed the motion to go to the vote may have enabled the right wing to claim that Liverpool had been heavily defeated given the power of the block votes cast by the union general secretaries. But by withdrawing the motion after the debate, but before the vote, the supporters of Liverpool's struggle at least had the best of a bad deal.

But in the atmosphere engendered by Kinnock's speech, 'open season' had been declared on Liverpool City Council and *Militant* supporters in particular.

16.
Forced to Retreat

NEIL KINNOCK'S attack on the Liverpool City Council at the October 1985 Labour Party Conference opened the door to an unbridled baiting campaign by the Tories, the Liberals and the media. They attempted to whip up what Engels called the 'enraged petit bourgeois' behind a hastily organised 'movement', called 'Liverpool Against *Militant*' (LAM). This body was supposedly indignant at the alleged 'antics' of the city council and particularly of the 'Militants'. However, the organisers were far from being the 'ordinary ratepayers' presented by the media. What ordinary ratepayers could afford an aeroplane for publicity on the day of a demonstration? Paul Feather, the principal spokesperson of LAM, was a failed Tory candidate and was also representing the Hotels and Restaurants Association within LAM. The local press, who had played down the massive demonstrations in the previous two years of 20,000, 40,000 and 50,000, gave huge publicity to the preparations for a LAM demonstration on 6 October.

The meeting of 400 people which initiated the demonstration was mostly composed of businessmen with a smattering of so-called 'Labour moderates' whom nobody had ever heard of. One, Mr Hugh McCafferty, a retired dockworker, was quoted in the *Daily Telegraph* as describing Derek Hatton as 'a *Militant* skunk'. The day of the demonstration saw a motley crowd, less than 4000 strong, gathering at the Pier Head, with a number of Labour activists counter-demonstrating. Assembling at the traditional meeting place of the labour movement, this rally was significantly different from the workers' demonstrations. This was obvious even by the number of golf umbrellas on display—a typical badge of the middle class. A lot of the demonstrators were elderly day trippers who had been bussed in for the occasion from the outskirts of Liverpool. They came from Southport, Crosby, Bebington, Maghull etc.

Every anti-*Militant,* anti-city council statement, was widely reported in the local and national press. The *Daily Mirror* reported: 'Godfather demo fury for Hatton', while the *Daily Express* gloated: 'Thousands turn out to rap chaos city lefties.' It eagerly featured the banners of the demonstrators: 'Mad Hatton and his allies in Wonderland' and 'King Hatton waives the rules.' However, Labour counter-demonstrators carried banners which summed up the mood of the majority of the population of Liverpool: 'Hands off Hatton. Concentrate on Thatcher's government.'

The Liberal leader, Sir Trevor Jones, and Chris Hallows, the Tory leader, were skulking at the back of the platform, pondering whether to speak or not. In order to maintain the spurious 'non-political' character of this fledgling organisation, they decided against it at that stage. But the blatant anti-Labour character of LAM was too much even for the opponents of *Militant* within the labour movement. Ian Williams for the Labour Co-ordinating Committee declared to the *Guardian*: 'We'll have nothing to do with demonstrations like this. While we are as distressed as anybody by the antics of Derek Hatton and *Militant,* the people who were involved in organising this campaign were consistently anti-Labour before *Militant.*'

The LAM demonstration once again underlined the political situation which existed in Liverpool where sharp class polarisation had developed as a result of the stand taken by the city council. The attacks of the media and their attempts to whip up the middle class in opposition against the council only reinforced support for Labour amongst the great majority of the working-class population.

Liverpool Labour Left

Despite Kinnock's attack at the Labour Party conference, the opponents of *Militant* within the Liverpool labour movement failed to make much headway. In October 1985, a new grouping, Liverpool Labour Left, became the focus of opposition to *Militant.* It was so 'left' that it included the witch-hunter Jane Kennedy in its ranks ! Realising that open support for Kinnock was the kiss of death in a city where the labour movement had been outraged by his attack at the Labour Party Conference, they went to great lengths to identify with the stand of the council: 'We consider the city council deserves the support of the Labour Party nationally in its attempt to defend jobs and services' said Ian Williams, a leading advocate of Liverpool Labour Left. According to the *Guardian,* the Liverpool Labour Left also 'believes Mr Kinnock has underestimated the mood of defiance in the city'. These 'left' lions were so confident of their ability to confront *Militant* that their first rally, at which David Blunkett and John Hamilton were invited to speak, was arranged on the very day when most *Militant* supporters would be in London attending their national rally.

The Liverpool Labour Left was to be stillborn. *Militant's* policies more accurately reflected the mood of the workers within the Labour Party and the working-class population of the city. Thrashing around to find points of support, this new left organisation was to end up as the finger-men and women for the right wing on the National Executive Committee of the Labour Party. Their 'evidence' was used later to expel leading *Militant* supporters, including several surcharged councillors.

Still £25 Million Short

In early October, a number of local authorities led by David Blunkett in Sheffield and under the auspices of the Association of Metropolitan Authorities (AMA) explored the possibility of a common loan from their 'reserve funds' to keep Liverpool afloat. A figure of £30 million was mentioned in the press, but no more than one-tenth of this would be forthcoming when the crunch came in early November. The situation of the council was critical.

Later the city council's opponents were to accuse spokespersons like Tony Byrne and Derek Hatton of deliberately concealing the real situation, and exaggerating Liverpool's financial plight. But not one 'expert' either then or since has been able, in examining Liverpool's books, to accuse the council of deliberately 'exaggerating'.

Tony Byrne pointed out that the normal running costs of the council were about £5 million per week. With the 9 per cent rate which had been set there would be a shortfall from December to the end of March which would have come to about £65 million. However, a new situation arose when the courts declared in October that the financial penalties which had been imposed by the government on Bradford District Council and Nottinghamshire County Council were illegal.

This extra money reduced the gap in the council's finances to under 90 days. This also reduced any period of possible redundancy to below 90 days and therefore enabled the council to use a proportion of the money set aside for redundancy pay. The consequence of this would be to reduce the period of any 'layoffs' from three months to four weeks.

But this did not satisfy some union leaders, particularly in the white collar unions. They were being egged on by the leadership of the Communist Party nationally. Gordon McLennan, Communist Party General Secretary, attacked Liverpool City Council policy in the *Morning Star* as 'disastrous and grotesque'. According to the *Morning Star* (17 October):

> He had first voiced these criticisms a year ago in the city, and not as a latter day convert to Kinnockism, although he was very pleased the Labour leader had said what he did at the Party's conference last week.

The NUT, with Communist Party member Jim Ferguson in the vanguard, had initiated legal action against the council to prevent any 'layoffs' (see Appendix 9). Yet there were 400 teachers in Liverpool who would have been made permanently redundant if government ceilings had been applied by the council! The NUT leaders spoke vaguely about an 'alternative plan' to solve the problems of the city. But they gave support to 'capitalisation'—using money earmarked for housebuilding to cover day-to-day spending. This would have meant sacrificing the jobs of building workers and condemning many families to the misery of living in slums. This course of action was rejected by the council and by the leaders of the manual workers' unions.

Faced with a financial situation changing almost daily, and with the capitalist press and labour and trade-union leaders systematically distorting the position, the Marxists in Liverpool took the historic step of producing a regular regional supplement to the *Militant*. Twenty-three issues of *Mersey Militant* were published in the autumn and winter of 1985-6.

It played a vital role, complementing the *Militant* with material relating directly to the rapidly changing events in Liverpool. Each issue was eagerly awaited by council workers and Labour activists who looked to it for answers to the lies of the press, especially the *Echo*. *Mersey Militant's* role was especially significant as it came out in a period of setback and retreat, its explanation of events helping to maintain the morale of the supporters of the stand of the council. The right-wing leadership of Labour's NEC paid a back-handed compliment to the role of *Mersey Militant* when authorship of articles in it was used as 'justification' for a number of expulsions from the Labour Party.

As Liverpool approached the abyss—the day when the money would run out—frantic activity took place between the 'left' authorities (hoping to raise a loan for Liverpool), the national trade-union and labour leadership, and even professional bodies like the Institute of Chartered Accountants. The *Evening Standard* reported that: 'Ken Livingstone says he would be ready to use some of the GLC's surplus millions to help the city of Liverpool avoid bankruptcy.' The attempt by other councils to bail Liverpool out was not entirely altruistic, as David Blunkett indicated: 'The credit of local government would be knocked for six. It would take years to get over the knock-on effect' if Liverpool was to be bankrupted.

Derek Hatton's statement on 17 October, that Liverpool could run out of money in two-and-a-half weeks was the signal for another 'mass meeting' of LAM at the pier head. Sensitive about the credentials of Paul Feather, who got a pathetic 236 votes for the Tories when he stood in Dingle Ward, the new spokesperson was Jeff Tinnion. The managing director of a car business in what the *Daily Express* (21 October) called the 'pleasant suburb of Allerton', Tinnion took a weekend off from his caravan and cod-fishing outings in Anglesey to sweep Liverpool clean of the baleful influence of *Militant* Marxism. The troops were rallied by a new theme song '*Militant* Out', specially composed for the rally. The lyrics ran: '*Militant* out—everybody shout *Militant* out, *Militant* out...M is for *Militant*, their image, their pretence; I is for Indifference, those who sit on the fence; N is for our nation, who play it by the rules, T is for the traitors destroying Liverpool.' Not exactly in the mould of The Beatles!

The purpose of the rally however was indicated by the speech of Tinnion: 'We are sending this message to Mr Kinnock and his National Executive—the vast majority of the people of Liverpool demand swift action from you to free the people of this city from its misery, unnecessary suffering and mental torment.' He demanded that Kinnock expel *Militant* supporters from the Labour Party. Another speaker declared, 'We are from all political persuasions, some of us from the Labour Party (murmurs around the crowd), some of us are Liberals (large cheers around the crowd), some of us are from the Tory Party (prolonged cheers from the crowd).'

But the flotsam gathered behind this organisation, along with the press, seemed to exercise a greater effect on Neil Kinnock than the mass of working people standing four-square behind their council. This was clearly shown when Kinnock visited the city a few days later. The city councillors saw it as a genuine opportunity to familiarise the Labour leaders with the real situation in Liverpool, rather than the media-inspired distortions.

Kinnock Visits Liverpool

In the meeting Neil Kinnock had been 'like a lamb' as one councillor put it and John Hamilton, council leader, announced afterwards: 'Neil Kinnock did not oppose the steps taken by the council so far.' Tony Mulhearn said: 'Twenty councillors met him and we impressed upon him the total unanimity of the Labour group over policies.' After the meeting Derek Hatton, speaking to the press, commented: 'Neil Kinnock listened and I think he understood. While much of the press would have loved this to have been a divided meeting or a witch-hunt against *Militant*, it was not. It was a proper discussion about the real problems of Liverpool, fraternal and very sympathetic.'

This impression of the meeting did not please Kinnock nor his advisers, who were eager to reinforce his 'strong man' image as a '*Militant* basher' which had been cultivated at the Labour Party Conference. Kinnock tried to create the impression at his own press conference that he had laid down the law to the Labour Group. Labour councillors emphasised the points of agreement, while Kinnock again reserved his fire and fury for fellow party members, in front of his favourite audience—the Tory press.

The next day John Cunningham indicated that one of the purposes of the visit had been to investigate the possibility of replacing the council leadership with a more pliable team which would carry out 'realistic policies'. Hidden away in Kinnock's statements was a token recognition that the government was responsible for the crisis, but the whole burden of his remarks was to paint the Labour councillors as the villains of the piece. However, as a consequence of meetings between representatives of the council and National Executive Committee members, the latter became 'convinced for the first time that Mr Tony Byrne Liverpool's Finance Chairman, is telling the truth when he says that bankruptcy is imminent'. (*The Times*, 22 October).

The government, the Labour leadership and right-wing national trade-union leaders, were all determined to rub the noses of the city council in the mud. All of them understood that big cuts were necessary without further resources from the government. They wanted the city council, and particularly *Militant* supporters, to be pressurised into carrying through cuts and thereby become discredited in the eyes of the working class.

There were other options open to the government, as *The Times* (22 October) commented:

> There is a fourth way, but no one, yet, dare touch it. Three high Court judges will declare at the end of next week that Liverpool's nine per cent rate is illegal. Liverpool disputes that, although Labour politicians privately accept that they are on dodgy ground over having agreed a deficit budget. The High Court will not, however, quash the rate because it has not been asked. It would take only one ratepayer, councillor or a parliamentary request to the Attorney General, to have the anomaly resolved with an application to the court. The councils' opposition parties and the government will not move because *Militant* could blame the rate rise on them and, in the present climate, it would take a courageous Labour politician to force the issue.

In other words, all the forces of 'official society' were refusing to act 'responsibly' and apply for a High Court writ for rate increases to cover the deficit. They were determined that the odium attached to big rate rises must be borne by the Labour group and in particular by the Marxists.

The stubborn refusal to go down this road, and in particular its refusal to heed the 'sensible' advice of the national labour and trade-union leaders accounts for the fury unleashed against the city council and *Militant* in October and November. The Tory press were quite clear as to what role they expected from the leadership of the labour movement. The *Daily Telegraph* jeered: 'The council has had to accept Mr Kinnock as the best man to arrange the terms of surrender.' Kinnock was to demonstrate his willingness to fulfil such a role. From the unlikely quarter of the *Economist* came an admission of the real plight of Liverpool: 'The Association of Metropolitan Authorities will deliver to Westminster and Whitehall a message much ignored when it is delivered by Mr Hatton. They will almost certainly say that Liverpool is not being treated like everybody else, but worse.'

The Stonefrost Report

As a consequence of the debate at Labour Party Conference, a commission to investigate Liverpool's finances was organised by trade-union and labour leaders, headed by Maurice Stonefrost, former Director-General of the GLC. When the findings of the Stonefrost Commission were finally published, Kinnock once again jumped the gun and launched a vicious attack on *Militant* supporters within the city council.

On 29 October, before the councillors themselves had even had a chance to read the *Stonefrost Report,* Kinnock's office leaked a statement claiming that the money was there all the time for those who 'really wanted to look'. This betrayed gross ignorance of the report's findings or a deliberate attempt to misrepresent its conclusions and to bounce the Labour council into carrying out a policy diametrically opposed to those upon which it had been elected. In fact, most of the material in the report had been provided by discussions with Tony Byrne, Derek Hatton, Tony Mulhearn and the city's financial experts.

John Edmonds, GMBATU leader elect, subsequently claimed to his union executive that '92 pence a week on the rates will solve Liverpool's financial crisis' and thereby save all the jobs. In fact the report demonstrated the opposite, and showed that it was impossible to balance the books without massive cutbacks, or attacks on living standards.

The report explicitly called for extra money to be raised through rent and rate rises, non-filling of job vacancies, and financial juggling which would inevitably have jeopardised the housebuilding programme and jobs. The report suggested a 15 per cent rate rise *in addition* to the 9 per cent rise that had already been agreed. This was described as the 'cornerstone' of the report's strategy and the authors claimed that it would bring in an extra £19 million. The additional 15 per cent rate rise would have severely hit big sections of the city's population. It would moreover have fuelled the opposition of Liverpool Against Militant, which drew most of its support from small businessmen who would inevitably be severely hit by the big rent and rate rises implicit in the *Stonefrost Report*.

The report also said that money could be saved by sacking workers—or by cutting 'employee costs', as it blandly called it. It calculated that 1000 redundancies would save the council £1 million in 1985 and £7 million in the next year. It proposed a freeze on employment and the non-filling of vacancies. It also suggested a £1 a week increase in rent to bring in £1 million in 1985 and £3 million in 1986.

Labour promises not to increase the already massive council house rents were supposed to be tossed aside like so many useless scraps of paper. Despite Kinnock's claims to support the strategy of building houses, the proposals of Stonefrost on capitalisation would have meant the effective ending of the housebuilding programme. Because of the council's building programme, thousands more building workers were employed than in 1983. No matter how much the report was dressed up, it represented a savage attack for the population of Liverpool through a combination of rent increases, jobs losses and rate rises.

The *Star* boldly declared, 'Take the medicine' and it went on: 'The principal requirement of any medicine is to cure the ailment—not to taste nice.' It viewed with equanimity the suffering of the working-class population of Liverpool. Even John Hamilton was constrained mildly to tick off Kinnock: 'The leadership has rushed into making statements that at this stage are not helpful.'

The District Labour Party, at a 400-strong meeting, carefully considered the report and rejected its main proposals. At the same time, mass meetings of the GMBATU and TGWU workers also rejected the *Stonefrost Report*. This unflinching attitude of the Liverpool labour movement, with the Marxists in the vanguard, provoked the ruling class and its acolytes to a new paroxysm of fury, but the real feelings of tens of thousands of workers throughout the city, were summed up in a letter by a Liverpool resident to the *Guardian*:

> Congratulations to Neil Kinnock and his team of experts for solving Liverpool's financial problems. It just didn't occur to us simple Merseyside folk that the answer to underfunding was a package involving selling off assets, cooking the books and raising the rates. Now I need worry no longer about the £1.2 million gap in arts funding which has been brought about by the abolition of Merseyside county council. Why didn't we all think about this when the government cuts were first announced?

The attacks on Liverpool by so many in the labour and trade-union leadership with the backing of the press only served to harden and steel support amongst the working class for *Militant* and for the council. Over five thousand workers and youth cheered the speeches of the leading figures of *Militant* at its biggest ever national rally in the Royal Albert Hall on 4 November. The stand of Liverpool City Council was the centrepiece of the rally. Derek Hatton received a standing ovation both before he started and when he concluded his speech. The audience were cheering the stand not just of one man but of the brave 48 councillors who remained firm in their support for the council's policies and the Liverpool labour movement. Derek Hatton called on Neil Kinnock to 'represent your people the same way that Thatcher represents hers'.

On the same day as the *Militant* rally in London the Liverpool Labour Left meeting discussed above was held in Liverpool. The platform speakers led by David Blunkett and Keva Coombes, Leader of Merseyside County Council, accepted the *Stonefrost Report* and called for its implementation. Two Merseyside MPs present, Bob Wareing and Alan Roberts, also suggested that the rates should be put up. This was met with opposition from the floor, with Tony Byrne putting the case for opposition to the *Stonefrost Report*.

The uncompromising stand of the Liverpool Labour group, stiffened by *Militant* supporters, undoubtedly convinced the leaders of the labour and trade-union movement to prepare for the expulsion of Merseyside *Militant* supporters.

But the Liverpool Labour Left was a very weak reed upon which the national leaders of the Labour Party could lean at a time when the whole of the labour and trade-union movement in the city had shifted decisively towards the left. The rank and file workers in the wards, constituencies and trade-union branches were behind the stand of the council. The Liverpool Labour Left only found its support amongst a gaggle of frustrated councillors or would-be councillors, trade-union officials who feared that control over their rank and file was slipping out of their hands, and some very middle-class ex-'left wingers'.

A Barrage of Lies

With the rejection of the *Stonefrost Report* another onslaught was launched against the council. As the city began to be starved of funds, the press began to use the inevitable cutbacks as a stick with which to beat the council. The first fiddle in this chorus was taken by Sarah Cullen, a commentator for ITV's *News at Ten,* a programme now commonly known by workers as 'Lies at Ten'.

The sick, the old and the infirm, whose facilities were threatened by the Tory government's cuts, were presented as victims of the council's policies. When a spina bifida children's home was threatened with closure because the council was unable to maintain grants, scenes of spina bifida children were shown on the television, with the implication that Labour councillors were about to turn them out of the home.

It became absolutely clear at this stage that the Labour and trade-union leaders were as much afraid of a Liverpool success for 'militancy' as the Tory government itself. There is plenty of evidence to show that the leaders of the labour movement behind the scenes were actually encouraging Baker and the ruling class not to give any concessions. One MP, an honest supporter of Kinnock, admitted in a private discussion with Tony Mulhearn that, through his contacts in the Tory Party, he had learned that the government would not be able to stand by and see a major city go into bankruptcy.

This discussion was confirmed by reports in *The Times* (19 October 1985) of suspicions 'that a plan forged between Mr David Blunkett, the Sheffield City Council Leader, and the Association of Metropolitan Authorities, is being sabotaged by the Labour front bench'. It reported that Kinnock and John

Cunningham 'want to delay any attempts to save the council', and instead 'leave *Militant* to hang themselves'.

Jack Straw and John Cunningham in particular did everything to frustrate David Blunkett in his attempt to put together a package which could bail out the city council. Tony Byrne angrily declared: 'Cunningham could have been far more helpful, but he and Straw are so blinded by hatred of the Militant Tendency that their political judgement has been warped. They hate *Militant* so much that they are almost prepared to see Liverpool run out of resources as a means of getting rid of *Militant.*'

As the money began to run out, the workforce began to prepare once more for a strike. The government was still refusing to give £25 million to Liverpool although it had just bailed out Johnson-Matthey, the bullion dealers, to the tune of £150 million! The press were baying for blood, raking up any blemish in the past of council and union leaders in order to discredit the council. The *Sunday Times* on 17 November screamed: 'Security boss was jailed for assault.' Under the signature of Lew Baxter, a Labour Party member who worked for the *Sunday Times* and used his attendance at Labour Party meetings to gather information for this scurrilous anti-Labour journal, the report indicated that Ian Lowes had once, 12 years previously, been jailed for assault.

No measure, no weapon, no dirty smear was too low at this stage to be used by the press against the Labour council. Only during the miners' strike did the press work itself up into such a lying frenzy. An atmosphere of impending doom was deliberately created. Church leaders even issued a united call for prayer to save the city from collapse. At the same time, the press gave prominence to the statements of the Liverpool Liberal leader, Trevor Jones, who accused the Labour group of 'a reign of terror' and the national Liberal leader, David Steel, who 'urged Mr Kinnock to expel the Liverpool *Militants* from the Labour Party'. Steel and Jones, demanded that the government should speed up legal action to surcharge the Liverpool Labour councillors and disqualify them from holding office so that by-elections could be held in the city. Labour countered this by demanding that these 'democrats' resign their seats so that a mini-general election could be fought in the city in the event of Labour councillors being disqualified.

General Secretaries of ten major unions were mobilised to exert pressure on the council. At previous meetings with the council's leaders they had been asked point blank to spell out how many of their members the city council should make redundant in order to balance the books. Fred Jarvis, leader of the NUT, escaped out of a back door at one meeting rather than answer this question! A meeting with the national trade-union leaders on 11 November broke up in disorder.

The new feature of this meeting was not the role of the right-wing General Secretaries, which was entirely expected, but that of the TGWU, previously supportive of the stand of the council, but now siding with the right wing. 'Left-wing' officials like Bobby Owens, soon to become regional secretary of the No 6 North West Region of the TGWU, demanded that the council retreat. His outburst was to cause much bitterness then and subsequently. He had been raised to his position by the left in the TGWU, within which *Militant* had played an important role. The General Secretaries in turn had been urged on by Labour's front bench, who made the most outrageous statements in the press. Jack Straw declared to the *Sunday Times* (17 November): 'Hamilton and Byrne have emerged as *Militant* pawns' and 'Without *Militant* this whole, unnecessary crisis need not have occurred.' The Liverpool delegation was united in rejecting the General Secretaries' demands. The *Guardian* reported on 18 November that John Hamilton:

> said the union leaders had told them they ought to raise rates by 15 per cent on top of the existing 9 per cent rise and implied other cuts to balance the books. That could mean £5 on a weekly rate bill of the average household. That is quite unacceptable to us. We are quite firm in our resolve.

The *Morning Star* correctly identified the mood of the trade union tops: 'Trade-union leaders furious as Liverpool talks fail'. The full weight of the national trade-union machinery was now brought to bear in order to pressurise the council into making cuts and to undermine its support amongst the unions' rank and file members. NUPE sent out a national circular reinforcing the demands in the *Stonefrost Report*. The General Secretaries issued a statement which, while making perfunctory reference to the responsibilities of the government, demanded that the Stonefrost proposals be implemented immediately. All their efforts were used to force the council to capitulate.

On 19 November, Jack Dromey travelled to Liverpool and convened a meeting in the Liverpool boxing arena of the 2500 TGWU members employed by the city council. Liverpool councillors, even TGWU sponsored ones, were refused the opportunity to speak to the meeting. Dromey managed to persuade the meeting with threats of 'chaos and ungovernability' to pass a resolution demanding rate increases to end the city's financial crisis. When similar demands were made to a specially convened meeting of councillors who were members of the TGWU, this was rejected.

But the barrage of propaganda began to have the desired effect. Even members of the GMBATU who hitherto had remained solid in support of the council began to bend. Four hundred workers in the Cleansing Department indicated that they thought that rate increases needed to be introduced to solve the crisis.

Commissioners and Troops?

If the ruling class had been terrified by the developments in Liverpool this was only outdone by that of the Labour leaders. This fear was best expressed in the shameful support of Kinnock for the government's threat to use Commissioners and even troops against the Liverpool working class in the event of the city going bankrupt. Asked whether he would back the use of Commissioners, Kinnock replied to a *Times* reporter (22 November):

> If the council cannot quickly balance the budget on the basis that it has been offered, and thereby save jobs and services, we are going to have to put in the Labour Party a complete emphasis on trying to prevent that massive addition to unemployment and misery, and therefore give consideration to proposals which the government may want to put.

What this meant was spelt out by Anthony Bevins writing in *The Times*:

> Mr Kenneth Baker, Secretary of State for the Environment, will be prepared to send Commissioners in to run Liverpool, ousting the *Militant* dominated Labour council when Mr Neil Kinnock gives a commitment to support the necessary legislation!

Kinnock railed against Liverpool council: 'I think sometimes I would have to employ the services of a psychiatrist to identify the motives of some of these people.' (*Daily Express*, 22 November.) Using precisely the language which the press had urged in the past, he 'disowned' the Labour group. These attacks were featured in the *Daily Mirror* with the simple headline 'Madmen'. However, the more far sighted strategists of capital, such as *The Times* cautioned the government (and Kinnock) against prematurely sending in Commissioners: 'It must choose exactly the right moment. The electors of Liverpool must see in action the consequences of voting for this council.'

The statements of Kinnock, Cunningham, Straw and others during the Liverpool crisis provoked a wave of revulsion throughout the labour movement. It brought back the memory of the Callaghan government using troops against the firefighters in 1977. It also raised the question in the eyes of many workers about the role of a Labour government with Neil Kinnock at its head. Would this mean that the next Labour government would be prepared to use troops against workers in struggle? It was certainly unprecedented that a Labour front bench could give tacit approval to a Tory government for the use of Commissioners and troops.

An Orderly Retreat

By 22 November, with the offensive launched by the trade union leaders, an entirely new situation had opened up. While sections of the manual workers, especially in GMBATU were still prepared to battle on alongside the council, it would have been lightminded adventurism to lead the most determined sections to inevitable isolation and defeat, given the desertion from and even opposition to the struggle by local, regional and national leaders of the movement. It became clear that in order to prevent a rout, an orderly retreat would be necessary. *Militant* supporters recommended such a course of action to the District Labour Party and the Labour Group. It was necessary to adopt a strategy which involved conserving the main gains of the previous two years. A package was prepared to balance the books based partly on capitalisation and partly on new loans to make up for the cash which the Tories had stolen from the city and failed to make available in the current financial year. The DLP pointed out that Liverpool could still have achieved a victory in 1985 if the resources of the labour and trade-union movement had been swung behind their fight, instead of behind the *Stonefrost Report.*

But the press were dumbfounded at the reaction of the Liverpool labour movement when they heard the decision. *Militant* (29 November 1985) reported the aftermath of a special DLP meeting:

> The scenes outside the Liverpool District Labour Party meeting on Friday 22 November were more akin to a victory rally than the climbdown or cave-in or surrender described by the Tory press. This was the biggest meeting in the history of the DLP, with 700 delegates and members inside and a further 200 outside the meeting.

The District Labour Party voted by 694-12 in favour of adopting a recommendation by the Executive for the council to implement a financial package to balance the council's books. This followed a meeting earlier in the day of the Joint Shop Stewards Committee which voted by 250-30 to support the council's proposals. The local authority trade unions and the labour movement of Merseyside recognised by this decision that they had to accept an orderly retreat given the monstrous campaign that had been waged against them.

Not just the Labour and trade-union leadership, but some who stood on the left had played a less than honourable role during the November crisis. They had also clamoured for the implementation of *Stonefrost*. If Liverpool had been completely successful in its battle, this would have raised questions about the position of councils like the GLC, Islington, Sheffield, etc, in the earlier part of the year. Right wingers leaned on some of the lefts as a means of bringing pressure to bear on Liverpool to capitulate. In a letter to the Parliamentary Labour Party, John Cunningham and Jack Straw quoted David Blunkett, approving his characterisation of Liverpool's stand as 'insane' and also 'an act of sabotage of the labour movement'. Margaret Hodge, Leader of Islington Council had earlier had the temerity to attack Liverpool's tactics as 'discrediting the left'. *Militant* retorted that it was the actions of leaders like Margaret Hodge earlier in the year, running away from the fight on rate-capping, who had discredited the left in the eyes of workers looking for an effective struggle against the Tories.

The Liverpool DLP, and particularly *Militant* supporters, believed in telling the working class the truth about the November financial package, the acceptance of which was undoubtedly a setback. The main element in the package was a form of capitalisation, which was made possible by a £30 million (£60 million over two years) loan from the Swiss banks. This meant that parts of the housebuilding and house repair programme would be carried out on the basis of a deferred payment scheme (the municipal equivalent of hire purchase) financed by the banks, while the original capital funds from government grants would be used for current expenditure. This in turn allowed the housebuilding programme for the following financial year to be completed.

The package incorporated the use of the small helping hand of £3 million transferred borrowing capacity from other local authorities, arranged through the Association of Metropolitan Authorities. It also involved another £3 million of 'unallocated cuts' which the Labour group openly explained would probably mean some 'unfilled vacancies' as well as other cutbacks. But there was no loss of jobs in the financial year 1985-6.

The £60 million which was loaned by the Swiss banks would have been impossible but for the preparedness of the council to go to the end in the struggle against the government. Pressure was undoubtedly used behind the scenes in Liverpool by the Tory government, notwithstanding its subsequent claims to 'non-involvement'. The *Guardian* and other capitalist journals jeered that the 'gnomes of Zurich had rallied to the Trotskyists in Merseyside'. Neil Kinnock echoed the same theme in attacking the details of the agreement.

The House of Lords devoted nearly a whole day to denouncing *Militant*, Liverpool council and particularly the Swiss bankers for seemingly bailing out the council. Beside himself with rage, Tory Peer Lord Beloff even delved into history: 'He thought that Lenin's remarks about the capitalist classes applied particularly to the bankers: They would sell the rope by which they would themselves be hanged.' (*Financial Times*, 12 December 1985). But then, hinted the ignoble Lord, perhaps the £60 million loan was some fiendish plot hatched 70 years before and just then coming to fruition: 'He reminded us Lenin had spent a considerable time in Zurich'! The fact remains that the loan only came through at one minute to midnight, when it appeared as though the city was going to go to the brink and over.

17.

The Months of the Great Slander

When it comes to a threat against their material interests, the educated classes set in motion all the prejudices and confusion which humanity is dragging in its wagon train behind it...the struggle of the other parties among themselves was almost like a family spat in comparison with the common baiting of the Bolsheviks. In conflict with one another they were, so to speak, only getting in training for a further conflict, a decisive one.

In the assault upon the Bolsheviks all the ruling forces, the government, the courts, the intelligence service, the staffs, the officialdom, the municipalities, the parties of the soviet majority, their press, their orators, constituted one colossal unit. The very disagreement among them, like the different tone qualities of the instruments in an orchestra, only strengthened the general effect...the slanders poured down like Niagara. (Trotsky, *History of the Russian Revolution,* 'The Month of the Great Slander')

CHEATED ONCE more of an ignominious *Militant* retreat, Kinnock prepared for revenge. Under a headline 'Kinnock outrage', he threatened expulsions: 'We'll handle it, we'll deal with it, we know we're going to deal with it—but these things take some time' (*Post*, 22 November 1985). The *Sun* declared, 'Kick him out', referring to Derek Hatton. Gavin Laird, right-wing General Secretary of the AUEW on *Question Time* on BBC television a few days later also came out for the expulsion of 'Mersey Militants'.

Remorseless pressure was to be exerted on the leadership of the labour movement to pursue precisely such a course. The National Executive Committee meeting of the Labour Party a few days later, on 27 November, saw the adoption of a resolution to enquire into the workings of the District Labour Party. The right wing obviously conceived this as a constitutional device to carry throught the swift expulsion of Derek Hatton and Tony Mulhearn, which in turn would break the back of Marxism in the labour movement in Liverpool.

But there are stronger forces at work in society than the bureaucratic whims of the few right-wing leaders of the labour and trade-union movement. The struggle in Liverpool was born out of the social conditions in that city, not because of any alleged conspiracy, manoeuvre or intrigue, as bourgeois thinkers would imagine. The attempt to 'root out Marxism' from the Liverpool Labour Party was to preoccupy the National Executive Committee of the Labour Party for over a year. It opened up a shameful chapter in the history of the Liverpool and national labour movement.

In the month of December 1985 the hue and cry against Liverpool reached a peak. In the wake of the Labour leadership's attack on the District Labour Party through the medium of its inquiry, every old slander was dredged up. Piled on top of them were new ones. Liverpool, like the miners' strike, illuminated the gross bias of the capitalist controlled mass media in the modern epoch. Enormous power has been concentrated in the hands of five millionaires who control more than 90 per cent of the press. Through an intricate web of interlocking companies, these five millionaires also exercise a decisive effect over the television and radio.

In the economic upswing of 1950-75, the anti-Labour media was able to create an illusion of a spurious neutrality. Their bitter class hostility to the socialist aspirations of the Labour Party was somewhat muffled in this period because of the right wing's domination of the labour and trade-union movement. The Gaitskellite 'Labour lieutenants of capital' who held sway both in the Labour Party and in the trade unions were recognised as the 'second eleven of capitalism', to be put in to bat whenever there was a sticky wicket, in other words when capitalism was in difficulties.

A decisive change in their attitude was effected, however, as the labour movement began to shift towards the left. The baying and the howling against the left began with the attacks on Jack Jones, Hugh Scanlon and Lawrence Daly in the late 1960s and early 1970s. When Tony Benn began to move towards the left, under the impact of the Upper Clyde Shipbuilders (UCS) struggles and the miners' strikes of 1972 and 1974, he became a prime target for the press.

These attacks were merely pin-pricks, however, compared to the venom which was displayed when Tony Benn stood for the Labour Party Deputy Leadership against Denis Healey in 1981. The press consciously set out to break the spirit of Benn's supporters and to personally demoralise Benn himself. The gutter press compared him to Hitler, Mussolini, and almost every other hate figure in history, combining this with the use of 'special psychiatrists' to diagnose Benn's 'personality disorders'. The same methods, only in an even more vicious fashion, were employed against the leaders of the Liverpool struggle. The way that this onslaught was met in Liverpool, however, was entirely different to the way in which other sections of the labour movement had reacted to abuse.

The possessing classes have concentrated in their hands colossal means of moulding public opinion. This even went to the extent of open censorship and of direct interference by former Tory Party Chair Norman Tebbit in the workings of the BBC. While Tebbit's statements have had the effect of terrorising and intimidating pliable journalists, they have also begun to shatter the myth of 'media neutrality'. The mass media has 'influenced' decisive changes in politics in the modern epoch. Its methods are to emphasise the role of the personality, and to lay bare deficiencies in policy before the eyes of millions. This was not possible in such a direct fashion in the past. The Kinnock leadership, bending to every twist and turn in slanted 'opinion polls', has danced to the tune of the ruling class.

The only way to counter effectively the pernicious effect of the mass media is to create a gigantic counter-weight in opinion, in the form of a conscious membership of a mass party. This would create its own 'public opinion' through campaigns in the factories, workplaces and on the doorsteps. Unfortunately, the slavish reliance of the Labour leadership on the 'mass media' as opposed to building a conscious socialist campaigning rank and file in its own party has resulted in setbacks for the labour movement.

The situation in Liverpool exposed the role of the capitalist media, but it also demonstrated something else: the ability of the labour movement, under Marxist influence, to counter it. Nowhere in Britain has the media gone deeper into the sewers in its attempts to malign the Labour Party and its leadership. Yet it is astonishing to see what little effect it had in shaping the outlook of the working class of Liverpool. They largely remained impervious to the vile propaganda, giving consistent and unprecedented support to Labour in elections.

Press Poison

The role of the media in December 1985 warrants examination because it is an example of the dirty methods that the ruling class will employ on a larger scale against the labour movement nationally in the future. The anti-Labour baiting had been encouraged by the decision of the Labour Party National Executive Committee to set up an inquiry into the Liverpool Labour Party. The right wing in the party still had to tread very gingerly at this time, but the Tribune Group of soft-left MPs (which was in the process of becoming the new right wing) resolved to support the inquiry into the District Labour Party although they required that there should be 'no action against individuals'. They were to sing a somewhat different tune after the inquiry report was completed.

The *Sun* kicked off with: 'Hatton on the couch'. It proclaimed: 'The *Sun* does Neil Kinnock a favour by calling in shrink'. In justification, it drew on Neil Kinnock's diatribe: 'I would have to employ a psychiatrist to identify the motives of some of these people'. Invariably, the ammunition for the press vilification of the left emanated from the mouths of right-wing Labour leaders themselves: 'Loony lefts', 'maggots', 'madmen', 'literal corruption' these were just some of the choicest phrases used again and again in an attempt to hammer Labour.

The *Sun* declared: 'We called on top London psychologist Jane Fairbank to analyse Hatton's words and deeds. And her verdict: "If you call him a loony lefty, you are absolutely right".' Naturally for any capitalist journal, they concluded that, like anybody who challenges the system, he 'displays all the classic signs of a man who is totally out of touch with reality'.

Using the normal divide and rule ploy of the ruling class one journal after another began to emphasise the role of John Hamilton as opposed to Derek Hatton. *New Society* carried an entirely false report which claimed that John Hamilton's phone was bugged and that he was watched by secret cameras. In fact, the cameras had been installed to avoid the attacks on leaders of the council similar to those made by the Black Caucus.

The *Daily Mirror*, while repeating the lies of *New Society*, was forced to concede: 'But Mr Hamilton denied last night that he had attacked Mr Hatton and *Militant* activists'.

Celebrities Against Labour

The press then wheeled in certain 'celebrities' opposed to the council. First the *Sun* declared: 'Jim [Saville] quits TV panto in Hatton storm'. This was because of alleged *Militant* 'excesses', but rumour had it that Jimmy Saville was more upset at the prospect of playing the back half of a panto horse behind Derek Hatton!

Expatriate Paul McCartney was also deployed against the city council. The attack of Paul McCartney perhaps came as more of a surprise to some. After all, The Beatles typified the rebellious and radical character of Liverpool's youth even during the economic upswing. But to the establishment, McCartney was always the smooth and acceptable face of The Beatles. It was John Lennon who penned some of the most radical Beatles songs, such as 'Power to the People' which was associated with the magnificent half-million strong demonstration in 1971 against the introduction of anti-union legislation. Lennon marched on this demonstration, campaigned against the Vietnam War, and would never have vilified those fighting for the oppressed and downtrodden in his native city.

In contrast Paul McCartney singled out not just Liverpool, but the miners and the teachers in his sweeping attack in the *Sun* (9 December 1985). He declared: 'I was quickly turned off the tactics [of the miners] that led to so much violence'. No condemnation of the violence of the police and the state which resulted in the deaths of miners! On the question of the teachers' strike he said: 'Their action has succeeded only in punishing innocent children'. Again, no responsibility is imputed to the government. On the issue of Liverpool's fight he declared that he was angry at the 'mismanagement' of his home city.

What we have here are the sentiments of a former working-class boy, now middle aged and comfortably cosseted by a millionaire's existence, incapable of comprehending the struggles of ordinary working people to defend and improve their meagre existence. McCartney's words are remembered with much bitterness by Liverpool workers coming as they did from one who should have identified with the struggle of the oppressed in the city.

Union Right Wing on the Offensive

The offensive against Liverpool came not only from outside the labour movement. The national leadership of the TGWU, the GMBATU, NUPE and NALGO, all sought in special union journals, letters to the membership, etc, to justify their role in the November crisis. In the December issue of the TGWU journal *The Record*, Jack Dromey, principal architect of the TGWU's retreat in November, stated: 'We argued that the council should balance its books to protect jobs, services, and the housebuilding programme...bankruptcy was unthinkable'. Dromey justified the retreat on the basis that, because Liverpool was isolated, any other course would have meant that 'the council would then have lost control because the government would have bided its time and then intervened—and we would have seen a new administration dominated by Conservatives and Liberals, which would have slashed jobs and the housebuilding programme'. Yet it was the capitulation of the originally defiant councils, tacitly supported by the national trade-union leaders, which isolated Liverpool and, following the refusal of the TGWU leaders and others to stand firm in November, it became inevitable that the council would be forced to retreat.

In attempting to justify NALGO's stand, the union's journal, *Public Service* even went so far as to suggest 'the council's line became crooked'. NUPE pursued a similar vendetta against the council. But the national GMBATU leaders were the ones who showed most the venom of a trade-union bureaucracy whose 'advice' is unheeded. The *GMBATU Journal*, in January 1986, had the headline, 'Spend now, Pay later'. It retailed the myth that the *Stonefrost Report* would have meant: 'As little as 92 pence per week on the rates, (and) would have solved the financial crisis, said John Edmonds'. All of this was music to the ears of the capitalist journalists who continued to savage Liverpool.

Occasionally a particle of Liverpool's case would find expression in the press. Thus front page headlines of the *Sunday Times* about 'Hatton's Army' were answered by a very brief but effective letter from Ian Lowes in the same paper in December 1985:

The static security force was renamed 18 months ago. It arose out of the old night watchman night security section—staff were regraded and put into uniform, and 75 extra jobs were created. The article refers to accusations that employees in the static security force have intimidated members of opposition parties. No official complaints have ever been made against any officer, no evidence has ever been presented to support such allegations. I challenge anyone, including your newspaper, to bring forward evidence of intimidation by any static security officer.

Needless to say, no such evidence was ever produced by any of the bourgeois journalists who continued to elaborate on the theme of 'Hatton's army.' Meanwhile, the more farsighted capitalist journalists recognised the long-term danger posed to them by the emergence of *Militant* as a mass force in Liverpool. Michael Jones wrote about: 'A labour movement that was slow to realise that Hatton's militants are, in deed as well as in word, a revolutionary force.' (*Sunday Times*, 1 December 1985). Nor did Kinnock receive much thanks from the capitalists for doing their dirty work in Liverpool. On the contrary, his denunciations of Liverpool were used against the whole Labour Party. David Owen declared: 'Liverpool is a ghastly reminder of what government by the Labour Party means' (*News of the World*, 1 December 1985).

Tebbit might continue to attack Kinnock on the 'loony left' issue but not so the more farsighted John Biffen, then Leader of the House of Commons. In a speech to business people, he ruminated on the achievements of Thatcherism. In the scheme of things due weight was given to the role of the Labour leadership: 'We now have the enviable situation where militancy does not intimidate its way to success. The whitened bones of Scargill will soon be joined by those of Hatton.' Referring to the dominant ideas of the Labour leadership he said: 'They seek a Wilson-style socialism, tailored for whatever circumstances can provide the chance of power. The Hattons, Heffers, Benns and Scargills are an impediment to such an ambition.' Vainly looking towards a Lib-Lab pact, Biffen went on: 'The Kinnock-Hattersley Labour Party, with its far left humiliated, will be in a far better position to come to a post-election understanding, should that be necessary with those other heirs of pragmatic Wilson socialism—the Liberal-Social Democrats.'

The bourgeois recognised early that Kinnock's role in attacking Liverpool and the miners was an attempt to sanitise the

Labour Party, ridding it of all that 'socialist nonsense.' But the purging of socialist ideas was precisely the reason why the Labour Party was to lose the 1987 General Election. This defeat will, after a delay, result in an enormous recoil towards the left by the ranks of the labour and trade-union movement. This will be one of the results of the enormous errors made by the labour leadership in their approach towards the struggle in Liverpool.

The main backers of Kinnock on the 'left' (or rather the ex-left) were in the Labour Coordinating Committee (LCC). The LCC was completely blind to the processes taking place within the movement. With 'perfect timing' the LCC decided to call a national annual meeting in Liverpool in early December 1985. After denouncing *Militant* for being 'a separate organisation' with members, it boasted in a press statement: 'We have been recruiting scores of *new members* in Liverpool who are fed up with *Militant*'s intimidatory and reactionary politics and want a genuine democratic left-wing alternative [our emphasis]. Even the *Guardian* was constrained to comment: 'Scores of new members? A total of 1300 nationwide...so the LCC is an organisation?' Such fine constitutional niceties were of course glossed over by the Labour leadership. The LCC were their friends!

Completely standing reality on its head, Peter Hain, vice- chair of the LCC, informed the rally: 'Liverpool marked the turning point for the Labour left. A new radical left is coming through the party.' This 'radical new left' was to agree with the abandonment of the Red Flag for the pink rose, the elimination of nationalisation measures for a new Labour government, and a virtual abandonment of unilateral nuclear disarmament by the Labour leadership before the 1987 election. Paul Lally and Paul Thompson of the Merseyside LCC used every occasion to go into the press to denounce the council. In the *Guardian* on 9 December, they took up a theme of Kinnock's and attacked the loan from foreign banks: 'The subsequent deal was a disgrace. Instead of the relatively painless step of a small rate rise, it has landed the city with crippling loan repayments that seriously threaten important housing and social programmes.'

When Islington, Sheffield, Camden and many other Labour authorities resorted precisely to such schemes in the subsequent two years, there was not a peep of criticism from Hain, Lally,

Thompson and the whole gaggle gathered around the LCC. According to Hain: '*Militant* and other leftists are in a timewarp. They are the old left, their methods are crossed between Stalinism and the boss politics of Chicago's Mayor Daley.' The fact that the real Stalinists in both wings of the Communist Party, Euro-communist and pro-Moscow, were baiting *Militant*, the fact that the LCC was itself a cross between 'old style' left reformism and Stalinism, particularly in its strongest base in Scotland—all this was an insignificant detail for Hain. Needless to say, not one scrap of evidence was produced to back up the slur about Liverpool councillors being comparable to the corrupt 'Mayor Daley of Chicago.' But comments of this kind gave the green light to the press to step up a gear in their campaign of vilification against the council and particularly its leading figures. On 9 December 1985 the *Daily Express* screamed: 'Police report on *Militants* goes to DPP (Director of Public Prosecutions).' It claimed that there was a probe into claims of corruption and threats in Liverpool. It went on: 'Police have investigated Liverpool *Militant*-run council for alleged corruption and intimidation.'

Every old slander against the council or Derek Hatton was regurgitated in what was claimed to be an 'exclusive.' Not one of the accusations was new or had any foundation. This did not dissuade the *Sunday Mirror*: 'Dandy Derek's night out on the town, he goes in council limousine to private dinner.' Derek Hatton was attending a boxing club dinner in his official capacity as deputy leader, for which he received not a penny in expenses. One of the milder comments appearing in bourgeois journals at this time was from David Lipsey who was then a *Times* correspondent: 'The City [Liverpool] landed up with a gang of rogues and deadbeats.' *The Economist* developed the 'Mayor Daley, Chicago' theme:

> Mr Hatton has none of the eccentric metropolitan charm of London's Mr Ken Livingstone. Ranting and philistine, he is a throwback to the politics of the Fedora and the bodyguard...corrupt city bosses...unreformed municipal government, long steeped in corruption but recently captured by a minority faction wholly dominated by trade-union delegates (many almost certainly phoney) to the District Labour Party. Any political machine given such power would be angelic to remain uncorrupt. *Militant* is by no means the first, even in Liverpool, to wallow in its delights.

These charges of 'corruption in Liverpool' were made precisely when it was being revealed that British capitalism was plagued with scandals and corruption. Billions of pounds were being embezzled from the government and the public. Even the Tory Attorney-General condemned the 'quite unacceptable level' of fraud in the City of London. The frauds involving the collapse of the Johnson-Matthey Bank alone were estimated to have risen to almost £1 billion. A Labour MP, Brian Sedgemore, was suspended from the House of Commons because, exposing the corruption and the rackets involved in Johnson-Matthey, he accused the Chancellor of the Exchequer of 'perverting the course of justice.' Scandalously leaders of his own party voted for the suspension.

Even greater sums had disappeared in the swindles at Lloyds of London. Yet not one single financier went to jail. In 1983 alone there were 324 cases of serious fraud. Yet only 37 led to prosecutions. The cry went up from the left within the party that instead of investigating the District Labour Party in Liverpool the Labour front bench should have been demanding a massive public and trade-union enquiry into a system which the corruption in the City of London revealed was sick to the very core.

World in Action

The barrage continued to pour down in an unremitting deluge against the council. The worst example was undoubtedly the *World in Action* television programme on 16 December 1985. Under the guise of a news report, a vicious character assassination of Derek Hatton was undertaken by this programme. All pretence of 'investigative journalism' was abandoned. *World in Action* in the past had a certain standing as radical and 'anti-establishment.' Never again. It regurgitated all the old allegations which had been answered many times. Most of the 'evidence' was based on the unsubstantiated outburst of a former 'friend' of Derek Hatton, Irene Buxton. All the claims of Buxton and other personal and political opponents of Derek Hatton were treated as fact. Any attempt by Derek Hatton to reply was either shouted down or edited out. Even the *Sunday Times*, not noted for its sympathies with the left—admitted on 22 December: This was not an interview, this was an interrogation.' Their television reviewer went on to comment:

Chief Public Prosecutor Irene Buxton...I saw Madame Defarge on Monday night. She was not knitting under the guillotine, she was too busy building the thing. No-one who saw *World in Action* will forget the vision of vengeance. 'Did you see the eyes?' asked a man in a pub in Stoke-on-Trent.

A reader of the *Glasgow Herald* described how:

Hatton had been approached first and told they would go ahead with all sorts of allegations whether he appeared on it or not. About how they managed to insinuate at one point that Hatton drank. There was an implication that he drank heavily in shady boxing clubs.

Another worker who attended a meeting that Derek Hatton had spoken at in Glasgow wrote to the Glasgow *Evening Times*:

I shook hands with Derek Hatton twice on Thursday evening. I attended a meeting organised by the Militant Tendency. Derek was the principal speaker. I sat on one of the front seats facing him and I paid particular heed to his forehead and feet. There was no sign of horns or the shape of cloven feet as I had half expected after reading so much about him lately.

It would take a book to answer the slurs and smears of *World in Action*. What was most shameful about this programme was that the producers never admitted that much of the 'evidence' was supplied by the bitter opponents of *Militant* in the LCC. One of their members was a researcher for this programme. The day after the programme the capitalist press were in full flight. First fiddle in the chorus of denunciation was once more taken by the *Daily Mirror*: 'Exploding of Hatton'. Maxwell's mouthpiece gloated: '*World in Action* on Monday night was a devastating destruction of Derek Hatton. Hatton may bluster and cling to office. But that programme finished him.' Neither the programme nor the *Daily Mirror* 'finished' Derek Hatton. It was the undemocratic legal servants of the ruling class who put Liverpool City Council out of office. Derek Hatton replied to the programme in a statement in which he said:

I restate my relationship with the *Militant* newspaper. I am not a 'member' of any such organisation and know of no members. I cannot therefore have 'recruited' anyone to a non-existent organisation. *World in Action* spent approximately one hour interviewing me and I answered all the lies and slander they presented. Virtually everything I said was not used.

When he declared that he was consulting his solicitors with a view to taking legal action against *World in Action,* the *Daily Mirror* was insistent that he should do so. They declared loftily that unless he took legal action then the accusations of *World in Action* would stand. Thus one individual, with limited financial means, must be expected to take on, in heavily biassed law courts, the might of the television and press moguls, backed up by the full weight of bourgeois public opinion.

Libel cases often have the heaviest costs. After due consideration, he decided to answer *World in Action* not through the courts but by mobilising the public opinion of the labour movement in a series of meetings up and down the country. The *Daily Express* on Christmas Eve could not resist reporting that the Director of Public Prosecutions was allegedly considering 'a decision about whether to bring charges against members of Liverpool's suspended Labour Party...in the New Year'.

Militant on the *Mirror*

In the New Year the *Daily Mirror* resorted to another disgraceful piece of character assassination, this time against *Militant* supporter Dave Cotterill. On 17 January 1986 it declared: 'Scandal of Dave Cotterill...the face of *Militant.*' Without the slightest shred of evidence it claimed: 'He's jumped the housing queue, he doesn't pay any rent, who foots the bill?' Secret photographs were taken of Dave Cotterill, his flat was staked out and his friends were harassed. There was also evidence to show that his mail had been interfered with. Dave Cotterill answered back:

> Incredibly the *Mirror* accuses me of privileges in obtaining a 15th floor flat. Could it be that jealous *Mirror* journalists would like to swap their modest abodes for my two-bedroomed flat? Liverpool has thousands of hard-to-let properties, most of them high-rise flats. Five people previous to me turned down this 'plum' flat. In some cases flats can be allocated within weeks. I waited nearly four months for my allocation. At the time I was living with two other adults and a child in a two-bedroomed flat which was clearly overcrowded. The *Mirror* asserts that the tower block is mainly housed by the elderly, yet the lifts only go to the 14th floor, so what use is the 15th floor to the elderly? Out of the last six housing allocations, two others have been single people.

Militant replied to the *Daily Mirror* with an article: 'Scandal at the *Mirror*'. This revealed the real 'secretive' role of Maxwell's empire, showing how the Pergamon Holding Foundation owns the *Daily Mirror*. The Foundation, the centre of Maxwell's business octopus, is incorporated in Liechtenstein. The laws of this tiny tax-haven statelet provides a cloak of secrecy for tycoons with a strong aversion to public scrutiny of their books. Moreover, in 1971 the Board of Trade had declared that: 'Mr Maxwell is not in our opinion a person who can be relied upon to execute the proper stewardship of a publicly quoted company.' This was the man whose journal spewed forth charges of 'corruption' in Liverpool! Turning Maxwell's charges back against himself *Militant* declared: 'Undemocratic? How does Maxwell champion democracy? "I am the proprietor 100 per cent. There can only be one boss, and that's me".' The article continued: 'On a visit to Poland in 1985...Maxwell broadcast his support for the authoritarian dictatorship of the Stalinist bureaucracy headed by Jaruzelski. He had no sympathy for the struggle of Polish workers for an independent democratic trade union.' Maxwell was quoted as stating that 'the problem of Solidarity is now solved'. This 'solution' of the Polish totalitarian Stalinist regime was based upon the arrest and imprisonment of the leaders of the independent Solidarity trade union, and the suppression of its organisation. But Maxwell loftily declared: 'We certainly will be devoting less space to Solidarity and more space to improving trade relations between Great Britain and Poland.'

The Old Swan By-election

The press barrage was a means for ensuring a Labour defeat in the forthcoming Old Swan by-election. The press devoted unprecedented space to this local by-election in Liverpool. Top political columnist in the *Daily Express,* John Akass, explained: 'Why Kinnock wants to lose this poll.' *The Times* said: 'Council poll vital test of *Militant* policy.' The fact that the candidate in Old Swan was not a *Militant* supporter was immaterial to bourgeois commentators.

It is doubtful whether at any time in the history of local government elections in Britain, national journals have devoted more time and space to the outcome of a relatively obscure election in one ward of a major city. On the eve of the by-election the *Daily Mirror* resurrected the allegations of corruption surrounding the Asda Superstore planning application. The police, with exquisite timing, announced that they intended to question Derek Hatton over the affair. This was linked to totally unfounded press reports that the police wanted to question him about expenses claims. On the very day of the by-election the *Daily Mirror* devoted a whole page to these allegations hoping that the 'new revelations' would 'yet deliver a knock-out blow to *Militant*'s fortunes in the city'.

Labour conducted a creditable campaign in Old Swan. More than 150 attended a public meeting in the area to hear Terry Fields the local MP, Dennis Skinner MP and John Hamilton, Leader of Liverpool City Council speaking. However, there was also a constant uphill battle to counter the SDP campaign, the centrepiece of which was their use of a prominent quote by Roy Hattersley at Labour's National Executive Committee alleging 'literal and actual corruption'.

The Labour Party candidate in the Old Swan was Ann Hollinshead who, whilst standing on the left was not a *Militant* supporter. Unfortunately, no serious attempt was made to counter the press campaign both against the city council and *Militant*. In addition, days of blizzards up to polling day hindered party activists from reaching enough voters. The result was a disappointment for Labour. The SDP candidate won with 3313 votes, Labour was second with 2358, while the Tories were way behind with 506 votes, with 126 votes for the Independent Liberal. The capitalist press used the results to go to town. The *Daily Mirror* declared triumphantly: 'Poll defeat for Hatton's Militants.' *The Times* commented; 'SDP wins a Liverpool seat after 30 defeats.' Telling the truth for once, the *Daily Express* declared; 'Poll defeat cheers Kinnock.' Flushed by victory, the SDP 'heralded the fall of *Militant*'. The Liverpool Liberals forecast 'early council control'. Even the *Morning Star* devoted an editorial to the theme of 'Labour right wing and Militants rejected.'

The result did not reflect a massive rejection either of Labour or *Militant*. In 1982 the Labour vote in the ward had been 1869, yet even in defeat 2358 turned out to support Labour in the 1986 by-election. The SDP victory was accounted for by the fact that they had patched up their differences with the Liberals, and more importantly, there was a staggering 43 per cent drop in the Tory vote. It was an enormously 'politicised' election with a high turnout of 53 per cent. Given the character of the media campaign, the 2358 who voted Labour must have known that they were voting for *Militant* socialist ideas.

The Old Swan defeat was not the only one suffered by Labour at this stage, nor was it the worst. In the previous week in Motherwell Labour had lost a seat to the Scottish National Party (SNP). Earlier, in December, Labour had lost another seat to the SNP in the Ladywell ward of left Labour MP Robin Cook's constituency of Livingston. There, Labour's vote collapsed by over 30 per cent, and the SNP took the seat by 61 votes. Even *Labour Weekly* was forced to comment that the campaign in Old Swan 'was a very dirty campaign'. At first glance it appeared as though the aim of the press to deliver a crushing blow to *Militant* in Liverpool had succeeded. They were baying and howling for the heads of Derek Hatton and Tony Mulhearn in particular. Yet the colossal reservoir of support, the capital which the marvellous campaign in Liverpool had built up, held many more surprises in store for the bourgeois and their echoes within the labour movement.

18.

Bring me the Heads
of Hatton and Mulhearn

I DEFY anyone to tell me how you can go to Liverpool and defeat
Militant by argument. (Tom Sawyer, speaking at the National
Executive Committee of the Labour Party in February 1986)
Labour is being crucified by demonologies of its own making; having
set up the targets for its enemies to attack, it can hardly complain
when they score a bulls eye...the Party leader has built a whole
political platform out of dissociating himself from and demonising
'extremists' for a whole year, Labour's enemy number one was not
Mrs Thatcher, not even Dr Owen (still less Mr MacGregor), but Mr
Hatton. (Raphael Samuel, *Guardian*, 20 April 1987.)

MERSEYSIDE, next to the coalfields, had been the main
arena of big class battles since Thatcher's reelection in 1983.
Unlike the Labour Party in many other areas, in Liverpool the
party was overwhelmingly working class in composition. The
scope and intensity of the struggle with the Tory government
had enormously radicalised the rank and file which inevitably
brought them into collision, not just with the right-wing national
leaders of the Labour Party, but with those in the area as
well.

In other parts of the country, with the collapse of the Bennite
left, the battle to de-select right-wing Labour MPs had subsided
but in Merseyside (apart from Liverpool where by 1983 all five
Labour MPs were considered to be on the left) it intensified after
1983. Frank Field in Birkenhead and Robert Kilroy-Silk in
Knowsley North, typified those smooth, polished self-seekers
who had rushed to become Labour MPs in the 1960s and 1970s.
They were a kind of political 'yuppie' before that term had been
invented. Kilroy-Silk had even given a famous interview when

he first entered Parliament frankly confessing his ambition to become Prime Minister!

A thin veneer of 'leftism', for both were members of the Tribune Group, masked only for a very temporary period their hostility to the socialist aspirations of the working class and the labour movement. Indeed, Frank Field was at the same time a member of the right-wing Solidarity Group! Both were terrified of the reselection procedures. Soon after the 1983 election, Frank Field, (according to the *Guardian,* 25 June 1984), 'signalled in the plainest possible way his willingness to force a by-election if he was not reselected to remain his party's official candidate in the Birkenhead constituency'. He said: 'I am confident of being reselected, but my advice to colleagues deselected is that they should fight a by-election as the Labour Party candidate if all local party members are denied a say in who should be their candidate.' In other words, he was prepared to accept the democracy of the Labour Party so long as it fitted in with his personal ambition. Once the membership demanded a candidate more in tune with their thinking, Frank Field and his like were prepared to 'do a Bermondsey'. There, Bob Mellish, the right-wing Labour MP, had resigned his seat at the most inopportune moment for Labour in 1983. In the by-election, all Labour's enemies combined with massive press support in a filthy campaign against Peter Tatchell, which resulted in victory for the Liberal, Simon Hughes.

Birkenhead Reselection Battle

In Birkenhead, Frank Field was threatening similar action safe in the knowledge that the might of the press would support him. Indeed, the *Echo* (20 February 1985) reported: 'some Liberals have suggested that Mr Field should be given a clear run if he is deselected by his local party to increase his chances of beating Labour—and of joining the Alliance later'. Moreover, Frank Field was an open advocate of the so-called 'Rainbow coalition'—a deal between Alliance and Labour. Yet the national leadership of the Labour Party, let alone Labour's headquarters at Walworth Road, never once publicly rebuked Field for his repeated attempts to blackmail his local party with his threat to force a by-election.

Throughout, the reselection battle was punctuated with threats and action against the left. In June 1986 the right wing in Birkenhead were successful in getting the party to accept a motion to ban sales of *Militant* at 'Labour meetings and events'. This in no way affected the sales of *Militant,* however, because it continued to be sold at the entrance of all Labour meetings. The left candidate opposing Frank Field was Cathy Wilson, a Marxist. She had an uphill struggle, having only moved back to the area in the previous month and was beaten by 53 votes to 21. Nevertheless, she had conducted an inspiring campaign.

The reselection meeting itself underlined the shift to the right of the trendy left within the Labour Party. Many of them, no doubt with a 'heavy heart', voted for Frank Field in preference to Cathy Wilson. Some of them were so-called 'radical feminists', who in their hostility to Marxism, voted for a male MP who had supported the reactionary anti-abortion Powell Bill.

Frank Field, like many others, only went into the 1987 General Election as the Labour candidate because of the shift to the right of the 'trendy left', who in their class outlook were now little different to Field himself. Like Nineteenth century Liberals, such people wish to help, to 'do service', to alleviate the terrible conditions of working people. But they do not see the working class as the main agency of social change, they wish to raise up 'the poor working class'. Yet once the working class moves beyond the safe parliamentary channels which they prescribe, they jump back in fright. They recoil from Marxism, which expresses in an unequivocal fashion the will of the working class to change society.

The British working class, once it becomes conscious of its own power, and understands that the building of a new society is the only way out, will force its leadership to rigorously account for itself. The socialist transformation of society will be the greatest struggle in the whole of human history. It will leave no room for half-heartedness, middle-class equivocation, or backsliding. It will require a leadership theoretically and organisationally firm. The Liverpool experience had demonstrated that only Marxism was prepared to go to the end.

The political amorphousness, not to say organisational looseness, of the 'soft left', never mind the right, will render them completely unequipped for such a test. Consciously or unconsciously, in Liverpool they saw the outline of the ruthless struggle between labour and capital that will unfold on a national scale in Britain in the next decade. The harshness of the conflict could not but help reinforce their sense of helplessness in the face of this struggle. Such people tend to ascribe the ruthlessness and bitterness of the fight however, not to the mutually antagonistic class forces which confront one another, but to the 'intolerance' and 'lack of sensitivity' of the Marxists.

Invariably, the 'soft left' find themselves either suspended in mid-air, or on the wrong side of the barricades. Hence their bitter and venomous hostility towards the Liverpool struggle and particularly its leadership.

To be sure, there was nothing new or unique in the Labour leadership attacking the left. Herbert Morrison savaged George Lansbury and the Poplar councillors as their modern-day counterparts have sought to do to Liverpool. However, Morrison's strictures against Poplar were largely kept within the labour movement and behind closed doors and were mild in comparison to the modern case of Liverpool. Even the attacks on the Clay Cross councillors in the early 1970s were a mere slap on the wrist compared to the savagery unleashed by the right wing and the ex-left against Liverpool council.

The opposition to Liverpool was buttressed by the feeling that *Militant* supporters were poised to replace known right wingers as representatives of the labour movement in Parliament in the area. Already the majority of Labour MPs in Liverpool stood far to the left of the great bulk of the Parliamentary Labour Party. With the exception of Bob Wareing, they were to stand four square behind the council right up to its ejection from office by the High Court.

Kilroy Must Go!

The challenge to Robert Kilroy-Silk in Knowsley North, with Tony Mulhearn as the nominee of the 'Broad Left' in the constituency, gave this struggle for reselection national prominence. The disbandment of the Liverpool District Labour Party (DLP) and the steps being taken towards the expulsion of Tony Mulhearn implicit in the setting up of an inquiry, was Kinnock's method of attempting to save the skin of Kilroy-Silk who would have been incapable of beating off the challenge of Tony Mulhearn through democratic debate.

A barrage of biased media reports flooded the press as Kilroy-Silk tried to avoid going through the selection process. In his book *Hard Labour* published a year later, after he had stabbed the Labour Party in the back by leaving to become a television commentator, Kilroy-Silk shows his real character. He boasts of how at the 1985 Labour Party Conference he hit an unnamed delegate who he described as a '*Militant* supporter'.

Both before and after he left the Labour Party, Kilroy-Silk sought to 'prove' that *Militant* had engaged in 'intimidation, chicanery, lying and cheating' etc. The only evidence he ever provided was that Derek Hatton and *Militant* supporters glared at him at the 1985 Labour Party Conference! What he does provide in his book, however, is more than enough ammunition which indicts him precisely on the charges he levels against his opponents on the left. Thus Eric Heffer is described as 'that bastard'.

In relation to the incident at the 1985 conference, he wrote: 'There was no way I could back down, so I hit him first. Just a left. He went down backwards so fast that unfortunately, he put an elbow through a window. I pulled him back by the throat, about to hit him again ...I was irritated.' Imagine the headlines if a *Militant* supporter had resorted to similar action! Yet those very same Fleet Street organs gave a very polite 'tut tut!' when the story surfaced. Right-wing Labour MP Joe Ashton said when Kilroy-Silk seemed reluctant to broadcast the facts: 'You put a *Militant* through a window...That will do you no harm. Do you a power of good, that. Want me to tell the press?' Don Concannon, soon to defect from Labour with Kilroy-Silk, said: 'Well done. Don't stand any bloody nonsense. Hit the buggers.'

Kilroy-Silk had never actually been selected for Knowsley North but, as the MP for the neighbouring Ormskirk constituency, he had been imposed by the Labour Party NEC when constituency boundaries were redrawn in 1983. When Kilroy-Silk was threatened with deselection, Frank Field floated the idea of him standing as an 'independent' against Labour if deselected. He revealed that 50 MPs would 'canvass for Kilroy-Silk' in this situation. At the same time, Neil Kinnock described Kilroy-Silk as 'by any standards a first-rate MP'. Like a rejected suitor however, Kinnock denounced him when he defected a few months later. But for the time being Kilroy-Silk

melodramatically resigned his front bench position in the House
of Commons to 'concentrate on defeating the militants'. His
determination however was soon to crumble when a lucrative
contract as a television presenter was dangled before him!

Within days of Kinnock's attack on Liverpool council at the
1985 conference, the right wing began to exert remorseless
pressure for expulsions in Liverpool. The press was screaming
for blood:

> Kick out the extremists, Kinnock...it is no use Neil Kinnock giving
> the extremists the odd tongue-wagging on television. He must do
> something. Specifically, he must tell the National Executive to
> renounce every revolutionary, every far out leftist. So that they are
> sent packing, bag and baggage, from the party they have disgraced.
> And he must make sure they are excluded for evermore.

This concern of the rabid right wing *Daily Express* (31 October
1985) for the internal health and future of the Labour Party was
most touching. The pressure of the capitalist press was reflected
by the right-wing leadership of the AUEW who wrote to the
NEC, demanding that action should be taken against Derek
Hatton and the 'Liverpool *Militants*'. But Kinnock, seeing at this
stage the danger of a split in the party, resisted the pressure for
immediate expulsions. He said on ITN television news that: 'a
general purge would be utterly impracticable, as well as illiberal'.
Pressed on the point by his interviewer, Kinnock said: 'The very
simple reason why Derek Hatton is still in the Labour Party is
that he wants to be in the Labour Party.' The bourgeois press
was having none of this, and was determined to maintain the
pressure.

The mechanics of the witch-hunt, and particularly the role of
bourgeois journalism, were revealed in a remarkable exchange
between Kinnock and Anthony Bevins. *The Times* journalist
declared (8 March, 1985):

> Mr Neil Kinnock said last night that there was no evidence that
> Liverpool's leading local politicians, such as Mr Derek Hatton and
> Mr Tony Mulhearn, were members of the Trotskyist organisation
> 'Militant Tendency' and he challenged *The Times* to provide the
> proof under which they could be expelled from the party.

Kinnock told Bevins:

If you would put your considerable talents and those of your newspaper at the disposal of the Labour Party in order to provide us with satisfactory proof of individuals' membership of an organisation, then we will consider that evidence and take action upon it.

The right wing have always dismissed *Militant's* suggestion that the witch-hunt began with Thatcher and was orchestrated by the capitalist media. Yet here we have a leader of the Labour Party, a party that is committed to challenge capitalist society, beseeching bourgeois journalists employed by the most ruthless capitalist organ in Britain to supply information for use against members of his own party! The bourgeois have set out to split and confuse the labour movement and Kinnock has been their unconscious tool in this process. He has fallen for every snare which has been set for him by the media.

The cynical calculation behind the witch-hunt was that if Labour was to draw a clear line of demarcation between itself and the 'extremists', this would mollify the millionaire press. This in turn would guarantee Labour 'fair treatment' in the media. But, as the Marxists continually argued, for the Labour leadership to give their little finger would only lead the bourgeois to demand everything.

The lurch towards the right at the top of the movement had not reconciled the strategists of capital to the prospect of a new Labour government. They understood that despite a few expulsions, the forces of Marxism remained intact. Moreover, they were terrified that a new Labour government, given the inevitable retreats it would make, would give an enormous boost to the left and particularly to the ideas of Marxism. The right-wing socialist governments in Greece, Spain, France and recently in Australia had carried out a draconian programme of counter-reforms. This in turn resulted in opposition currents within the socialist parties. In Britain a powerful Marxist force would have acted as a catalyst which at a certain stage would result in a mass left wing opposition to the right wing. They were therefore not prepared to hand over control to the Labour leadership at this stage.

Thatcher summed up the long-term 'strategy' of the ruling class when she declared that it was her ambition to 'eliminate socialism' in Britain. She looked towards the Labour Party becoming the British equivalent of the American Democratic Party. Indeed, she rebuked the SDP leaders for not staying in the Labour Party to accomplish this task! The purpose of the witch-hunt was to make the Labour Party once and for all 'safe for capitalism'. In a most astonishing fashion Kinnock was attentive to the latest whims of the editorial writers in the bourgeois press. He danced to their tune between 1983 and 1987. Nowhere was this more graphically revealed than in the persecution and prosecution of the witch-hunt against the Liverpool *Militants*.

Inquiry into the DLP

In November 1985, the National Executive Committee of the Labour Party, after prompting by the TGWU General Secretary Ron Todd, and the GMBATU General Secretary David Basnett, set up a Committee of Inquiry into the Liverpool District Labour Party. This was decided by 18 votes to 9. None of those who voted against the inquiry were included in the inquiry team. At this same meeting, shamefaced at their role, the soft left backed the right wing on the NEC to end the practice of automatically recording who voted for or against a resolution. In future, a recorded vote would only be made if agreed by a majority vote!

The press and media spoke of the imminent demise of *Militant*. Norman Tebbit said: 'I wish Neil Kinnock luck in purging the extremists from Liverpool's District Party.' Only Sid Tierney, normally on the right wing of the NEC, expressed hesitations about a purge at this time. He referred to the 1950s, when there were interminable hearings and appeals and when the Labour Party regional staff spent all their time keeping dossiers on and 'policing' their own members and warned that a return to those days would lose the next election. Despite these warnings however, when it came to the vote he proceeded to vote with the majority for an inquiry!

There is nothing particularly new in the current witch-hunt against the Liverpool militants. The same ingredients were there in the war of the right-wing Braddock apparatus against the left, the followers of Aneurin Bevan, in the 1950s. Bessie Braddock fell foul of her predominantly left-wing Liverpool Exchange constituency party. Even her election agent Kenneth

Counsell opposed her. Naturally in her joint biography with Jack Braddock, *The Braddocks,* she claimed that this was not because of differences on policy but was a carefully constructed 'left wing' plot: 'Counsell brought Bevan supporters into the constituency and arranged for them to be elected to the management committee.' Shades here of *Militant's* later alleged 'bed-sit infiltrators'!

Braddock confessed that she was isolated from the constituency party and a motion was passed calling on her to resign at the next election. The regional Labour Party officer Reg Wallis stepped in and declared that the motion was 'unconstitutional' but the party proceeded to pass a vote of no confidence in Braddock. This in turn prompted Labour's National Executive Committee to set up an inquiry and in October 1955 the NEC, predictably, came out in favour of Braddock. Labour's officialdom was deployed to ensure that she received the necessary support at a specially convened meeting on 27 March 1955. Exactly the opposite process is unfolding in Liverpool today with the full resources of the North West Regional Labour Party, bolstered by many full-time trade-union officials being deployed by Neil Kinnock's 'political policeman' Peter Kilfoyle in an attempt to remove Terry Fields as Labour's MP for Broadgreen.

In the Braddock case, at a specially convened meeting in 1955 Exchange Party members: 'decided by 40 votes to 39 not to adopt me as a parliamentary candidate for the forthcoming election'.

The NEC then decided on a new inquiry. To the chants of 'Heil Hitler' Reg Wallis announced to the management committee that the NEC had imposed Braddock as the candidate of the party. The meeting carried a resolution of protest by 37 votes to 26. Such defiance was intolerable for the right wing and: 'ultimately the committee was disbanded and reformed without the communist and Trotskyist elements'. Notwithstanding this as Bessie Braddock ruefully comments: 'Unfortunately, we found no way of removing them (the communists and Trotskyists) from the Liverpool Labour Party or the trades council.' Is there not a lesson here for Neil Kinnock and his Liverpool ciphers!

Organisational measures cannot suppress ideas, particularly those which are confirmed by the march of events. Bessie Braddock was obsessed with the 'spectre' of Trotskyism to the end. The very last sentence of her biography warns: 'The purpose of this book is to bring home to the rank and file how wide the influence is and to warn them that unless positive steps are taken by workers themselves, ultimately these communists and Trotskyists will triumph. Democracy will be dead.' Her peculiar notion of defending 'democracy' was to cut a swathe through the democracy of the labour movement, yet this did not prevent the later emergence in the city of a far more powerful Marxist force than the one she had confronted in the 1950s and 1960s. Similarly, the attempted repression of the Liverpool *Militants* today will not fare any better in the long run given the stormy epoch which has been ushered in by the 1987 Wall Street and world wide stock market crash.

Kinnock was carried away by his war against *Militant*. One of his aides said on Granada Television: 'Kinnock hates *Militant* more than he hates the Tories.' In prosecuting this war against the Liverpool Marxists Kinnock was prepared to ignore the interests of millions of workers who were looking to a Labour government for their salvation. On Channel 4 on the night that the inquiry was announced, Kinnock indicated that he hoped that it would be all over by January 1986. He predicted that the future for *Militant* in Liverpool would be: 'very bleak and very short term. We are saying: *Militant* is on the way out and democratic socialism is very much on the way in.'

The inquiry was to drag on for almost a year and was to bedevil and split the labour movement throughout this period. The media had a field day in creating the impression of a Labour Party divided and riddled with 'loony lefts' and 'crooks'. Every enemy of Labour welcomed the inquiry. David Steel, ever solicitous for Labour's health, arrogantly declaimed that 'expelling *Militants* was not enough'. Jeff Tinnion, leader of Liverpool Against Militant (LAM) was ecstatic: 'I am absolutely delighted. The revolution stops here. We are very pleased Neil Kinnock took our advice to be strong.' With the headline 'The Enemies Within', the *Daily Mail* (28 November) congratulated Kinnock:

At last, yesterday, with a boldness born of desperation, he started to hurl something other than words against the *Militant* citadel in Merseyside...has he the stomach or the support on the NEC for a thorough-going purge of the *Militants*? Will he try to break their hold, for instance, not only on Merseyside, but also on the Young Socialists? Will he expel from the Parliamentary Labour Party the two MPs who support *Militant.*

The *Daily Mirror* expatiated 'Expelling the poison'. It went on: '*Militant* is a conspiracy, deceitful and secretive. It lies, it manipulates, it manoeuvres, it twists.' Uncharacteristically attempting to give a political basis to its charges, the *Daily Mirror* declared: 'Trotsky's theories were undemocratic and unworkable. His disciples' policies are the same. As the citizens of Liverpool have now found to their cost.' Unfortunately for Maxwell the 'citizens of Liverpool' continued to give their support to the *Militant* 'conspiracy'. The *Daily Mail* (28 November) featured Roy Hattersley's much quoted comments: 'We know that there has been intimidation. We know that there has been political corruption. We know there has been literal corruption—particularly in terms of employment practices.' Hattersley's words never be forgiven!

Under this barrage the leaders of the Liverpool labour movement remained firm. Tony Mulhearn declared: 'Liverpool Labour Party's democratic processes were second to none.' He described the NEC's decision as an attempt by the right wing to drive a wedge into the party: 'It is absolutely incredible. Rather than calling for an inquiry, they should have been striking a medal to pin on the chest of every single Liverpool Labour Party delegate because of the magnificent campaign it has fought.' Like Lewis Carroll, author of *Alice in Wonderland,* the press had adopted the motto: 'I'll be judge, I'll be jury, said cunning old Fury. I'll try the whole cause and condemn you to death.' The inquiry itself was to observe another maxim of Carroll: 'Sentence first—verdict afterwards.'

On 'Mafias, Safe Houses and Crooks'

A verbal lynching took place in the press with a conscious attempt to stampede the inquiry into a quick decision. The *Sunday Express* (1 December) proclaimed: 'Kinnock purge on crooks'. This created the impression that an inquiry was being conducted not into members of the Labour Party, but into some kind of 'mafia' that controlled the city. The *Daily Telegraph* declared: 'Labour seeks "safe house" for *Militant* inquiry.' This tale was obviously inspired by right-wing Labour Party officials.

The *Sunday Times* confidently predicted: 'evidence against *Militant* may go to police'. The *Mail on Sunday* went further: 'Grass on Hatton. A senior Kinnock aide said they would even take down evidence themselves and send it to the Director of Public Prosecutions.' Each of the tabloids attempted to outdo each other in the zealousness of their attack on *Militant* supporters.

Kilroy-Silk was mobilised by the *Sunday Mirror*. Without a shred of evidence, he wrote: 'They refuse to acknowledge—let alone tolerate—a different point of view to that of their own warped ideology. In my own constituency they falsify the minutes of meetings and refuse to correct them when challenged.' He had the neck to assert, with his record of hitting opponents in the labour movement through plate glass windows, that when *Militant*'s arguments failed: 'Members may be asked to "step outside". Intimidation of Labour Party members by *Militant* has now become everyday practice on Merseyside.' His *coup de main* was: 'This is not the Labour Party. It is more reminiscent of Oswald Mosley's Nazis in the thirties. And if thuggery is not enough, there is always patronage.'

The atmosphere of a witch-hunt surrounding the inquiry was created by this press campaign, yet the inquiry had supposedly been set up not to investigate the activities of *Militant* supporters, but to examine the workings of the District Labour Party. It was of course, in reality, merely a cover for an assault on what the bourgeois and their echoes in the labour movement considered to be a *Militant* stronghold. The *Daily Telegraph* revealed the real purpose of the inquiry on 2 December: 'Mr Kinnock seems adamant that Mr Hatton and Mr Mulhearn in particular should be expelled from Labour in the interests of the party's image to the electorate at large.' The baying and the howling of the press reached such a pitch that the Labour Party General Secretary, Larry Whitty was forced to step in and disavow the more lurid claims of 'safe houses' in Liverpool as 'melodramatic'.

The labour movement in Liverpool reacted angrily to the inquiry and the atmosphere of 'intimidation' of *Militant* whipped up by the media. The inquiry was also condemned by Labour party wards, regions and constituencies up and down the country. Hampstead Labour Party for instance condemned the NEC's action, and demanded that NEC member Tony Clarke of the Union of Communication Workers, and a delegate to the Hampstead party should not aid the witch-hunt in the party. The Greater London Labour Party Executive Committee, representing the biggest region in the country, passed a motion condemning the inquiry by 19 votes to 13. Symbolically Frances Morrell, of the Labour Coordinating Committee (LCC) and former adviser to Tony Benn, voted against. This was in anticipation of her further shift towards the right which would culminate in the Inner London Education Authority, under her stewardship, beginning a retreat which would result in cuts in education in London.

The bitterness of those councillors in Liverpool who were not *Militant* supporters, was expressed in a letter to the *Guardian* by Dominic Brady, Chair of the Education Committee. He declared:

> I am not a member of the Militant Tendency, most people are now aware that the vast majority of the members of the Labour group are not members of *Militant*. But on behalf of all other non-*Militant* members of the Labour group, I will say this to Neil Kinnock: If he continues to use the media to attack life-long socialists, if he continues to attempt to destroy Liverpool Labour Party and its achievements, he will end any possibility of a Labour government. And if he continues to consider expulsions of our comrades in the Labour group, he will do so over our dead bodies.

The offensive against Liverpool also began to unfold on the union front. The *Daily Express* (2 December), obviously on the basis of information from the summits of the unions themselves, reported: 'Unions join in all-out war on the Militants.' From this report it became clear that in the TGWU, GMBATU and the CPSA, the right wing were beginning to organise to combat the growing influence of *Militant*.

The internecine warfare within the labour movement was a gift to the ruling class. It presented the image of a split and divided labour movement in the teeth of the Tory offensive. The dispiriting, not to say demoralising, effect of these developments on the labour movement was expressed in the Tynebridge parliamentary by-election on 5 December 1985.

Incredibly, Anthony Bevins in *The Times* declared: 'Labour last night won Tynebridge with an increased share of the vote, an achievement which is bound to bolster Mr Neil Kinnock as he launches his struggle with the party's *Militants.*' To be sure, Labour had won by a majority of 6575, but far more significant was the turnout of only 38 per cent in this inner city seat. Thus two-thirds of the population had not felt motivated to vote.

Undaunted, the media, fed by a series of 'shock-horror revelations', timed another barrage to coincide with the opening of the inquiry on 9 December. Two successive issues of the *Daily Express* detailed what it called a 'dossier of dishonour'. The first melodramatically proclaimed 'Ousted—by a huddle of men beneath a street lamp.' The other one was entitled 'Hatton's inferno'.

Mixed in with all the old, and in Liverpool, discredited charges, were some new features. Thus the Labour council was accused of discriminating against Labour councillor Paul Orr, one of the 'scabby five' who had abandoned the fight against cuts. He claimed that he had applied four times to the Housing Department for a 'priority certificate' for his disabled wife. In fact, his application had been processed in the normal fashion and in effect what he was asking for was 'special treatment', and in particular the right to jump the queue—something that the *Daily Express* and the *Daily Mirror* had denounced *Militant* supporters for allegedly doing in the past.

Another spicy ingredient was the heartrending tale of Liberal councillors Pam and John Bradley. The *Daily Express* (11 December) claimed:

> At first they clashed verbally with *Militant* councillors who told them they would be put against the wall and 'shot' come the revolution. Death threats began to arrive with the morning post. Then came attacks on their cars. John's royal blue Jaguar was daubed with black paint, which cost £450 to repair. Pam's red TR7 was attacked with paint a few nights later. Windows in their shops and their home were smashed repeatedly.

Again not a shred of evidence was produced. Yet at the same time the *Daily Express* in an editorial declared:

> As we revealed today, the Merseyside police are about to submit to the Director of Public Prosecutions a file containing details of alleged

corruption and intimidation within the *Militant* controlled Liverpool City Council. The Labour Party team believe they can wrap up their inquiry in a mere two days. We hope they are right. In any event, they are most welcome to supplement their own finding with ours. Anything to help. Clearing the 'maggots' out of the Liverpool Labour Party is not just an internal Labour Party matter. It concerns the political public health of the whole country.

Joining in, the *Daily Mirror* (9 December) declared:

Militant is a political menace—a dangerous, revolutionary conspiracy burrowing away inside the Labour Party...They include corruption, the misuse of public funds and providing jobs for people who are supporters at the expense of those who aren't.

It then went on to reveal why this mud was thrown at Liverpool City Council and *Militant*:

That is a long way from *Militant's* public face of pure, clean-living socialists, working nobly for the poor and oppressed. These allegations do not apply only to one or two leading *Militants*. The charges are widespread. They point the finger at the whole *Militant* organisation.

No Evidence

This Tower of Babel of lies and misinformation was a deliberate smear campaign against the *Militant*. The bourgeois understood that *Militant* represented a new force in British society. Its demand for MPs and union officials to be paid no more than the average wage of a skilled worker had found a big echo within the labour movement. The bourgeois were therefore concerned to link *Militant* with allegations of 'corruption' and politicians 'on the make'.

Despite the avalanche of innuendo and of outright falsifications, not one single charge was ever brought by the police, and none of those raised by Labour's 'internal police' through the inquiry was upheld. Every single accusation was refuted. But this did not stop every opponent of the labour movement rushing forward to 'help' Labour and the inquiry. Thus, a particularly virulent representative of the Liberal Party, Rex Makin, a solicitor, arrived at the Labour Party's inquiry with a 'dossier' of complaints against the Liverpool Labour Party. Even the *Morning Star* joined in, reporting allegations without comment.

Tony Benn correctly forecast that: 'What the NEC's action has put at stake is not just the future of the Liverpool District Labour Party, but the future of the Labour Party itself.' Thus *The Times* demanded a far wider purge. Its editorial singled out Diane Abbott and Bernie Grant for expulsion, referring to the democratic governing bodies of local Labour Parties as: 'the ideological cabals passing themselves off as General Management Committees'. Sure enough, the right wing soon moved to begin expulsion proceedings against Birmingham Sparkbrook members who supported black sections in the party. *Militant* correctly warned that 'the attempt to purge the Labour Party of Marxism could cause Labour to lose the next general election'.

A rally organised by the officers of the Liverpool District Labour Party and the Labour group to protest against the actions of the NEC was attended by 700 Labour Party members. Why then did the District Labour Party, under the pressure of *Militant* supporters, decide to participate in the inquiry? It was not without opposition, and quite forceful opposition, not just from the left within Liverpool, but also from some *Militant* supporters.

An Independent DLP?

Militant is usually pictured in the press as grey and monolithic. Like all political groupings within the Labour Party, *Militant* is 'organised', in so far as *Militant* supporters meet together and with other left wingers to discuss and to debate the way forward for the labour movement. There have been occasions when *Militant* supporters have been at variance with one another, have disagreed, sometimes quite sharply, on key tactical questions. Indeed at each decisive turn in the last three years, there have been different views amongst *Militant* supporters as to what would be the correct course of action. There were for instance differences over how the Liverpool labour movement should respond to the inquiry by the Labour Party National Executive Committee.

Some, including Derek Hatton, believed that the colossal authority enjoyed by the DLP would have enabled it to have defied the disbandment edict of the National Executive Committee. They argued that thousands of workers would have rallied to the DLP despite any 'expulsions' of leading DLP figures or delegates to this body. The majority of active workers in the Labour Party, a significant section of active trade unionists as well as other leading figures in the movement, would have supported the DLP. Any rival organisation that would have been established by the NEC, at least in the first instance, would have been a very feeble affair. This would have enabled the DLP and the Labour group to have continued virtually undivided in its task of defending the city against the Tory onslaught.

The DLP would have been temporarily 'isolated' from the Labour Party's official organisation at national level. There have been times in the past when precisely such a development has taken place. Thus when Stafford Cripps was expelled from the Labour Party with Aneurin Bevan in 1939 for campaigning for a 'Popular Front', he took with him the Bristol Labour Party. The rival 'official' Labour Party in the area was a stillborn affair. The Bristol Labour Party was taken back into the Labour fold when Stafford Cripps, along with Aneurin Bevan, was allowed to rejoin the Labour Party.

The contrary view was advanced by leading local and national *Militant* figures. They argued that it was an unquestionable fact that the DLP would have rallied a significant layer of workers to its banner, possibly numbering 10,000. But an act of defiance of the National Executive Committee of the Labour Party, particularly given the swing towards the right on the NEC, albeit of a temporary character, would allow the right wing to separate some of the best left fighters from the Labour Party nationally. An 'independent' DLP would undoubtedly meet with initial success, they argued, in the short term, but would have undermined the long-term struggle to transform the Labour Party in a leftward direction. Through the trade unions, the Labour Party possesses a big reservoir of support.

Six million workers are affiliated to the Labour Party through the political levy. Superficial commentators, both of the capitalist class and the ultra-left fringe outside of the Labour Party, usually dismiss this as being a mere relic of the past political allegiances of workers to the Labour Party. However, when the Tories attempted to break the link through enforced political fund ballots, the results not only astonished them, but also the leadership of the movement and the assorted critics of the political levy. Every single union with a political fund recorded majorities, sometimes of a quite spectacular nature, in favour of retaining the levy. Some trade unions that did not even have a political fund adopted them as a result of the Tories' attempt to break the link between the unions and the Labour Party.

The mass of the working class, so the *Militant* Editorial Board argued, while passively supporting the Labour Party, had not yet actively moved into its ranks. They argued that for one worker who supported an 'independent' DLP, there would be another five, ten and perhaps 100 at a later stage who would move into the official Labour Party. These workers would be denied contact with the best fighters who would have constituted themselves into an 'independent' DLP. This left wing, particularly with the tremendously rich experiences of the last three and a half years, could be a vital yeast for the rise of an even more spectacular mass movement in Liverpool in the future.

Therefore, despite the heavy blows of the expulsion of Derek Hatton and Tony Mulhearn, together with other *Militant* supporters, it was necessary, argued the *Militant* Editorial Board, to accept the expulsions under protest. It was this view that won majority support amongst *Militant* supporters in Liverpool. However, the discussion was conducted, as with all issues which *Militant* confronts, in a comradely and serious fashion. It was done in such a way that all workers could learn and the labour movement as a whole could clarify these issues.

The issues were thrashed out amongst *Militant* supporters and between *Militant* supporters and sections of the Broad Left. To imagine that it is possible to impose the views of a 'narrow, dogmatic sect' onto the Liverpool Labour Party, which historically has pulsated with so much life, is to fail to understand just how the working-class movement functions. Many times *Militant* has adopted a position, only for this to be modified and sharpened in the course of discussions and debates with others on the left through the various Broad Left organisations in the Labour Party and the unions.

Right wing Labour Party spokespersons will, no doubt take this as confirming their contention that *Militant* is 'organised' and therefore, as they would claim, in violation of the Party's constitution. Before the introduction of the 'Register of unaffiliated groups' in 1982, the leaders of the right declared hand on heart,that unlike *Militant* they were not organised. Since the Register was introduced, however, it has been decreed that organisations within the Party *are* acceptable—provided they are not *too* organised. This is sanctimonious hypocrisy!

In reality the mis-named Solidarity Group and the LCC, which both have members and subscriptions, and the Tribune Group, have always been just as 'organised' as *Militant* and its supporters. The real complaint of the right is that *Militant* is more successful in 'organising' to get support for its ideas. The right wing in reality do not complain that *Militant* organises, but that it has been far more successful in gaining support among working people. While using organisational pretexts for disciplinary measures against *Militant* supporters, the right wing's real objection is to the *ideas* which are the key to *Militant's* success.

It is incredible just how much time and energy the NEC was prepared to devote to the attack on the Liverpool District Labour Party. But the venom of the bourgeois press and the right wing of the Labour Party was directed as much towards the control exercised by ordinary Labour Party members over their leadership as against *Militant*. The annual Municipal Policy Conferences of the District Labour Party made binding decisions. The DLP delegates in effect elected the leader and deputy leader of the Labour group, as well as the chairperson of the main council committees. *The Economist* bemoaned the fact that the DLP 'through its discipline can set the policy line' but the right wing never understood that the 'discipline' exerted by the DLP was entirely based on its political authority, gained through earning the respect of its members. While supporting Kinnock, *The Economist* pointed out that:

> Mr Kinnock's logic is bound to take him farther, into a proscription of all those who adhere to something like *Militant* policies. And if he really wants to do what no Labour leader has ever managed—rid his party of its Marxist wing—he will have little time before the general election to fight the Tories or the Alliance.

No wonder the bourgeois were prepared to give massive publicity throughout the inquiry to every bit of gossip and tittle-tattle of Liverpool's opponents.

On the very first day of the inquiry, the *Sun* reported: 'Shock 150 page blast at *Militant*'. This dossier had been drawn up by Jane Kennedy and the NUPE leadership in Liverpool probably with the connivance of the union leadership at national level. Jane Kennedy was more than eager to detail the alleged 'crimes' of the Liverpool District Labour Party in the safety of the inquiry's private sessions.

When the leaders of the District Labour Party appeared at the inquiry, they were given an assurance that they would be allowed to question their accusers and the 'evidence'. When this was revealed to Jane Kennedy by reporters, she was alarmed and threatened to withdraw the 'dossier'. The inquiry was a show trial.

Stalin himself would have been proud of the way that Charles Turnock, Tom Sawyer and others proceeded. Michael Crick reveals in *The March of Militant*, that they secretly visited Irene Buxton in Scotland. There was no opportunity for Derek Hatton, Tony Mulhearn or any *Militant* supporter to question the evidence of Irene Buxton. Nor was it the whole inquiry team who visited her but only those on the right wing, Turnock, Sawyer and Whitty.

The methods of the inquiry were even worse than those used by the Diplock Courts in Northern Ireland. This infamous court system prevented the accused from actually seeing accusers. However, at least the accused were allowed to hear the evidence and to question it. This was not permitted in the Liverpool investigation where the norms of natural justice appeared to be non-existent.

Militant Answers Back

Militant supporters did not take this lying down. Tony Mulhearn wrote to *Labour Weekly* refuting all the charges levelled against the District Labour Party. Not one of the vociferous critics of the council was prepared to go into the columns of *Labour Weekly* and answer the very detailed statement which he made. Once the real case of the council was explained in detail to workers, there was overwhelming support. Thus Ian Williams of the LCC failed to get even his own railway union branch to back the NEC inquiry. He was quite at home amongst the literati who were supposed to read the *New Statesman*, the *Guardian* and *Tribune*, which he regularly wrote for, but he was utterly rejected by workers in Liverpool. Shortly afterwards he was removed by his union branch as a delegate to the body the NEC set up to replace the DLP—the Temporary Coordinating Committee (TCC).

Jack Straw, prominent critic of Liverpool, saw his own Oval Ward in the Vauxhall Labour Party pass a resolution which dissociated itself from his comments. It declared: 'Jack Straw's time and energy would be better spent attacking the real enemy—the Tory government and their policies of mass poverty.' Where the inquiry and the subsequent expulsions received support, it was not out of genuine conviction on the part of ordinary Labour Party members. At best it was 'reluctant acquiescence', the 'price', argued the leadership, of achieving a new Labour government.

Every day of the inquiry saw more speculation—'inspired leaks' from right wingers, as to what the inquiry was likely to find. On 19 December, the *Echo*, in an 'exclusive' predicted that the inquiry would recommend to:

> i) ban the District Labour Party dictating day-to-day Labour decisions,
> ii) stop the DLP from vetting council candidates, leaving the job to local wards and constituencies,
> iii) limit the number of DLP trade-union delegates—which dominate the Liverpool DLP—to a certain number from each constituency,
> iv) ban Liverpool-style aggregate meetings open to all party members, not just delegates.

At this time the NEC expelled, by only 14 votes to 13, *Militant* supporter and Sheffield City Councillor Paul Green, this time with the opposition of David Blunkett, who felt the breath of his local labour movement hot on his neck. Also two constituencies in St Helens, which were in opposition to MPs John Evans and Gerry Bermingham, were suspended. The clear intention was to guarantee the sitting MP the candidature for the next election and the method the NEC was prepared to use was to suspend uncooperative parties one after another.

The *Sun* predicted, as the New Year approached: 'Hatton heading for heave-ho!' Just to demonstrate the impeccable 'democratic' credentials of the AUEW, a public meeting planned with Derek Hatton speaking in the Coventry AUEW hall was banned by the national leadership of the union. This did not prevent a very successful meeting from taking place at another venue.

By now the witch-hunting atmosphere was beginning to unnerve some of those on the left who had previously supported Kinnock. On 2 January 1986 even David Blunkett warned Kinnock that he could not expect the support of the 'soft left of the Labour Party if he embarks on a purge of the Militant Tendency after the current inquiry into the Liverpool District Party'. He said:

> One thing clearly upsets the electorate more than believing that there are a minority of well-organised, well-disciplined Trotskyite operators within the Labour Party. That is quite simply that the Labour Party is grievously divided and presents itself as a shambolic and feuding morass.

However, he was not to heed his own advice once the inquiry had met. Even the *Tribune*, rattled by the spate of revelations surrounding the inquiry declared: 'Why not shut up and wait for the evidence.' But it indicated precisely how it would react when the necessary 'evidence', no matter how shallow, was forthcoming: 'But the left naively call for "no expulsions." If the inquiry into Liverpool comes up with hard evidence of practices unacceptable in a democratic party, then disciplinary action must be taken against those found guilty.'

The inqury did not come up with the necessary 'hard evidence' but, contrary to its previous record under the editorship of Michael Foot, and Chris Mullin, *Tribune* now supported expulsions. This put it outside the real left in the labour movement. It has since vegetated as the home of the 'soft left' who have formed a kind of 'league of abandoned hopes' and become the new right wing. With all the deficiencies which a left reformist journal like *Tribune* possessed in the past, its current political line is a million miles removed from those who gathered around the journal in its heyday.

The great majority of the rank and file of the Labour Party, who consider themselves on the left, recognised the witch-hunt for what it was. One letter appearing in *Labour Weekly* from a former Labour Party local government officer, summed this up:

> The dubious merits of this foray must be questionable when leading party figures are calling their Liverpool colleagues maggots and psychiatric cases, indulging in lofty sentiments about restoring the good name of local government and unbelievably accusing Liverpool of confronting the government...If the appointment of political

sympathisers to posts and a lack of vigour and skill in equal opportunities policies, for example, is to be a reason for an NEC inquiry, there will be no shortage of Labour authorities to be visited. Where was the NEC inquiry when a Labour authority had a discrimination notice served on it by the Commission for Racial Equality for its housing allocation policies, when even Her Majesty's Inspectors of Education singled out a Labour authority for the poorness of its educational provision, when Labour authorities were charging the very poorest old and disabled on social security for home helps and an authority was banning a gay festival as 'a threat to public order'.

Labour workers had to pinch themselves to remember that the insane witch-hunt was taking place against a background of massive splits in the Tory government. An rupture split had occurred over the collapse of the Westlands helicopter company which was to cost Michael Heseltine and Leon Brittan their Cabinet positions. This and many other opportunities for Labour to savage the government both inside and outside the House of Commons were to go begging because of the colossal expenditure of energy of the Labour Party leaders on the Liverpool District Labour Party inquiry.

19.

The 'Lefts' Move Right

There is a ruling class and a working class. There are elements within our own movement who have clearly not grasped the significance of events taking place. The witch-hunt is something I thought had gone out of the Labour Party forever. (Arthur Scargill, President of the National Union of Mineworkers, 12 January 1986)

ARTHUR SCARGILL, Tony Benn, Eric Heffer and a few others were in a minority amongst the 'left' in adopting a principled position towards the witch-hunt at the beginning of 1986. A sea change had taken place in the approach of the 'soft left', including those on the NEC, towards expulsions. This was the decisive factor which allowed Kinnock to pursue his vendetta against *Militant*. At the time of the expulsion of the *Militant* Editorial Board, Michael Meacher correctly wrote in *Labour Weekly* (18 February 1983) that leading witch-hunter John Golding was 'bleeding the Party's election prospects to death'. Moreover, in Labour's magazine, *New Socialist* (September-October 1982) an editorial denounced the witch-hunt:

The expulsion of leading *Militant* supporters [is] wrong. The Labour Party always has been a broad collection that includes Marxists amongst its ranks. The Militant Tendency, drawing as it does upon Trotsky's critique of Stalinism, belongs to this Marxist tradition, and has a legitimate place within the Labour Party. The charges being levelled against *Militant* that it is 'a party within a party' is one that can be levelled with equal justification against other groups within the Labour Party on both the left and right...The very existence of *Militant* and other groups within the Labour Party is a source of strength rather than a weakness. By working for the adoption of alternative policies and candidates, they assist the democratic functioning of the party.

The LCC 'Dossier'

An entire epoch seemed to separate the lefts of 1983 from the 'soft left' of 1985-6 and particularly from the Labour Coordinating Committee (LCC). The 'evidence' supplied by the Merseyside LCC, a small band of discontented petit-bourgeois without real roots in the labour movement in the area, became the principal source of information used by the majority on the DLP inquiry to justify expulsions. The LCC had come a long way from its left phase of 1979-81. Then it had been attacked by the millionaire press, along with other tendencies on the left, for daring to recommend in a letter to constituencies of the Labour Party that they should ask their MPs how they intended to vote in the elections for the deputy leadership of the Labour Party. Then they were fawning on Tony Benn. This was the route whereby they hoped to ride to power and influence in the labour movement.

The same press now lionised the LCC, reprinting its alleged 'evidence' against Liverpool District Labour Party (DLP) 'malpractices' at enormous length. The *Sun* approvingly stated that '*Militant* moles' were 'in control'. The LCC's kindred spirits, *Guardian* journalists Martin Linton and Alan Dunn, gleefully reported: '*Militant's* rivals claim exposure of party plot.' Philip Webster in *The Times* wrote: 'Militant Tendency accused of physical attacks on Labour opponents.' In a later report, Martin Linton went much further: '*Militant* grip on Liverpool gained by usurping power of local parties.' All of this and two special issues of *Tribune*, was based on an LCC 'dossier' submitted to the inquiry with advance copies sent to the capitalist press. *Tribune* however, refused *Militant's* request for an advance copy. Nor was the DLP Executive given the opportunity of answering the allegations in the report.

Marxism of course has had a long experience of vilification by its capitalist enemies. It has had to contend with constant attacks from the right wing of the labour movement. But rarely in the history of the British labour movement has a supposedly left-wing organisation stepped into the gutter to the extent that the LCC did in relation to the Liverpool DLP.

Marx, Engels, Lenin and Trotsky also had many occasions to devote thousands of words to refuting the slanders of their opponents. Marx was compelled to devote a whole book, *Herr*

Vogt, replying to a slanderer. *The Case of Leon Trotsky* is a monumental and lengthy answer to Stalin's Frame-up trials. Likewise *Militant* was compelled to devote considerable time, space and effort to refuting the slanders of the LCC. Like the capitalist press the LCC attempted to bury the magnificent experiences of Liverpool under a heap of slander and misrepresentation. They attempted to build up a picture of 'malpractice and corruption' maintained through the undemocratic manipulation by *Militant* of the Labour group and the DLP.

However not one of the allegations of the LCC was ever made directly either to the DLP or to the Executive of the DLP. The small band of LCC supporters waited until a witch-hunt was in full swing before regurgitating what Tony Mulhearn described as 'almost every lie and distortion spewed out from the Liberals and Tories and faithfully recorded by the press over the past three years'.

Not once before the September 1985 crisis did the LCC raise an alternative political perspective for the struggle of the council. On the contrary, they had gone out of their way to reject the attacks on *Militant* as a diversion from the struggle against cuts. Needless to say, they were not at all overjoyed at the colossal influence exercised by *Militant*, but the pressure of the mass movement compelled them to hold back.

It was only after the set-back of September 1985, when all-out strike action was rejected, that the LCC began to stir themselves to become the stalking horse for the right-wing leaders of the labour and trade-union movement. Incapable of winning the argument on political terrain, the LCC took to the road of vilification.

What then were the main charges against the DLP in the LCC's dossier? Echoing bourgeois hostility to the links of unions with Labour, the LCC incredibly objected to 'unions having a disproportionate influence' in the DLP. Paying a back-handed compliment they went on: 'In effect it [the DLP] acts as a general political Parliament on all aspects of policy, ranging from local and national, to international issues.' The DLP was accused of the crime of discussing issues such as South Africa, Nicaragua, the struggles of workers in France and Spain etc! The LCC wished to confine the DLP to deliberations of such issues as the bins and pavements!

These accusations were coupled with criticisms that the DLP did not have 'properly constituted meetings' but big aggregates. Speaking about the massive 22 November 1985 DLP meeting which ratified the budget settlement, the LCC complained: 'Some delegates were locked out because the hall was full.' This was a packed meeting, with over 700 delegates and visitors present. The stewards made every effort to ensure that delegates were admitted. Not one single complaint was received by DLP officers about delegates who were unable to get into this meeting.

The gist of the LCC criticism was that the DLP meetings were 'too big' for a handful of frightened petty-bourgeois, lacking confidence in their ideas, and more used to the cosseted atmosphere of the university seminar. To them the massive working-class meetings must indeed have seemed like 'intimidation'. Throughout the history of the Labour and trade-union movement, right-wing leaders have always been organically suspicious of the involvement of the masses in their own organisations. This has applied not just to the full-blown bureaucracy at the top of the labour movement, but also to the incipient bureaucrats such as those who control the LCC.

They accused the DLP of not 'functioning normally'. They also alleged that the Executive of the DLP treated the DLP 'in a cavalier manner...even before the suspension, there has been no DLP meetings since September'. There were in fact only two ordinary business meetings which did not take place prior to the suspension, which was imposed just before the December meeting. These were in October, at the time of the Labour Party Conference in Bournemouth, and in November when the budget crisis came to a head. In both cases the meetings had not been held because of the need to deal with these other important events. They were not 'ordinary' months when 'normal' business meetings could take place. The financial and political situation changed from day to day, sometimes from hour to hour. The leadership of the DLP had a far from 'cavalier attitude' to the rest of the DLP. In fact, between October and December 1985 the DLP Executive met seven times and convened eight aggregate meetings, five public meetings, a national conference, and numerous meetings with the trade unions.

The LCC spoke of the 'danger' of DLP aggregates. It stated: 'It is impossible to scrutinise the actions of the Executive and council leadership particularly when meetings are called at short notice and are presented with complex financial and other information on the night itself.' But as *Militant* in its reply asked:

> What really is the LCC's complaint? The Labour group's general policy was clear—to oppose cuts and fight for this Tory government to provide the necessary resources. The aggregates were called because of events—which often meant rapid changes in the position. How many other Labour groups consult the widest number of DLP delegates and members on the details of policy and tactics, and publicly present the ranks with 'complex financial and other information?'. If the LCC had their way, DLP delegates would meet behind closed doors, without the scrutiny of rank and file members, and 'democratically' vote to abandon the fight against cuts.

Their accusations regarding 'intimidation' at DLP meetings amounted to objecting to the occasional heckling which had been no greater than that traditionally experienced at large meetings of the labour movement. Tony Mulhearn commented in relation to this allegation:

> Ordinarily, the whinging of an insignificant rump organisation containing a handful of disaffected individuals would not be of any concern to a large democratic vibrant socialist body such as the Liverpool DLP. Unfortunately though, the jaundiced views of the LCC rump seem to carry more weight than those of hundreds of good, honest, working-class Labour Party members.

The crux of the LCC's conclusions was the paragraph which suggested that:

> Any measures taken by the NEC must be capable of gaining the consent of the majority of non-*Militant* members...At the moment large scale expulsions fail to meet that criteria. However, we recognise the rights of the NEC to take action against individuals on the basis of breaches of the party constitution and rules.

In a nine-page document, the DLP gave a point by point answer to the LCC. The LCC complained that prospective councillors had to swear 'a loyalty oath' to the DLP because, like many other DLPs throughout the country, the Liverpool party required prospective councillors to answer three standard questions. The DLP showed in detail that there was no prospective councillor who supported the LCC who had been 'debarred' from the panel of candidates.

The criticism of council policy, particularly on 'nomination rights' and that council employees who do not support *Militant* policies were sent to a 'leper colony' were completely refuted. In relation to this charge, the DLP commented:

> There are several council employees who have scabbed on trade unionists in the anti-privatisation struggles under the Liberal council and the protest strikes to defend jobs and services. Trade unionists will not work with these individuals. Are the LCC demanding that good trade unionists be forced to work with scabs?

Despite the huge publicity given to the LCC, not one of their charges was later to be upheld in the full hearings of the National Executive Committee meetings! The real purpose of their 'evidence' was revealed in their list of organisational changes they required. *Militant* pointed out: 'These add up to a charter for frustrated careerists. If adopted, these proposals would set the labour movement back 30 years to the period of right-wing domination.' A crucial proposal was: 'That a new DLP constitution should restrict its powers to making policy guidelines and supervising the Labour group, coordination of city wide local government campaigns, and the municipal panel.' This was a covert way of advocating the autonomy of the Labour group. It flew in the face of the struggle of the left to bring public representatives under the control of the ordinary members of the party. What *was* the ferocious struggle on the issue of reselection of MPs, but an attempt to bring all public representatives of the movement under the control of those people who select and work for them? The press were hostile to the idea of reselection and in favour of 'autonomy' of MPs and Labour Groups. They recognised that this was the only way that the pressure of bourgeois 'public opinion' could be exerted to water down and render harmless the socialist aspirations of the Labour movement.

The LCC's proposals went hand in hand with support for Neil Kinnock's efforts to establish the independence of the parliamentary leadership from the Labour Party as a whole, with the necessary freedom to then go on to ditch radical conference policies and override democratic processes. Without the attack on the Liverpool *Militant* supporters, and a subsequent witch-hunt against others on the left, the right wing leadership would not have been able to carry through a massive revision in party policy in the period 1985-7. The attack on Liverpool paved the way for the defeat of Labour in the 1987 general election.

Buried in the LCC's massive dossier of complaints and allegations, there is one paragraph, significantly not quoted in the *Tribune* extracts, which says it all:

> A theory of organisational conspiracy, however, has limited explanatory power. *Militant* has very deep roots in the Liverpool party, and has gained considerable respect for its commitment and its association with ridding the party of the discredited right-wing machine. Furthermore, its workerist, bureaucratic but anti-capitalist policies have great appeal among many party members in the city. Many members see them as the left—militant with a little 'm' rather than *Militant* with a big 'M'. This false image is naturally cultivated carefully by their organisation. More recently it has been strengthened by alliances made with local authority activists, mainly in the manual unions, for whom their top-down socialism has immediate appeal and material benefits in terms of jobs and conditions.

Leaving aside all the waffle about *Militant* being an 'organisation' and the jibes about 'workerist' and 'bureaucratic' policies what the LCC are admitting through gritted teeth is that despite all the attacks, *Militant* had deep support for its ideas amongst the workers of Liverpool.

It did not bother the LCC that in attacking alleged '*Militant* full-timers' in Liverpool, they singled out a South African student whose position in this country would have been in jeopardy had they been allowed to continue with their slander. The LCC's 'evidence', together with leaks from the right wing on the inquiry team, led to open speculation in late January that a list of expulsions had already been drawn up. This was to lead to members of the suspended DLP having to have recourse to the High Court in late January.

Legal Action

In the three months up to January 1986, repeated requests had been made for the DLP to be given assurances that anyone facing disciplinary charges arising out of the inquiry would be given a fair hearing 'according to the rules of natural justice'. The right-wing dominated NEC refused to give such categorical assurances so the accused had no alternative but to go to the High Court to demand them.

Faced with this application for an injunction, Larry Whitty produced an affidavit giving the necessary assurances. Although the affidavit was not a binding undertaking, the judge commented that if the NEC did not stick to its word, there would be an 'open and shut case' for the DLP to return to the court to overturn any action against them. Some on the left, such as Blunkett, who were afraid now of the consequences of their ill-judged support for the witch-hunt, joined Tony Benn in a campaign against expulsions. A joint statement was drawn up, but the 'soft left' insisted that it be toned down to one which would reject the expulsion specifically 'of socialists...for their political beliefs'. In other words, an escape clause was still left to justify support for expulsions on the basis of unsubstantiated organisational charges or claims of 'violence and intimidation'. It is as well to remember that the Liverpool *Militant* supporters were eventually expelled not for 'intimidation, malpractices and violence' but specifically for speaking on *Militant* platforms, that is, for their 'political beliefs'. Having once made a compromise with the right, the soft left were compelled to go the whole hog and support expulsions at a later stage.

While the inquiry was taking place *Militant* supporters did not sit on their hands waiting for the blow to fall. On the contrary, an enormous fightback campaign was launched throughout the country. This kicked off with an enthusiastic meeting of 800 people who poured into the Manchester Free Trade Hall to hear Derek Hatton and Peter Taaffe, together with John Tocher, Broad Left candidate in the AUEW Presidential elections. This was followed by meetings of more than 1000 in London, 1300 in Glasgow, 1300 in Edinburgh, 1000 in Newcastle and one of the biggest meetings of the labour movement ever in Sheffield, of 700.

Even in Neil Kinnock's own constituency of Islwyn, 500 Welsh workers turned out to greet enthusiastically the speeches of Derek Hatton and Peter Taaffe at a meeting in a local school hall. The mean-minded local right-wing supporters of Kinnock on the local council took their revenge later by prosecuting Peter Taaffe, as the Editor of the *Militant*, for posters which had been put up advertising the rally. This was not the first nor the last example of Kinnock's highly 'personalised' brand of politics whereby individuals were picked out for attack rather than ideas. Undaunted, *Militant* supporters in the first six months of 1986 organised over a hundred meetings up and down the country opposing the witch-hunt. These meetings were attended by 50,000 or more workers and comprised the biggest meetings since the miners' strike, in some areas the biggest for 40 years!

Some of the most oppressed and down-trodden layers of the working class, who had not been involved in the organisations of the labour movement before were drawn to the banner of *Militant*. Derek Hatton and Tony Mulhearn were attracting the biggest meetings of any figures in the labour movement. This was an indication of the process of transformation which will encompass the whole of the labour movement in the next decade, as Marxism becomes the predominant force within the movement.

The deeper that *Militant* penetrated the ranks of the working class, the greater the warmth and the ardour for its ideas. The bourgeois could see this, and demanded that Kinnock should not flinch from the 'necessary task of purging *Militant*'. The *Daily Express* (13 February) summed up their attitude:

> Neil Kinnock will shortly face the acid test of his Labour leadership. Within two weeks he will have to decide whether or not to back demands for the expulsion of 20 leading Trotskyists from his party. Such a wholesale purge of the Liverpool Militants is certain to lead to a bitter left-right clash, and could even cost Mr Kinnock his job, even if the Executive votes for expulsions, *Militant* is certain to challenge their verdict in the courts—ensuring a bitter and prolonged battle. Last night, two *Militant* supporters from Ipswich won a court injunction stopping their local party from expelling them.

The bourgeois were egging on Kinnock, conscious of the fact that this would split and divide Labour and play into the hands of the Tories and the Liberal-SDP Alliance. The right wing decided to go ahead with the National Executive Committee meeting to consider the inquiry, despite an impending by-election in Fulham and the pressing political tasks which confronted the labour movement.

The intimidatory tone and manner of the inquiry sessions was a disgrace to the labour movement. Eric Heffer accompanied Derek Hatton during his DLP 'interview'. He commented:

I went along with Derek Hatton as a witness to his interrogation by the inquiry team and I must say that from the behaviour of one person in particular, it would not have been out of place for him to have been wearing jackboots. As a former chair of the Organisation Sub-Committee, I have conducted a number of such inquiry's in various areas, but I have never seen anything like this person's behaviour. It was disgusting, nothing but a McCarthyite inquisition. I shall be raising the whole matter at the NEC.

Eric Heffer was referring to the inquiry Chair, Charles Turnock. His objectionable manner was displayed not just towards Derek Hatton. During Richard Venton's 'interrogation' he said: 'Natural justice is not a thing that you are concerned with at the moment.' When the victims of their interrogation asked for documentary evidence of allegations, or what the implications of questions were, they were refused an answer and badgered with demands like: 'Are you refusing to answer our question?' One source of evidence produced by the right wing was an article in Murdoch's *Sunday Times*. When the 'accused' Richard Venton denounced the lies in this article, Charles Turnock made the absurd suggestion that he should take legal action against Murdoch—the same Murdoch who had just secured the sequestration by the courts of the entire £17 million assets of the print union SOGAT!

NEC member Audrey Wise completely dissociated herself from the tone of the interrogations. At one stage Cathy Wilson, who had challenged Frank Field in the parliamentary selection for Birkenhead, was reduced to tears by the disgraceful behaviour of members of the inquiry team. The bogus character of the proceedings was indicated by the fact that some people named in written allegations were not called in, including DLP delegates. Yet others, such as Tony Aitman and Lesley Holt, who were called in, had not been DLP delegates for at least the previous six years.

Even before the inquiry had completed its work, the intentions of the right wing were clear. Well informed leaks about expulsions were featured prominently in the Liverpool and national press: 'About 12 Liverpool *Militants* face expulsion from the Labour Party following the probe by national chiefs.' (*Echo*, 17 February) The *Daily Star* was in the vanguard: 'Kinnock to boot out Hatton'. The 'quality' *Guardian* commented: 'Labour ready to disband Liverpool party.' Derek Hatton condemned the inquiry as 'a kangaroo court' and accused it of reaching a verdict before hearing any of the evidence. The *Morning Star* also was convinced: '*Militant* faces expulsions.'

The national and local press began another offensive against the leading *Militant* supporters on the council as a means of reinforcing the expected 'expulsion' decision of the inquiry. For a whole month, the *Echo* had conducted a vicious personal campaign against Tony Mulhearn, running lurid headlines: 'The man who wants to stop you reading your *Echo*...Town Hall keeps gag on *Echo*.' The *Echo*'s editor, Chris Oakley had been incensed by Tony Mulhearn's stand on two issues. Firstly, because Tony Mulhearn had refused to speak to the *Echo* as a result of a request by the National Graphical Association (NGA) which was in dispute with the management of the paper. However, what rankled even more with the *Echo* editor, was the analysis which had been made by the council's campaign unit, of 37 editorials published between 1 October 1985 and 22 November 1985, in which the *Echo* had only twice acknowledged that the city deserved more cash than the government was providing! Dropping all pretence of 'neutrality' the *Echo* waded in:

> Mr Mulhearn simply wants the bullying, the wheeler dealing and the incompetence which characterises *Militant's* handling of the city's affairs to go unreported. Neil Kinnock calls Militants like Mr Mulhearn maggots within the body of the Labour Party. True Labour supporters are about to squash those maggots, perhaps partly because of the *Echo's* stand. It cannot happen a day too soon.

They carried a headline a few days later of 'How you're whacking *Militant*', which was connected with the sales drive for the *Echo*.

As the witch-hunt clouds gathered, Eric Heffer wrote to general secretary Larry Whitty:

> What concerns me is the serious effect all this is having on the future electoral fortunes of the party. A witch-hunt against Liverpool party members and some MPs will not satisfy the right-wing press. Today's *Daily Telegraph* leader makes that absolutely clear. What can happen is civil war within the party, and if that occurs, we shall be handing electoral success to the SDP-Liberal Alliance, not to Labour...I therefore appeal to you as General Secretary to do all you can to steer the party away from this self-destructive course.

Despite the fact that at least 100 Constituency Labour Parties, four District Labour Parties, 65 trade-union organisations, 15 women's sections, over 100 ward Labour Parties, 107 LPYS branches and 9 Labour Clubs had passed resolutions against the witch-hunt and the inquiry, the right wing and the 'soft left' were hell-bent on expelling the Liverpool Militants.

The DLP Inquiry Report

After months of allegations in the press of 'massive intimidation' and 'physical abuse', not to say Roy Hattersley's accusations of 'literal corruption', not a shred of evidence was produced by the inquiry team to justify these claims. The inquiry was like the mountain that had laboured and brought forth not a mouse but a flea. After 60 hours of questioning 120 Labour Party members, tens of thousands of pounds wasted on wages, hotel bills, fares, including air flights to Liverpool and Scotland, the investigation team did not produce a single shred of evidence to back up the dirty allegations made against Liverpool *Militant* supporters. Moreover, the inquiry team was sharply divided. Two members, Audrey Wise and Margaret Beckett, rejected the witch-hunting of the right-wing majority and produced a minority report.

The report of the majority repeated some allegations, but in a roundabout, vague and nit-picking way. Tucked away in it was the admission that:

> the investigation team did not take seriously all allegations made of *Militant* activities in Liverpool...There are undoubtedly a large number of supporters of the broad line taken by the *Militant* in Liverpool, and others who are prepared to go along with most of the policies, particularly whilst *Militant* has appeared to be the only credible focus of left-wing activity within the party in Merseyside.

The report made the record in acknowledging the terrible social problems in Liverpool and the difficulties confronting the city council. *Militant* (28 February) commented:

> Then the report gets down to real business: manufacturing from thin air a series of tissue-thin arguments in order to reach its predetermined conclusion that very serious and deep-rooted

problems exist in the party. And yet the inquiry team acknowledged that the rules [of the DLP] differ little from the rules of other District Labour Parties of large conurbations.

But what really concerned the inquiry was the control exercised by the DLP over the Labour group. As to the charge of 'intimidation' at DLP meetings, the investigation team were reduced to complaining about 'indications' that there were complaints—but only over issues like the right of reply, the time limits of speakers, and the fact that Executive Committee members and officers were having the 'last word'. *Militant* replied:

> Without a single shred of evidence, without a time, a date, place or person involved, the best the investigation team can come up with is that there was some physical violence on 'one' occasion! Indeed, the inquiry team's report amounted to taking at face value gossip, malicious rumour and tittle-tattle, and elevating this to the level of official allegations. But the purpose of the inquiry was not to establish the truth about Liverpool. It was an exercise, merely a pretext, to wheel in a new apparatus of expulsions. Although the section on *Militant* occupies only four pages out of the whole report, this is the key section. The right wing are terrified that *Militant* has assumed such widespread influence within the labour movement in Liverpool and the whole charade of the investigation and report boil down to an attack upon the political influence of this newspaper. But the authors of this shameful report are making a big mistake if they imagine they can emasculate a whole city Labour Party and expel some of its best activists without a long and bloody struggle.

The conclusion of the majority report was that 16 party members be re-invited to answer questions, with the clear implication that expulsions would follow. This was merely a case of going through the motions of a trial in order to meet the requirements of 'natural justice', in other words, to prevent a successful challenge in the courts. Other recommendations were that the DLP remain suspended and that two full-time organisers should be appointed to police the party in Liverpool. While the DLP was suspended, a 'Temporary Coordinating Committee' was to be established. Unlike the DLP which had wide participation, this new body was to have only two delegates from each constituency, two from each of the larger unions and a few other delegates as well as the full-time Labour Party regional and local officers. It was also proposed that the 'all-member' aggregate meeting should not be held more than once a quarter. Outside speakers were to be banned, so that speakers from CND, trade unionists in dispute etc would no longer have a platform at the most important Labour Party body in the Liverpool area.

The report went on to recommend that there should be a restrictions on the influence of the DLP over the Labour group. It also suggested that those unions who had a block affiliation to the DLP, particularly the GMBATU and the TGWU should be asked 'to check rigorously the delegation to both the DLP and the CLPs as against their branch membership and to check the method of appointment, in consultation with the North-West regional office'. A similar check was to be made on the student Labour clubs and the women's council. There was no suggestion that any such rigorous check be made on right-wing delegations.

The Minority Report

The minority report made a number of proposals about the reorganisation and efficient running of the DLP, but completely rejected any idea of unelected full-time agents. The most notable feature of this report was that it pointed to the 'terrible dangers' of expulsions based on unprovable assertions and it notes that even many of those interviewees who were critical of the DLP were nevertheless opposed to expulsions. It went on:

> If expulsions are contemplated, where doubt exists to the quality of the evidence...we are on a very slippery slope where such proposals might be made on more and more tenuous evidence and thus, in reality, on the grounds not even of real political conviction, though that would be dangerous enough, but even of personal likes and dislikes.

The right-wing majority on the NEC were impervious to such warnings. They also turned a completely deaf ear to the growing opposition of the rank and file to the suicidal path they had chosen. They were listening to the orchestrated campaign of the Fleet Street editorials which, like the *Sunday Mirror* (23 February 1986), claimed, 'all that would happen is that even fewer people would vote for the party than the abysmally low total of 8.4 million in 1983', unless Kinnock expelled *Militant* supporters. Like most of the bourgeois press it linked the winning of the next election to expulsions: 'To win power at the next general election Labour must gain the support of at least a further 3 million voters, most of whom thoroughly dislike extreme left- and right-wing policies.' In the light of the defeat of Labour in the 1987 General Election, these comments are of some interest to the rank and file of the party.

As always, the *Daily Express* (24 February) expressed the self-satisfied mood of the capitalist press. John Akass wrote:

> It would be hypocritical to deny that I am looking forward to the public humiliation of Liverpool's weird tendency this week...If the National Executive Committee decides on Wednesday that Liverpool's *Militants* should be hanged in public, I will be in the queue for tickets.

Fortunately the right wing on the NEC of the Labour Party were not yet quite ready to go *that* far! To maintain the outward appearance of 'fairness', and to avoid legal action, the right wing were preparing to approve the report but defer expulsions until after 'a personal hearing' at a later stage. Nevertheless, the smell of left-wing blood had the right wing in full cry. George Robertson MP, leading light of the right-wing Solidarity Group, called for an investigation into Tony Benn because of his opposition to NATO. The Labour Party's head of information, Peter Mandelson, even approached the BBC *Question Time* programme to try and get Tony Benn taken off the panel in the week when the expulsion issue was coming up at the NEC. The same Mandelson had the gall to give press briefings accusing *Militant* of being 'anti-democratic and supporting totalitarianism'.

The February NEC

On the morning of the 26 February, more than 1000 *Militant* supporters together with other Labour and trade-union activists gathered outside Walworth Road to lobby the National Executive Committee who were meeting to discuss the outcome of the inquiry. Neil Kinnock chose to march in the front door, heavily flanked by police, in order to demonstrate his 'determination' to stand up to *Militant*. The bourgeois press and media played up to him with headlines about 'gauntlets of hate' with the *Bournemouth Evening Echo* even screaming '*Militant* mob vent rage on Kinnock'. In reality, the lobby was conducted in a very democratic and good-natured fashion.

The attitude of the majority of the NEC was summed up in the immortal words of ex-left winger Tom Sawyer: 'I defy anyone to tell me how you can go to Liverpool and defeat *Militant* by argument.' In other words, it was impossible to defeat the ideas of Marxism in open democratic discussion and debate. This clearly demonstrated the real meaning of this 'trial' of the Liverpool *Militants*. There was the spectacle at one stage in the NEC meeting of a resolution moved by David Blunkett, urging 'tolerance in the party', being passed with Neil Kinnock supporting it! This was just another example of the blatant hypocrisy of the right-wing majority on the NEC who then proceeded to set in motion steps towards expelling people who they politically disagreed with.

A whiff of reality penetrated the proceedings when Audrey Wise declared that none of the NEC members except the miners' representative knew anything about running Labour organisations in the midst of a crisis such as that which Liverpool faced in the budget campaign the previous year. But the right wing were impervious to such arguments, with Union of Communications Workers representative Tony Clarke, launching into a vitriolic attack on Tony Benn for allegedly repeatedly criticising the party leadership. After seven hours of debate, by 19 votes to 10, the NEC instructed General Secretary Larry Whitty to draw up evidence against the 16 who were then invited to another special NEC meeting on 12 March.

In a display of breathtaking irresponsibility, that evening Neil Kinnock dismissed the damage being done to Labour, boldly declaring: 'I am not even considering the electoral costs and losses,' (*Financial Times*, 27 February). That statement should be engraved on Kinnock's memory in the aftermath of the defeat of Labour in the 1987 General Election.

The media had a field day in once more presenting the Labour Party as a camp divided against itself. Vincent Hanna, typical of the cynical opportunists who pass for journalists in the British media, commented on the *Newsnight* television programme that evening:

> The trouble with the *Militant* issue is that the Labour Party, being what it is, there is a certain amount of dissembling and indeed, some

hypocrisy on both sides. The official line from the NEC is that members of the Labour Party aren't condemned for their political beliefs, but rather for the running of a party within a party, the organisational point. But everyone knows that the right wing and indeed some of the left, hate the *Militant* precisely because of their Marxist beliefs.

Reflecting the behind-the-scenes gossip after the meeting he also commented: 'Michael Meacher did not support his leader, and may now lose his shadow cabinet seat.' Meacher in the NEC meeting indicated that he opposed the decision to enquire into the 16 because Sylvia Sharpey-Schaefer, a nurse who he had met in the past, was on the list. He was to swallow any doubts later on once the expulsions had been narrowed down to the leading *Militant* supporters in Liverpool. Eric Heffer ripped into the majority of the NEC on *Newsnight*:

> The inquiry was set up into the runnings and workings of the Labour Party, the District Labour Party in Liverpool. The minority report by Audrey Wise and Margaret Beckett certainly had said that there were a number of infringements that could be discussed and in no way came out against individuals or thought that there should be any expulsions and did not raise the question of *Militant* because they did not distinguish between *Militant* members and other people...it says that action should be taken against the officers for infringements. There are five officers, two of the officers apparently are alright—there is nothing wrong with them—how can you say you are going to have three officers in front of you, because they may happen to be in the Militant Tendency and two, who are not. That is not logical and it is not fair and is not natural justice and cannot be natural justice.

At the NEC meeting earlier in the day Heffer had occasion to remind the meeting that although the inquiry team was sent to Liverpool to investigate the local Labour Party, they had not appeared at all interested in the houses or nurseries, which had only been built because the council had fought the Tories. The whoops of delight of the bourgeois journalists were evident in the next day's papers. But like Oliver Twist they were always demanding 'more'. The *Daily Express* said:

> Fine. The trouble is that *Militant's* influence does not begin and end in Liverpool. It runs virtually country-wide. It extends to Parliament itself where two *Militant* supporters sit openly on Labour's benches.

When will Neil Kinnock and his friends find the guts and inclination to eliminate all that?

The *Daily Mail* complained about the 'mild character' of the witch-hunt. They singled out the Labour Party Young Socialists in particular for the same treatment as was being planned for *Militant* supporters in Liverpool. The *Daily Mirror* (26 February) said that the inquiry decision was a 'vote for votes'.

The rage of the Liverpool working class at the decision of the NEC on 25 February was revealed at a meeting convened the next evening when a resolution condemning the NEC's decision to begin expulsion proceedings was passed by 400 votes to 4! This completely shattered the idea perpetrated by Kinnock and his supporters that a 'silent majority' was waiting to step in and brush *Militant* aside once the leaders had been dealt with.

The minuscule Liverpool Labour Left welcomed the decision to bring charges against *Militant* supporters. This earned them the well-merited contempt of the great majority of Labour Party members and their 'stand' has not been forgotten by the active workers in the Labour Party in Liverpool. Nor have the vicious comments of the *Tribune,* which outdid many of the editorials in the capitalist press. Without a shred of evidence, they repeated the legend: 'What the inquiry does show is that there have been systematic and organised abuses and breaches of the Labour Party's rules and constitution...Therefore it is essential that the party acts against this conspiracy. Some expulsions are probably inevitable.'

Eric Heffer at the NEC spoke for virtually all Labour Party members in Liverpool when he said to Kinnock: 'I shall never forgive you for what you've done to my party in Liverpool.' Charles Turnock, after the NEC's marathon meeting, showed the real intentions of the right wing when he declared that the recommendations in the majority report would 'lead to the elimination of the Militant Tendency in the city of Liverpool'. He must have had a strange vision because that scenario, despite all the efforts of the right wing, has not and will not materialise in Liverpool.

Every enemy of Labour seized upon the expulsions to discredit the Labour Party. That night on *Question Time,* Roy Jenkins of the SDP called *Militant* 'a cancer in the Labour Party', adding however that ten or 16 expulsions was an 'absolutely hopeless' way to deal with it. This stung Tony Benn into denouncing Jenkins: 'You left the [Labour] Party—that is the cancerous growth—not personally. But I think that people who betrayed those who gave them power are the real threat.'

Jenkin's Alliance partner, David Steel, also demanded more: 'Equally, in the Labour Party, getting rid of a dozen or so *Militants* in Liverpool isn't going to change the nature of the Labour Party. Again we have seen speeches from some leading figures recently which indicate that there is a desperate wish to move onto our ground.' A few days later Tory Chair Norman Tebbit attacked Neil Kinnock for not being tough enough on the left.

The desperate search to prove that the attack on *Militant* was 'electorally popular' was led by Maxwell's *Sunday Mirror*. Try as they may, in an opinion poll only 27 per cent of Labour supporters said they were more likely to vote for the party if there was a 'crackdown on *Militants*'. In other words, more than three-quarters of those polled were impervious to the siren song of the bourgeois press that 'expulsions were good for Labour's health'. Even this figure of 27 per cent was probably bogus.

The mass of the working class were more interested in the issues of jobs, housing, education, etc, rather than the preoccupation with so-called extremists by the bourgeois press which unfortunately was echoed by the leadership of the movement. The press were virtually unanimous in support of Kinnock's measures. Even the so-called 'left' joined in. Thus, while formally opposing the witch-hunt, Ken Livingstone could not desist from a side-swipe at Derek Hatton in his column in *Tribune* (7 March 1986), particularly disgraceful after Livingstone's own experiences of personal vilification. He described Derek Hatton as having: 'Possibly one of the most attractive faces since Oswald Mosley.' However, contrary voices were also heard. Indicating the problems which lay ahead for the right wing, Audrey Wise in a letter to the *Guardian* (4 March), stated:

> Until now, the Liverpool District Labour Party has never been advised or warned that its interpretation of the rule book was in error. To go, without any warning, straight into effective disbandment of the DLP and other disciplinary proceedings seem not to accord with natural justice or common sense...Your

description of the incorrect practices is far more lurid than the facts. For instance, you talk of 'false accounting of membership'. The District Labour Party did not falsify any membership figures. You do not, of course, speak as supporters of the Labour Party. When elections come, you will not be helping towards a Labour victory. Why should the Labour Party listen to its opponents on how best to conduct its affairs?

But this was precisely what Kinnock was doing in his vendetta against Liverpool. Another letter in *Labour Weekly,* 11 March indicated the growing consternation at the actions of the NEC:

> The way the defendants were proclaimed guilty before the investigation started and the way they were guilty by association because they were in the Militant Tendency, has all the ingredients of a show trial; I do not know the truth about the Liverpool DLP. The Party nationally seems to me to want to prove that it stands up against extremists who get bad opinion poll ratings. It wants to occupy the middle ground in politics which is being quite adequately fielded by the SDP. In other words, the trappings of a judicial farce are used for political expediency.

Twelve Charged

Undaunted, Larry Whitty proceeded to lay charges against the Liverpool *Militants* for the forthcoming NEC. For some mysterious and hitherto unexplained reason, four of the original 16 were excluded from the list. The four were Pauline Dunlop, Sylvia Sharpey-Schaefer, Josie Aitman and Paul Astbury. The 12 was further reduced later when Richard Knights was removed from the list. It seemed a 'mystery' the way that the NEC had drawn up the charges against some individuals and yet not against others. Thus DLP secretary Felicity Dowling was one of those on the list, yet John Hamilton, DLP Treasurer, was not included. One Vice-President, Terry Harrison, had to face charges while the other Vice-President, Eddie Loyden MP did not.

Contrary to all the promises made at the beginning of the inquiry, legal representation was not to be allowed for the defendants and no 'live' evidence would be presented. Nothing was left of Turnock's promise that those charged would have the opportunity to challenge any spiteful smears and allegations made against them. One of the charges against Derek Hatton was that he was a 'full-time or part-time worker for the Militant Tendency'. Yet everybody knew that he worked for Knowsley Borough Council. All of this was taking place at a time when the Liverpool councillors, together with the Lambeth councillors, were fighting to defeat the District Auditor's surcharges in the courts.

Fighting for Natural Justice

It was quite clear that the show trial being prepared by the right-wing majority on the NEC would not conform to natural justice. The Liverpool 12 therefore decided to seek an injunction in the High Court to prevent the NEC from proceeding. The case for seeking the injunction was made on three grounds: they had not been allowed to see the evidence against them; they would not be allowed witnesses in their defence; and that nine members of the inquiry team would not be able to vote impartially at the NEC meeting because it was they who had drawn up the charges against the accused. The twelve declared: 'It is a scandal that we have had to go to court to get a fair hearing. If they were to simply accept the NEC's procedure without access to the allegations or evidence against them, it would mean accepting the same justice as you would get in a Diplock Court or a Star Chamber.' Lynn Walsh, writing in *Militant,* commented:

> The procedure to be faced by the 12 at the NEC meeting on 26 March would be like that of the Star Chamber. Originating in the murky feudal era, the Star Chamber was used by Tudor monarchs as a tribunal to deal with potential rivals. The court was used by James I and Charles I as a tool of absolute government, and became notorious for its arbitrary procedure and the oppressive punishments inflicted on its victims.
>
> The High Court judge, Vice-Chancellor Sir Nicolas Browne-Wilkinson in effect agreed with this analysis. He ruled that: 'It is contrary to the rules of natural justice in a case such as this to find a man guilty of a charge on the basis of evidence not disclosed to him.' The NEC's proposed procedure, he went on, was 'manifestly dangerous' and unfair. The entire case against one of the twelve was based on such evidence. The judge himself only found out on the second day of the court hearing that even the NEC members were not going to be given the evidence. Larry Whitty was to have read out a summary of the evidence, informing the NEC that in his opinion it went against the twelve! The judge even likened this

procedure to a 'supergrass' system. He further ruled that there would be reasonable suspicion that the nine investigation team members could have prejudged the issue before attending the NEC. Therefore they should not be allowed to sit in the NEC hearing. It was against the principle of natural justice for the same people to be both prosecution and judges.

NEC in Turmoil

This judegment, just 24 hours before the NEC was due to meet, threw the Labour leadership into turmoil. A sensible leadership, would have cancelled the proceedings in order to ponder the implications of the judgement. Not so Kinnock and the right-wing majority on the NEC who later claimed that the judges had in effect upheld the NEC's right to proceed as long as those who sat on the inquiry team had withdrawn. He had done nothing of the kind and had indeed criticised the NEC for its failure to observe the basic principles of 'natural justice'.

Kinnock's attempt to proceed resulted in the most open, public and visible split in the NEC ever seen. Frances Curran, Tony Benn, Eric Heffer, Eric Clarke, Jo Richardson, Joan Maynard and Dennis Skinner dramatically walked out of the meeting. They did this because Kinnock was insisting on proceeding, despite the judgement of the day before. This made the National Executive Committee inquorate and therefore incapable of proceeding.

The right wing and the bourgeois press foamed at the mouth at this tactical ploy by the left. Yet the right were hoist by their own petard because when the right took a majority on the NEC in 1982, fearing that the left would win votes by delaying key decisions until 'busy' right-wing trade-union leaders had left for other business, they increased the quorum from ten to 15.

As the left wing walked out of the meeting, the right began to hurl insults at them and even David Blunkett screamed, 'Get out, get out'. That evening on television and radio, Kinnock fulminated: 'Their protest was pathetic. A deliberate and planned wrecking tactic. It was a case of if they couldn't win, they would take their ball back home.' However, in the wake of his defeat it was Neil Kinnock who was threatening to move the goalposts. He promised to change the rules at the next NEC to ensure that there would be a quorum to carry through expulsions.

The immediate trigger for the walk-out involved the case against the first of the accused, Felicity Dowling. The chaos which reigned as a result of the court judgement was such that she and the friend accompanying her were three times called to the NEC room, only to be told to go back as the NEC was not yet ready. When they were finally admitted, the General Secretary Larry Whitty announced they were dropping the charges relating to her working full-time for *Militant*. He then outlined that they were proceeding with some of the charges but not with others. They were relying only on written evidence and the majority report of the Committee of Inquiry.

Felicity Dowling challenged the use of the report in the light of the judge's ruling and asked for time to withdraw in order to sort out the carrier bag full of papers in view of the revised list of charges. At this stage one of the left-wing members of the NEC shouted loudly 'This is a farce', and the seven left wingers walked out.

The most politically advanced workers in the labour movement looked on them as 'The Magnificent Seven'. The bourgeois press had other thoughts. The *Star* urged: 'As for Eric Heffer, Tony Benn and Co, they should continue walking out—out of the Labour Party.' The *Sun* gloated: 'It must be rare for even a Labour leader to suffer the humiliation inflicted yesterday on Neil Kinnock.' *The Times,* hitherto right behind Kinnock in his war against *Militant* said that 'Kinnock loses control.'

The attitude of the bourgeois was perhaps best summed up by Marcia Falkender, adviser to Harold Wilson when he was Labour prime minister. Writing in the *Mail on Sunday* (30 March), the headline of her article was: 'Neil, you're still not fit to govern.' She went on, 'Just when Labour was beginning to win the match, it was deeply dispiriting to watch *Militant* mauling Neil Kinnock last week.' Revealing just how deep was the 'comradely feeling' of Harold Wilson for the organisations of the labour movement, she repeated a comment of his: 'I love my Cabinet, but I hate my NEC.' Revealing the open contempt that the more serious bourgeois representatives felt about the Labour leadership she wrote: 'It is beyond me why Neil, whose party is not short of lawyers turned MPs, could not have arranged the *Militant* inquiry so the unwanted dozen did not have recourse to the courts. *Militant's* lawyers are obviously smarter.'

An exasperated Kinnock urged *Militant* to 'quit the party and fight under their own colours'. He had never made a similar request for the potential SDP-Tory elements on the right wing to take that path. But *Militant* supporters were not about to oblige the right wing by leaving the field free for them to disappoint the hopes of millions of workers without opposition. *Militant*, the modern expression of the ideas of Marxism, is an integral part of the labour movement.

It began to dawn on the more serious bourgeois commentators that a new force had arisen in British politics. Unlike other groupings, *Militant* had deep roots not only in Liverpool but throughout the country, and was not going to be dislodged from its rightful position in the mass organisations of the working class by paper resolutions concocted in secret and imposed upon the membership of the Labour Party.

There had of course been many expulsions in the past, when the right wing had complete sway. Following the defeat of the 1926 General Strike, there was a purge conducted against Labour Parties then influenced by the Communist Party. Twenty-seven Constituency Labour Parties were disaffiliated. However, the Communist Party, particularly in its 'Third Period', of ultra-left tactics, played into the hands of the right wing by breaking away from the Labour Party. The whole basis of *Militant's* opposition to the witch-hunt was to demonstrate not just to the active workers in the Labour Party but to the mass of workers who look towards the Labour Party as 'their party', that *Militant* considered itself a viable wing of the movement.

Lessons of the Spanish Witch-hunt

It is one of the ironies of history that in preparing his blow against *Militant*, Neil Kinnock had consulted Felipe Gonzalez, leader of PSOE, the Spanish Socialist Party. Gonzalez had carried through the expulsion of virtually every supporter of the Spanish Marxist paper *Nuevo Claridad*. Nevertheless the supporters of this tendency still considered themselves to be the Marxist left wing of the PSOE. They had not turned away from the mass organisations as so many ultra-left sects had done in the past. While energetically intervening in the workers' movement, they had linked this to the demand to be accepted back into PSOE. Intransigence on programme and flexibility in tactics enabled this tendency to play a role completely out of proportion to its numbers in leading the mass movement of students in late 1986 and early 1987. The movement and the victories of the students burst the dam which had been building up, not just for the eight months since the PSOE government had been re-elected to power, but for a period of ten years. Once the floodgates were opened, the heavy reserves of the working class burst onto the political arena. The victory of the students was used by workers going into struggle in 1987 as a means of extracting wage increases and forcing a retreat on lay-offs and sackings.

This movement of three million students was led by a tendency which was formally outside the Socialist Party. At the height of the school students' struggle, PSOE Ministers were forced to negotiate with people they had expelled from the party! Thus even mass expulsions did not prevent the Spanish Marxists from finding a road to those workers influenced by and supporting the PSOE. This will also prove to be the case in Liverpool, notwithstanding any measures to expel *Militant* supporters from the labour movement.

20.
Towards Expulsions

IN THE wake of the walk-out from the March 1986 NEC, some serious bourgeois commentators began to recognise, somewhat tardily, the roots of *Militant* in Britain. David Selbourne, writing in *The Times* (26 March) commented:

> *Militant* is not just a reflection of scouse Labourism in general; it incorporates a Liverpool tradition of bare-knuckled ardour in defence of the city. If Derek Hatton and company had not existed, someone would have had to invent them. In Liverpool itself, across the entire spectrum of the party's supporters, the *Militant's* scouse chauvinism still commands substantial favour. *Militant* has the capacity not merely to give its (lame) pursuers a good run for their money, but to outlast Kinnock himself in the struggle for political survival. The net consequence of the imbroglio has been to exacerbate party divisions, duck the main isssues of Liverpool's appalling economic privations and hand the city council to the Liberals.

Precisely because of the durability of *Militant*, the latter prediction was not borne out. In a very telling comment, however, David Selbourne also said:

> And what is certain is that *Militant* will not be dislodged from the city—investigations, surcharges, expulsions and disqualifications notwithstanding it will go marching on; across a political and economic landscape ransacked by unemployed and devastated by indefensible central government neglect and revenue losses. One way or another, *Militant* will survive the huffing and puffing of its critics.

At the same time, from a most unusual quarter, came confirmation of the popularity of Liverpool's struggle. In a poll in the *New Musical Express*, under the section, 'Most wonderful human being' Derek Hatton was rated way ahead of Neil Kinnock! While the tabloids took great delight at the difficulties for Kinnock and the Labour Party, which the walk-out had revealed, the serious bourgeois commentators sounded a warning note. Michael Jones, Political Editor of the *Sunday Times* said:

> The war Kinnock must never lose...[if] as it could, Labour ended up shackled to *Militant* because its party constitution cannot cope with secret groups of entryists and the courts make matters worse, Britain's body politic would be sick indeed. Only those who want Labour's downfall at any cost will want to see him [Kinnock] beaten.

This warning was to be heeded later on, particularly by the judges who, as the witch-hunt continued, abandoned any semblance of 'neutrality' or even-handedness between *Militant* and the Labour Party NEC.

The Temporary Co-ordinating Committee

The day after the NEC meeting at which the right wing had hoped to expel the twelve *Militant* supporters, the Liverpool Labour Party Temporary Co-ordinating committee (TCC) held its first meeting. Tony Mulhearn, President of the suspended District Labour Party and one of those facing expulsion, was elected Chair. The meeting praised 'the magnificent seven'—the members of the NEC who had walked out of the March meeting in protest—and called for the reconvening of the DLP.

All the constituency delegates present and many of the trade unionists were absolutely opposed to the witch-hunt. Only four voted to oppose electing officers. Ted Mooney, a *Militant* supporter, was elected as the Treasurer, Phil Rowe from West Derby, another *Militant* supporter, as Secretary, Tony Hood and Mike Carr (who later turned into a witch-hunter) as Vice-chairpersons. The right wing's very carefully constructed plan to supplant *Militant* supporters in the new body was therefore coming apart at the first meeting.

This latest turn provoked the *Daily Mail* (28 March 1986) to storm: 'Second coup puts *Militant* back into power again.' Eddie Loyden answered:

> This makes a nonsense of what the Executive were trying to do. They do not understand the Liverpool situation at all—that is quite

plain. And it shows the whole affair to be a sham on the part of the Executive. It was a scatter gun exercise with them shooting off indiscriminately in all directions.

Not just the right but the 'left', particularly David Blunkett, wrote and spoke energetically in support of expulsions of the Liverpool Militants. His attack in the *Guardian* on the seven who had walked out of the NEC meeting had called forth a shower of letters in opposition to him. Louise Christian, the solicitor who accompanied Felicity Dowling to the NEC, completely shattered the case which Blunkett attempted to make against her client. She pointed out:

> Felicity Dowling faced some 39 charges. She had no time to arrange for witnesses to attend which had only been allowed by the NEC the day before. When she appeared she was told that her charges had been 'rearranged' into groups, and some dropped.

To the embarrassment of the right on the NEC, even legal experts such as Professor JA Griffith, politically opposed to Marxism, were forced to question the fairness of the expulsion procedure. He wrote to the *Guardian* (25 April 1986):

> When, many weeks ago, I first read of the procedure that the NEC was adopting for the investigation, I was, as a lawyer, most surprised. It seemed obviously contrary to the rules of natural justice that members of the NEC should both investigate and then sit in judgement. As details began to emerge of the way the investigation was being conducted, dismay succeeded surprise. So I expected the court to find as it did. What I did not expect was that the NEC would seek to persist, without proper presentation of the charges and without giving the accused the elementary rights associated with such hearings, but if members of the party are to be dismissed, it is absolutely essential that they be given a fair hearing by an unbiased tribunal. The earlier incompetence makes this difficult. Those members of the NEC who protested about the procedures should be regarded as protectors of the constitution, not as its enemies.

But the most devastating reply came from Tony Mulhearn in an open letter printed in *Militant* which Blunkett never answered. He particularly debunked Blunkett's attack on the 'pernicious nominating rights' which had been given to the trade unions. Tony Mulhearn wrote:

> He [Blunkett] then, in a confused amnner, attacks the 'nominating rights' which the trade unions had secured by negotiation. These

rights were accepted by all unions at local, regional and national levels, certainly I don't recall any union objecting to them. If they were abused—and he does not seek to prove it—that is a matter between him and the unions. For my part, if abuse did take place it was never brought to the attention of the DLP. Had the DLP been aware of any abuse it would have made its position clear in no uncertain manner.

A statement was also issued in the name of the Tribune Group of MPs, condemning the walk-out of the seven from the NEC. However, Ian Mikardo in a letter to the *Guardian* stated that the Group had taken no such decision because, as a Vice-chair of the Group, he had not been consulted on any statement.

Roland Boyes, the Chair of the Tribune Group, Chris Smith, Islington South MP, and Richard Caborn, Sheffield Central MP, had signed the statement. Boyes was unapologetic, saying: 'It had been essential to issue a statement immediately while the issue was urgent, rather than wait till a meeting of the Group could be convened.' This Tribunite, a paragon of 'democracy', issues a statement on such a fundamental question without even going through the procedure of discussing it within his own Group or even with the Vice-chair of the Group!

It was one more sign of the evolution of the Tribune Group towards the right. The Group secretary was Chris Smith who was himself under criticism from within his own constituency party at this time for threatening to go against the party's wishes. Despite the attacks and the continued threat of expulsion hanging over the head of Liverpool *Militant* supporters, Derek Hatton received a tumultuous welcome at a 'Labour Unity Rally' at the Labour Party Young Socialists' national conference which met in Bournemouth in early April. At this meeting he issued a challenge to Neil Kinnock to openly debate with him so that 'the rank and file can decide what they want'. He stated: 'Intimidation has become a new word for democracy. If the right win a vote, it's democracy. If they lose it's intimidation.'

There was no real support for the witch-hunt in Labour's ranks. However, other sentiments prevailed within bourgeois circles. It was not at all accidental that just at this stage the local government editor of the *Liverpool Echo*, Peter Phelps, was named as 'Journalist of the Year' at the 1985 British Press Awards. He was awarded a prize of £1000 for his coverage of the city's political scene during 1985 'and for his investigations into the Militant Tendency and the city council'. The bourgeois were rewarding one of their own for a systematic campaign of vilification to undermine the influence of Marxism in Liverpool. By rights, Kinnock and Hattersley should have shared in the prize!

Meanwhile, the National Executive Committee, which within a year was attempting to sack staff at the Labour Party Headquarters, spent over £160,000 in circulating every Labour Party branch with a copy of the majority report on Liverpool. By the end of May, the bill for the Labour Party for legal fees, travelling and accommodation expenses, the inquiry itself, publication and circulation of reports, additional NEC meetings etc, had reached well in excess of £100,000. In other words, the Labour Party had been prepared to spend £35,000 per expulsion!

It was not just money but the most valuable commodity of all—time—which was being expended and which could have been more profitably deployed combating the Tory enemy. Nevertheless the Kinnock majority on the NEC proceeded to pursue the witch-hunt. They changed the quorum figure at an NEC meeting in early April in order to ensure that another walk-out could not scupper the vote for expulsions. The sixth meeting of the NEC to discuss the expulsion of Liverpool party members took place during the crisis over the American bombing of Libya, and in the wake of the Thatcher government's defeat in Parliament on student grants.

Majority Report Dropped

A drastic alteration of the NEC's expulsion procedure completely vindicated the walk-out of the left-wing members at the previous meeting. The NEC completely changed tack. They altered both the charges and the nature of the evidence on which they were to rely in pursuing the twelve. The NEC would no longer be relying on the majority report of the inquiry team as evidence. The evidence that the NEC was now relying on consisted of advertisements and leaflets for *Militant* meetings, and press reports of these meetings and rallies. The pretence that the twelve were being expelled for 'malpractices' in the running of the DLP, 'intimidation' and 'reprehensible trade-union nomination rights' was exposed. The NEC had also conceded that the twelve would be able to call witnesses on some points.

The Unacceptable Face of Labour

The 'unacceptable face' of the Labour Party was shown not by *Militant* supporters but by the actions of the right's 'appointed official' in Liverpool, Peter Kilfoyle. He walked into the DLP office and ripped a phone from the wall, a sign of desperation and of the brutal methods that the right wing were prepared to employ in the battle against the Marxists. Meanwhile, *Militant* supporters up for expulsion prepared for the NEC that was to hear their case in late May.

The main criteria for carrying through expulsions was to be that people like Derek Hatton and Tony Mulhearn had spoken at '*Militant* meetings', and yet it had been revealed that Kinnock himself had spoken on a platform at a meeting organised by *Militant* supporters at Swansea University in October 1980! At that meeting, attended by 150 people, Neil Kinnock had even given £5 to the *Militant* Fighting Fund. Tom Sawyer, one of the chief witch-hunters, had also spoken at *Militant* Readers' Meetings.

The witch-hunt was organically connected with the swing towards the right on policy and programme. The party's 'freedom and fairness' campaign involved the replacement of the red flag with grey symbols, the abandonment of renationalisation and of the idea of public ownership. Only the demand for unilateral nuclear disarmament remained intact, but with the right continuing its offensive to have this abandoned.

It was in this atmosphere that the NEC met on 21 May, to consider for the tenth time the first of the cases, that of Tony Mulhearn. If some on the right had had hesitations about driving Tony Mulhearn from the party of which he had been a member for 23 years, his advocacy at this meeting must have hardened their resolve. The hearing took a total of seven hours. Even some on the right grudgingly conceded that he had brilliantly rebutted the charges, although they were still determined to give the bourgeois his head. This they duly did at one o'clock in the morning.

The next day the NEC proceeded to hear the case of Ian Lowes, who again stunned the right wing by refuting in detail every one of the allegations made against him. He was nevertheless expelled for his efforts. In an attempt to create a smokescreen of 'fairness' they dropped the charges against Harry Smith. By now it was late in the day and Tony Aitman returned to Liverpool having been hanging around for 36 hours waiting for his hearing. After his departure, Tony Aitman—22 years a party member—was expelled without a hearing.

By now, even the most obtuse right winger realised that the proceedings were likely to drag on and on. The *Daily Telegraph* reported (26 May 1986): 'Mr Kinnock and his supporters on Labour's national executive are resigned to a war of attrition lasting well into the summer as they try to complete their disciplinary action against Mr Derek Hatton and his Liverpool comrades.'

The bourgeois press, of course, applauded Kinnock as a 'man of principle'. They were quite happy to see the continuing divisions within the Labour Party. At the same time, the party in Liverpool refused to accept the expulsions. Tony Mulhearn's constituency, Garston, voted by 36 votes to 2 not to recognise 'this insane action of the right-wing dominated NEC'. Moreover, Peter Kilfoyle was thrown out of a Labour group meeting which he had barged into. Nevertheless, the expulsion proceedings dragged into June.

Derek Hatton was finally expelled in his absence (while on council business) in late June. This recalls the experience of the Irish writer, Brendan Behan, when he was expelled from the IRA in the 1950s. They held a court martial and sent him a note saying he had been condemned to death in his absence. He sent a note back saying, 'Then you can carry out the sentence in my absence'! Derek Hatton and the Liverpool labour movement had a similar contempt for the proceedings on the NEC.

Richard Venton 15 years a party member, Terry Harrison 28 years a member and a former leader of the apprentices movement on Merseyside, and Roger Bannister, 15 years a member and a NALGO activist were all expelled at the same meeting. The charges against Carol Darton, a party member for only a few months, were too much even for some of the right wing to swallow, and her case was dropped by 11 votes to 9, Neil Kinnock amongst those seeking to proceed.

At the same time, an offensive was launched by a number of union leaders who perceived *Militant* as an increasing danger within the union movement. First, the GMBATU General Secretary John Edmonds attacked the 'poison of *Militant*...' This was part of the softening-up process to launch an attack and investigation into the GMBATU No 5 branch in Liverpool which had been the backbone of the council's campaign.

More surprising perhaps, given his past 'left' credentials regarding the battle on reselection, was the vicious campaign of Sam McCluskie. Accepting the hospitality shown by the Liverpool City Council in providing a hall for the Annual General Meeting of his union, the seafarers (NUS), he used the occasion to launch a diatribe against *Militant*. He condemned the amount of money which *Militant* allegedly raised for itself, yet as party Treasurer he was responsible for allowing the misuse of party funds on the enquiries and expulsions.

Incredibly, he declared: 'You do not achieve democratic socialism in Britain by flouting the laws of the land', an open criticism of the stand of the Liverpool City Council. Twenty years earlier the NUS leaders had been subjected to slanderous attacks about 'conspiracies'. In 1966, Labour prime minister Harold Wilson had attacked the seafarers strike, denouncing it as the work of a 'tightly-knit group of politically motivated men'. McCluskie was now using similar language against the Liverpool City Council and those who had defied the law in the interests of working people.

The press hailed the expulsion of Derek Hatton of course. But even Larry Whitty finally recognised that it was foolish to pretend that concentration on 'the internal affairs of the party have not been a major diversion from achieving some of our aims' (*Guardian*, 9 June 1986). He even admitted, 'There is a near obsession with Liverpool'(*Daily Mirror*, 13 June 1986), again an implied criticism of the right wing. In Liverpool itself there was virtually no support for the witch-hunt. In fact, over 150 people attended a public meeting in Tony Mulhearn's ward, St Mary's, giving him massive backing.

Even the expulsion of Derek Hatton did not satisfy the jackals of Fleet Street. They demanded more. They were up in arms at the endorsement of Pat Wall as parliamentary candidate for Bradford North by the June NEC. Peter Phelps, rewarded so hugely for his attack on *Militant*, commented (*Daily Mail*, 14

June 1986): 'The Labour Party with a long history of expulsions has a habit of turning its rebels into leaders.'

In Liverpool *Militant* supporters and the left had to confront difficult tactical questions. The right did not just want expulsions but the closure of constituency parties as well as the DLP. Therefore after taking the opposition to expulsions as far as was possible, Tony Mulhearn convinced the Garston constituency that it was necessary to accept his expulsion 'under protest', rather than be shut down.

When it came to Broadgreen, Terry Fields' constituency, the right wing were not prepared to accept even a minimal resistance. They used the attendance of Derek Hatton at a meeting of the constituency—he had come to protest at his expulsion—as a pretext for closing down the Constituency Labour Party. Thus in the run-up to a general election, the Labour Party members' ability to mobilise to re-elect Terry Fields in a marginal seat was sabotaged by the right wing. Cheryl Varley was expelled at the July NEC. Felicity Dowling's case dragged on until after the Labour Party conference in October 1986 where, as a delegate, she was able to protest against the witch-hunt.

In September the *New Statesman* carried an article which completely exposed the bogus character of the attacks and the undemocratic methods of the NEC. The author, Quentin Mc Dermott had acompanied Cheryl Varley to the NEC as her 'friend':

> The hearing itself was eye-opening. For the expulsion to be credible, the evidence against Ms Varley should have been thorough and pretty well irrefutable, the voting 'fair'. In fact, what evidence there was at best arguable at worst flimsy; the voting—with the notable exception of Michael Meacher who opposed her expulsion—predictably pre-ordained. If anyone was enjoying themselves it was the left wingers, who seized every opportunity to expose the weakness of the evidence as presented. The right seemed faintly embarrassed by the whole affair, while Gwyneth Dunwoody, if she was listening at all gave no evidence of it, as she crocheted throughout, never once, according to my tape, pausing to ask a question.
>
> The evidence arrayed against her boiled down to the allegation that she was a 'regular' contributor to *Mersey Militant*, and therefore in Whitty's words a 'significant' supporter of *Militant*. By 'regular', he meant the author of three articles. Cheryl Varley read out each of

them, and challenged anyone on the NEC to point out anything which was distinctively different from Labour policy. No one did.

She detailed how, in her period of office, Liverpool's FE students had won free nursery provision throughout the FE sector, free meals, free transport, free stationery and books, an increase in the students' union budgets, an increase in grants—particularly for students with children—and financing for sabbatical officers to be elected in every college in Liverpool. 'That might not mean much to some members of this NEC, because some members of this NEC might not have experienced what it's like to be an unemployed student, trying to get through further education, but it means a lot to the young people of Liverpool', she said.

At the end of the hearing, Cheryl Varley asked to be allowed to hear the verdict in person from the Executive—not to have it relayed to her, as the others had, by a 'messenger boy'. The request was turned down. The messenger boy turned out to be Larry Whitty, who told her somewhat sheepishly that the case against her had been deemed 'proven'.

Miners' Support

The Durham Miners' Gala in July gave a striking example of the opposition to the expulsions by ordinary Labour workers. Derek Hatton had been invited to march with the Wearmouth Lodge. Suffering a broken leg from playing football, he still hobbled on crutches at the head of their contingent. A local paper, the *Sunday Sun* (13 July 1986) commented: 'Derek Hatton, expelled from the Labour Party for supporting the Militant Tendency, got one of the biggest cheers of the day at the Durham Miners' Gala yesterday.' When he marched past the guests standing on the balcony of the Royal County Hotel, Neil Kinnock prominent amongst them, he waved his crutches and shouted 'You won't get rid of me that easy, lad.' He was applauded not just by the crowd but by almost all the guests on the balcony. Neil Kinnock looked acutely embarrassed and retreated into the hotel.

Throughout the day Derek Hatton was received enthusiastically, with workers congratulating him on the Liverpoool struggle and urging him to keep on fighting. At the rally in the gala field, Dennis Skinner won wild applause for denouncing the 'childish witch-hunt mentality' within the Labour Party. This enthusiasm for Dennis Skinner contrasted sharply with the lukewarm response for the final speaker, Kinnock. By the time he finished his second sentence, hundreds were streaming away and at least one lodge banner struck up and marched off the field, banner flying proudly.

The Kent miners also supported Liverpool at their gala in the same month. At the same time, throughout Liverpool, meetings were held with enthusiastic support for all those expelled. But just after Derek Hatton's expulsion there was an incident which demonstrated clearly the mechanics of the witch-hunt, and the link between the attacks by the state on *Militant* supporters and the actions of the Labour right on the NEC. In late July, the case against Derek Hatton over his expenses claims was dropped by the Director of Public Prosecutions! There were no banner headlines in the press: 'Hatton is Innocent!' Yet for the previous 18 months, the press had carried lurid, but completely unfounded, allegations against Derek Hatton. Nor did Hattersley apologise for his disgraceful comments about 'corruption'.

Kilroy-Silk Resigns

It was at this time that Kilroy-Silk decided to quit as an MP. Of course, he made the ritualistic claim (*Daily Express*, 31 July 1986) that '*Militant* made me quit.' As a man of 'principle' he could take no more. In reality, his motive for resigning as MP was the little crock of gold waiting for him on becoming a TV interviewer. Not that *Militant* supporters were unduly worried by his claim. After all, *Militant* had played a prominent role in the exposure of right-wing trade-union general secretaries Sid Weighell (NUR) and Alastair Graham (CPSA), both of whom had taken themselves off to greener pastures. Even Kinnock was moved to describe his allegations as 'rubbish' (*Daily Mail*, 31 July 1986).

It can be predicted with some certainty that Kilroy-Silk will join a long list of those like Reg Prentice and Neville Sandelson who will end up in the camp of the Tories. His resignation was greeted enthusiastically by the workers in his constituency in Knowsley North. But it panicked the right wing, who now feared a left candidate would be chosen in a highly publicised by-election. In *Tribune* Hugh MacPherson summed up the feelings of betrayal among those who had been supporting Kilroy-Silk against the left. He quoted Robert Browning's famous *Lost Leader*: 'Just for a handful of silver he left us, just for a ribbon to wear in his cap.'

August and September witnessed a running battle between the Liverpool labour movement and the agents of the right wing National Executive Committee. At the same time, the right wing began to plot Eric Heffer's removal from the NEC. They had never forgiven him for his walk-out at the 1985 Labour Party conference and his principled criticism of Kinnock since.

Just before the Labour Party conference, writing in *Campaign Group News,* Heffer commented:

> The Liverpool and Lambeth councillors are in the tradition of the Poplar councillors of 1919-24. Councillors who went to prison fighting for the working class. They fought for the unemployed, the poor and for a real redistribution of wealth. The interesting thing is that in the municipal elections of 1922, Labour's vote in Poplar was 51.5 per cent, but in London as a whole it was an average of 36.4 per cent.

Having compelled the constituencies of Garston, Broadgreen and others to accept the expulsion of the eight, Larry Whitty and 'strong man' Kilfoyle attempted to force the eviction of Tony Mulhearn and Derek Hatton from the Labour Group. This was not successful in time for the forthcoming Labour Party conference. Before the conference, Eric Heffer in his new book *Labour's Future,* also warned of his fears that 'Labour is taking the road to defeat.' (*Guardian*, 24 September 1986). This only fuelled the campaign to remove him from the NEC.

One of those leading the attack was Albert Williams, General Secretary of Heffers own union, the building workers (UCATT). He released to the press a letter expressing 'his concern' (*Daily Telegraph*, 25 September 1986) about Eric Heffer's criticisms of the Kinnock leadership. Eric Heffer only received the letter after it had appeared in the press! He also commented that he did not understand UCATT's attitude as, since his walk-out at the last party conference, he had attended dinners of the UCATT executive and also the union's biennial conference and had been given no indication of criticism. He declared defiantly: 'We are not living in the Soviet Union. We are still free to adopt positions freely arrived at, and if UCATT wants to withdraw my sponsorship that's a matter for them. I don't take kindly to threats and won't be giving any assurances.' (*Guardian*, 25 September 1986)

But one effect of the NEC's intervention was to split the Labour group. This was something that the Tories, the District

Auditor, the courts, the Liberals and every opponent of the Liverpool City Council had failed to do in the previous three years. Fourteen councillors, including Leader John Hamilton, broke ranks and met Whitty for what they claimed were talks to 'clear the air' (*Morning Star*, 19 September 1986). This, they claimed, was in order not to be 'isolated' from the broad labour movement. But in Liverpool their connivance with the right wing represented real isolation from the advanced workers. John Hamilton, who had played a role in the campaign in the previous three years, became an increasingly sad and isolated figure.

Meanwhile, on the eve of the Labour Party conference, Tony Mulhearn declared that despite the likely decision to uphold the expulsion, he and the other expellees would eventually be reinstated back into party membership. He declared:

> The Labour Party conference will only be a page in the chapter of our campaign to win reinstatement. Neil Kinnock will have the block vote in favour of expulsion, that is a foregone conclusion – but our campaign will go on. What they (the right) fail to understand is that we are a product of the social and economic conditions that exist in Liverpool. The economic crisis will continue to worsen, as well as unemployment, and the prospects for lower paid workers will become grimmer. We can see a stormy period ahead for British politics which the right wing will be incapable of coping with. There will be a massive shift to the left which in part will open the way to our reinstatement. (*Guardian*, 22 September 1986)

Personal Vendettas

On the eve of the Labour Party conference, the right wing suspended the selection process for a successor to Kilroy-Silk. Tony Mulhearn had been removed from the scene. However, another left, Les Huckfield, had the most nominations and was likely to be selected to replace Kilroy-Silk. He had earned the abiding hostility of Kinnock, if for no other reason, because in 1982 he had been one of ten MPs who formed a group called Labour Liaison '82, with the intention of getting Kinnock and Joan Lester voted off the National Executive Committee after they refused to support Tony Benn in the Deputy Leadership contest.

A number of Kinnock's actions were obviously determined by personal hostility, even hatred, as we have seen in the case of the

Liverpool *Militant* supporters. For a political leader of a mass party to allow himself to be swayed by personal considerations is fatal. Personal spite in politics is the worst and most dangerous quality for a leader. It clouds the judgement and elevates personal feelings, personal envy, before the interest of the working class.

This was demonstrated again when Kinnock vetoed Sharon Atkin as a candidate for the 1987 General Election, because of her remarks that 'the Labour Party was racist'. She had a previous personal clash with Kinnock on the issue of 'black sections'. Atkin's remarks were mistaken, but a serious leader of a mass workers' party would have dismissed them as of no consequence whatsoever. Once more Kinnock acted partly through personal antipathy, partly in response to the goading of the press.

Appeal To Labour Party Conference

The approach of the Labour Party Conference in October 1986 posed a number of difficult tactical questions for the Liverpool *Militant* supporters. The hearings at the NEC had merely been a show trial. The conference was likely to be an extended version of this. Many of the union block votes had virtually been counted and weighed beforehand.

The right-wing general secretaries had not consulted their rank and file on the issues raised by the Liverpool inquiry. Nor had the case of the Liverpool eight been properly put even to those union conferences which considered the matter. Indeed, some unions, like the TGWU, were to vote for expulsions in contravention of their policy. There was no enthusiasm or support for a witch-hunt at the union conferences in the summer, nor at the Labour Party conference itself. Many rank and file delegates in the conferences 'reluctantly acquiesced', while outside they expressed sympathy and gave money to the *Militant* Fighting Fund. The right-wing union general secretaries were prepared to use the block vote in order to crush the Liverpool Militants.

For *Militant* supporters, the vote itself was of little consequence. Far more important was the opportunity to present the case, both to the delegates but also to the mass of the working people who would be following the conference on live television and radio. After all, they had been bombarded throughout the previous 12 months with an avalanche of distorted facts and impressions of what Liverpool *Militant* supporters stood for and had achieved in the city. Therefore, Derek Hatton and Tony Mulhearn demanded half an hour each in order to defend their record, in Tony's case after 23 years' party membership, before the conference. They also demanded that the NEC should allow the media, particularly the television and the radio, to carry the debate live.

Despite their abhorrence of the capitalist media, Marxists will use any opportunity, no matter how limited, to put their case to the mass of the population. They were confident that the case of the Liverpool Militants would shatter the image which had been created about Liverpool and its leadership.

In the period prior to 1983, Labour had abolished the 'closed session' (closed to the media and visitors) at conferences. Their argument had been that a democratic party had nothing to fear by open discussion and debate. The secret session was re-introduced in 1983 in order to carry through the 'secret expulsion' of the *Militant* Editorial Board.

The five members of the *Militant* Editorial Board availed themselves on that occasion of the *five* minutes each, which was completely inadequate, to reply at least to some of the slanders to which they had been subjected. These slanders, however, were merely pin pricks compared to the deluge which had fallen on the heads of the Liverpool *Militant* supporters. It was therefore only fair and reasonable that they be given adequate time and the opportunity to explain their case. The NEC of the Labour Party were terrified and completely dismissed the request.

When the eight arrived at the conference on the morning of 28 September, they repeated their request. This was refused by Larry Whitty on behalf of the NEC. Derek Hatton and Tony Mulhearn then led a sensational walk-out of the eight from the conference hall. They were met by the world's press, mingling with many Liverpool *Militant* supporters cheering them to the echo. Derek Hatton's statement was carried in all the papers and on the television that evening: 'We were not prepared to give credibility to a farce. We are not prepared to see a British labour movement that is more akin to Stalinist Russia.' Tony Mulhearn forcefully declared 'The National Executive is petrified by the ideas that have won us so much support in Liverpool.' (*Evening Standard*, 26 September 1986)

This bold action earned the vitriolic attack of Kinnock, who accused the eight of being 'spineless' (*Daily Star* 30 September 1986). This from a leader who refused to allow an open, democratic discussion and debate of ideas. Moreover, as he was leaving the conference hall and was being mildly barracked by two *Militant* supporters, Kinnock reacted furiously. As he got in his car he waved his fist and pointed to one *Militant* supporter, indicating that he was next for expulsion.

The conference passed a motion overwhelmingly endorsing the expulsions, but the comments of the right wing indicated that they had been cheated of the expected show trial. Instead of the vote being triumphantly featured in the media, it was the dramatic walk-out and the statements of Tony Mulhearn and Derek Hatton which appeared on the television and in the press. Moreover, while the union block votes were mobilised to crush the Liverpool Militants, 263 constituencies, nearly half of the total, still voted against expulsions.

Without much conviction Larry Whitty declared 'We have broken the inner ring of *Militant* control over a large part of the Liverpool Party.' (*Daily Mail*, 31 September 1986). Subsequent events, not for the first time, were to confound the right wing's perspectives. Once more the press went into action: 'You are finished,' declared the *Daily Star* (30 September 1986). 'Good riddance', screamed the *Daily Mirror* (30 September 1986).

Having exhausted all suitable adjectives to describe *Militant* supporters—'maggots, corrupt, termites, intimidators'—the *Daily Mirror* editor decided that *Militant* supporters must come from outer-space! Its headline read, 'Defeat of the aliens' (30 September).

Renegade Kilroy-Silk, who was at the conference launching his book '*Hard Labour*', welcomed the expulsions. He had been protected, indeed cosseted, by the Kinnock leadership before he decided to resign as MP. In the vote for the National Executive Committee, Eric Heffer lost his seat, a product of the scheming of the right and the 'new right' of the LCC. On the day the NEC results were announced, *Militant* held one of its most impressive readers' meetings ever at Labour Party conference. Denied access to any of the hotels, sometimes on the most flimsy pretext, the meeting took place in a school far from the conference hall.

Nevertheless, more than 500 cheering Labour Party members, youth, older trade unionists and *Militant* supporters listened to Derek Hatton, Tony Mulhearn, Peter Taaffe and Ted Grant outline the perspectives for the labour movement and the future of Marxism in Britain.

It was not at all the 'wake' which the opponents of Marxism hoped for. The expulsions were seen in the proper historical context. Paradoxically they indicated the enormous strength and potential for Marxist ideas within the labour movement. The right wing were incapable of answering these ideas and therefore resorted to organisational measures to suppress them. But the speakers indicated that the political and social situation, no matter who won the next general election, would open up a favourable scenario for the growth of Marxist ideas. *Militant* supporters, however, would still be the most energetic workers for a Labour government. The return of Labour was seen as the most favourable outcome of an election, both from the point of view of the working class and for Marxism.

Meanwhile, the spotlight on Liverpool was even more intense in the aftermath of the Labour Party conference than before. Party officials Larry Whitty and Joyce Gould walked out of a Labour group meeting in early October because it still continued to recognise Derek Hatton and Tony Mulhearn. The meeting was lobbied by more than 100 Liverpool Labour Party members. At this meeting, we saw real intimidation; against *Militant* supporters! Cllr Harry Smith was entering the Labour group meeting. He was confronted with a 'bouncer' on the door. He recounts:

> When I got there, I noticed a number of people from the Vauxhall area who had been vocal in attacking the council. I went upstairs with about a dozen other councillors. An ex-Communist Party member was standing on the door. As I went up to the door he put his arm across my chest. I asked him to take it away and to mind his own business. And as I walked into the room he hit me in the chest—I kept my arms by my side and he grabbed my jumper. I was fuming. I went straight up to Larry Whitty and said 'who are you, putting these thugs on the door?' Whitty said nothing and just looked up at me.

The stand of the Labour group, particularly of non-*Militant* supporters like Tony Byrne, enraged Neil Kinnock and his entourage. At the NEC meeting later that month, Kinnock proposed that the new National Constitutional Committee should investigate Byrne's membership. Tony Byrne declared:

> I can understand why, from Neil Kinnock's point of view, Derek Hatton could be seen as the devil. I abhor personality politics in Liverpool or nationally, but Derek has become in Liverpool our Labour programmes personified. To allow him and Tony to be crushed is to allow all we stand for to be crushed. If the NEC is determined to be vengeful and is not prepared to find a productive and constructive way forward, then a number of us will stand and say that it is not of our making. If we are so offensive to socialists, then I personally would rather go with Derek and Tony (*Guardian*, 20 October 1986).

However, while welcoming this solidarity, *Militant* supporters were not prepared to see unnecessary expulsions from the Labour Party. The struggle in Liverpool is part of a long war of attrition against capitalism and its greatest ally—the right within the Labour Party. It was essential that the gains of 1983-7 should be preserved, and particularly that the leading councillors should remain within the Labour Party to continue the battle.

With great reluctance, Derek Hatton and Tony Mulhearn agreed not to attend Labour Party meetings. *Militant* supporter Paul Astbury was elected in Derek Hatton's place as the Deputy Leader of the council. *Militant's* support was as strong at the end of the year of witch-hunting as it had been when the battle began. Indeed, it was immeasurably stronger, with the accumulated experience and qualities of leadership retained both by *Militant* and also by the Liverpool labour movement.

The Knowsley North By-election

Kinnock's right wing domination of the Labour Party will be seen merely as a short historical episode. The right wing did not secure the defeat of Marxism or the council in which its ideas had such a sway. It was the House of Lords and the bourgeois legal system that did the job for Kinnock. When the Kinnock-controlled NEC imposed George Howarth, a rabid right winger as the candidate for the forthcoming Knowsley North by-election, Les Huckfield and the Knowsley North Executive Committee decided to take court action. Despite his overwhelming case, the courts found against him. The judges had switched tack from an earlier period when injunctions were granted for the left against the right. While the bourgeois wanted to portray the Labour Party as split, they had decided that in the long term to give succour to the left would be more dangerous. The right was the reliable prop of capitalism, which in general must be supported by the bourgeois and its institutions. The judges in a whole series of cases acted accordingly.

Nevertheless, the Knowsley North party still refused to endorse Howarth, and wrongly refused to campaign for him in the forthcoming by-election. *Militant* supporters, on the other hand, urged the left to concentrate in the election on defeating the Tory and Liberal candidates. An occasion would be presented at a later stage for the Knowsley party to select a candidate of their choice. To boycott the election, however, would strengthen the hold of the right, and provide a pretext for the right wing on the NEC to begin the process of reorganising Knowsley North Labour Party.

On 27 October, almost a year after the inquiry had been set in motion by the NEC, Felicity Dowling's case came up. At this NEC meeting, Tony Benn had suggested that on the day of the city 'Big Bang', the day on which Jeffrey Archer was resigning as the Tory Party's Deputy Chair, and the day of bus deregulation, the NEC should wind up the proceedings and return to the House of Commons to debate the issues really confronting working people. His appeal was rejected by 11 votes to 7.

Felicity Dowling then outlined her work as Secretary of the Liverpool DLP, having given up far higher paid work as a teacher. She detailed her involvement as a councillor in education, the urban regeneration strategy, in organising support for the miners' strike, and as a former activist in the National Union of Teachers. Even right wingers were forced to concede that she had made a big contribution to the labour movement in Merseyside. Yet they then proceeded to expel her on the spurious grounds of 'membership of Militant Tendency'. The evidence amounted to one leaflet signed by numerous Liverpool councillors, acknowledging the support given by *Militant* to the city council, and a public meeting in Winsford, at which she had spoken in an official capacity as a councillor.

So thin was the evidence of the NEC against her that Neil

Kinnock dragged in by the hair the council's 'no-rate' policy. He was taken aback to learn that this policy had originated from Labour councils such as Sheffield, and had initially been opposed by Liverpool. He even suggested that the city council was being run by a 'democratic centralist organisation' and they wouldn't let anybody else hold a position of secretary. Dennis Skinner reminded the meeting of the NEC's 'democratic' centralist imposition of George Howarth, as candidate in Knowsley North. On this occasion Michael Meacher voted against expulsion. After 60 wasted hours, therefore, the round of expulsions of Liverpool supporters was complete.

The Knowsley North by-election campaign was a mixture of tragedy and farce. The Liberal candidate, Rosemary Cooper, accused Howarth of 'running away from *Militant*'. Howarth vehemently denied this, saying that he had bashed *Militant* and would bash as hard, if not harder, than the Liberals. The press used Labour's divisions to demoralise Labour voters. The *Guardian*, for instance, while enthusiastically supporting the expulsion of *Militant* supporters, jibbed at the imposition of Howarth on Knowsley North Labour Party.

Faced with a boycott from party members, apart from *Militant* supporters, the Kinnock leadership substituted the national party machine for an active rank and file. On 6 November, Kinnock addressed a famous pre-election rally. As *Militant*, 14 November reported, 'Knowsley North's pre-election rally must rate as the most secret in history. In Liverpool, election rallies have been 1000-plus strong and open to any party member or voter. Getting into the Kinnock rally in Kirkby was like getting out of Colditz.' Labour Party officials, aided by lines of police, turned away local party members. Kilfoyle, Merseyside's Labour policeman, was on the door pointing out undesirables with the comment, 'He is one of the comrades.' One blind man, the local leader of the blind and disabled, was dragged across the road outside by at least six policemen for trying to get near the door.

Yet even in this hand-picked audience there were protests. One interjection from the floor brought down on the head of the heckler the comments of a furious Kinnock: 'You may be able to get away with shouting where you come from, but you've got the wrong man.' It was Kinnock who'd got the wrong man—it was the local vicar he attacked! After the meeting, according to his biographer, Michael Leapman, 'Kinnock drove to the Derby Lodge at Huyton, the smartest hotel in the area, where he and his team from London were staying. He drank at the bar with Straw and some of the key campaign workers.' The next day 'he disclosed how, at the Derby Lodge the night before, he had his first disappointing encounter with a Jacuzzi'. Kinnock and his entourage were as remote from the working people of Knowsley North and Liverpool as it was possible to be.

The campaign was conducted by the full-time party machine, with the aide of outside 'yuppies'. The character of the 'campaign workers' was typified by an encounter which one of them had with a local fish and chip shop. Jack Straw had bought some mushy peas when one of the 'yuppies' decided that he too would have some of 'that avocado'! (*Independent*, 18 November 1986)

The outcome of the election was an absolute disaster. Labour held the seat, but with a swing of 14 per cent to the Liberals. The turnout fell from 69.5 per cent to 57 per cent. Labour's share of the vote went down from 64.5 per cent in 1983 to 56 per cent. And this was proclaimed as a 'triumph' by the right wing! The disaster of the Knowsley North by-election was a precursor for the general election in 1987. It was a fitting epitaph for the right wing's campaign of expulsions against *Militant* supporters in Liverpool. The *raison d'être* of the witch-hunt was the prospect of massive electoral success for Labour. Instead, even more than 1983 it had divided Labour, turned the movement in on itself, and given the weapons to the bourgeois parties which they would successfully use against Labour in the run-up to the 1987 General Election. Marxism, however, was not crushed.

Temporarily weakened on the council plane, the support for *Militant* was being reinforced and extended industrially and above all amongst the youth. No organisational measures are capable of defeating an idea whose time has come. Liverpool has indicated that the time of Marxism has come. The collapse of capitalism and the incapacity of the right wing to solve the problems of the working class provides a fertile soil upon which a mass, powerful Marxist movement will develop in Britain in the next period.

21.
Surcharged

> They do not object to a Labour Government if it is a nice Pleasant
> Sunday Afternoon Government that is content to leave untouched
> the sacred ark of the covenant of Capitalism...Our governing class,
> with the ingenuity and cunning they know so well how to exercise,
> allow the workers to retain all the outward signs and symbols of
> democracy. We elect municipal councils and other authorities, but
> after election if they dare to put Socialist principles in operation,
> then the 'artful dodgers' who rule us scheme and plot to overthrow
> Labour majorities. George Lansbury (*Lansbury's Labour Weekly,* 6
> March 1926).

REPRESSION against the Liverpool *Militants* through the
Labour Party National Executive Committee's inquiry went
hand in hand with an open assault by the forces of the capitalist
state. The medium for this offensive was the District Auditor,
McMahon. He had been deliberately chosen by the Audit
Commission in consonance with the government. In 1984 the
previous District Auditor Leslie Stanford had made threatening
noises when the council delayed setting a rate. However, his
hand was stayed by pressure from the government which was
not at all eager to open a 'second front' during the miners'
strike.

By the autumn of 1985, with the miners' strike out of the way
and the Liverpool council isolated, the new hard-line District
Auditor Thomas McMahon prepared the ground for the 'legal'
dictatorial removal of the Labour councillors from office. This
battle was to be a long and tortuous one, extending over a period
of 18 months. The full panopoly of the law, together with the
invaluable assistance of the right-wing leadership of the Labour
Party, were to be brought to bear in order to reinforce the very
flimsy 'legal' case of McMahon for the removal of the
councillors.

For Marxists the law is not at all neutral as the reformists would have us believe. The judges, selected from social classes 'A' and 'B', in their overwhelming majority trained at Oxford or Cambridge, are steeped in the outlook of the possessing classes. In the final analysis, defence of 'private property' supersedes in their outlook any moral precepts about 'fairness' or 'justice'.

Bourgeois judges played a viciously repressive role against the first attempts of the working class at the end of the Eighteenth and the beginning of the Nineteenth centuries to form their own independent class organisations. From the Tolpuddle Martyrs, the 1906 Taff Vale judgement, the one-sided interpretation of the Public Order Act of 1935, to the imprisonment of dockers in 1948 and 1972, the judges have overwhelmingly been in favour of the rich against the poor.

The judges, not to say the professors of jurisprudence, have attempted to embellish capitalist law with eternal moral precepts, particularly of 'natural justice'. However, if the law were implemented in a crude class fashion, it would eventually become utterly discredited. Hence the law, and particularly the judges, have to balance the interests of capitalism, and particularly the 'sacred rights of property', against the need of being seen to act 'fairly'.

With the intensification of the class struggle, and particularly when the balance of forces appears to be in favour of the capitalists, the mask of the judges drops. The Thatcher government has used the law to attempt to weaken the unions and infringe democratic rights. Bolstered by this law, the judges sequestrated the assets of the miners and then the printworkers.

The green light for the legal repression of the Liverpool and Lambeth councillors was given by the leadership of the labour and trade-union movement. The signal they sent at each critical juncture was that if the councillors were 'legally hung,' no help would be forthcoming from the summits of the labour movement. It was not accidental that McMahon began to probe and test out the ground in July of 1985, when it appeared that Liverpool was isolated. McMahon addressed a four-page letter to all Liverpool's Labour councillors on 19 July 1985, in which he wrote:

> Whilst not wishing to pre-judge the issue at this stage, I must say that
> in view of the advice provided by the council's officers, by my
> predecessor and by me, the failure to make a sufficient rate appears
> to be so deliberate as to call into question the issue of wilful
> misconduct. I must make it clear, therefore, that if losses arise as a
> consequence of the council's actions, it may be necessary for me to
> consider whether further action may be required of me under the
> provisions of Section 20 of the Local Government Finance Act
> 1982.

Despite this clear threat, McMahon was not at all confident
nor, we may assume, were his Tory masters, that they could
proceed against Liverpool. After all, such threats had been
made in the previous year but in the light of the agreement
between the council and the government, the District Auditor
was no doubt instructed to ignore the councillors' delay in
setting a rate. He summed up his hesitation, 'Such possible
action against individual members is not now my most
immediate concern.' His letter amounted to warning the
councillors that the expenditure that they had set would run out
unless the rate were to be increased. Having gone through the
various options facing the councillors, he then wrote:

> There would seem to be a third course of action available. Having
> regard to the City Solicitor's advice that the council's rate resolution
> was unlawful and open to challenge, the council's problem could be
> solved if the present inadequate rate were challenged and quashed
> and the council were then to make a rate at a level to meet whatever
> level of expenditure it considered appropriate.
>   A challenge to the present rate could be made by any person with
> an appropriate interest and this would appear to include any
> member of the council. A failure to make a further rate if the
> present rate were quashed would be likely to be followed by
> consequences similar to those following the council's earlier delay in
> making the present inadequate rate.

But as we have seen earlier, none of Labour's opponents was
prepared to be saddled with the responsibility for 'raising the
rates'.

£106,000 Fine

On 8 September, McMahon imposed a fine of £106,000 against
the Liverpool councillors dismissed them from office and

banned them from holding any office for five years. 'Coincidentally', on the same day, the Lambeth councillors received a fine of £126,947 from the Metropolitan District Auditor, Skinner. The fingerprints of the government's concerted campaign against both councils were all over the measures taken by the two District Auditors. All the hesitations of the District Auditor disappeared after the failure of all-out strike action at the end of September 1985.

The reaction of the tabloid press was predictably jubilant. But it was *The Times* (10 September), baring its fangs, which displayed malicious pleasure at the predicament of the councillors:

> The gamesmanship is over. Mr Ted Knight and Mr Derek Hatton and their municipal followers have long deserved a come-uppance for their extravagant refusal during the 'rate-capping' campaign to act responsibly in office.

Reflecting also the determination of the ruling class to make the Liverpool working class pay, it commented:

> While the financial crisis plays itself out, nothing must let the Liverpool councillors off the hook they fashioned for themselves two years ago when they announced their intention to 'confront'. Liverpool, this sad city, must be an object lesson of the consequences of irresponsible administration: if its people return a *Militant* dominated council, they must be the first witnesses of the result. The spectacle for the rest of us may be unhappy, but how else can the public's education, in financial and administrative necessity proceed?

The District Auditor was quite clearly an arm of the government. Indeed, they had never been genuine auditors, that is accountants merely checking the books of local authorities. They had been installed in the Nineteenth century as a means of keeping down relief to the poor to an absolute minimum. When the Poplar councillors fought in the early 1920s for decent levels of outdoor relief to the unemployed, they were constantly harassed by the auditors. Between 1922 and 1926, 5 surcharges were imposed on Poplar Borough councillors and 9 surcharges on Poplar's Labour Poor Law Guardians, for paying "too generous" wages and unemployment relief. These accumulated to tens of thousands of pounds, and successive Liberal and Tory ministers, including the hard nosed

Neville Chamberlain, were forced to "remit"—that is, waive—the surcharges as unrecoverable. However, after the defeat of the 1926 general strike, which also undermined the struggle of councils like Poplar, the local bosses, organised in the Municipal Alliance, went onto the offensive. Among other things they challenged Chamberlain's right to remit the surcharges, and the judges ruled against the Tory minister. Ironically, in view of the renewed clamour about "retrospective legislation", Chamberlain was forced to introduce legislation to legitimise his illegal remission of successive surcharges. At the same time, however, his Audit (Local Authorities) Act of 1927 gave District Auditors drastic new powers, notably introducing for the first time the power to disqualify democratically elected councillors for 5 years.

In the 1930s, the District Auditors were used to fend off reforms being pressed by the increased Labour representation on councils. During the post-war economic upswing the role of the District Auditor receded into the background when councils dominated by Labour were under control of the right wing, who were prepared to merely manage the system. But beginning with the surcharging of the Clay Cross councillors in the 1970s, and particularly in the 1980s, local government has increasingly become a battleground between labour and capital as the capitalists have attempted to snatch away the reforms given in the post-war upswing.

Under the 1982 Local Government Finance Act the District Auditor was given new and draconian powers, becoming, under the control of the National Audit Commission, an instrument for promoting 'local government efficiency', 'value for money', and 'good housekeeping'. This was capitalist code for slashing jobs and services. The District Auditor was the local representative who would enforce the rolling back of the 'boundaries of the welfare state'.

The Tory government armed the auditors with a battery of new legal powers which allowed them to investigate local councils and to act as judge, jury and executioner in issuing certificates of surcharges and disqualification. As the case of Liverpool and Lambeth demonstrated, this was without even giving councillors the right of an oral hearing!

The District Auditor's actions in Liverpool created a sense of unease throughout the labour movement. If Liverpool could be successfully prosecuted by the District Auditor, what fate lay in store for other councils like Sheffield, Camden, Hackney, Lewisham and Islington. They may not have gone as far as Lambeth and Liverpool, but they had also delayed setting a rate. There were those, like David Blunkett and others on the 'soft left', who had capitulated on the rates battle in order to safeguard their parliamentary futures. Now it appeared as though the District Auditor was coming for them. No wonder Blunkett was to the fore in denouncing the surcharges. He correctly pointed out in the Guardian (10 September)that it was a

> totally unnecessary and vindictive attack on individual councillors who are doing their best to defend local communities and vital services...the penalties of surcharge and disqualification do not apply to MPs, businessmen, or indeed others in public life, but fall selectively on councillors who now face financial ruin and disqualification.

A major Labour spokesperson on local government, he attempted to warn the judges to desist from attacking the councillors:

> This action confirms our long-held view that the Audit Service is being used as a political tool by the Tory government. I want to give notice now that any penalties imposed on councillors will be remitted by the next Labour government. There is no ambiguity about this.

The Labour leaders were ambivalent, if not completely hostile, to Blunkett's correct interpretation of the decisions of the 1984 Labour Party Conference. He reinforced his position, by sending a letter to the NEC which extracted relevant sections from recent conference decisions to underline the point. He summed up the decisions of the Labour Party Conference as follows:

> (1) The next Labour government (will) indemnify those councillors defending local government as outlined in this statement, threatened with disqualification and surcharge. (NEC Statement, *The Defence of Local Democracy, Services and Jobs*).
> (2) (The next Labour government will) recompense from central government funds, individual councillors penalised for resisting the rates legislation (Composite 42−Conference 1984).
> (3)(Conference) commits the next Labour government to repeal repressive legislative measures ... and indemnify Labour councillors defending local government (Composite 30, 1983 Conference).

(4) Labour will also enact legislation to abolish the penalty of personal surcharge of individual councillors (Labour *Manifesto*, 1983).

(5) We will also retrospectively cancel any penalties imposed on councillors for actions taken by them—in furthering their own local manifesto policies—which conflict with local government laws introduced by the Tories ... (*Labour's Programme 1982*).

The Labour leadership were at this stage concerned that the councillors should 'pursue their case against disqualification and surcharge through the courts rather than 'bring their communities to a standstill'. According to the local government correspondent of the *Daily Telegraph*, 'The Labour front bench argue that recent judgements show that the court believe that the fixing of local rates is a matter primarily for local councillors.' This touching faith in the law was not borne out. Moreover, after the councillors had heeded the advice of the Labour leadership and had been crucified by the judges, the reaction of Kinnock, Cunningham and Straw was 'I told you so.'

Labour's main opponents in Liverpool, the Liberal-SDP Alliance, were eager to get their hands back on the levers of power. John Cartwright, the SDP's national spokesperson on local government, pressed for an early hearing of the Lambeth and Liverpool cases, a call echoed by Liberal leader Steel. The Alliance also demanded that the Audit Commission reveal all the details of other Labour councils which had delayed setting a rate. All of this of course was in the 'public interest' and had nothing to do with the fact that the Alliance were hoping for ammunition that they could use in the May 1986 elections.

Labour's opponents were confident that they would ride back to power on the backs of the District Auditor. Not so Anthony Bevins in *The Times* (27 December). He quoted 'government sources' who he claimed believed:

that even if the courts disqualify Labour's 48 Liverpool council rebels from office, there are many more *Militants* waiting in the wings to take their place...and they suspected the hard core of Labour voters in the city will have been so taken in by the extremes of *Militant* propaganda that they will automatically replace the Labour rebels with their sideline 'substitutes'.

However, the ever hopeful Sir Trevor Jones confided to *The Times* that he expected a 'breakthrough in the May elections'. It was not the first or the last time that he was to be proved wrong.

Pursuing the case through the courts was extremely costly. By the end of 1985, it had risen to £40,000. The councillors applied to have the case heard in Liverpool because almost half of them were unemployed. Lord Justice Mann turned down this appeal.

The press, in view of the colossal financial burden on them speculated hopefully that the councillors would be out of office before the beginning of 1986. However, the labour movement rallied round and the necessary finances were provided to carry the fight to the High Court. Prominent was the Transport and General Workers Union which lent £50,000 to the councillors' Appeal Fund. A special issue of *Liverpool Labour News — Not the Echo* was distributed widely throughout the city and nationally.

During this period the Liverpool councillors and the miners occupied a special place in the hearts of the labour movement. As the High Court appeal opened, the *Daily Mail* (15 January 1986) made the heartrending appeal 'Don't disfigure the High Court', referring to the fact that 'Banners festooned the High Court railings. Placard carriers crowded the pavement outside.' The protest of the Liverpool and Lambeth working class was 'disfiguring the splendid sculpture of the High Court'.

More in touch with reality was Arthur Scargill when he declared at a special rally in Lambeth on the eve of the case that: 'like the miners' strike the attack on Liverpool and Lambeth councils was an attack on civil liberties in Britain...the unelected District Auditor, acting in parallel with government wishes, issued surcharges on the councillors in September'.

Unconcerned about the plight of the Liverpool councillors the right wing were still hell bent on pursuing their vendetta against Liverpool *Militant* supporters. This earned them the undying hostility of those, like Eric Heffer, who were close to the workers of Liverpool. Incensed at Hattersley's charge of 'political corruption' which was a factor in the defeat in the January 1986 Old Swan by-election, at a Labour Party NEC meeting Heffer slammed his fist on the table white with rage, and said to Hattersley: 'You should feel ashamed of yourself. If you don't, I feel ashamed for you, you stinking little swine!'

The Labour leadership may dissemble about the 'non-political' character of the law, not so the serious representatives of the bourgeois. *The Times* (13 January) in a significant editorial headed 'Fiat Justitia' (let justice be done) gave its instructions to the judges. It commented that four years previously the court had come out against the District Auditor who had charged Camden councillors, among them Ken Livingstone, for acting 'contrary to the law'. It commented, 'That decision gave a green light to conduct in a number of urban local authorities which has embarrassed defenders of the principles of local self-government and encouraged those calling for further centralisation of the administration of Britain.' It then shattered all the pleas of the bourgeois experts, echoed by the right wing of the Labour Party, that the courts were 'above politics'. It said, 'Whatever the court says, it will be making a judgement about the legitimate distribution of power in society. In short, it will be engaging in politics.' And those sitting in judgement on the Liverpool and Lambeth councillors acted accordingly.

The first time that the councillors appeared in court was to appeal against the arbitrary judgement of the District Auditor! Both sets of councillors had been surcharged and disqualified, fined and stripped of an important democratic right, for losses of a little more than £100,000 for each council. The main charge of the District Auditor was that because the council had delayed setting a rate by something like two weeks, the government delayed paying £8 million in housing benefits. The District Auditor decreed that because of this, the city had lost interest of just over £100,000. And yet the government had still received the interest. Thus from the standpoint of public funds in general, there was no 'loss' at all!

Crown Agents Losses

In a series of articles by Lynn Walsh, *Militant* showed how government ministers had been responsible for the loss not of £100,000, but millions of pounds in circumstances which highlighted 'the blatant double standard by which the machinery of justice operates, along clear class lines. There is one law for the rich and another for the poor.' £180 million was squandered in the Crown Agents scandal. But the 75 people under criticism and considered to be at risk were granted immunity from prosecution on charges of fraud, corruption, exchange control avoidance, etc.

Moreover, when the Smith white settler regime declared unilateral independence in Rhodesia, now Zimbabwe, an oil embargo was sanctioned by the Wilson Labour government. The major oil companies, particularly Shell and BP (then 51 per cent owned by the British government) broke the embargo. An investigation took place, but when the Tory government came to power in 1979, they announced there would be no prosecutions and in effect 'retrospective immunity' was granted to all those involved in a twelve-year conspiracy. This netted millions of extra profits for the oil companies and prolonged the agony of the black population of Zimbabwe.

There was no trial for the racketeers and stock exchange swindlers—the real criminals of the 'millionaires tendency' who were involved in a series of scandals at the time when the Liverpool councillors were being dragged before the courts. As mentioned earlier, multi-million losses of Johnson-Matthey Bank were headline news in the press, and yet no prosecutions were undertaken against those who perpetrated this massive fraud.

The council's case was ably prepared by solicitors Mike Fisher and Louise Christian of Christian Fisher, together with barrister Beverly Laing. Presenting the arguments in court Steven Sedley QC completely undermined the case of the District Auditor. He showed that the claims that the councillors had 'deliberately set out for confrontation' and 'refused to manage the local economy' were completely false. He gave an outline of the social conditions which led to the return of the Labour council in 1983. He showed in great detail that far from acting 'irresponsibly' the council was barely able to provide minimum services that would constitute a civilised existence.

However, much of the proceedings revolved inevitably around the entangled framework of local government legislation. Sedley showed that the councillors had to contend with a whole range of duties, and with often irreconcilable legal demands. As democratically elected representatives, they had the right to use their own political judgements on what course to take.

Moreover, there had been no legal deadline for setting a rate. In 1984 they had delayed setting a rate, had continued to campaign and had forced the Secretary of State (Patrick Jenkin) to think again. As a result they had won extra resources.

Sedley also dealt with the role of the District Auditor as prosecutor, judge and jury rolled into one. The District Auditor was obliged to give the councillors a hearing—but incredibly failed to do so. He had accused the councillors of lying, but had given them no chance of answering back. Seasoned observers considered that the case outlined by Sedley on behalf of the council was quite devastating. Felicity Dowling commented:

> It's ironic that after the argument has been won several times over among the people of Liverpool, who recognise the council's real achievements, the issues now have to be put all over again in the court. But the evidence shows just how impressive the council's case is. We were quite justified in delaying the rate to demand further negotiations with the government. It is unfortunate that there is not a much wider audience than this courtroom for all the evidence on our side.

Despite the very effective presentation of Liverpool's case the court found, predictably, in favour of the District Auditor. The capitalist press lifted the veil of silence which had surrounded the case and greeted the verdict as 'appropriate...municipal punishment'. It was in fact an act of unparalleled class spite. Three unelected High Court judges declared 80 Labour councillors guilty in the words of Derek Hatton of providing jobs, housing and opposing Tory government cutbacks. They had been surcharged and banned from holding public office for five years. The total estimated cost at this stage awarded against them was approximately £4,000 each. When the verdict was announced, some, like John Hamilton, broke down in tears.

Mr Justice Corfield made a scandalous personal attack on Lambeth Council Leader Ted Knight, accusing him of having 'reached a pinnacle of political perversity.' There were gasps, even amongst some of the lawyers, at the completely biased political character of some of the comments of the judges. Mr Justice Russell astonishingly said: 'It is entirely wrong for such a majority to regard themselves as bound to exercise their discretion in relation to that policy in accordance with their election promise, whatever the cost and other considerations may turn out to be.' In other words, the Liverpool and Lambeth councillors were found guilty, severely fined and banned from office for daring to implement the promises upon which they had been elected. The 'norm' was to promise one thing in opposition and do the opposite in power.

The *Daily Mail* gloated, 'A punishment well deserved.' It devoted the whole of its front page on 6 March 1986 to the case with the banner headline, 'Not fit to rule.' Lord Justice Glidewell wept hypocritically over the 'severe social deprivation in Liverpool and Lambeth' but declared nevertheless: 'However great our sympathy for those in need, this is an area into which we may not enter. Considerations of this kind play no part in our decision.'

Even *The Times*, while welcoming the decision, was forced to comment on the severity meted out to the councillors: 'There are many public officials who, without penalty, have lost the public purse considerably larger sums than the £230,000 involved here.' Nevertheless, the government were obviously pressing the Audit Commission to take action against the 300 or so other Labour councillors in other authorities who had also delayed setting a rate. The *Daily Telegraph* reported:

> Government ministers are at odds with the members of the Commission on the issue. The ministers feel that the High Court judgement on Wednesday leaves the Commission with no option but to move for further sums against the Liverpool and Lambeth councillors and against others for money allegedly lost.

The mood for vengeance in the government ranks was indicated by the *Daily Telegraph*'s comment: 'Some Tories feel that the Commission has become soft on the issue.' However, even Banham, the head of the Audit Commission and future Director-General of the Confederation of British Industry, had some glimmer of an understanding of the widespread anger at the sentences and their severity. The *Daily Telegraph* summed up his unease when it reported that: 'It feels that it has been cast into the role of an arm of the government, rather than an independent adviser.' Like some modern Pontius Pilate, Banham could wring his hands and weep at the prospect of councillors being fined and possibly jailed, but nevertheless generally supported the action of the courts.

But it was the reaction of Labour's front bench spokespersons which particularly outraged the Liverpool labour movement. Keva Coombes not known for his *Militant* sympathies, on the day the councillors were surcharged, threw a 'temper tantrum' at a Merseyside County Council press conference for a Hong Kong businessman who was setting up a joint venture with Littlewoods in Knowsley. He declared, 'On the very day they face the court's decision in London, our members are sitting here giving comfort to some of the people who have been opposed to our existence. I am always in favour of jobs, but we are not here to feed the fat.'

The Labour leadership were absolutely silent about the vicious anti-working class implications of the High Court's decision to uphold the District Auditor's surcharge and disqualification of the councillors. Their attitude encouraged the ruling class to consider going further in their attacks on the other 300 councillors. Indeed, the Liverpool Labour councillors counsel, Stephen Sedley, had privately told the councillors that the intervention of the Labour leadership had been 'absolutely disastrous'. *Militant* commented on the attitude of the Labour leaders:

> While the Tories are using the courts to crucify councillors, Kinnock is misusing the Labour Party's constitution to do the same. On the same day that this judgement was made, a Tory minister announced the diversion of £500 million from the cash-starved inner cities to the Tory shires. What were the Labour Party and trade-union leaders doing? The General Secretary of the Labour Party was busy cooking up charges to expel some of these councillors from the Labour Party.

Retrospective Legislation?

Those councillors next in line for surcharge began to exert pressure on the leadership of the labour movement. David Blunkett declared, 'No one has been found guilty of corruption or any criminal offence. Local councillors are subject to rules and laws which apply to no other body of people. The Labour Party is committed to reform the law.'

The *Guardian* (7 March) gloated over the difference between the attitude of Labour's front bench at the time of the Clay Cross affair and their current posture. It pointed out that at the 1973 Party conference, Edward Short, Deputy Leader and not remotely left wing, told the delegates that 'the next Labour government would see the rebel councillors right. In the event, it was Mr Anthony Crosland, also a man of Labour's right, who lifted the automatic disqualification for office that had been imposed.'

Applauding the attitude of Kinnock and Cunningham, the *Guardian* went on: 'The Labour Party is now beginning to learn that lesson [and] could ultimately become a much healthier party than it was in 1973.' That is from the standpoint of the bourgeois! To be sure, Cunningham had said that the next Labour government would abolish the power to surcharge and disqualify, but he said that it was 'unthinkable that a Labour government would lift penalties from surcharged councillors on the grounds that this would be "retrospective legislation".'

Lynn Walsh, in an article in the *Militant* pointed out that Cunningham's claim 'even from the point of view of liberal jurisprudence is nonsense'. He went on:

> The traditional obfection to retrospective legislation is based on the generally fair principle that no-one should be convicted and punished for doing something that was not a crime under the law at the time. But if a future Labour government abolished a law which, as John Cunningham admits is reactionary and oppressive, what legal principle stands in the way of that government giving recompense to those who suffered under an outdated, oppressive law.

The Bournemouth 1985 Labour Party Conference had demanded that a future Labour government lift the fines on the councillors. But Kinnock was deaf to all but the capitalist press. The *Daily Mirror* said: 'The 81 Labour councillors who lost their legal fight against personal surcharge and a ban from office have no one to blame but themselves.' In a vitriolic editorial entitled, 'Councils of despair' which was no different to a *Sun* editorial, it declared that the councillors 'deserve what they get —from the courts and the voters'. And yet legal experts, who were a thousand miles removed politically from the Liverpool councillors, were protesting about the political interference of the courts in council business and their bias against Liverpool and Lambeth councillors. Owen Lomas, a lecturer in law at Birmingham University pointed out in the *Guardian*, 'It has quite literally led to unelected, unaccountable and faceless QCs performing policy and decision making functions which are the province of elected councillors.'

Not once did Labour's front bench spokespersons make

similar speeches. David Blunkett was also faced with the possibility of surcharge. However, in his usual fashion, he attempted to water down conference pledges on the issue. On the television programme *This Week Next Week* he stated that the party conference had decided to lift 'the iniquity of surcharge and disqualification'. But he went on, 'You can't retrospectively lift disqualification. You would instead have to deal with the question of whether you compensated people who had been made bankrupt.' It was left to Dave Nellist, Labour MP for Coventry South-East, to state clearly on the same programme:

> The Conservative government had introduced retrospective legislation for people who had lost their jobs because of trade-union closed shops. Now if it's good enough for the Tories to support and defend their class, then nothing short of that is going to be good enough for the majority of the rank and file in the party.

When a vaguely worded resolution was moved at the Labour Party Local Government Committee, Kinnock was found to be the only one voting against. He declared that there was no possibility of any government led by him indemnifying councillors for breaking the law: 'We owe it to the people concerned not to entertain fantasies or kid people, but to back and help those in greatest hardship.' When pressed over conference resolutions which were clearly on the side of the Liverpool and Lambeth councillors, Kinnock hid behind the fact that none of the resolutions had got a 'two-thirds majority on a card vote' which could have included them in a manifesto.

After the meeting, Blunkett and Cunningham explained to Kinnock that he was not being tied down by giving verbal support to this resolution. He then changed his mind and agreed to support the resolution! He was mollified by the fact that the resolution said that 'disqualification of any elected councillor carrying out party policy will be lifted upon the passage of appropriate legislation'. In other words, a bill would be introduced into Parliament to lift the surcharges. This would mean that only the remaining period of disqualification would be lifted and therefore Kinnock was safe in not supporting the principle of 'retrospectivity'!

On compensation, Blunkett with weasel words declared 'consideration will be given to the best and most equitable method of dealing with compensation for loss incurred in a way which does not undermine the labour movement's clear commitment to the upholding of the law'. This was an attempt to square the circle, a classic fudge by Blunkett. Kinnock also agreed to support the setting up of a 'hardship fund' for the Liverpool and Lambeth councillors. However, a similar fund for the Clay Cross rebels had netted just £200. In reality it would be left to the efforts of the councillors and the labour movement in Liverpool and Lambeth to raise the colossal sums to continue the legal battle.

Even this minimal measure earned Kinnock the denunciations of the *Daily Express* which declared that he was 'aiding the lawbreakers'. Thus on this critical issue, the reformists once more neither satisfied the working class or the labour movement, but irritated the bourgeois. A clear and simple class position on the law would have enormously encouraged the active workers in the labour movement in the battle against the Tories and capitalism. But the fudging of Kinnock, Cunningham and company, combined with the witch-hunt and retreats on policy, paved the way for the discouragement and demoralisation of the active Labour workers which was to be a key factor in the defeat of Labour in the 1987 General Election.

The disquiet of the ordinary members of the Labour Party filled not just Labour journals but the letters columns of the bourgeois press. One letter to The *Guardian* (12 March) declared:

> Retrospective legislation is not, in ordinary circumstances, acceptable; but it is no novelty. How, in this case, it can be morally wrong to use it to remedy so serious an injustice, it is not easy to see.

Another referred to the Liverpool and Lambeth councillors:

> They have been grossly and unfairly victimised. That an elected officer can be disbarred from office and brought to financial ruin for doing what he honestly conceives to be his civic duty, must dismay all who believe in the democratic process...The spectacle of well-heeled Labour front benchers turning on their cold little smiles as they murmur 'I told you so' is not edifying. These gentlemen seem more bent on weeding out and expelling the foot soldiers of the poor than on fighting the real enemy. I am a member of no political party, group or tendency, but I do know a Welsh hawk from a scouse handsaw.

Another wrote:

I do not write in support of *Militant*, neither am I opposed to disciplinary action being taken against Labour Party members who break the rules. However, it can be argued that the greater contribution to Labour's defeat in 1983 came from the disloyal intervention of Messrs. Wilson, Callaghan and Healey, rather than from the ultra-left.

David Skinner, one of the surcharged Clay Cross councillors, came to the support of his Liverpool and Lambeth comrades in an interview in the *Guardian*:

'Anybody who breathes socialist air should be saying, "Stand up and fight Thatcher as the miners did". It is no good saying that and then stopping when it gets too hot—you cannot have it both ways.' He [Skinner] sees the Lambeth and Liverpool situation as identical to Clay Cross, albeit with a different stance from the Labour leadership. 'Kinnock and Cunningham do not own the Labour Party. It belongs to us. What will happen will be decided at the Party Conference.' He also appealed to the other 300 councillors facing the threat of surcharge: 'They should say they don't want preferential treatment. They should point out that their colleagues and comrades in Liverpool and Lambeth have been hammered. They should say "We broke the law and demand to be sentenced".'

The 'careerist left' not unnaturally did not heed David Skinner's advice! Nor would the Labour leadership need to have looked into the annals of local government to find more than one precedent of 'retrospective' legislation.

Militant showed that 'Transport Minister Nicholas Ridley was found to have acted unlawfully in taking £50 million from the Greater London Council for London Regional Transport. He merely changed the law retrospectively to avoid having to repay the money.' Moreover, in early 1987, Ridley once more introduced 'retrospective' legislation on a gargantuan scale. His officials had discovered that the Department of the Environment had been acting 'illegally' in its dealings on the Rate Support Grant since 1982! When he announced this in the House of Commons there was uproar. Heseltine, who had been the Environment Minister, declared: 'If I am to understand the thrust of my Rt Hon Friend's remarks, is it that I have spent £30 billion illegally?'

To the Court of Appeal

Faced with enormous costs for the case, Labour began to organise bucket collections in the city centre. The vengeful Liberal councillor Rosemary Cooper demanded the police stop such collections. Indeed, when they enjoyed a brief tenure of office by courtesy of the House of Lords in March and April 1987, the Liberals used their powers to suppress street collections. Nevertheless, Labour continued to receive enormous support from the working class. In view of this, a decision was taken to go to the Court of Appeal. No great faith was placed in the judges, but it would give more time to develop the campaign in Liverpool and nationally. And it was necessary to test out all the organs of bourgeois law in order to give a visible demonstration to the labour movement of its class character.

The councillors appealed to the courts for legal aid. In the meantime, the right wing in the TGWU attempted to have the financial lifeline which had been given to the Liverpool councillors, withdrawn. The fact that 48 working men and women had put their position on the line to defend the jobs of thousands of TGWU members, was nothing to them. But the pressure from the union membership stayed the hand of the right wing.

The bourgeois continued their offensive against Liverpool and other councils which had delayed setting a rate. The *Daily Telegraph* (17 April) demanded that the Audit Commission proceed against the 300 Labour councillors in the other authorities who had delayed setting a rate:

> There will be some, including those on the government's side, who will argue that it is enough to make examples of Liverpool and Lambeth. They will say there is nothing to be gained from more court cases which the opposition can present as a further attempt by the government to erode local freedom. But it is not for the Auditor, or any of those who may influence him, and that includes the Audit Commission, to listen to these siren cries. He must resist the temptation to follow the dictates of political caution. Ratepayers have a right to see their case presented if there is a legal case to answer. This must be the only criterion for the auditor.

The Audit Commission's Liverpool satrap McMahon, responding to this pressure, produced a venomous report, just before the local elections stating: 'The council's financial and management systems and style is seriously out of hand and urgent steps are needed to correct the situation.' Tony Byrne declared, 'This is an election document in its timing and tone.' John Hamilton pointed out that although McMahon had been District Auditor for twelve months, he had not approached him or any other leader of the council to discuss the figures in his report.

The Association of Municipal Authorities (AMA) were outraged at McMahon's intervention. David Blunkett on a visit to the city commented, 'To present a distorted picture at the time of an election is very worrying.' The AMA was concerned that the Auditor had not followed 'parliamentary guidelines' in consulting with councillors and officers before publishing the report. Labour unequivocally demanded the removal of McMahon and a public enquiry into the report. Even Trevor Jones, while seizing on the documents as election ammunition, conceded that the language of the Auditor was 'a little strident'.

In the May 1986 local elections, as explained in Chapter 22, Labour once more scored a stunning victory. Nevertheless, the witch-hunt against *Militant* supporters by the Labour Party NEC and the hounding of the councillors by the High Court, continued. In the midst of this battle on 13 June *Tribune* took time out to speculate: 'Left candidates prepare to take over from *Militant*'. *Tribune*'s predictions in this respect were on the same level as Sir Trevor Jones' predictions of an imminent Liberal takeover.

The *Tribune* confidently announced 'one member of the group predicts this week that if the councillors lose their appeal, the *Militant* organisation will collapse'. They were to eat their words, because of the enormous development of support for the councillors amongst all layers of the labour movement in Liverpool, despite the witch-hunt. The comments of *Tribune* were an indication of the degeneration of this formerly 'left' journal. They were now looking towards the organs of the bourgeois state to deliver them the positions which they hankered for in Liverpool and which they could not get on the basis of political support.

In a series of meetings throughout June and July, the tremendous support amongst the Liverpool working class for the councillors was demonstrated again and again. Even in the Mexico World Cup, Liverpool fans supporting England gained an enormous amount of publicity for a flag with 'Liverpool City Council' emblazoned on it.

At a public meeting a Liverpool woman got up and simply said, 'Thank you to the Liverpool councillors' and sat down again. In other words, the avalanche of filth which still continued to pour down on the councillors had as much effect on the mass of the Liverpool working class as a dewdrop on a hot stove. Even a local radio interviewer, on leaving the area, declared that the city council had done 'a brilliant job'.

Although denied legal aid by the High Court, the councillors took their case to the Court of Appeal in July. Their case was presented in a very effective fashion by leading QC, Louis Blom-Cooper. He stressed in particular that the councillors had never been given an oral hearing before the District Auditor. If they were facing criminal charges they would have got much fairer treatment. The District Auditor would have had to have proven their guilt, not the councillors to prove their innocence, as was the case under existing local government law.

On the charge of 'wilful misconduct', the allegation that they not only acted unlawfully but deliberately did so, the District Auditor would have had to have proved his case 'beyond all reasonable doubt'. Above all, in a criminal trial the verdict would lie with the jury. The councillors were already innocent before the court of the labour movement. But no jury, after considering the detailed evidence, would have convicted them of wrong-doing.

Blom-Cooper pointed out that the District Auditor had erred in law by saying that the rate should have been fixed by the end of May:

> He is imposing a date beyond which it would be wilful misconduct not to fix a rate. But there is no date by which a rate must be fixed. It depends on reasonableness. To be wilful misconduct it must be in the minds of those denying a rate that it will be unlawful.

Despite the crushing case of the councillors, and its able presentation in the court, the Court of Appeal judges as far as the Liverpool councillors were concerned, were 'hanging judges'. Their blatant class bias was shown by their interventions. One of the three was the infamous Lord Justice

Reaction takes to the streets. 19 October, 1985.

No Comment!

25 September 1985.

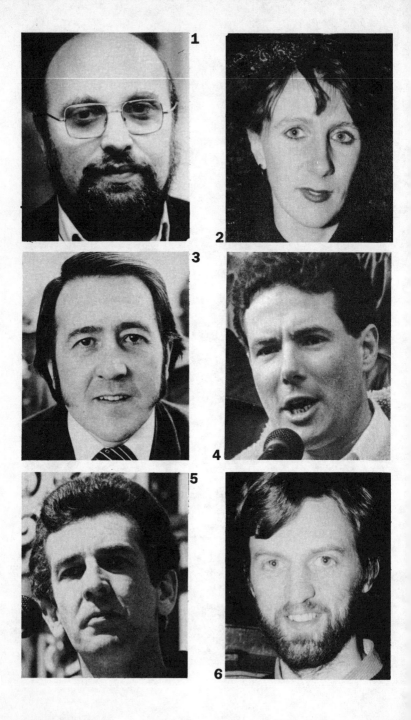

The Victims of the Labour Party NEC's Purge Trials

1. Tony Aitman, 22 years a Labour Party member, expelled.

2. Cheryl Varley, 3 years, expelled.

3. Terry Harrison, 28 years, expelled.

4. Derek Hatton, 15 years, expelled.

5. Ian Lowes, 10 years, expelled.

6. Richard Venton, 15 years, expelled.

7. Tony Mulhearn, 23 years, expelled.

8. Roger Bannister, 15 years expelled.

9. Felicity Dowling, 20 years, expelled.

The NEC spent ten meetings and £250,000 to expel these nine socialists who had 141 years' membership of the Labour Party between them.

The councillors were thrown out of office and surcharged £106,000, with £242,000 costs by the District Auditor.

26 January, 1987. The councillors and MPs make a final appeal to the House of Lords. It is rejected on 12 March.

Lawton, who was a fascist candidate for Hammersmith in 1936. Labour councillors asked how such a judge, with his ingrained hostility to the labour movement and democratic rights, could possibly give a fair hearing to councillors on trial for carrying out socialist policies. One of his more liberal interventions was to picture Derek Hatton as a Viking bent on pillaging taxpayers' money!

But he was extremely even-handed: he also described former Environment Secretary Patrick Jenkin as 'Ethelred the Unready', presumably for giving concessions to Liverpool in 1984. An indication that Lawton took his line straight from the authoritative organs of the bourgeois was shown by his comments: 'If Ethelred the Unready paid Danegeld one year, they could get it from him another year. That is the issue.' The term 'Danegeld' was lifted from *The Times* editorial of two years earlier.

Innocent but Guilty!

On July 31, the three Court of Appeal judges upheld the decision of the District Auditor. Their written judgements reinforced all the fears of Labour councillors that they could not get a fair hearing before judges who were biased against them and poured scorn on democracy itself. They dismissed the idea that the District Auditor had acted in an unfair fashion: 'The majority party seem to have had their thinking dominated by the mandates on which they have been elected,' said Lord Justice Lawton. He gave a classic expression of the capitalists' insistence that defence of their system must take precedence over any promises to the electorate: 'Pursuit of their political objectives was not a valid excuse for not performing their statutory duty.'

The judges dismissed the fact that 'losses' which the councillors were being surcharged for arose from the government deliberately withholding DHSS housing rebate and Crown property payments. Blom-Cooper's restatement of the fact that the Treasury had collected the interest on this money was airily dismissed.

The Court of Appeal accepted that in 1984 Liverpool gained more cash from the government after refusing to set a rate, but then went on to say, 'By 16 April 1985 no rational member of the majority party could have believed that there was any hope of persuading central government to make further grants out of central funds.'

The judges made a stream of hostile comments during the trial. Lawton remarked, 'It is a matter of human experience that political zealots, as some of these councillors are [presumably unlike himself when he was a fascist candidate in 1936], so delude themselves about reality that lying is unnecessary for them.'

Two of the three judges conceded the central points of the councillors' appeal—that they had not been given a fair hearing by the District Auditor. Lawton and Dillon agreed that McMahon should have allowed an oral hearing. But having accepted that the District Auditor had acted unfairly, they then decided that the hearing in the Divisional Court (the first High Court Appeal against the surcharge) 'cured' this unfairness. The Court of Appeal's rejection of the councillors' case caused widespread anger in Liverpool and nationally. The councillors were, however, given leave to appeal to the House of Lords in early October.

Meanwhile, the *Post* shrieked at the end of August, 'New bid by *Militant* to keep power.' They had woken up to the fact that in the event of the removal of the 47 councillors, the replacement panel of candidates included a high proportion of well-known *Militant* supporters. The national press picked up this theme in an attempt to embarrass Kinnock. The *Daily Mail* on 23 August said '*Militant* gang defeat Kinnock's purge'. Its editorial lamented, 'The *Militants* who never give up...they never tire and they never go away. These people never give up. As Derek Hatton, Deputy Liverpool Council leader says, "there are ten waiting in the wings for every sidestep which one has to make".' For once, Labour workers in Liverpool could agree with the *Daily Mail*!

The Liberals, ever eager to get their hands on the council pie, demanded through David Steel that the House of Lords should meet to throw out the Liverpool councillors. Liberal MP David Alton declared that the councillors needed to be dismissed immediately, otherwise under 'Labour leadership Liverpool ratepayers faced a 60 per cent rate rise and a £50 million budget deficit for the next financial year.' In the event, Labour set a budget with a 5 per cent rate increase in early 1987. No apology for this slander was forthcoming from Alton.

The House of Lords Appeal began in late January 1987. Blom-Cooper once more outlined the case of the councillors. He pointed out that 'over the past 140 years every District Auditor, with one exception, had given the opportunity of an oral hearing to everybody likely to be surcharged for misconduct'. In summing up Labour's case, the *Echo* (22 January 1987) for once reported accurately:

> He [the District Auditor] did not give them the opportunity of an interview. It was a sensible decision not to make a rate in 1985. The loss of income in the short term would have been outweighed by extra money in the long term. It is uncertain whether there was ever a real and measurable loss.

Guilty!

One redeeming feature of the House of Lords appeal was that after the third attempt, legal aid was granted for this hearing for at least 30 of the councillors. The five Law Lords examined the Liverpool council's appeal in the first three months of 1987. The verdict of 'guilty' on the 47 councillors came as no surprise but caused widespread anger within the labour movement and particularly on Merseyside. A staggering £242,000 estimated legal costs claimed by the District Auditor was added to the surcharge of £106,103.

Councillors who were democratically elected in successive elections from 1983 onwards were debarred from office for five years by an unelected District Auditor, a decision enthusiastically endorsed by unelected judges. The highest 'court' in the land had carried through a 'legal coup' not just against the 47 councillors but against the population of Liverpool as well. The 47 were denied the elementary democratic right to stand for elected office in their native city. Moreover, the legality or otherwise of the council's budget of 14 June 1985, according to Lord Keith of Kinkel, was not the issue: 'the point is that the delay in setting the rate led to delay in receiving various items of income, including government contributions in respect of rates on crown properties and...rate rebates'. But as we have shown, there was absolutely no loss to the public purse whatsoever.

Lord Keith claimed that the non-making of the rate was used deliberately 'as a lever to prise additional money from central government'. But as *Militant* commented, 'Wasn't the government using the deliberate withholding of payments as a lever to force Liverpool into a cuts budget?' Lord Templeman accepted that Liverpool had delayed in 1984 and received more cash as a result. But the Auditor had taken no action then, yet he had in 'changed circumstances' in 1985.

The argument that the District Auditor had acted unfairly by not offering them an oral hearing was dismissed. These unelected Lords also declared that neither the mandate of the councillors, nor the sincere beliefs that they were acting in the interests of ratepayers was a defence. In justification of their decision Lord Templeman took an excursion into history: 'Political leaders from Robespierre the sea-green incorruptible to Gandhi the prophet of non-violence have acted in the sincere belief that it was necessary to break the law in the interests of the nation's citizens.' He added, however, that after breaking the Salt Laws (imposed by Britain's colonial government in India), Gandhi, 'acknowledged the correctness of his conviction and appropriate sentence'. But even he had to admit that Gandhi's illegal campaign had 'hastened the repeal of the salt tax and the dawn of independence for India'.

The *Echo* printed the frustrations voiced by one youngster on hearing the Lords' judgement: 'It's too complicated. It's sub-section this, clause that. What I want to know is, what's happening to my dad?'

The press had waited for this moment for four years and they were determined to extract the maximum potential capital. The *Sun* declared, 'Labour blow as Hatton's sacked by Law Lords.' The *Daily Express* stated, 'Final defeat for Hatton's shock troops.' Derek Hatton's reaction, however, was to declare that the 47 were proud to be found 'guilty' of building houses, schools and defending the working class of their native city. Tony Mulhearn declared defiantly, 'They cannot expel us from the working class.' While there was widespread disappointment in the labour movement, with relatives of the 47 breaking down in tears at the savagery of the judgement, the leadership kept their heads, pointing out that this decision of the Lords was only the end of a chapter. They stated: 'For the next six weeks, there might well be a Liberal-Conservative pact to run the city, but that will be short-lived'. They were cetain that Labour would be returned to power at the May elections. This was dismissed as wishful thinking at the time, but the prediction was born out to the letter in the May 1987 elections, when the colossal sympathy for the council within Liverpool engendered by the Lords' decision was undoubtedly the key factor in the sweeping victory of Labour

Militant summed up the case: 'The Lords' judgement is one thing; the judgement of history will be different.' Such was the feeling in the city that the Catholic and Protestant Bishops declared that the enormous financial burden imposed on the 47 was 'without parallel' in the government system. They also praised the former Labour council for its housebuilding policies. However they also called for prayers for the city and for 'cooperation across party barriers for the good of the city as a whole'. Not for the first time, the working class of Liverpool was to ignore this advice of the Bishops in the elections six weeks later.

The anger directed at the Law Lords was only exceeded by that which labour activists directed at the Labour leaders whose comments on the Law Lords' decision fuelled the sense of outrage. Cunningham in a press statement put the knife in:

> the disqualification of these councillors, and their surcharge, was the inevitable result of a course of action pursued by the City Council at the behest of the now wholly discredited Militant Tendency...As a party, we also have to live by our rules. Members of the Militant Tendency, against whom there has been sufficient evidence, have been expelled. Neither the Labour Party, nor the people of Liverpool, will again tolerate a *Militant*-manoeuvred council.

But the support of the labour movement for the councillors was shown a few days later at the North-West Regional Conference of the Labour Party. The conference voted to support the 47 surcharged city councillors. Against the advice of the Regional Labour Party Executive, it also voted to press a future Labour government to lift the surcharges on the 47, as well as the five-year ban on them holding office. Unions such as the TGWU, AUEW, TASS, NUR and the National Union of Seamen, voted solidly in favour of the councillors. The right-wing officials were embarrassed at the success of the resolution. Walworth Road's policeman, Peter Kilfoyle, even told the mover of the successful resolution, Pete Tyson from Mossley Hill, 'that he would now be on his way' in a none too veiled threat of disciplinary action.

Tory-Liberal Junta

With the dismissal of the 47 Labour councillors, a Tory-Liberal junta took control until the May elections. They immediately set in train their promised 'counter-revolution'. They announced the sacking of Sam Bond, Liverpool's Principal Race Relations Officer, and Beryl Molyneux, who was employed in the Education Department and who had committed the ultimate crime of defecting from the Liberals to Labour three years before. Sir Trevor Jones, the Liberal leader, installed his wife as the Lord Mayor. He demanded immediate preferential treatment from the government to solve the problems which he claimed had been inherited from Labour.

Thatcher refused to meet a delegation. But on television on the evening of the councillors' dismissal, Rhodes Boyson, Tory Local Government Minister at the time, indicated that he would 'lend a sympathetic ear' to any approaches from the new council. The *Financial Times* (14 March) even hinted that:

> in Whitehall, it has been suggested that options might include a judicial review of the council house contracts to get them quashed. Mr David Alton, Liberal Chief Whip said yesterday one action might be one-off government help towards clearing loans of the city of £30 million from a Swiss and a Japanese bank.

The Liberals were searching desperately for a way to end Labour's housebuilding programme. This in turn set alarm bells ringing in the private building companies which had done remarkably well out of Labour's housebuilding programme which had created an extra 10,000 jobs in the building industry. Their pressure was probably one of the factors in the incredible *volte-face* of the *Echo* when it came out against the Liberals on the eve of the May elections.

While the Liberals were protesting at Liverpool's 'mountain of debt', statements by government ministers had revealed that Liverpool was not at all unique in this respect. The city's loan debt of £680 million compared quite favourably with £816 million for Manchester, and £575 million for Sheffield. These amounts were dwarfed, however, by right-wing controlled Birmingham's £1.3 billion debt. Moreover, a government minister, Chope, revealed that 'when the Liberals left office in 1983 Liverpool's loan debt was £557 million'. But the Liberals still continued their noisy campaign against Labour alleging that it had put the city 'in hock' to international bankers.

The labour movement continued its campaign to help the 47 councillors. A magnificent social, organised by *Militant* supporters, attracted the support of Ricky Tomlinson and Tony Scoggo who were actors in the television series *Brookside*. Letters flooded in to Labour papers commenting on the unfairness of the judgement against the councillors. A rates clerk wrote to *Militant*:

> Many big firms only pay their rates when they receive a court summons, which could be three months after their rates are due. Even then the courts treat big firms in a different way to ordinary workers. A firm summoned to court with a rate demand of £30,000 pays the same costs as a person who owes £10 on their house. Of course, the interest that you can earn on £30,000 is a lot higher than the couple of quid that the court costs come to.

In the street collections in Liverpool, there were numerous examples of the enormous support and devotion that was felt by ordinary working men and women for the stand of the councillors. Collectors were approached by a woman and her son, who gave them a moneybag full of pennies and twopences: 'Can you give this to the councillors—it's not much, it's just the kids' pocket money.'

Even in bourgeois circles there were worries about the implications of the Law Lords' decision. One letter in the *Financial Times* summed this up:

> It is not unreasonable that those elected are responsible for their actions, but the electorate's sanctions (except in the case of fraud) should surely be limited to non re-election, coupled with disqualification for those who refuse to attempt to operate within rules that existed at the time of their election...if the principle of surcharge were to be applied to MPs, would they be as quick to accept responsibility for their actions? If 'failure to set an oil depletion policy' carried the same penalty as failure to set 'a legal' rate, the bailiffs would be descending on a house in Dulwich [Thatcher's retirement residence] as well as a few in Liverpool.

However despite the contradictions in the law, the bourgeois as a whole were not concerned about legal niceties. Having failed through the use of the mass media to evict the Labour councillors from office, they had set their minds on carrying through a legal coup. By crushing the Labour councillors they hoped thereby to crush the spirit of resistance to the Tory government which the councillers stand had engendered in the majority of the Livepool population and had reverberated through the length and breadth of Britain. They had their judgement, they temporarily were successful in expelling the councillors from office. But they had not and will not succeed in crushing *Militant* either in Liverpool or elsewhere. Indeed the stand of the councillors was to prove an enormous inspiration in the battle not only in the May elections of that year but in the subsequent battles that opened up in the aftermath of the 1987 general election.

22.
Labour Victory—Again

BETWEEN MAY 1986 and May 1987 Neil Kinnock and his advisers were obsessed with the need to 'root out' the Liverpool Militants. Kinnock's preoccupation with Liverpool dominated developments within the labour movement nationally. All else was to be subordinated to this question. Prime Minister's Question Time was missed on two occasions by Neil Kinnock and Roy Hattersley. Opportunities to attack the government in the House of Commons were neglected. The mobilisation of the resources of the Labour Party for the expected general election was virtually forgotten, but the expulsion of *Militant* supporters was vital!

However, the Liverpool working class again and again revealed an embarrassing 'tendency' to support the Militants. The solid achievements in the field of housing, education, sports centres, etc had deepened support for Labour, and particularly for the most militant, fighting elements like Tony Mulhearn, Derek Hatton, for *Militant* supporters in general and for those close to them like Tony Byrne.

Flying in the face of all the evidence, Kinnock and Hattersley believed that they would climb to power over the 'whitened bones' of Scargill, Mulhearn and Hatton! But the moguls of Fleet Street who were urging Kinnock on in his 'war against the left' had no intention of supporting Labour as an alternative to the Thatcher government. They merely used the expulsions to demand 'more' and to portray Labour as a divided party.

The bourgeois in Britain hope to convert the Labour Party into a version of the American Democratic Party. In vain! The Labour Party came into being as the political outgrowth of the trade unions. Even with the drift to the right of the labour and trade-union leadership, the dream of the capitalists, frequently echoed by the right wing of the movement, to separate the unions from the Labour Party, will be stillborn.

The worsening of the economic and social situation in Britain will radicalise the unions, which in turn will be compelled to transform the Labour Party. The movement of the working class back into the Labour Party will develop in waves, over months and years, transforming it from top to bottom not once but many times. Nevertheless, Kinnock's assault on *Militant* in Liverpool temporarily had a disastrous effect on the labour movement nationally. Combined with the jettisoning of left policies, the witch-hunt disheartened many active workers within the movement, who fell into inactivity or were elbowed aside by Kinnock's new 'whizz kids' who controlled the public presentation of Labour's policies. Falsely basing themselves upon the experience of 'presidential elections' in America, Kinnock and his entourage developed the notion that it was possible to supplant a mass party by television campaigns.

An essential element in the plans of the right wing to discredit the Liverpool Militants, was to secure the electoral defeat of Labour in the city, proving the 'unelectability' of Labour with the *'Militant'* tag. But all the carefully constructed plans of the national leadership of the Labour Party were to go awry in the May 1986 local government elections, which once again confirmed the colossal and deep-rooted support which existed for Labour and the ideas of *Militant* in Liverpool.

Even those unions, like NUPE, which had stood aside from the struggle, knew what was at stake. The NUPE journal (number 4 1986) outlined the record of the Liberals in slashing jobs and services. In calling for support for Labour it also quoted Heseltine who in 1981 had declared: 'The private sector cannot play the prime role. Only public funds can buy out the accumulated legacy of decay and dereliction.' Incredibly it also recorded the fact that in 1984 the city council had forced the government to retreat; 'the government stepped in and bailed the council out with money through the back door'. It then outlined the tremendous record of the council: 'Despite the government's financial squeeze the council has: built new homes, frozen rents and kept rates down. Opened new nursery classes. Built four new sports centres.' It called for mass support for Labour.

NUPE was singing a different song in these elections, with the Tory and Liberal enemy at the gate, than in the previous two years. Not so the political opponents of *Militant* within the Labour Party. Phil Kelly, local government correspondent for *Tribune*, derisively wrote about the 'mess in Liverpool'. An Islington councillor and a refugee from the Young Liberals with his LCC mentor Peter Hain, Kelly had denigrated *Militant* in the columns of *Tribune* for more than a year, echoing criticisms of Liverpool's decision to borrow from the Swiss banks. Yet three months after his article Islington council borrowed £200 million from city banks! In the May elections in 1986, the Labour Party in Islington unfortunately lost 13 seats including Kelly's to the SDP-Liberal Alliance. Not a word of 'explanation' of the Islington disaster was to be forthcoming in Kelly's future columns in *Tribune*.

In the run-up to the May 1986 local elections, Cunningham once more distanced himself from Liverpool and Lambeth, saying derisively that they represented less than one per cent of Labour councillors and were 'atypical. They are not and never will be the norm for us.' (*Morning Star*, 19 April 1986). Buoyed up by the attacks of the Labour right, a Liberal leaflet shrieked: 'Remember all Labour candidates have been approved by Mulhearn and Hatton. They all support *Militant's* council policy. Votes for them put all jobs at risk.' Sir Trevor Jones' confidence was unbounded: 'By any assessment, Labour's days are numbered. This is a chance at last, make or break for the city.'

Like a gramophone needle that was stuck, this was the constant refrain of Jones from 1983 right up to 1987. Labour canvassers, in contrast, encountered on the doorstep the deep-seated support for Labour and its leading *Militant* figures. One canvasser met a middle-aged woman who asked if he supported Derek Hatton. Given the vicious personal diatribes against Derek Hatton, the canvasser was just a little cautious but explained that Derek Hatton carried out local and national Labour Party policy, so he did support him. The woman replied that if he did not support Derek Hatton, she would not be voting Labour! Another old man told a canvasser: 'I am not voting Labour if they're getting rid of Derek Hatton and Tony Mulhearn.' After discussion he was convinced that the candidate was not a witch-hunter and supported the city council. Another unemployed man said, 'It's militants that have won all that the working class have at the moment.'

The Liberals produced 100,000 leaflets with a headline from the *Echo*: 'Gangsters run our town hall.' It also featured Roy Hattersley's infamous comments about 'corruption'. Labour conducted a vigorous counter-attack, exposing the record of the Liberal-Tory coalition council in Hammersmith where the Liberals had voted 300 times with the Tories and only once with Labour. In four years no council houses had been built, purpose-built accommodation built under Labour had been sold off, and the direct labour building organisation had been cut from 516 in 1982 to 183 in 1986.

Any frivolous point was seized on in order to attack Labour in the city. The *Daily Express* (22 April) asserted that: 'Soccer stars snub Hatton' after Liverpool Football Club had refused to participate in a joint civic reception for Liverpool and Everton, who were competing in the FA Cup Final. Not for the first or last time Liberal councillor Rosemary Cooper declared, 'By the time the final is played on 10 May, Mr Hatton knows he will be out of office—so he has organised this last ditch effort to win votes.'

The *Daily Telegraph* (5 May) predicted, '*Militant* at crossroads in Liverpool.' The widely expected defeat in Liverpool was linked to the final push against *Militant* supporters: 'such a defeat would break the *Militant* stranglehold on the city and add impetus to Mr Kinnock's campaign to rid the party of the Trotskyist Tendency.' The day before the elections the *Echo* called for a massive vote against Labour:

> *Militant*, masquerading under the banner of Labour, have taken the city to the brink of bankruptcy, saddled it with an impossible debt burden, damaged its education service, left its streets dirty, its dustbins unemptied and given it an international image of industrial anarchy. And that takes no account of the jobs for the boys scandals, or the intimidation of council officers, of the revenge on those who dared to step out of line and of the anxiety inflicted on thousands of families who for months never knew for certain whether they would be paid.

In the interests of 'balance', local government editor Peter Phelps interviewed leading figures from the three main parties in the city. Trevor Jones declared:

> We will switch the housing programme to cooperative housing and that should release capital which can be used to remedy the deficit. We have always had cooperation from the workforce in the past and have no reason to doubt we will get it in the future.

This breathtaking example of the Liberals' political amnesia left out of account the numerous industrial battles of the council workforce against the Tory-Liberal coalition prior to 1983, such as the typists' strike and the one-day general strike of the council workforce against the threat of privatisation. Tony Mulhearn, speaking for Labour, clearly enunciated the reasons for Labour's success in the city:

> I believe the people of Liverpool have seen through the diatribe of distortion and downright lies which has been hurled at Labour and certain individuals. What the Tories, the press and the right wing of the NEC cannot do is fantasise away the major problems which continue to affect the city of Liverpool.

Asked by Phelps why people should vote Labour when most councillors were expected to be thrown out of office within months, if not weeks, Tony Mulhearn replied:

> The voters will cast their votes on the basis of policies, not individuals. They will see, cutting through all of the propaganda, that we have a Labour council which, come hell or high water, has attempted to stick to the promises it made in 1983 and 1984. The fact that people may be removed at a later date—and that is not a foregone conclusion—will not weigh heavily at all.
>
> When you challenge those responsible and their enormous power, then that becomes a very controversial situation. When people realised we were serious, that we were not just going through the motions, they began to worry because nothing is hated more by the establishment. Once the people in the establishment believe that certain individuals are leading a force which threatens their wealth and privileges, they will mobilise all their forces against anyone who threatens them.

Phelps resorted to sarcasm: 'So councillor Mulhearn is saying the Liverpool Labour Party is the most misunderstood Labour Party organisation in Britain.' Tony Mulhearn simply replied: 'Yes—by its enemies.' Phelps tried another ploy: 'Could not the party share some blame for its own predicament, could it be they are unable to explain themselves properly.' Tony Mulhearn replied 'No it is the media. A lie is half way round the world before the truth has got time to put its boots on.'

A real demonstration of *Militant's* support in the city was given at a magnificent rally held by the paper in the week prior to the elections, attended by 1000 Labour Party members and trade unionists. A standing ovation was given to Labour councillors threatened with disqualification from office and for the twelve *Militant* supporters threatened with expulsion by the Labour Party leadership. Alongside Tony Mulhearn and Derek Hatton were Peter Taaffe, Ted Grant and a speaker from the long-running Addenbrooke's Hospital strike. A collection raised £1785 for the *Militant* Fighting Fund, including a donation of £100 from Ricky Tomlinson who plays Bobby Grant in the Channel 4 television serial *Brookside*—and was one of the two Shrewsbury building workers jailed in 1974.

'A Confounding Victory'

Labour held on to its gains of the previous three years, winning a seat in Breckfield from the Liberals and losing one in Dingle. In the atmosphere of the council's financial difficulties, the witch-hunt in the Labour Party, and the surcharge case against the councillors it was a stunning victory for Labour. All the experts had been confidently expecting a rout. In an editorial headed 'A confounding *Militant* victory' the *Echo* declared:

> However experts may analyse the votes, there is not a shadow of doubt that Liverpool's town hall election results were a success for *Militant*...nowhere else were the local issues more sharply defined and more important than in Liverpool...no scouser could have been under any illusion that a vote for Labour in this city yesterday was a vote for *Militant*.

The *Echo* had to say this. It had made the issue of *'Militant'* the dominant theme of the election by its vicious diatribes during the campaign. It went on:

> The scope of *Militant's* victory still confounded all the experts. Independent experts say Liverpool is the worst run city in Britain and no one who went to the polls yesterday did so in ignorance of the price Liverpool would have to pay for endorsing *Militant* misrule.

The 'independent experts' were sitting in the editorial chairs of the *Echo*! Moreover, the Liverpool working class through their own experience had seen that it was far from being the 'worst run city in Britain'. Tony Mulhearn triumphantly declared, 'We said we would be judged on jobs, services and houses. The courage shown by councillors was not lost on the people of the city.'

The council elections were an absolute disaster for the Tories. Their vote was halved. Six of the seven seats they were defending were won by the Liberals who have become the new Tory party in Liverpool. The only Tory to hold his seat, the leader Chris Hallows, saw his majority slashed to about 300. Thatcherism as a political creed had been well nigh obliterated in Liverpool. The only Labour seat lost to the Liberals was in Dingle, by 31 votes—with the 'Communist' party taking 44 votes!

The Times, reflecting the consternation of the bourgeois and the Labour leaders, declared:

> The results were welcomed by Mr Derek Hatton, the council's Deputy Leader, but will not help Mr Kinnock, the Labour Leader, in his campaign to rid the local party of its *Militant* influence. Mr Hatton said 'The District Auditor and the Courts may have rejected us, but the people have supported us.'

Labour had done well in other parts of the country, but according to the *Daily Telegraph* (10 May) 'Labour's elation at the local election results was tempered by the continued success in Liverpool of the Militants.' Even the doubting Thomases in the *Morning Star* declared 'Liverpool beats smear campaign.' David Butler in *The Times* (10 May) summed up the attitude of the Labour right: 'Indeed, it might have preferred a worse result in Liverpool—it may even look forward to one later this year if the Appeal Court ousts their surcharged councillors.' One of the most remarkable results was the re-election of Felicity Dowling, secretary of the disbanded DLP and one of the eleven facing expulsion from the Labour Party. She said: 'Everyone knew exactly who I was and that I face expulsion from the party. I got 71 per cent of the vote. What more need I say? We would have won more if the DLP had not been suspended and I had been able to do my job.' (*Financial Times*, 10 May)

Incredibly, Kinnock commented to the *Guardian* (6 May): 'With the absence of the *Militant* element I think our strength will be even greater.' His local acolyte, Kilfoyle, spent most of his time in subsequent weeks dedicating himself to rubbishing Labour's splendid victory. *Tribune* (16 May) carried a long article from him which claimed to show in detail that Labour's Liverpool performance was dismal. The same arguments were repeated in the *New Statesman* (16 May). They all drew the conclusion that in a general election Labour MPs in Liverpool would be vulnerable to the Alliance.

It was true that the Labour vote had gone down from 90,187 (46.2 per cent) in 1984 to 73,617 (41.7 per cent) in 1986. But the main explanation for this, as the *Echo* had conceded, was the large drop in the turnout, from 195,000 (50.1 per cent) to 171,655 (44.3 per cent). Thousands of Labour voters did not come out to vote, which is not unusual in council elections. Over the same period the Alliance vote rose from 67,204 (33.4 per cent) to 78,571 (44.6 per cent).This was largely due to the collapse of the Tory vote from 37,023 (19 per cent) to 21,118 (12.5 per cent). To see the real progress Labour had made, the 73,000 vote should be compared with the years before they controlled the council. In 1982, in exactly the same seats as in the 1986 election, Labour polled 54,780 (38.8 per cent), and in 1978 when the Labour vote was only 46,488 (33.4 per cent). It was impossible therefore to maintain that there had been a serious erosion of Labour's vote.

Labour's vote in the 1986 council elections, as *Militant* (16 May) pointed out, was 'little short of marvellous'. Kilfoyle was answered in detail by Tony Mulhearn in a letter to *Tribune* and *Labour Weekly*.

It was considered not worthwhile replying to the *New Statesman*, which was the home of those petit-bourgeois cynics who no longer believed in the socialist aspirations of the labour movement. He wrote:

> Peter Kilfoyle picks out Speke Ward, and its candidate Felicity Dowling, as doing particularly badly. This is no doubt an attempt to justify support for their expulsion from the party. Unfortunately, Peter's figures are incorrect. For example, Labour's percentage share of the poll in two other wards dropped by a larger margin than the ten per cent in Speke.
>
> Any serious analysis of the results would have highlighted five factors:
> i) the collapse of the Tory vote into the hands of the Alliance;
> ii) the Labour vote in marginal wards held up: the percentage turn-out was higher in these wards;

iii) the areas of massive Labour support—Dovecot, Abercromby, Netherley, Speke, Valley, Vauxhall, etc, all suffered large decreases in Labour's vote compared to 1984, though still maintaining massive majorities. This was due to the drop in the turn-out in these areas to a pre-1984 level. This was attributable in some wards to the outflow of people rehoused under the council's urban regeneration policies;

iv) the effect of the Liberal propaganda in prominently headlining outrageous statements by Roy Hattersley ('There has been political corruption and literal corruption') and Neil Kinnock's 'Liverpool councillors need psychiatric treatment';

v) the continual problems with the refuse collection and housing repairs service. We explained the problems of the refuse service and housing repairs and we displayed a united party determined to oppose all cuts in jobs and services and for the advancement of socialist policies as opposed to some 'light grey' version of social democracy...

Peter Kilfoyle has already shown the party membership in Liverpool that he is a dab hand at ripping telephones from walls, removing typewriters to 'safe places' and closing down party offices that have been in existence for years. We only hope his next 'analysis' is more factual and constructive than his performance so far.

Militant Gains Elsewhere

'Anti-*Militant*' candidates in other parts of the country did badly. In Gateshead, Ken Buckingham, a 'rent and rate payer' on Gateshead Council for 19 years was defeated by 27-year-old *Militant* supporter Neil Waite, standing for the first time. In a 43 per cent poll (very high for council elections thanks to the Labour campaign), Neil Waite polled 1936, the second highest Labour vote ever, to Buckingham's 1153. Buckingham had gone out of his way to stress that his opponent was a Marxist: 'If you vote for Labour, you are voting for the *Militant*.' In North Tyneside, seven of thirteen right-wing councillors who were expelled from the Labour Party and called themselves 'Labour against *Militant*' were thoroughly thrashed. Amongst the Labour victors, with substantial majorities, were two *Militant* supporters.

In Glasgow the outstanding result for Labour was the victory of Margaret Dick 'a self-confessed *Militant* supporter'. The local press, the Tories and Liberals joined in denouncing her and the *Glasgow Evening Times* believed it would be a 'political shock' if she was returned. In the event, she turned a Tory majority of 1612 into a 643 Labour majority. Pollock's parliamentary candidate described it as by far the best result of the night. Also in Scotland, in Musselburgh, where *Militant* supporter Keith Simpson was standing for Lothian Regional Council, the Alliance struck a deal with the Tories who did not stand a candidate for the first time in decades. Despite this and a hostile local press, Keith Simpson increased his majority over the Alliance candidate, former Musselburgh Labour Party Chair, Andrew Coulson, from 700 to nearly 1700. *Militant* supporters were also elected in Hackney, Southwark, Greenwich and Tower Hamlets.

Black Caucus Candidate Defeated

One of the most important results was the victory for Labour in the Granby ward in Liverpool, where more than half the city's black population live. The Black Caucus stood an independent candidate. It was admitted by leading Black Caucus member Liz Drysdale, who became a Labour councillor after the disqualification of the 47, that the independent candidate was selected to stand against Labour, not the Liberals or the Tories. They hoped this would split the Labour vote and let the Liberals in, as part of their contribution to what they imagined would have been an overall Liberal victory in Liverpool. The main plank of their platform was 'the sacking of Sam Bond'. But in the event Labour increased its majority to 938, more than twice that of the vote of 427 for the independent black candidate. The campaign had been characterised by vicious attacks on LPYS members who had been flyposting the area. The attackers emerged from the Independent candidate's campaign van, resulting in one LPYS member being slashed above the eye with a stanley knife.

The victory for Labour in Liverpool, the other council victories for Labour, and the collapse of the Tories' vote, together with the Tories' Parliamentary by-election loss of Ryedale and near loss of West Derbyshire, could have become a platform for a campaign to defeat the Tory government. But the Labour leadership were to squander the opportunity.

Some sections of the bourgeois press like the *Daily Mail* (10 May) began to recognise that:

The extremist scare just did not work. Labour held on in Derek Hatton's Liverpool, gained seats in Ted Knight's Lambeth. And even Bernie Grant increased his majority. People are looking for something more today than a political slanging match. What we saw on Thursday was a much more politically sophisticated electorate than Mr Tebbit or Mrs Thatcher seem to credit. Protest politics has come of age.

Despite this the Labour leadership continued their war against *Militant* in Liverpool. The bourgeois also understood the necessity of 'crushing Liverpool' because of what it represented. Environment Minister Kenneth Baker was reduced to saying that the vote was 'a sad day for democracy', a remark reminiscent of the East German Stalinists who, in the wake of the East Berlin uprising in 1953, declared that they had 'lost confidence in the people'. Bertold Brecht's riposte could just as well be applied to Kenneth Baker: 'Why don't you dissolve the people?'

Meanwhile, the Liverpool Liberals were in turmoil. The lure of the council feedbag once more being in their hands induced the Alliance partners in Liverpool, the SDP and Liberals, to sink their differences over the division of seats. But this outbreak of chumminess, both between the Alliance partners and within their respective parties, did not last long.

In the autumn a ferocious struggle broke out among Broadgreen Liberals as to who was to be their candidate at the general election. At their constituency Annual General Meeting, Richard Pine, the candidate for the seat in 1983, was punched in the face and kicked in the backside by the leisure services spokesperson, John Jones! Jones' supporters claimed that fellow councillor Pine and his supporters had packed the meeting! There were of course no banner headlines in the *Echo* or the *Post* about 'Liberal thugs and gangsters' wanting to run 'our town hall.'

Notwithstanding Liverpool's striking victory, the right wing pursued its vendetta against *Militant* supporters to the end. While wrestling with the enormous problems of the city, Derek Hatton, Tony Mulhearn and others also had to fight against the expulsions and prepare their defence in the capitalist courts against disqualification and banning from office. Even after the expulsions in October 1986, the Labour Party national officials, Larry Whitty, the General Secretary, and Joyce Gould, Director of Organisation, were more preoccupied with the drive against *Militant* than in preparing Labour for the forthcoming general election. Their attention was particularly concentrated in ejecting Tony Mulhearn, Derek Hatton and others from the Labour group.

Knowsley North

Kinnock also linked this with a drive against the left in Knowsley North, promising 'direct and effective action'. The by-election result there was hailed as a great victory, despite Labour losing over eight per cent of its 1983 vote. Immediately the result was known, regional officials declared that the Knowsley North Labour Party would be disbanded. On the basis of inside information, the *Sunday Times* (16 November) declared: 'It will be reconstituted when *Militant* supporters have been flushed out.' According to this journal, 'around a dozen expulsions are likely after allegations made in a sworn affidavit by Tony Glover, a former ward secretary who has broken with *Militant* and gone into hiding in Leicester'. Glover's lurid tale of alleged 'Trotskyite plotters' was splashed across the *Today* newspaper. Glover's subsequent claims that he had been beaten up, led to Dave Kerr, vice-chair and press officer of Knowsley North Labour Party being interviewed by the police and charged although the charges were later dropped. The character of the main witness against him, Glover, is indicated by the fact that he had been convicted of stealing £200 from a moneybox belonging to the housing charity Shelter.

Glover's testimony was just another 'five minute wonder', another tale of a 'former extremist' which the Liverpool working class had become habituated to. However, it was to provide the excuse for the National Executive Committee on 26 November to set up an inquiry, adding Knowsley North to the three other constituencies on Merseyside (Broadgreen and the two St Helens seats) already suspended by the NEC.

In the midst of this turmoil Roy Hattersley dashed the hopes of those 'left' council leaders who had gone along with the expulsions as the price they were prepared to pay for a Labour government. They confidently expected that a Labour government would cancel the massive debts which most councils had accumulated during the Thatcher years. Hattersley

declared, however, on 19 November: 'We are not in the business
of bailing any councils out, whether they be Labour-led or hung
councils like Hampshire, which have very similar problems.
What we are interested in is providing funding for councils that
come to us with job creation packages.' Hattersley promised a
maximum of £1 billion to these councils. Yet the total debt of
councils amounted to more than £2 billion. His statement
indicated that a right-wing dominated Labour government
would not meet the needs of councils for more resources.

Tony Byrne Elected Group Leader

Meanwhile in Liverpool, Larry Whitty and Joyce Gould sallied
forth once more, like some leaky battleship, to do battle with the
Labour group. According to the *Echo*, 'Labour's national rulers
are fuelling up for more action in Liverpool following a night of
Militant chaos.' This followed a Labour group meeting from
which Tony Mulhearn and Derek Hatton absented themselves,
where the inept handling of the meeting by Whitty resulted in
Tony Byrne replacing John Hamilton as leader of the Labour
group. The majority of the group wished Tony Byrne to chair
the meeting. They were not confident that John Hamilton
would be tactically adroit in the face of manoeuvres from the
national Labour Party officials. In contravention of all normal
procedure, Whitty insisted that only the leader of the Labour
group could take the chair. After much wrangling, Tony Byrne
was then nominated for this position and was subsequently
elected.

The capitalists immediately set up a hue and cry in defence of
John Hamilton who they had previously vilified, as had the
supporters of Neil Kinnock, for not 'standing up to *Militant*'.
The *Echo* said, 'Derek Hatton's supporters ran rings round
Labour's General Secretary Larry Whitty last night as he tried to
complete his purge of *Militant*.' In reality, while John Hamilton
was respected for his stance in defence of the record of the
council, he had angered many by siding with the right-wing
cabal who were collaborating with the national Labour Party
officials in seeking to have Tony Mulhearn and Derek Hatton,
together with other *Militant* supporters, evicted from the Labour
group.

Once more, Neil Kinnock was faced with screeching headlines

from 'Liverpool's Left outflank Kinnock' *(Daily Mail)*, to 'Liverpool Militants beat Labour ban' *(Financial Times)*. The *Echo* summed it up as 'a night of disaster'.

Nor was Kinnock having it all his own way in assembling the machinery to carry through 'democratic' expulsions. Alan Quinn, a left winger nominated by the Transport and General Workers Union, despite frantic efforts by Kinnock aides to prevent this, was elected with other unions' backing onto the National Constitutional Committee, the body established after the 1986 Labour Party Conference to deal with disciplinary matters—expulsions—without troubling the whole NEC.

It soon became clear that Labour's frenzied right wing were prepared to strike out in all directions if they were thwarted in their ambition to chop off '*Militant's* head.' They were, if necessary, prepared to wreck the Labour group and the labour movement on Merseyside. Therefore it was necessary, concluded the Marxists, once more to beat an orderly retreat. While the Labour group of 20 November had in effect continued to recognise those expelled councillors, not making any moves to replace Derek Hatton as Deputy Leader, he now formally resigned his position. Tony Mulhearn explained: 'In no circumstances were we prepared to allow other councillors to be expelled from the party for continuing to be loyal to us.' Derek Hatton summed up his feelings with the words:

> Proud, sad and bitter. Proud that we have achieved so much in the city. Sad to be leaving a position which I've held for three-and-a-half years. Bitter that our Labour group has been split by the National Executive of our own party. Even the Tories, the Courts, the media and the District Auditor could not do that...We will be around when Kinnock moves faster towards the right than MacDonald did in the 1930s.

The national press could proclaim this as a great victory, but the *Echo* was not so sure:

> Another coup for *Militant*...On the face of it, councillor Hatton's resignation is a body blow to *Militant* and a triumph for Labour leader Neil Kinnock. But Mr Hatton is going because it best serves the cause of *Militant* that he should step down. For the first and perhaps the last time the interests of *Militant* and the Labour Party coincide ... it is a further demonstration, if any were needed, that while Mr Kinnock may be publicly defied, when *Militant* say 'jump' it is time to go without argument.

The editorial creatures who write this kind of material imagine that a Marxist tendency operates in the same way as big business and capitalist journals. An editor says 'jump' and bourgeois journalists dip their pens in poisoned ink to malign the labour movement. Derek Hatton's conduct in stepping down from his position as Deputy Leader, also that of Tony Mulhearn and Felicity Dowling, was an indication that they placed the interests of the labour movement and the working class of Liverpool before any personal ambition. It was devotion to the cause of working people, to raise them out of the dirt into which capitalism had thrust them, that had generated the struggle in Liverpool and hoisted Derek Hatton, Tony Mulhearn and Felicity Dowling to positions of power in the Labour council. In stepping down they remained faithful to the cause for which they came into politics in the first place. It was this inflexibility and intransigence in the face of the venom and the hostility of the capitalists, together with adroit tactics, which so enraged the bourgeois and their props within the labour movement.

Their formal resignation from the council leadership positions in no way diminished the colossal support which they and Marxism had built up in the city. The *Independent* could use Derek Hatton's resignation as an indication of the alleged 'decline and fall of *Militant*'. Yet the resilience of Marxism in Liverpool was to convince the *Independent* that Kinnock had scored merely a Pyrrhic victory in Liverpool. Anthony Bevins, its political editor was to write, 'He [Kinnock] has not broken the Trotskyists and never will.' Like the bourgeois, the Labour leadership secretly looked towards the House of Lords to do the job for them: 'The unspoken hope in the Labour leadership that [through] a House of Lords ruling in January that most of the party's Liverpool councillors should be barred from office...could render further expulsions unnecessary.' (*Daily Telegraph*, 27 November)

The attack on the left was connected with the political drive towards the right of the leadership. Thus at the quarterly meeting of the Association of Metropolitan Authorities, Jack Cunningham said that 1987 would be an election year, and the local leaders should think very carefully about statements that they made, 'or commitments entered into by Labour councils in advance of the next Labour government'.

While the press was full of the Labour leadership's denunciations of *Militant*, sometimes as we have seen in the most vitriolic terms, *Militant* supporters concentrated their attention in the main on the Tory and Liberal-SDP enemy. In its comments on the Knowsley North by-election, the *Independent* was constrained to remark: 'It [*Militant*] differs perhaps most sharply from other ultra-left journals in reserving the major thrust of its venom, in print at least, for Conservative rather than Labour policies and leadership.'

Despite the blows which rained down on their heads, the Marxists in the Merseyside area continued to score remarkable victories. At the North-West Labour Party Women's Conference, two-thirds of the delegates voted in favour of Marxist ideas. An emergency resolution from Liverpool Women's Council was passed, which reaffirmed support for the 47 surcharged Liverpool councillors. The enormous progress of Marxism in the student sector was reflected in the election of Cheryl Varley on to the Further Education sector National Committee of the National Union of Students. This was achieved despite her recent expulsion from the Labour Party. The convenor of 72,000 Merseyside students, she received the highest vote ever recorded, with 83 first preference votes out of 199 cast, double the number of her nearest rival.

In Liverpool, despite the boycott of a handful of party members, 300 people from Liverpool, Knowsley and St Helens attended a rally to mark the anniversary of the suspension of the Liverpool District Labour Party (DLP). Despite the constitutional bickering of the NEC and the bureaucratic manoeuvres of Kilfoyle, the colossal authority of the city councillors, and particularly the Marxists, remained undiminished amongst the mass of party workers and working people on Merseyside. Paul Astbury, who had been investigated by Labour's NEC as a suspected *Militant* sympathiser, was elected as the Deputy Leader of the Council. Harry Smith replaced Derek Hatton as Industrial and Public Relations Committee Chair and Tony Jennings replaced Felicity Dowling as Deputy Chair of the Education Committee. Moreover, the expected 'moderate backlash' against the election of Tony Byrne for Leader of the council group evaporated. On 8 December he was confirmed as Leader by 27 votes to 21. These actions infuriated the right on the NEC.

Kinnock was determined to pursue his vendetta against the Liverpool Militants, even if this extended to a 'non-*Militant*' such as Tony Byrne. By 21 votes to 6, he forced a decision through the NEC to refer Tony Byrne to the incoming National Constitutional Committee. Once more he reserved his passion for members of his own party: 'Let us not forget what was done to John Hamilton. That has not been forgotten or forgiven in Liverpool. It is demoralising for people in Liverpool to see that John Hamilton has been kicked out because there is a little clique who, for one reason or another, want to keep Derek Hatton in the public eye.' But to have Kinnock acting as his latter day attorney only served to undermine John Hamilton's position in the eyes of the advanced workers. There was, however, genuine regret when Derek Hatton and Tony Mulhearn stepped down from their positions at a special council meeting called on 10 December.

John Hamilton's rather pathetic campaign to 'humanise the machine of local government in Liverpool' fell on deaf ears, particularly as his main advocate now was Peter Kilfoyle who, in a letter to the *Echo*, accused *Militant* supporters of using 'fascist methods'. He ignored the fact that *Militant* supporters had recently been hospitalised as a result of confrontation with fascist groups in the city: Kilfoyle himself had never once organised any anti-racist activity in Liverpool in his capacity as a Labour Party official. But even out of office, Derek Hatton still managed to proselytise on behalf of Marxism. Much to the chagrin of the *Echo* and its TV column, he appeared before an audience of 15 million people on the *Wogan* show.

Within the limits of a light-hearted, not to say frivolous show, he managed a partial explanation both of the social conditions from which *Militant* sprang and some of the ideas of Marxism. The *Echo* believed that it had buried Derek Hatton and his ilk. But here he was, rising from the dead to haunt them and Neil Kinnock. They devoted a whole editorial to the subject of 'Wogan and Hatton', entitled 'Hatton help for Tories'. But the *Echo*'s readers did not agree. One wrote from West Kirby: 'Neil Kinnock is finding that a Taffy is no match for a Scouser in the battle of wits.' The *Daily Mail* carried a letter from a somewhat confused opponent of *Militant*:

> Derek Hatton and his fanatics are using today's problems to gain
> power. They must be stopped, but—God help me—I had to agree

with him as I watched the Wogan interview. He is right. In Liverpool, which I have seen change from a thriving city to a dead end town, apathy abounds. The likes of Hatton must not be allowed to dupe us, but for once he did make sense.

Having hounded Derek Hatton from office, and out of his job, the bourgeois press at the same time attacked him for attempting to set up a business to earn a living. Yet here the sound instinct of the Liverpool workers was displayed in a letter to the *Echo*:

> Travelling through this city, everywhere you look there are new council houses either completed or being built, new sports centres, housing offices, landscaped areas etc. In order to achieve these for the city of Liverpool, Derek Hatton and other Labour councillors have put their livelihoods at risk. Because Derek has been the focus for the attack, which has resulted in him being expelled from the Labour Party and losing his job in Knowsley, he will probably be debarred from office and is unlikely to find suitable employment in the future. I am sure the media would love to see him miserable and on the dole, but instead he has made the most of one of the few avenues left open to him. I am sure he'll do well in the future and will always have the backing of the rank and file.

Alongside the attacks on the Marxists, the Liverpool press was compelled to feature the terrible social conditions which had nurtured Marxism and which sustained it. During the bitterly cold winter of 1986-7 the *Echo* reported:

> Hundreds of families on Cantril Farm are risking prison just to keep their children warm. And they don't care. In the words of one desperate mum of five, fighting to keep her family from freezing: 'They can throw us in jail—at least it will be warm there.' Welfare workers reckon as many as half the estate's households are running up huge debts by buying warm clothes for their children which they cannot afford.

An Unemployed Resource Centre worker commented: 'It is simply a matter of life or death to them...if they don't run up these debts, they don't keep warm—and in this weather, that is an almost certain way to die.'

This worker summed up the widespread feeling in Liverpool at this stage:

> It is disgraceful that families have to live like this. The ideal solution to these terrible problems is to bring work to the area—but that

doesn't seem very likely. The government must start to pay out adequate allowances so that people can live in dignity and comfort. It is not right to punish the poor in this cruel and heartless way.

Strike Wave

In early 1987 a wave of strikes swept through the area. In the British Telecom dispute, Merseyside was one of the most solid areas. A whole series of strikes broke out in small factories.

To add to the widespread grievances in the city, bus deregulation in December 1986 resulted in massive fare increases, some as high as 90 per cent. It also resulted in a lowering of pay and a lengthening of the working day for bus crews. The simmering discontent of the busworkers resulted in strikes every weekend. The disaffected mood spread to the Crosville Bus workers where the management provocatively closed a whole depot.

Given the central importance of the local council workforce in the city, this mini-strike wave was bound to affect them as well. A sense of insecurity pervaded the workforce, given the expected eviction of the Labour council from office by the House of Lords. Some union leaders, who had been implacably hostile to the Labour council from its inception, attempted to exploit this mood. They wished to embarrass the Labour council in its last days, and thereby *Militant*, and at the same time extract concessions from Labour which they believed the Liberals, if they came to power, would be forced to maintain. The Marxists pointed out that this was a chimera. Some of the council leaders were enraged by this attitude. They had sacrificed everything in defence of the jobs of council workers and the services provided to the workers of Liverpool. Now, it seemed that they were being rewarded with an approach which would cast them in the worst possible light, putting them on a par with right-wing Labour councillors who were prepared to carry through cuts and sit out strikes of their own workforce.

A series of disputes broke out amongst NALGO members, working in the housing benefit offices, bin drivers, gritters and social workers. Teachers also came out on strike, over the issue of 'cover', even though NUT Branch Secretary Ferguson had agreed and accepted a recommendation of ACAS on the issue. All the enemies of the council, from the right to 'left' sought to exploit this situation. The Communist Party journal the *Morning Star* proclaimed 'Liverpool set for strikes.' It went on: 'Troubles are piling up for *Militant*-led Liverpool council as more industrial action is threatened by key groups of workers in protest over council policies.' It confidently predicted that 1000 GMBATU workers would march out on indefinite strike action. It also looked towards the 6500 NALGO members taking industrial action.

The *Echo* for once came out in favour of strikes! They supported council security guards, organised in the mobile force, who were allegedly fighting in opposition to being merged with the dreaded 'Hatton's army', the static security force. The *Echo* even carried photographs of two horses used by the mobile security, under the headline 'Rebels told their horse must go.' The tear-jerking impression was given that the horses were about to be turned into dogmeat! Trevor Jones was wheeled in to declare 'It was just an act of vindictiveness.' No such decision had been taken by the council. The philosophy of the council's opponents was to use anything and everything considered to be even remotely damaging to Labour. George Knibb, with tremendous energy and patience used great skill as a concilliator between councillors and the unions in settling a number of disputes. He was a veteran of the Croxteth Comprehensive School battle who subsequently was employed in the Central Support Unit of the council. A combination of firmness and a preparedness to grant reasonable claims resulted in most of the disputes being solved before the House of Lords decision.

During the dispute between British Telecom and the National Communications Union (NCU), the fear of bold socialist ideas was revealed in an incident in the House of Commons. At the request of NCU members in Liverpool, Terry Fields took the initiative of drawing up a motion which condemned British Telecom and supported the union. This was supported by 21 Labour MPs. But to his astonishment an amendment, in the name of NCU-sponsored Labour MPs, right wingers Roger Stott and John McWilliam, added at the end 'but notes that our union, the NCU, sees this totally as an industrial dispute and not a political matter and does not wish the Tory government to intervene in any way whatsoever.' This was followed up by a letter from Deputy Chief Whip, Norman Hogg, to Terry Fields, advising him that sponsored MPs from the NCU had protested about the motion. The letter stated: 'It is the view of the union...that no parliamentary initiative of any kind should be taken at this time in the dispute.' But the very reason why the unions formed the Labour Party at the turn of the century was in order that they could have a political and a parliamentary voice. Terry Fields was showing precisely how Parliament could be used as a platform in defence of basic rights and conditions of workers in struggle. The action of the NCU leadership caused outrage amongst the union's members, and won enormous support for Terry Fields.

But it was not just the traditional opponents of *Militant* on the right, but former allies in the GMBATU who began to distance themselves and attack *Militant* supporters. Most prominent was Peter Lennard, convenor of Branch 80 of GMBATU, responsible for education. He now collaborated with the NEC's inquiry into the DLP and was an ally of the right-wing opponents of *Militant*. Afraid that his union branch, which he ruled with an iron and undemocratic hand, would be broken up by the GMBATU local full-time officials, he did a 180 degrees turn and began to collaborate with them. Early in 1987 he recommended the expulsion from the union of *Militant* supporter, Mick Hogan, for the crime of writing an article in the *Mersey Militant*. The article protested at the split, at Lennard's initiative, of Branch 80 shop stewards from the Joint Shop Stewards Committee, without even consulting members of the branch. Mick Hogan was compelled to take legal action, with the courts finding in his favour and preventing his expulsion.

The general discontent, simmering just below the surface, was reflected in the strike wave at the beginning of 1987. Conscious of the way the wind was blowing, the Liverpool Bishops once more launched a 'one nation' pre-election campaign to heal what they saw as 'divisions caused by political extremism'. Facing both ways they attacked both the government's dismissal of the North-South divide and '*Militant*-inspired policies of confrontation pursued by Liverpool City Council.' David Sheppard once more condemned the 'rule of a political group committed to confrontation with the government of the day'. At the same time he praised 'the council's fine programme of building council houses'. Attempting to square the circle, he regretted that this had been achieved at great cost by 'taking resources from other important services in the city, ignoring the wishes of local people, trying to block the way for other good forms of housing development'. Sheppard also let slip the real reasons for *Militant's* support within the city: 'Comfortable Britain need to ask why ordinary people vote for *Militant*. If pragmatic and cooperative councils have their resources so reduced that they can no longer achieve anything but cuts in services and jobs, voters turn to those who make bigger promises.' The Liverpool City Council didn't just make 'bigger promises' but carried them out! That was the 'secret' of the enduring support for *Militant* in Liverpool, and the reason why these stinging attacks on *Militant's* policies were not to be heeded by the Bishops' flock in the elections in May 1987. Because they desperately attempted to straddle the class divide, the Bishops were neither capable of understanding this, nor the political outlook of the workers of Liverpool.

The Bishops were joined in their assault on the council by the leaders of NALGO. Graham Burgess accused the council of reducing the workforce by 744. He ran to the *Guardian* to declare: 'This exposes the council's claim to be defending jobs and services; they are shown to be making cuts of massive proportions.' While Burgess was making his completely unfounded claims, 'left-wing' Hackney council had over 1000 vacancies. What Burgess did not say was that at any one time two per cent of posts, about 600 jobs, are always vacant because of the movement in the workforce. Nor did the NALGO leaders mention that two vacancy sub-committees, which had been held recently, filled 300 posts, or that the council was committed to filling the rest.

1987 Budget

Within a matter of days the council was able to give the lie to these claims, with the introduction of an early budget. This budget, which fundamentally protected jobs and services for the next year and involved a small rate increase of five per cent, was an incredible testimony to the stand of the Labour councillors. A number of windfalls accrued to the city through the abolition of the Merseyside County Council. Monies which went formerly to the boards in transport, fire service and police were divided amongst the different Merseyside authorities.

But the main reason why Labour was in this position was because of its fighting stance and its refusal to carry through the cuts outlined in the *Stonefrost* package preferred by the Labour and trade-union leadership a year previously. Many of those councils who had abandoned the struggle were now in financial difficulties, such as Sheffield, Manchester and many London boroughs. Others, faced with savage cutbacks in the rate support grant, resorted to huge rate increases to maintain council workers' jobs and services.

In the borough where Neil Kinnock lives, Ealing, the rates were increased by 60 per cent. Waltham Forest, where Labour had regained a majority in May 1986, increased the rates by a colossal 62 per cent. Whipped up by local businessmen, demonstrations of 5000 and 10,000, the biggest in the history of the borough, besieged the Town Hall. The leader of the Labour group, Neil Gerrard, had his house attacked with a fire bomb. The Asian Mayor received death threats. The size of the demonstration in this borough dwarfed the puny attempts of Liverpool Against Militant who had organised in Liverpool in 1985. Yet not one word of criticism of these two Labour boroughs was forthcoming from the national leadership before the 1987 election. Both Ealing and Waltham Forest had increased their rates in one year by more than Liverpool had in a period of four years! There was not even a hint of any praise for the magnificent achievements of the Labour council in defending the past gains of the council or keeping rates down to five per cent. Nevertheless this achievement did not go unnoticed amongst the workers in the city and was recognised in the incredible victory of Labour in the May elections.

Once more the bourgeois press attempted to deflect attention from the achievements of the council. First the *Echo* and then the *Sunday Times* attempted to resurrect the 'Asda Affair'. Both suggested falsely—the *Echo* in another 'exclusive'—that the police were conducting fresh investigations into Derek Hatton's alleged links with Asda. Derek Hatton completely denied these allegations and threatened to sue the *Echo*. But the attempts to muddy the waters was to no avail. The 'new' allegations against Derek Hatton were dropped as quickly as they were raised. The mass of the population were now inured to such 'shock horror' tales in the local press.

Despite their imminent eviction from office by the House of Lords, Labour councillors still took the gospel of Liverpool far and wide. Tony Mulhearn spoke to meetings throughout the length and breadth of Britain and took the message to the international plane as well.

As well as meetings in Spain, in early February 1987 he visited Amsterdam to speak to a very successful meeting of members of the Dutch Labour Party and workers employed by the Amsterdam council. The international significance of Liverpool was emphasised by the attendance at the meeting by Ernst van Damme, who represented the joint shop stewards' committee for council services (the ABVAKABO—the civil servants' union, and the biggest union in Holland). They were experiencing similar problems to their British counterparts. The 'socialists' in the Amsterdam council were carrying out a cuts policy. Cuts in council services and the consequent redundancies amongst many council workers went hand in hand with the waste of money on prestige projects such as trying to become the venue for the 1992 Olympic Games.

Ernst Van Damme commented:

> We want to establish a form of cooperation with Liverpool, to learn from each other in order to fight the policy of Lubbers [the Dutch Prime Minister] and Thatcher. We ask the council to support the population, support the services and ensure that they acquire more money from the state for Amsterdam, instead of increasingly little. This will have to happen in cooperation between the unions, the council and the people of Amsterdam. The PvdA (Labour Party) is, as far as I am concerned, still the party of the workers and has to become again the party that supports the workers. We can learn an awful lot from Liverpool.

Meanwhile, even *Brookside*, a Liverpool-based television serial, finally mentioned *Militant* and the struggle of the city council. Throughout the previous four years, the producers of the programme had studiously avoided any mention of these issues. Ricky Tomlinson, as mentioned earlier, had remained extremely friendly and sympathetic to the struggle. Now, in one incident, playing the character of trade-union official Bobby Grant, he was asked if he was 'a member of *Militant*'. He replied,

> What if I am? What have they ever done to you? All they have done is build houses. Anyone with the bottle to stand up is branded as a

Militant. I'm not talking about the tendency, I'm talking about ordinary people with heart and guts to say we're not begging for jobs, we're demanding them, but not at any price. We want good jobs, good wages and good conditions. If that's a Militant, count me in.

Militant commented, 'That's a militant and a *Militant* too. Become a *Militant* supporter!' And this is precisely what workers in Liverpool continued to do, particularly after the Liberal-Tory junta was installed in the Town Hall by the decision of the House of Lords on 12 March.

Liberal Junta takes Power

Jones and his acolytes immediately set in train their expected 'counter revolution'. They assured the workforce that all jobs were 'safe' with them: all jobs except those of Sam Bond and Beryl Molyneux! These two were immediately given their marching orders. But no sooner were the Liberals installed in power than the storm clouds began to gather.

A ballot of Liverpool branch NALGO members voted by 3 to 1 in favour of non-cooperation with an unelected Liberal-Tory administration. This was a shot across the bows of the Liberal junta. The Liberals went ahead with the restoration of the Mayor's office with the wife of Liberal leader, Trevor Jones, Lady Doreen Jones, receiving the chain of office. Ribald jokes about 'jobs for the family' were widespread in the city. The Marxists christened her 'Doreen the Brief'. Her reign was the shortest since Lady Jane Grey (queen for 9 days in 1553). At a parade organised by the Liberals at St George's Hall, to re-emphasise the pageantry and splendour of the Mayor's office, replete with horses etc, the hymn 'Abide With Me' was played. One working-class woman asked her friend why they were playing such 'miserable music'. Her friend replied: 'It is because she (Lady Doreen) is about to lose her job!'

Despite what the pundits and experts might say, the mass of working-class Labour voters were determined to see a Labour council once more restored to office. *The Times* correspondent, Peter Davenport, wrote on 18 March: 'Lord Mayor helps to bury Liverpool's *Militant* era.' Exactly the opposite was to happen in the council elections less than a month later. The more discerning commentators, such as Michael Parkinson, understood the invidious choices facing the government and their local agents: 'Cuts in the council workforce would increase unemployment in a city with 60,000 already out of work. Any kind of concessions to Liverpool would infuriate other Labour cities.'

It was not just the government and the local Liverpool Tories and Liberals who were determined to prevent the return of *Militant*, so also were the right wing of the Labour Party. Completely neglecting, and indeed sabotaging, the campaign for the local elections, the time of Peter Kilfoyle was spent in attempting to 'weed out' *Militant* supporters as council candidates and also imposing right-wing candidates on some wards in the city. He was reacting to the goading and the jeering of the *Echo* and the Liberals and Tories. On 18 March the *Echo* declared 'City's Trots on march again.' Extreme right-wing members of the Vauxhall Labour Party, such as John Livingstone, wrote to the national leadership of the Labour Party, 'We are told *Militant* is only a splinter, but in Liverpool it's more like a log.' The Labour Party national leadership responded to this by barring Josie Aitman and Richard Knights from the panel of councillors. Others were eliminated on technical grounds by Kilfoyle. And shamefully in Anfield and Gilmoss, notorious right wingers Malcolm Kennedy and Eddie Roderick were imposed on the wards.

And yet even in the midst of all these manoeuvres, the *Echo* was forced to carry letters indicating the depth of support which the previous Labour council had built up. One was from a Liverpool worker now based in Sheffield, who commented:

After a number of years of being unemployed I was forced last year to take up work in Sheffield and leave Liverpool. On my regular trips I am always amazed at the new achievements that I see. Only last week I saw for the first time the new sports centre at Millbank. There are always more new houses going up and more slums like Gerrard Gardens coming down. These achievements are a result of the principles, commitment and hard work of the Labour councillors who have now been undemocratically removed from office by three Tory judges. As an ex-Liverpool Labour Party member I am bursting with pride to count some of those 49 men and women as my friends.

Vote Against Labour

While the national leadership continued the campaign of persecution against *Militant* supporters, Frank Field, right-wing Labour MP for Birkenhead was allowed to get away with murder. In the *Catholic Herald* (9 January) he had revealed that 'ever since 1983 I thought that the smart money should be on a hat trick for the Tories'. He gave as an explanation for the success of the Tories 'The Falklands apart, trade-union reforms and council house sales are probably the two most important. I regret not voting for them.' Asked why he did not vote for the Tory measures, he declared: 'Perhaps simple cowardice accounts for why I didn't. I prefer, however, to believe that, being already locked in a brutal struggle with my local party, I would have totally demoralised those people who are fighting to retain me as their MP by opening up another front where I was out of step with the national party.' He didn't reveal his real political position in order to save his political skin! He then went further and in violation of the Party Constitution urged Labour voters not to support Labour candidates who supported *Militant* in the May elections. But Field did not receive even so much as a limp slap on the wrist.

In their short tenure of power, the Liberals gave just a glimpse of what they would do if they were installed in office for any lengthy period of time. They immediately withdrew the financing of the trade-union centre which was vital for the unemployed in the city. The Urban Regeneration Strategy was threatened by Jones. NALGO came out in opposition to this and other measures of the Liberals. Cleansing workers and security guards were involved in strike action or the threat of strike action. At the same time, the Liberals unashamedly used council property to put up posters with an implied anti-Labour bias. In their party colours of gold, huge slogans such as 'stop rubbishing our city' plastered the city.

Attempting to cash in on some of the problems which the bins service had experienced under Labour, the Liberals conducted a 'clean-up campaign'. This sometimes took the most ludicrous forms. On 24 April the *Echo* reported 'Sir Trevor blows his top in loony bin war.' It went on to report, 'Mountains of rubbish were carted into Liverpool city centre and scattered over shopping streets to sabotage the Spring clean campaign, Liberal leader Sir Trevor Jones claimed today.' He conjured up the vision of Militants secretly stealing into the city centre with bags of rubbish over their backs intent on discrediting him! He commented to the *Echo*, 'In Paradise Street, there were mounds of fast food cartons, which you don't usually get there. I am convinced it was deliberate, but it won't happen again. We'll ask the police to keep an eye on the situation. There is no doubt that this was a deliberate act of sabotage.'

Liberal hopes were raised by the defeat of the Labour candidate in the St Mary's ward by-election on 9 April. Despite an effective campaign, Ian Rogers lost with the fourth highest vote that Labour had ever got in this marginal seat. Labour's setback was accounted for by two factors. On the one side, the Tory vote had collapsed from 1283 in 1980 to 276. But also many Labour workers who had indicated solid support for Labour thought that Labour was home and dry and therefore didn't bother to turn out and vote. But in the meantime, the Liberals and the capitalist press, seizing on the St Mary's result, began to celebrate their 'inevitable' victory in the forthcoming council elections. The task in the council elections was made enormously difficult by the 'stand' of the national leadership of the Labour Party. They made no attempt to concentrate on the Tory 'raving right' who were savaging jobs and the living standards of workers up and down the country. Instead, the Labour leadership attempted to mollify the press and its campaign against the 'loony left'. But this only led to demands for further action. Tory Minister Nicholas Ridley said: 'They like to pretend that expelling a few Militants on Merseyside has rid them of this cancer in their own party. When are they going to expel the Labour members of Brent, Haringey, Hackney, Lambeth, Southwark, Manchester, Bristol, because they are just as bad?'

In Liverpool, the 'loony left' tag would not stick. The council had consistently concentrated on those issues close to the working people of the city: jobs, local council services, education, and the marvellous housebuilding programme. The real question in the 7 May elections was: Would Labour be vindicated for its historic stand in the city? All bourgeois commentators, without exception, were convinced that Labour was heading for a resounding defeat. Even those on the 'left' expected dismal results. Thus the *Morning Star* proclaimed:

'Labour faces uphill battle in Liverpool elections.' Cunningham, according to *The Times*, 'declined to predict whether Labour would regain control of Liverpool, where the national party has been fighting a running battle to expel local Militants'. He further commented to the *Financial Times*: 'We are determined to reconstruct a genuine Labour Party in Liverpool That process is going on and we are determined to see it through and to see *Militant* off. That makes it difficult electorally.' I decoded this meant that the Labour leadership were quite prepared to countenance a Labour defeat in the city as the cost of driving *Militant* out of the Labour movement. In the *Guardian* he 'did admit that Liverpool City Council was a very hard result to predict'.

Trevor Jones, desperate to cling to power, denounced Labour's 'scaremongering tactics'. He wrote to all council employees 'assuring them that there is no intention to have redundancies, and that the Liberals are totally opposed to privatisation of council services'. This is true only in words. It represented a complete *volte-face* of the Liberals in comparison to the past. In reality, they had cancelled the Urban Regeneration Strategy, which was worth £25.2 million. They also carried through retrospective cancellation of other URS programmes worth £14 million. They had cancelled vehicle replacement, about half of it involving cleansing wagons worth about £2 million in total. They cancelled the Education Capital Programme and improvements to school buildings, which was worth an additional £1.6 million.

Tony Byrne calculated that they had frozen around £50 million of projects, which would probably affect 4000 jobs directly, and indirectly many construction jobs. He commented: 'All this has been decided by a body with absolutely no mandate from the people of Liverpool.'

Victory!

Labour workers, with *Militant* supporters prominent, threw themselves into the campaign, and the result on 7 May was a magnificent victory for Labour, in some respects eclipsing Labour's victories in the previous four years. In some wards the turnout was 59 per cent and 60 per cent, something which was unique to Liverpool in council elections. While there was gloom in many Labour committee rooms throughout the country, there was euphoria and celebrations late into the night in the Labour Clubs of Merseyside. Against all the odds, Labour emerged with a majority on the council. The Labour vote increased in every single ward in the city.

The most spectacular results for Labour were in those wards in which well-known *Militant* supporters were candidates. Moreover, a significant body of workers had consciously differentiated not only between Labour and the Liberals and Tories, but between right-wing Labour and those who stood on the left. It was not uncommon on the doorstep for Labour councillors to be met with the statement 'I am Labour, but I am Militant Labour.' Others demanded to know where the Labour candidate stood on the issue of the defence of the debarred 47 councillors. Many commented that they were reluctant to vote for imposed candidates such as Malcolm Kennedy, husband of Jane Kennedy.

When the votes were counted on 7 May, there was a mixture of bewilderment and gloom amongst Liverpool Labour's opponents. On television, Professor Anthony King could only mumble that the Liverpool results were an indication that 'the city had declared political UDI'. Cunningham attempted to claim the results as a 'victory for moderate Labour' in the city. Neither the *Liverpool Echo* nor the *Post* could share his delusion. Moreover, a close examination of the figures revealed that those who stood on the left, and particularly those who supported *Militant* had done spectacularly well. In Anfield, *Militant* supporter Jackie Smith was victorious over the Liberals. Unfortunately, in the same ward Malcolm Kennedy, the imposed candidate, was defeated! In Kensington, *Militant* supporter John Blackhall cancelled out an 800 Liberal majority to score a spectacular Labour success. The other Labour candidate was not successful. In St Mary's, Labour took the seat lost in the by-election back from the Liberals. Trotsky once said, 'Revolution sometimes needs the whip of the counter-revolution.' The 'Liberal counter-revolution' had lasted for a matter of six weeks in Liverpool. That was enough! The workers of St Mary's and the rest of the city turned out to put a Labour council back in power. The right wing of the Labour Party, such as Cunningham and Kinnock, may have suffered from the delusion that *Militant* had nothing to do with this splendid victory, but not so the bourgeois. *The Economist* commented:

> Liverpool produced the most paradoxical result. The Alliance had a lead of 0.1 per cent over Labour, but Labour regained control of the city council by a majority of three seats. The three point rise in Labour's share of the votes since last year suggests that most of Liverpool's working-class voters have accepted *Militant's* explanation of Liverpool's financial crisis. The continuing collapse of the Tory vote—only 9.5 per cent of Liverpudlians now vote Tory—shows that the government's version has been rejected by Liverpool's middle-class too. Liverpool's present bewildering local mood deserves much more attention than it has received. It cannot comfort Mr Kinnock.

The Times (8 May) also reported: 'Sir Trevor Jones, Liberal Group Leader of the city council, said he was astonished by the results which he contended had been directed by *Militant* supporters.' He also commented, 'The only way to end *Militant* rule in Liverpool is to abolish the Labour Party in this city.' Undoubtedly some of the right wing were prepared to entertain such a prospect, but they were checked by the pressure of the rank and file of the labour and trade-union movement. And the looming general election stayed their hand.

23.
Let History Judge

FOLLOWING THE May 1987 elections, the Liverpool Council Labour group had a much more right-wing complexion than the group evicted from office by the Law Lords. There had been a marked shift to the right in the trade-union officialdom, particularly in the Transport and General Workers Union, where Bobby Owens, the ex-left regional secretary, was almost as obsessed as Kinnock about the influence of *Militant*. The weight of this machine was brought to bear to assist Peter Kilfoyle, in 'constructing' a 'moderate' Labour group with 'realistic' policies.

The right wing were successful in having one of their own, Harry Rimmer, former deputy leader of the defunct Merseyside County Council, installed as the new leader of the Liverpool Labour group. But like Banquo's ghost sitting in Macbeth's place, the debarred 47 and their achievements haunted Labour's right wing. Their militant stance had left an indelible imprint on the consciousness of the whole of the Liverpool labour movement and checked the right wing's attempt to carry through cuts. Tony Byrne addressed the first meeting of the new council on behalf of the 47 debarred councillors. Thirty of the 47 councillors were also present, including Derek Hatton and Tony Mulhearn. In a speech enthusiastically supported by the Labour benches, Tony Byrne detailed the record of the council since 1983, of 5400 new homes built and the securing of at least 10,000 jobs. He declared: 'The way to thank the 47 is to commit yourselves to the same policies.' (*Independent*, 20 May).

Rimmer, to the annoyance of the debarred councillors and their supporters, while claiming that the 47 had been harshly treated, also pointed to an unspecified 'error of judgement' on their part. Nevertheless, two days later contracts for the building of 800 new homes, 20 refurbishment schemes and 15 demolition projects, which had been frozen by the 'caretaker Liberal administration', were ratified by the Labour council. The Liberals vehemently objected to this step but there was jubilation in the contracting industry, with an estimated 2000 jobs saved. Tenants who now could move into decent housing conditions instead of being forever trapped in the hell of high rise flats were similarly delighted.

The 1987 General Election

Hostilities on the council front were temporarily suspended as the Liverpool labour movement girded itself for the forthcoming general election battle. As in 1983 the press predicted Labour defeats in Liverpool, particularly in the key marginal of Broadgreen. In a painstaking examination of the electoral entrails, The *Independent* (15 May) concluded with an analysis that was shared by most of the press: 'Richard Pine [Liberal candidate for Broadgreen], 34, is virtually certain to defeat Terry Fields, *Militant*-supporting Labour MP at Liverpool Broadgreen.'

They not taken into account the lasting effect which the mighty struggles between 1983 and 1987 had had on all strata of the population. This was the main factor in the sweeping victory for Labour in Liverpool and indeed the Merseyside area on 11 June. However, Labour appeared to have an uphill task in Broadgreen where, unlike in 1983, the Alliance partners fought a 'united campaign'. Moreover, the Liberals were starting from the position of holding 13 out of 15 council seats in the constituency. It would require an election campaign on a much higher plane than even the victory in 1983 for Labour to guarantee victory. The Broadgreen and Liverpool labour movement were not found wanting. The local Broadgreen Labour Party had been suspended for more than 12 months before the election, and its officers were under the threat of expulsion, yet there could not have been a greater contrast between the campaign in Broadgreen and Labour's disastrous national campaign. The leadership of the Labour Party relied predominantly on 'media' and 'photo opportunities'. The Broadgreen campaign was a model, both in political content and organisation.

Alan Hardman's cartoons were a feature of the campaign. Originally drawn for *Militant*, the cartoons here and others were reproduced in leaflets and pamphlets by many sections of the Liverpool labour movement.

CAN YOU HELP US? WE'RE INVESTIGATING
THE UNCONSTITUTIONAL PRACTICES OF THESE DAMN MILITANTS

JENKIN AND

I HAVE NEVER
SEEN HOUSING
CONDITIONS THE
LIKE OF THESE

LIVERPOOL SENSATION—
MANAGER TO SACK WINNING TEAM

HYDE

RIGHT TOOL FOR THE JOB!

LIVERPOOL

Alan Hardman.

Mass canvassing on a higher scale than 1983 covered every part of the constituency, detailed discussions on policy taking place on the doorsteps. The constituency was canvassed many times before 11 June. There was no poster 'war' this time, unlike 1983: the opposition parties were simply crushed by the sheer numbers of Labour posters displayed throughout the constituency. Even in so-called Liberal or Tory areas new posters had to be ordered at least twice. Six special leaflets on youth, women, health, education, the Tories' threatened poll tax and other issues were distributed throughout the constituency.

The consciousness of the Liverpool workers was indicated by the reply of an older woman to a *Daily Telegraph* reporter who asked if she was still voting for Terry Fields even though he was a 'Militant': 'He's just a good socialist...like we used to have in the old days.' (*Militant*, 19 June)

Dozens of workplace meetings were organised and meetings of trade-union activists were held at Fords Halewood, Green Lane Cleansing Depot, Plessey, GMBATU Branch 5, FBU Bank Hall, Edge Lane Bus Depot. Over 1000 workers were addressed by Terry Fields in special meetings of this character during the campaign. In addition there was a magnificent 400-strong meeting addressed by Tony Benn, and 1000 attended an electrifying meeting addressed by Arthur Scargill. Arthur Scargill and most of the Labour candidates spoke to a 2000-strong audience in the Philharmonic Hall. One of the greatest ovations at this meeting was when Tony Byrne introduced surcharged councillor Tony Mulhearn, who wasn't even on the platform, to the audience.

The capitalist parties reworked the theme of '*Militant* extremism' in the course of the campaign. *Militant* was attacked from all sides, not the least by Neil Kinnock, in an infamous American presidential-style broadcast during the campaign. Learning absolutely nothing from the previous two years, Neil Kinnock's advisers had come to the astonishing conclusion that, in the midst of the general election, 'bashing the left' would see him into No 10 Downing Street. The media egged him on with the clear intention of then presenting Labour as a divided party.

His attacks on Liverpool City Council were similar to Michael Foot's attempts in 1983 to distance himself publicly from the

Labour candidate for Bradford North, Pat Wall. Kinnock was to make just one fleeting visit to Liverpool, to an old people's home in the Mossley Hill constituency.

Labour workers in Liverpool barely concealed their disgust at a Labour leadership which all but openly sabotaged Labour's campaign in the city. Neil Kinnock gave the impression that he would not lose too much sleep if Liverpool Labour, and particularly Terry Fields, were to go down to defeat.

Labour's national campaign was absolutely ruinous. The razzmatazz, all tinsel and very little content, was of course praised to the skies by the media. The Labour leadership's occasional excursion into the field of policy was catastrophic. Long before the election Kinnock and Hattersley had announced that they would reverse the Tories' tax cuts, in effect saying, 'vote for us and we'll increase your taxes'. The lessons of the Presidential election in the USA in 1984 were completely lost on the labour Leadership. The 'courageous' Mondale had fought on precisely such a programme, and had lost every state except two, his home state of Minnesota and the District of Columbia.

The Labour leadership's campaign, designed to win the middle class, had exactly the opposite effect. The skilled workers and the houseowners were alienated. The number of skilled workers voting Tory increased from 38 per cent in 1983 to 42 per cent in the June 1987 General Election. Even in comparison to previous election campaigns under the stewardship of the right wing, Labour's performance nationally was abysmal. Ruthless control was exercised from the top. There was very little canvassing, with few election leaflets and the 'public meetings' were ticket-only affairs with audiences that were meticulously vetted by Labour Party officials. A media campaign, little different from those conducted in America by the Democratic Party, was supposed to usher in a Labour victory.

In Liverpool, however, when Labour candidates turned to the media it was usually to counter the distortions of their opponents. It was to be on the doorstep and in the factories and workplaces that Labour would get its message across in the teeth of the media's colossal anti-Labour campaign.

National Alliance leaders attempted to bolster their candidates in the city on 'whistle stop' tours. Owen claimed Labour had 'governed with such arrogance and contempt for the people of Liverpool.' (*The Times*, 23 May). Cyril Smith also lumbered into town to launch a broadside 'against the *Militant* influenced Labour strongholds in the city'. He stated that 'We have our eyes particularly on Terry Fields' 3800 majority in Liverpool Broadgreen.' (*Sunday Times*, 2 May) However, when Cyril Smith stepped into a hotel lift it refused to take off—just like the Alliance campaign in the city in the next few weeks! On one of his two visits Liberal leader David Steel informed the *Echo* (26 May) that the Alliance 'have decided to focus upon Merseyside as a prime example of Labour's extremism at its worst'.

Even the Tories discussed 'a plan for Mrs Thatcher to drop in on Merseyside' but this never materialised. Try as they might the 'extremist' card made little impression in the city. Although the *Guardian* (29 May) declared: '*Militant's* man is the issue in battle for Liverpool Broadgreen', the complete ineffectiveness of the Liberals' red scare campaign was underlined by a Granada television poll which revealed that only two per cent in the Broadgreen constituency thought that '*Militant* was an issue'. This could be accounted for by two factors. On the one side, there was a bitter anti-Tory mood, which was expressed in outright hatred of Thatcher herself. Sometimes this was revealed in the most unlikely fashion. Thus in the midst of the election campaign the *Echo* featured a 57-year-old former unemployed man who had set up his own business making T-shirts and baseball caps. One T-shirt, with a 'Maggie No Go Zone' logo, sold like hot cakes. The owner of the company, to be fair, had also produced a pro-Thatcher cap but said, 'You try selling those around here. I've had a few orders from down South, but only a few.' On the basis of his sales he declared: 'If my caps are anything to go by then the sales show an overwhelming result—the Tories are going to lose this election!' Although not exactly 'scientifically based', it was more accurate than the usually fiddled opinion polls as far as Liverpool was concerned.

The other factor which determined the complete ineffectiveness of the 'anti-*Militant*' campaign of the Tories and Liberals was that the mass of the electorate were now impervious given the deluge of such campaigns in the previous four years.

Violence?

Labour's opponents did not hesitate to use the slightest pretext
to throw mud at Labour and particularly to present the Marxists
as 'proponents of violence'. Thus a few days before the election
the *Sunday Express* (7 June) front page headline screamed
'Labour's Bullies in New Terror'. It declared:

> The uncanny silence of Labour's hard-left exploded into uproar
> yesterday with a plea from an Alliance candidate for police
> protection against *Militant* thugs. Richard Pine, Alliance candidate in
> Liverpool's Broadgreen—scene of one of the most bitterly fought
> election campaigns in Britain—wants protection for his
> canvassers.

Pine had alleged that he had been forced to order his
supporters 'not to go out alone in areas of the constituency
where gangs of *Militant* thugs are gathering'. This hysteria had
been prompted by a lobby, organised outside one of Pine's
election meetings, by the Labour Party Young Socialists, some of
whom were dressed as a pantomime horse. This was in response
to an earlier comment from Richard Pine who, frustrated at the
ineffectiveness of his campaign, characterised Labour voters as
'donkeys'. Attempting to introduce a little humour into the
campaign, Labour's youth were now denounced by the *Sunday
Express* as '40 thugs [who] tried to kick down a school door and
get at the Alliance supporters'. The *Echo* (5 June) carried
Labour's rejoinder to this:

> Broadgreen's Labour candidate Terry Fields said his supporters
> took a pantomime donkey to the Liberal meeting. Mr Fields said
> 'The Alliance candidate has made an ass of himself. The donkey was
> there to make a lighthearted protest. Richard Pine made a mistake in
> talking of "donkey voters". Ee-Yor-To know better than to criticise
> voters like that.'

Even the Tory candidate in Broadgreen, Mark Seddon, was
forced to complain publicly about the Alliance's smear
campaign. According to the *Echo* (9 June) he claimed that 'an
Alliance supporter has been telling voters that his family has ties
with the Trotskyists'. Moreover, he was so disgusted at the
Alliance's tactics that he 'blasted recent Alliance claims of
Militant intimidation: "I have seen Militants around, and they
have been good humoured. But the Liberals claim they are

being intimidated by them. I believe it is a cheap publicity stunt'. For once a Tory was telling the truth!

The press was forced to record the bedrock of support for *Militant* in the Liverpool area. Thus following the Broadgreen rally where Arthur Scargill had spoken, a *Times* reporter had gone into a pub with 'plenty of confirmed Fields supporters'. When asked to comment about *Militant* these workers declared, 'They promised to build thousands of new houses in the rotten slums and create thousands of new jobs for people on their knees for work and they did it.' (*The Times*, 3 June) The reporter then asked:

> What about the cost of all those controversial loans from French, Swiss and Japanese banks to get around Whitehall's spending restrictions that have now landed Liverpool with a debt that some estimate at about £800 million and crippling interest repayments?, 'Look pal', a large man said not unkindly, 'everyone in this bloody pub is up to their eyes in debt and looking for work. Who gives a stuff how much we owe the gnomes of Zurich?'

The Liberals' final masterpiece was a leaflet showing a photograph of Terry Fields with Derek Hatton, over the comment, 'What you see is what you get', and absolutely no political comment. This was distributed the day before polling day. Thus there could be no misunderstanding as to what the choice was. Labour's candidate was clearly identified with the stand of the heroic 47 councillors. He was a well-known Marxist who stood on a clear socialist programme and on a slogan of 'a workers' MP on a worker's wage'.

As the general election results flashed up on the television screens on the night of 11 and 12 June, a pall of gloom descended on the working-class areas of Britain. Only small gains were made, leaving the Tories clearly in power. Nationally the Tories percentage of the vote was virtually the same, at 42.3 per cent, as the 42.4 per cent they got in their 1983 landslide. But Labour only inched up from the disastrous 27.6 per cent in 1983 to 30.8 per cent. But the mood in Liverpool was entirely different. Labour's share of the vote increased in Liverpool by a colossal 9.5 per cent compared to 1983. The Tories, second in 1983, were reduced to third behind the Alliance. The *Financial Times* (13 June) commented: 'Their share of the citywide poll dropped by a massive twelve points to only 17 per cent.' The Alliance, who were eagerly looking to profit from a Tory collapse, increased their share of the poll by only 2.5 points to 25.5 per cent. Massive swings towards Labour were recorded in all Liverpool seats. The 57 per cent share of the vote won by Labour in Liverpool was the party's best ever result in the city, comfortably surpassing even the result of 1945 which gave Labour a landslide victory nationally.

Eric Heffer stormed to victory in Walton with a magnificent 64.4 per cent of the vote. Walton had been a marginal seat when he won it for Labour in 1964! He had been villified by Labour's right for his courageous defence of the Liverpool Labour movement. He had been stitched up in the elections to the National Executive Committee at the 1985 Labour Party Conference by the 'soft left' who never forgave him for his public display of opposition to their idol Kinnock. Yet the Liverpool working-class rewarded Eric Heffer, someone who unflinchingly championed their cause, with this large vote of confidence. Eddie Loyden, who enjoyed a similar reputation amongst the Liverpool working-class, saw his Garston majority 'rocket from 4002 to a substantial 13,777' (*Echo* 12 June 1987). Victory was all that much sweeter in Garston in view of the fact that the defeated Tory candidate was Paul Feather, one of the leading lights of the 'Liverpool Against Militant' (LAM). He was 'lamblike' in defeat, while Eddie Loyden declared. 'We fought on the policies that affect the people of Liverpool. The voters saw throught the smears against the hard left.' (*Echo* 12 June) 1987). Bob Parry in Riverside also won a massive 73.2 per cent of the vote and Bob Wareing in West Derby 65.3. It was in Broadgreen, however, where Labour scored its greatest triumph. This had been a Tory marginal in 1983 and was the seat of mainly owner-occupiers. Terry Fields increased his majority from 3800 to 6047 with 48.6 per cent of the vote. Little wonder that Eric Heffer could claim that the Labour vote was no longer counted but 'weighed' in Liverpool!

The five Liverpool Labour MPs although Bob Wareing wavered at the later stages, had remained unshakeable in defence of their council comrades. On 11 June they were rewarded with the most outstanding victory for Labour in the whole of Britain. Even Alton, the Liberal Chief Whip, saw his Mossley Hill majority slashed. Only defecting Conservatives managed to save his skin. In the 17 Merseyside constituencies Labour increased its vote by 72,477 (a 22 per cent increase), while the Alliance dropped 4505 votes and the Tories lost 43,021, a 15 per cent drop. If the swing to Labour from the Tories had been the same across the country as in Liverpool this would have meant 133 seats fewer for the Tories in the new parliment. Well known Tories such as Lynda Chalker, Malcolm Rifkind, George Younger, William Waldegrave, Winston Churchill, Edwina Currie, Peter Bottomley, Terry Dicks and Geoffrey Dickens would all have lost their seats. Labour would have won an extra 116 seats which would have put Neil Kinnock into number 10 Downing Street.

The contrast between the spectacular performance of the Liverpool labour movement and the dismal performance of the right wing's campaign elsewhere was too transparent to pass over in complete silence. The immediate reaction of the *Post* (12 June) to the Liverpool result was clear: 'Liverpool voters gave Labour a big pat on the back last night.' Gerald Kaufman, right-wing front bench spokesperson, had the grace to point to 'the splendid victory in Liverpool'. Even Thatcher, according to the *Echo* on 12 June 'had a special word about Liverpool. She accused the city's Labour Party of stifling private enterprise, but admitted they had the voters on their side.' The right wing, however, were far from pleased at the triumph of the left, and particularly of the Marxists.

Indeed, a *Guardian* correspondent present at Labour's Walworth Road headquarters, as the results came through reported 12 June that, a 'Labour Party manager' responded to the victories of the left with the comment 'it's been a good night for the nutters'. This 'fraternal attitude' was extended by the right to their feeble attempt at explaining the election results. Implicit in the comments of the leader Neil Kinnock also was the idea that the 'ignorant' working class were really responsible for Thatcher's third victory: 'many people, for reasons best known to themselves, have voted to maintain divisions'. Yet the architects of Labour's defeat was the leadership of the Labour Party itself. No real alternative to the Tories had been spelt out by Labour nationally. This had however been done in Broadgreen, in Coventry South East, where Dave Nellist was the Labour candidate, in Bradford North, where Pat Wall was the candidate, and in Southwark and Bermondsey, where John Bryan fought an excellent campaign.

The campaign in these four seats was entirely different to that conducted by Labour's national leadership. Kinnock did make some telling agitational points on the health service, on unemployment, poverty, etc. But there was no attempt to explain the nature of the crisis of world and British capitalism, as the Marxists had done. *Militant* had consistently warned, even before the Stock Market crash of October 1987, of an impending economic catastrophe on the basis of capitalism. Even former Tory Minister, Sir Ian Gilmour, had warned in the Commons before the election: 'There is therefore a great deal of consolation for the Opposition and the Alliance in the fact that they are going to lose the next election. There will be a nasty crisis in the next Parliament and the opposition parties can count themselves lucky that not they but my Right Honourable Friends will be dealing with it.' But the question on the lips of workers on the doorsteps and in the factories was 'how would Labour do better?'

Subsequent analyses of voting intentions have shown that the majority believed that the Tories would handle the economy better than Labour. Labour leaders struck a high moral tone, believing that an appeal to the so-called 'have-lots' on behalf of the 'have-nots' would do the trick.

Capitalist commentators, and Labour's right wing, maintained that the secret of Thatcher's success lay in her naked appeal to homeowners, shareholders and so-called 'property owning democracy'. How then to explain Terry Fields' victory in Broadgreen, where nearly 73 per cent of constituents own their own houses? The right wing also put the defeat in London down to the so-called 'loony left'. Alf Dubbs in Battersea, Eric Deakins in Walthamstow and Nick Raynsford in Fulham were, it was claimed, defeated because of the so-called 'yuppie factor'. In making this claim the right wing performed an amazing somersault. The main reason they gave in shifting Labour's policies to the right was in order to 'win the middle ground'. Now the 'yuppies' to whom Labour's policies were meant to appeal, were given as the main factor for the defeat.

Yet in those seats where Labour stood on the left, and particularly on a Marxist platform, the middle-class was won to the banner of Labour. Good results for the left, and particularly for Marxist candidates, were not just achieved in Liverpool but in other areas also. Thus Dave Nellist recorded the biggest pro-Labour swing in the West Midlands, 5.2 per cent from the Tories. The campaign, including a rally attended by 750 from all over Coventry, at which the main speakers were Tony Benn and Dave Nellist, contributed to the success of the other Coventry seats, which all recorded big swings to Labour. Contrast this with the dismal performance in right-wing dominated Birmingham. In Birmingham Northfield, formerly a Labour seat, where the Labour candidate was the right-wing EETPU guru John Speller, there was a swing of 0.34 per cent from Labour to the Tories. In Roy Hattersley's Sparkbrook seat there was a 1.5 per cent swing from the Tories to the SDP! This cannot be ascribed to the 'homeowning' and 'skilled worker' factors. These were just as much in evidence in Coventry South East as in Birmingham. And yet the swing to Labour in Coventry was more than three times that of Birmingham.

The question was posed in the aftermath of the election: if the policies of the right wing were so attractive to working people why didn't the working class flood out in Sparkbrook to vote for Roy Hattersley? The turnout in this seat was barely 63 per cent compared with turnouts of almost 73 per cent in Coventry South-East, 75.9 per cent in Broadgreen and even 70 per cent in inner-city Bermondsey. But what a contrast there was between Labour's performance in Liverpool and in right-wing dominated Birmingham! In Birmingham there was an average increase of 1202 in the Labour vote, whereas in Liverpool there was an average 4436 increase per constituency. *Militant* commented: 'We eagerly await the comments of Roy Hattersley and his right-wing agent Peter Kilfoyle about the Merseyside results.'

The right wing had wasted the enormous political capital that had accumulated to the labour movement from the miners' strike. This was reflected in the support for the retention of the political funds by the unions. The Tories had attempted to cripple the Labour Party financially. They compelled the unions to ballot on their retention, hoping that the vote would go against and the unions would therefore cut off Labour's financial lifeline. But 90 per cent voted in favour of retaining their political fund. Moreover, some unions which did not have political funds decided to set them up! The Tories' attempts to cripple the Labour Party rebounded on them. This heightened political awareness was a product of the miners' strike which, by laying bare the brutal reality of Thatcherite capitalism, had politicised the working class like no other event in decades. This represented colossal potential support for Labour within the trade unions. Yet only 43 per cent of trade unionists voted Labour in the general election. A campaign along socialist lines would have mobilised a big majority of trade unionists to vote in their class interest and against the parties of big business. But the class issues were never raised. The defeats in Walthamstow, Fulham and Ealing did not arise from any major 'demographic changes', as the Labour right feebly claimed. Even the most zealous Tory estate agent could not have wrought such changes to guarantee the victory of the Tories in these seats. Labour's losses were due mainly to the massive rate rises of 62 per cent, 50 per cent and 65 per cent that had been imposed by Labour councils in these areas, in line with the 'dented shield' philosophy of Neil Kinnock, Jack Cunningham and Jack Straw.

They had recommended a 60 per cent increase in rates for the Liverpool City Council in 1985. If the much reviled 'Militants' of Liverpool had heeded this advice, Labour in this city would have faced the same fate as Eric Deakins in Walthamstow and Nick Raynsford in Fulham.

After its initial dismay at *Militant's* success in Liverpool, the Echo once more attempted to throw dust in its readers' eyes. On the one hand, the defeat of Keva Coombrs in Hyndburn and Sylvia Renilson in Pendle was due to their alleged association with the *Militant*, yet both were well known opponents of *Militant*. On the other hand, the victory in Liverpool supposedly had nothing to do with *Militant*. The *Echo* (12 June) declared: 'The increased votes for Liverpool's Labour MPs are less a sign of support for *Militant* revolution than a cry of despair and anger.' But Terry Fields was much nearer the mark when he declared, 'The people of Broadgreen have sent a message to the rest of Britain tonight. A message nobody can ignore. The Tories are the Millionaire Tendency. I am with the majority tendency, the working class.'

Undoubtedly, the profound anti-Tory mood was the most dominant factor among Liverpool workers. But the colossal swing from Tory to Labour cannot be ascribed to this alone. To some extent, the same factors were present in Merseyside as in Scotland. The struggle of Liverpool City Council had the same effect as a large stone dropped in a pond. The ripples from Liverpool reached out to touch most areas of Merseyside. The 47 were seen not just as champions of the interests of the area, but as people who had successfully extracted concessions from the Tory government and had therefore been persecuted by them. They raised sections of the population from their knees and inspired many who might otherwise have stood aside from the struggle in despair and resignation.

Similarly, the big swing to Labour in Scotland had very little to do with the influence of Kinnock's policies, contrary to the claims of his attorneys in the Labour Coordinating Committee. The heroic struggle of the Caterpillar workers, occupying their factory against closure, played a very similar role to that of the Liverpool City Council, both before and during the election. The whole of the Scottish labour movement was compelled to come behind the Caterpillar workers, although Neil Kinnock, as during the miners' strike, only gave very lukewarm support very late in the day. Their struggle was perceived, by the middle class included, as the last ditch attempt to maintain the semblance of a manufacturing base in Scotland. It was this that resulted in the decimation of the Tories throughout Scotland on 11 June. The victories in Liverpool and Scotland were an indication of what Labour could have achieved nationally if the leadership had put the full weight of the labour movement behind the miners and their heroic struggle.

The election revealed not so much a 'North-South divide', as the Labour leadership argued, but a colossal class polarisation. It was this that accounted for the crushing of the SDP. Roy Jenkins, the inspirer of the SDP, had once compared the launch of his party to an aeroplane taking off. In the general election the plane crash-landed, ditching Roy Jenkins in Hillhead, Shirley Williams, who lost in Cambridge, and Bill Rodgers, who was defeated in Milton Keynes. Only one of the original Gang of Four remained, David Owen, who subsequently constituted himself as a Gang of One, breaking away from an alliance with the Liberals. Even in London the class polarisation was evident. While the Tories' total vote increased by 163,035 across the capital, Labour's vote also went up, by 105,353. The Alliance was crushed between the millstones of Labour and the Tories, losing 81,887 votes in the capital.

In the avalanche of hostile criticisms of Liverpool, occasionally a shaft of light would appear in the press. In the *Sunday Times* (5 July) Professor Ben Pimlott confessed, 'Blame for defeat cannot simply be laid at the door of the hard left. Witness the remarkable swing to Labour in Liverpool.'

Indeed Terry Fields' successful campaign in Broadgreen and particularly his call for Labour representatives to accept no more than the average wage of a skilled worker, found an echo well beyond the borders of Merseyside. An article in the *Daily Telegraph* (8 May) pointed out that Terry Fields 'does not even accept all his £18,500 salary but keeps his pay in line with that of a firefighter—a job he did for 26 years'. In response to this a Tory-voting *Telegraph* reader from Essex wrote to Terry Fields to:

> wholeheartedly applaud the attitude you take. It's a refreshing change to hear of an MP with the courage of his convictions and to practise what he preaches. If more MPs did the same instead of caning the taxpayer for all they can get, fiddling car mileage etc, etc, Parliament and indeed the country as a whole would be a lot better place...If you ever put up for my constituency you could rely on my vote and that of many of my friends...Good luck and best wishes for the future.

This merely underlined the case of Marxism: if Labour were to adopt a clear socialist position and Labour representatives to live the lifestyle of those they sought to represent, many Tories, not to say Liberals, could be swung behind the banner of Labour.

New Council Crisis

No sooner had the election clamour died down than a new crisis loomed on the council front. Despite the new 'moderate' tone struck by Harry Rimmer, the government was impervious to all Liverpool's pleas for concessions. Lord Young, a clone of Thatcher, spoke about money 'wasted' on Liverpool. But the budget gap for 1988-9 would be of the order of £51 million, which would mean big cuts.

All the gains of the previous four years were once more threatened by the Tories. Would the new Labour group stand up to the Tories as had the previous one? The omens were not favourable. At a seminar for new councillors, chief officers warned the councillors that their first duty was to uphold the law, not to carry out election manifestos. The new right-wing dominated Labour group moved immmediately to take back some of the concessions given in the previous period. There was growing concern in all departments over the delay in filling vacancies. Disputes broke out in the careers service, leisure centres and in the City Estates Department.

In a sharp departure from the previous council, Rimmer and other right-wing chairs of committees, in the words of one council worker 'listen to management and deal with the workers', as opposed to the old council which 'listened to workers and dealt with management'. In the final ten minutes of one Labour group meeting, the right wing decided to withdraw funding for three of the four sabbatical positions of elected Student Union presidents at Sandown, South Mersey and City FE colleges. This effectively amounted to the sack. One of those dealt with in this way was NUS Executive member, Colette Williams. The right were nibbling at the gains of the previous four years: they wished to travel down the same road as other Labour councillors throughout Britain who were following Kinnock's advice and passing Tory cuts on to the workforce and council tenants. All those who had abandoned Liverpool in the rate-capping battle in 1985 were now busily carrying through cuts. In Islington Margaret Hodge presided over cuts, while in Haringey it was members of the Labour Coordinating Committee who proposed amendments calling for a three per cent cut to ensure that the council 'acted within the law'. Both Hodge and the Haringey leaders, as with many other councillors in London, claimed that they were carrying out 'socialist cuts'.

In Haringey, Bernie Grant voted with the ex-lefts for cuts. He was bitterly denounced by white and black workers at the council meeting. Subsequently, in an interview with Darcus Howe on the television programme *Bandung File*, he tried to justify this policy by claiming that he had not, and would never, vote for cuts which affected the council's 'anti-racist' policies. The clear implication was that anything which adversely affected black people Bernie Grant would oppose. This was an attempt to ingratiate himself with blacks by giving the impression that he was still championing their cause, despite his vote in favour of a cuts' budget. Cuts will bear down heavily on the poor. Among the 'black population' there is a higher proportion of poor people, council tenants facing massive rent increases and cuts in council services, than among the white population. Moreover, Bernie Grant's attempt to differentiate between the effects of cuts on blacks or whites is also extremely dangerous, opening up the danger of splits between different sections of the working class In reality, having climbed to power as an MP, Bernie Grant placed this above responsibility to the black and white workers in Haringey who put him there in the first place.

The obstacle to Rimmer following a similar path in Liverpool was the colossal achievements of the previous council and the martyred 47. The total surcharge, together with court costs imposed on the 47 amounted to £348,000 in total. In addition the councillor's own legal costs were £240,000.

The District Auditor, in a deliberate attempt to crush the councillors and make an example of them, demanded the immediate payment of £20,000 and a minimum of £4000 a month. Failure to meet his demands would result in court action which in turn could result in bankruptcy, confiscation of property, homes, and even eviction. A campaign was therefore launched both in Liverpool and throughout the country to come to the assistance of the councillors. Foremost in this campaign were the left. The right wing spent most of their time manoeuvring for the forthcoming reconstitution of the Broadgreen and District Labour Parties rather than concentrating on speaking and organising financial defence for the councillors.

At every turn the right wing came up against the achievements of the 47 and what they meant for the people of Liverpool. But this did not prevent Rimmer from recommending in late August 1987 that the council apply to the government for 'redetermination'. This would have meant the council handing over control of all its spending plans to the Secretary of State for the Environment, Nicholas Ridley, who then *might* give small concessions in some areas, while demanding cuts in others. It would have certainly meant massive increases of at least £13 a week in rents, or 5000 job losses. The right wing, while not facing up to the government, was quite prepared to take on its own workforce. Thus they were prepared to countenance a strike of council parks department drivers in September 1987 which resulted, for the first time since the 'Winter of Discontent' in 1979, in the dead not being buried in Liverpool. Their response to the strike was to threaten all drivers with 'summary dismissal' for 'gross misconduct'. One worker declared: 'We might have had our disagreements with the last council on a few occasions, but they would never have acted like this'.

The *Daily Mirror*, which had formerly hounded the council, decided in September to praise the efforts of the previous council, of course without mentioning the crucial role of *Militant*. Contrasting the desperate plight of many who still existed in slum dwellings in parts of Liverpool, the *Mirror* journalist Barry Wigmore commented:

> In 1983, when the Labour Party took over, Liverpool embarked on the biggest rebuilding programme in the country. It had its Urban Regeneration Strategy long before inner cities became a Tory buzzword. Today the city's one vast building site. Everywhere you turn there is the new beside the vanishing old and ugly...Labour took over the city in 1983 and boldly decided to smash it [the Piggeries] all down and start again. That Labour council which has taken so much abuse, also went into partnership with private companies. The only criticism of the council might be that it has tried to do too much too fast—but it desperately needed doing...Since May 1983, nearly 22,000 flats, maisonettes and houses have been done up or knocked down and replaced. Quietly, with no fanfare or trumpets. (*Daily Mirror*, 21 September)

The abuse which Barry Wigmore spoke about emanated amongst others from the *Mirror*, probably directly inspired by Robert Maxwell, its multi-millionaire owner. Moreover, a little over a week after this article, one of those responsible for the 'biggest rebuilding programme in the country', Felicity Dowling, was dragged before the Labour Party Conference and her expulsion confirmed, to plaudits from the *Mirror*.

She was the last of the Liverpool nine who were expelled as a result of the DLP inquiry. Her speech to the conference, however, was punctuated with loud applause from both constituency and union delegates. At the end of her speech she received a standing ovation from parts of the conference, while Eric Heffer left the parliamentary benches, went right down to the rostrum at the front of conference and embraced her. She had challenged Kinnock, 'to debate our differences in front of the workers of Liverpool, and if they vote for my expulsion only then will I accept it'. Her reception was in stark contrast to that received by National Executive Committee member Jack Rogers when he was replying to the debate on housing at the conference. Rogers was a UCATT leader who had spent a large part of his time in the Liverpool area, denigrating and attacking the council despite the enormous benefits that had accrued to his members. In a 20-minute speech, allegedly replying to the housing debate, he vilified the Liverpool Militants and was constantly barracked and slow handclapped by a large proportion of the delegates.

David Blunkett once more sullied his reputation as a 'left'. When he replied on behalf of the NEC to the debate on Liverpool, he recommended rejection of a resolution which called for support for the 47, while at the same time supporting the NEC's call for contributions to assist the surcharged councillors. He could not resist the temptation to attack some councillors, who he claimed, 'arrange their affairs to avoid the consequences of bankruptcy'. This merely echoed the theme of the capitalist press. No councillor, not Derek Hatton, Tony Mulhearn, or those on the right who were known to be comfortably off, would escape the seizure of all their assets if they were made bankrupt.

This charge was answered by Tony Mulhearn and former council leader Tony Byrne in an open letter to Blunkett demanding that he justify his shameful remarks in a debate, either in Liverpool or Sheffield. Needless to say, this request was turned down.

Shortly after the Labour Party Conference Harry Rimmer resigned as leader of the City Council, when the Labour group voted by 42 to 6 against his recommendation that the Labour Group seek redetermination. He even said: 'Mr Ridley [the Environment Secretary] was kind enough to say our approach was the right one.' However, Ridley repaid this 'kindness' by ratecapping Liverpool and leaving a huge gap between income and expenditure. John Hamilton commented, 'By 1990 the city will only have sufficient revenue to service its debts, with nothing left for expenditure on housing maintenance or services'. Not one single constituency Labour Party voted for 'redetermination'. Not only the left and the Marxists, but also 'moderate' Labour members rejected redetermination. The majority of the Labour group reflected this pressure. *Militant* commented:

> Implicit in Rimmer's resignation is a recognition that Liverpool's crisis, together with that of other cities, is so severe that it cannot be

solved by 'cooperation' and talks. There are only two roads—either 'cooperate' with the Tories and make cuts, or fight for extra resources.

John Hamilton in an interview with the *Post* revealed that he had never fully understood the implications of the stand which the previous council had made. In a bemused fashion he declared 'So...we're victims of an accident of history. I've sat down many times and asked myself why, out of all the leaders of Liverpool council over the generations, I should have been the one to be caught up in this turmoil.' He then went on, however, to hint correctly that the upheavals of 1983-7 were rooted in the situation itself: 'One individual couldn't have stopped the bandwagon of *Militant* or the train of government.' This has not prevented John Hamilton, in a bloc with Kilfoyle and the right-wing cabal which surrounds him, from organising against *Militant* in a vain attempt to prevent a repetition of the events of 1983-7.

This culminated with the right-wing coup in Broadgreen in November 1987, which installed John Hamilton as Chair and vicious right winger Malcolm Kennedy as Secretary of the constituency. In a clear threat to Terry Fields, John Hamilton declared:

> If Terry Fields is hoping to retain his seat as an MP, he will have to take note of the new membership of the constituency, particularly the Executive, and work closely and harmoniously with them if he wants to have their confidence. This can happen to any MP—he has got to recognise the winds of change.

This temporary victory for the right had been achieved by expulsions, debarring some delegates on flimsy technical grounds, for instance rejecting applications that had initials instead of the full Christian names, by allowing trade-union delegates supporting the right wing to affiliate later than constituency delegates; and by refusing application for membership from dozens of left wingers and supporters of Terry Fields. The same methods were employed to secure a narrow victory for the right in the reconstituted District Labour Party in December 1987.

It took two years of the most ruthless repression, including expulsions, to secure this victory. Moreover, as we have shown, it is not the first time that the right wing have carried through such a coup to supplant the left. They did this in 1955 in Bessie Braddock's Exchange constituency. They divided the old Trades Council and Labour Party in 1969. This did not prevent the re-emergence of the left and the development of a powerful Marxist force around *Militant* in the city. The objective situation in Liverpool today is far less favourable for the right than in the 1960s, the 1970s, or for that matter the early 1980s.

This is indicated by the sheer pessimism of bourgeois economists and commentators, reflected in the comments of Noel Boaden, Professor of Continuing Education at Liverpool University. According to the *Post* (14 September):

> His detailed report pours cold water on the growing belief that a boom is just round the corner for Merseyside. There seems never to have been a time when Merseyside didn't have problems, nor a time when the professional groups and even some politicians were not concerned to look for solutions...Small business and tourism may be desirable but it is not likely to reduce unemployment significantly or provide economic support for a population even as big as that which remains in the city...Despair is an easy emotion to feel in Liverpool.

The professor, like the effete British capitalists, dreams of a re-industrialisation of Liverpool and the British economy. But such a perspective is utopian on the basis of capitalism. He admits:

> The problem of Merseyside remains our inability as a society to find a solution. I am afraid that the independent pursuit of personal benefit will never translate into a society where problems such as those of Liverpool will be solved.

In other words, Thatcher's support for 'individualism' as an alternative to Labour's 'collectivism' will be incapable of delivering the goods. Reflecting the utter pessimism of bourgeois commentators he says: 'We might do better to acknowledge that and avoid consequent disappointment. Only if we recognise the marginality of our efforts will we create the impetus for more fundamental solutions.'

This is the background against which the future of Liverpool will unfold. The replacement of Harry Rimmer by Keva Coombes in early October 1987 will not fundamentally alter the scenario. The Coombes regime is on the same plane as the

Kinnock-Gould ascendancy in the Labour Party at national level. Almost as soon as he had taken power Coombes was confronted with the warning from the Chief Executive, Michael Reddington, that 'a legal budget could be reached only through cuts in the workforce and increases in rents'. (*Post*, 13 October 1987). However, any attempt by the council to go down this road will be met with the bitter opposition of the great majority of the Labour workers in the city. The rigging of the District Labour Party is an attempt to insulate the Labour council against pressure from the wider labour movement. This may succeed temporarily. But even if the voice of the rank and file is muffled in the Constituency Labour Parties and District Labour Party, the Labour group will not get an easy passage in carrying through cuts or rent increases. They will be met by a bitter opposition from the radicalised rank and file members of the trade unions and particularly the shop stewards.

The successful occupation of Millbrook College early in November is an example of the opposition that the right wing will meet in attempting to unload cuts on the backs of the workers. The previous Labour council provided a creche at all Further Education colleges. This evoked a tremendous response from ordinary working-class women, with 2000 extra students enrolling in Millbrook College at the beginning of the term in 1987. However, as a result of the cuts, the creche was closed for an hour at lunchtime. Following an occupation by students, supported by Terry Fields MP, Keva Coombes was compelled to come down and personally ratify the opening of the creche at lunchtime.

This will be as nothing compared to the hurricane of opposition from the aroused Liverpool working class that this Labour council will meet should it squander the enormous capital which has been built up by the heroic sacrifices of the 47 councillors between 1983 and 1987. The bourgeois, and echoing them Neil Kinnock, have written obituaries for *Militant* many times. Neil Kinnock has claimed that the series of expulsions nationally and in the area have either 'marginalised' *Militant* or that the Marxists have been 'pushed to the sidelines in Liverpool'. Yet in late November 1987, 1200 workers gathered at the Liverpool Empire to commemorate the 70th Anniversary of the Russian Revolution and the stand of the 47. Some sideline!

At the height of the battles in 1984, 500 had attended a similar rally. The doubling of the turnout at this rally represented the real support which Marxism had built in the city. The move to the right had been mainly at the top in the Labour and trade-union official machine. The hammer blows of events, particularly the looming recession, will completely shatter not just the Tory government but the grip of the right wing at the top of the labour movement. Despite their colossal efforts, they have not been able to remove Marxism from the movement. All they have succeeded in doing is providing ammunition to the capitalist enemies of labour and squandering the movement's resources. Never in history, however, has organisational repression defeated ideas, particularly ideas whose time has come.

One trade unionist, not a *Militant* supporter, commented to Tony Mulhearn in late 1987: 'No matter what happens to you people, no matter what measures are taken against you, like a cork you keep reappearing in the river, and usually at the most turbulent stretch.'

The essence of the Marxists' criticism of capitalist society is that it is incapable of ensuring rising living standards and a lasting period of social tranquillity for working people. It will provoke upheavals, social convulsions and 'turbulence'. And it is precisely in those conditions that the programme, perspectives and policies of the Marxists find an echo amongst working people.

Karl Marx once said that an idea becomes a material force when it grips the mind of the masses. Such a process developed in Liverpool between 1983 and 1987. It represented the fusing together of an aroused and embattled working class with a class conscious leadership in which the Marxists played a decisive part.

It was this aspect of the Liverpool conflict which sent shock waves through the British ruling class. It also haunted, as we have shown, the right wing of the labour movement. Without their direct assistance the Thatcher government would never have succeeded in their legal coup against the Liverpool council. Nevertheless, this axis has not broken the spirit of the magnificent Liverpool working class. Nor has it cowed the forces of Marxism gathered around *Militant*. The Marxists would have been severely weakened, if in the course of this movement they had advocated that the Liverpool labour movement should shrink from the battle with the Tory government. Some erstwhile 'lefts' eventually embraced Kinnock's 'dented shield', but at the cost of some damage to their 'left credentials. No such suspicion is attatched, however, to the battling Liverpool councillors and particularly the lefts and *Militant* supporters within that group, by the advanced workers.

But it is not just as courageous fighters but as strategists and tacticians that the Liverpool conflict put the Marxists to the test. Mistakes, it is true, were made; but as we have shown, they were openly recognised and corrected in the course of the battle. In general, however, it was the strategy and tactics of the Marxists which determined the course of the struggle and which confounded Liverpool's critics at every turn. In any mass movement mistakes are inevitable. But contrast the approach of the Marxists with that of the right wing of the labour movement. They have drawn a veil of silence over Labour's disastrous election campaign. In so doing they will prepare the way for similar but bigger blunders.

The Marxists, on the other hand, have used the Liverpool experience, both the victories and the setbacks, as a means of educating the advanced workers for future battles. The lessons of Liverpool show that the working class are prepared to fight. But victory can only be assured if they have at their head a leadership which fully understands the terrain on which the battle is to be fought, is armed with a clear perspective, correct strategy and tactics, and will not flinch from going to the end to defend the rights and conditions of working people.

The lessons of Liverpool are not restricted to one city. There will be many 'Liverpools' in the next five or ten years. The struggle will not necessarily take the form which it has done in Liverpool. Indeed, the most likely course of events will be that developments in the next period in that city will be on the industrial plane. The historical parallels for the working class will be more that of 1911 than even 1983-7. However, the council as the biggest employer in the area, will still be an important area for the Labour movement. The working class throughout Britain will find in a study of the experiences of Liverpool the political weapons to guarantee victory overy capitalism and usher in a socialist planned economy for Britain. This is our purpose in recounting the Liverpool drama.

Appendix 1: Chronology of Key Events 1979-87

May 3 1979: Taking 46 seats in local elections, Labour becomes largest party on Liverpool City council. Although without a clear majority, they take control of the council committees.

May 3 1979: Tories win general election.

March 26 1980: Minority Labour council in Liverpool raises rates 50 per cent.

May 1 1980: Labour loses six council seats. Liberal-Tory coalition takes control.

May 7 1981: County Council elections. Labour gains control of Merseyside County Council.

July 1981: Riots in Toxteth.

May 6 1982: Labour makes two net gains in city council elections, making the council Labour 42, Liberals 36, Tories 21. After the experience of 1980 Labour refuses to take the Chairs of committees.

August 1982: Croxteth Comprehensive occupied to prevent its closure.

1983

April 27: One day city-wide strike against privatisation.

May 5: Labour gains 12 seats on council to take control. New council: Labour 51, Liberals 30, Tories 18.

June 9: General election. Landslide for the Tories nationally, but Labour wins five out of six seats in Liverpool, including the Tory marginal Broadgreen won by Terry Fields. For the first time this century there are no Tory MPs representing a Liverpool seat.

November 19: Demonstration called in support of the council by the Merseyside Labour and Trade Union Movement Campaign Committee attracts 25,000.

1984

February 26: The 'scabby seven' make their first public statements against the stand of Labour's proposed budget.

February 28: 100,000 take action on Merseyside in support of the GCHQ workers.

March: Beginning of the miners' strike.

March 29: Budget day. One day strike throughout the city. 50,000 march to the Town Hall to support the deficit budget proposal. No budget from any party gets a majority.

May 7: Local elections Labour gains 7 seats. New council Labour 58, Liberals 28, Tories 13.

July 9: A deal is reached with Patrick Jenkin. The council makes a 17 per cent rate rise. The government makes concessions worth up to £60 million.

October 9: Sam Bond appointed as Principle Race Relations Adviser.

November 17: London Bridge Shop Stewards organisation calls a one day strike against rate-capping and the abolition of the GLC. 100,000 take action and 30,000 demonstrate in London.

1985

March 7: ILEA sets rate, breaking the 'No-rate' front.

March 7: Democracy Day. 50,000 march in Liverpool in protest at rate-capping and government cuts.

March 30: The National Local Authority Workers Combine Committee (NLACC) founding meeting.

April 25: National school student strike. 250,000 take action under the leadership of YTURC and LPYS. In Liverpool 25,000 strike and 10,000 march through the city.

April 29: Heysel Stadium tragedy at the European Cup Final in Brussels between Liverpool and Juventus leaves 38 dead.

June 14: After the complete collapse of the 'no-rate' front, Liverpool sets a rate rise of 9 per cent, which results in a deficit budget.

September 8: 49 councillors are surcharged £106,000 for their delay in setting a rate until June.

September 24: As the council's cash crisis deepens, a narrow majority of the workforce reject an all-out strike.

September 25: Despite the rejection of all-out strike action, almost the entire council workforce come out on a 24-hour strike in support of the council's fight against the government.

October 1: Neil Kinnock makes infamous 'Grotesque chaos' speech attacking the council at Labour Party Conference.

November 22: A budget is set with a £30 million loan.

November 27: The Labour Party NEC votes to set up an inquiry into the Liverpool District Labour Party (DLP).

December 9: First meeting of the NEC inquiry.

1986

January 28: DLP officers go to the High Court to seek the right to reply to the NEC's charges.

February 26: NEC meeting adopts the report of the majority of the inquiry team.

March 5: The High Court upholds the District Auditor's action against the council.

March 25: Council sets a budget with a 5 per cent rate rise.

March 26: Seven left-wing members of the NEC walk out of its meeting in protest at the flagrant breeches of natural justice, making the meeting inquorate.

May 8: Local elections. Labour win one seat and lose one. New council: Labour 54, Liberals 37, Conservative 7.

May 21-22: Tony Mulhearn expelled from the Labour Party at 1 am, followed by Ian Lowes and Tony Aitman.

June 12-13: Further NEC hearings. Derek Hatton, Richard Venton Roger Bannister and Terry Harrison expelled.

July 9: Councillors go to the Court of Appeal to challenge the surcharge.

July 24: Cheryl Varley expelled.

July 31: Court of Appeal rejects the councillors' case.

October 27: Felicty Dowling expelled.

1987

January 26: Councillors appeal to the Law Lords.

March 12: Law Lords dismiss councillors' appeal and imposes £242,000 costs on top of the original £106,000 surcharge. The councillors are dismissed from office. A Liberal-Tory junta takes control.

March 13: Sam Bond sacked.

May 7: Labour wins historic victory in local elections and the by-elections to replace the surcharged councillors, to regain control of the council. New council Labour 51, Liberal 44, Conservative 4.

June 11: General election. A huge swing to Labour in Liverpool, which if repeated nationally would have meant a landslide Labour victory. Labour keeps all its five seats in Liverpool with massively increased majorities. Liberal David Alton only just hangs on in Mossley Hill.

Appendix 2: Liverpool City Council Election Results

	Labour	Liberal	Conservative
pre 1979	40	35	24
1979	46	30	23
1980	40	38	21
1981	No local elections		
1982	42	36	21
1983	51	30	18
1984	58	28	13
1985	No local elections		
1986	54	37	7
1987	51	44	4

Appendix 3: General Election results in Liverpool 1974-87

Year	Electorate	Lab	Tory	Lib	Other	Total
1974 (Feb)	414,590	140,901 48%	96,784 33%	52,196 17.9%	1,803 0.6%	291,684 70.3%
1974 (Oct)	418,950	149,780 54.6%	89,388 32.5%	34,374 12.5%	921 0.3%	274,463 65.5%
1979	399,380	137,202 49%	100,290 35.8%	40,504 14.4%	1,553 0.5%	279,549 69%
1983	389,199	128,467 47.3%	79,627 29.3%	62,410 22.9%	1,050 0.3%	271,554 69.7%
1987	371,933	155,083 56.7%	47,568 17.4%	69,814 25.5%	699 0.2%	273,164 73.5%

In 1951 the Tories got over 207,000 votes (51%).

In the two elections since Thatcher came to power in 1979, the Tory vote in Liverpool has more than halved, while Labour's has risen by 13%, gaining over 17,000 votes. In the same period nationally the Tory vote has risen by 0.3%, while Labour's has fallen by 12.8%. Labour's 1987 result was the party's best ever in Liverpool, surpassing even 1945.

Labour Votes 1983-87 – A Comparison

	1983		1987				
	Votes cast	Labour vote	Votes cast	Labour vote	Labour inc	Labour share	Labour swing
Broadgreen (%)	45,944 (71.98)	18,802 (40.88)	47,890 (75.91)	23,262 (48.57)	4460 (23.72)	+7.7	+12.4
Garston (%)	46,051 (71.59)	21,450 (46.58)	46,387 (75.70)	24,848 (53.57)	3402 (15.86)	+7.0	+10.5
M'ley Hill (%)	46,059 (73.36)	12,352 (26.82)	45,803 (75.14)	17,786 (38.83)	5434 (43.99)	+12.0	+13.2
Riverside (%)	38,454 (62.39)	24,978 (64.96)	34,834 (65.32)	25,505 (73.22)	527 (2.11)	+8.3	+7.1
Walton (%)	51,158 (69.57)	26,980 (52.74)	53,827 (73.59)	34,661 (64.42)	7681 (28.47)	+11.7	+11.2
West Derby (%)	43,838 (69.49)	23,905 (54.53)	44,443 (73.43)	29,021 (65.30)	5116 (21.40)	+10.8	+9.6
Totals	271,504 (69.76)	128,467 (47.32)	273,164 (73.37)	155,033 (56.77)	26,616 (20.72)	+9.5	+10.7

If the 10.7% swing to Labour achieved in Liverpool in 1987 had been repeated nationally, Labour would have won over 325 seats and formed the next government.

Appendix 4: Interview with Jimmy Deane

'IN 1937 I met Eric Brewer and joined the Labour Party. I had already formulated ideas in my head about socialism and fighting for Marxism. I joined the Labour Party because at that time the Labour Party in Walton was more left than the ILP. At that time politics in Liverpool were very different. There was a Protestant party, led by Longbottom which had a large base of support amongst Protestant workers. Vauxhall was the base of the old right wing, and was largely a Catholic area. Bessie Braddock represented Exchange which was made up of really run-down areas, but for a time she played a progressive role and built up a support amongst ordinary workers.

'For many years we had a broad basis of support inside Walton. For example, John Hamilton and his father, John Hamilton Snr supported us. There were other sympathisers, for example Hywel James, who was a member of the Co-op and a former sympathiser, George Bradshaw of the National Council of Labour Colleges. But a lot of comrades slipped through the fingers of the RCP, but not the youth—they stayed with us—people like Alan Giles, Brian Deane and so on.

'For a short time in the war, the Trotskyists set up an organisation called the Militant Workers' Federation. It conducted very effective work but was in no way as successful as the BLOC today, but we were obviously working under very different conditions, more difficult in some respects. In 1940 there was a large apprentices' movement mainly based among apprentices in the AEU and the ETU. However, the movement was dissipated among the youth by the call-up. But for two years in this period the Trotskyists had big support among the young workers in Liverpool.'

Appendix 5: Interview with Tommy Birchall

Tommy joined the Independent Labour Party Guild of Youth in 1934, and became a supporter of Trotskyism around 1935, joining a group called the Marxist League. His father was a Stalinist and there were many rows in the household. 'By 1937 less and less activity was being organised by the ILP. It was becoming a talking shop. The comrades in the Marxist League decided to join the Labour Party. There we came into contact with Jimmy Deane and his mother Gertie Deane and others, including Arthur Leadbetter. Here they were able to build great influence, including getting five comrades on the Trades Council and Labour Party, which in those days was a joint body, from Kirkdale. In Walton, there was a good grouping around Jimmy and Gertie Deane with representation on the Trades Council.

'The comrades developed a good base on the Trades Council Labour Party. By the 1938 May Day demo, we were strong enough to organise our own section on the march. We hired a horse and wagon and one comrade made a huge plywood tank and we marched with the slogan 'Not a man, not a gun for imperialist war'. The comrades also carried banners and photos of Marx, Engels, Lenin and Trotsky. It was about this time we became linked to the Workers' International League (WIL). By now our group had grown to about 35-40 in number, of which Kirkdale made up 14-15, the rest being distributed between Granby, Walton and Fairfield. This was just about prior to war taking place.

'When war broke out, there was a political truce declared nationally between the major parties, but we still continued our work changing our emphasis to the industrial struggles. I was declared unfit for service because of a bout of rheumatic fever and went into Harland and Wolff. Jimmy Deane as an electrician was in a reserved occupation and went to Cammell Lairds. And Frank Forster, who had recently joined the WIL went into ARN Browns. Bob Shaw and George McCartney were sent up from London and both went into telecommunications. Alan Christianson was employed at Vesteys cold stores and docks and he was invaluable as a working-class militant. Regular lunch hour meetings were held at that time.

'In 1944 the RCP was launched, the leaders being Ted Grant, Jock Haston, Harold Atkinson, Roy Tearse and Millie Lee. *Socialist Appeal* was launched and at least 2000 copies were sold in Liverpool of every edition, with 15-20 comrades selling inside the factories, the docks and other workplaces. The comrades sold in pubs, outside the dock gates and so on. As a result of the activity during the war, I became Secretary of the Harland and Wolff shop stewards' committee, representing 100 shop stewards and 5000 workers. Jimmy Deane became a shop convenor at Cammell Lairds, Frank Forster became a shop steward at Browns. Alan Christianson had an important role in the docks in the cold storage works. The Communist Party controlled the port shop stewards' committee at this time, with leaders such as Creighton and Marshall. But we were able to make big sales of the *Socialist Appeal* at the big meetings on the docks.

'The peak of the struggle on the docks was the 1945 dock strike. I organised meetings in Bootle, Bromborough and South End. In the end there were meetings with six speakers from the six major docks, where we explained the situation, bringing all the strands together. These meetings were held at 1pm and by 2pm there was a standstill at all the docks of Liverpool and Birkenhead.

'Once Liverpool was closed, the employers decided to divert the ships but the dock workers realised the need for quick action. Delegates were sent to the major ports of Glasgow, Leith, London and so on to explain the situation. One of our leading comrades in the docks was Charlie Martinson. Charlie had been a member of the Communist Party and had gone to Spain with the International Brigade. He had observed the Barcelona uprising, but when he saw the Communist Party attacking the POUM, he went over to the POUM. On his return to Britain he joined our group. During the port dispute he went to London, Frank Ward went to Glasgow and other dockers went to Leith, Hull etc. By 8am the next morning, nothing was moving in any of the docks and the dispute had broadened out to demand a 25 shillings per day guaranteed wage, a guaranteed working week, holidays with pay and so on. After 5 weeks the strike had been won with all the claims met.

'After the war the political truce ended. I went back to Bootle and was active in Litherland Labour Party where I became chairman of the ward. I re-joined the printing trade working at John Gardeners and became Father of Chapel. Through Marxist discussion classes young apprentices were won to the ideas of Marxism. They later in turn played a part in winning Tony Mulhearn.'

Appendix 6: Statement of Richard Venton to the NEC

1. I joined the Labour Party in 1971, the day after I came to Liverpool from Ireland, in order to campaign for socialism as an answer to the poverty I witnessed as a child. I have devoted 15 years to the party, in order to change society, not to change my income, as unfortunately too many in the party have done.

2. I am a member of no political organisation except the Labour Party and the TGWU. I have held numerous positions of responsibility in ward and constituency Labour Parties, and in the Labour Party Young Socialists. I was elected delegate to the North West Regional Labour Party Conference on numerous occasions, and national conference three times—from Garston CLP once, and Birkenhead CLP twice.

I have actively organised canvassing, leafletting, street meetings, factory gate meetings and public meetings in support of Labour candidates in council elections and every general election since February 1974. I have done this regardless of which strand of opinion within the Labour Party the individual candidates represented, because I am a loyal Labour Party activist who relies on democratic debate to convince members of my socialist beliefs, and I accept majority decisions. Indeed, I received written thanks from Frank Field MP in 1979 for playing a key role in his election victory, despite my profound differences of opinion with him on many policy questions.

The same loyalty to Labour is lacking in many of those who seek my expulsion; the same Frank Field, for instance, threatened to stand against Labour unless his GMC selected him as a candidate in 1985!

3. I fully accept Labour's constitutional commitment to socialism, embodied in Clause IV, part 4, on every membership card I have held in 15 years. Unfortunately, I believe this is the real reason some people on the NEC would favour my expulsion; they want to abandon socialist policies, so they want to first purge socialists from Labour's ranks.

No other reason is given in the charges against me, as I wish to demonstrate.

4. I make no denial of having 'participated in meetings and rallies organised by *Militant*'. There is nothing unusual about Labour Party members speaking at such meetings: Tom Sawyer has spoken at a *Militant* rally, and yet now calls for the expulsion of others for doing so, because, to use his own words, 'you cannot hope to defeat *Militant* in Liverpool by debate and argument'. Numerous miners, printers, Addenbrookes Hospital workers have spoken at *Militant* meetings. The logic of the charges levelled against me is a wholesale purge of these comrades, which I fear is the intention of some on the right of the party.

5. I regard speaking at *Militant* public meetings as an honour, not a crime. I have helped to recruit hundreds of youth and trade unionists to Labour over the years at such events—people who were duly accepted into the party because they agree with its 'programme, principles and policies'.

6. Neil Kinnock, our party leader, has shared a public platform with Professor Eric Hobsbawn, 'theoretician' of the Communist Party of Great Britain. Yet nobody has suggested that these are grounds for expulsion of Neil on the basis that the CPGB is a 'political organisation with its own programme, principles and policies for distinctive separate propaganda and being ineligible for affiliation to the (Labour) party'.

One of the many differences between *Militant* supporters and the Communist Party is that the former have NEVER stood against Labour candidates of ANY wing of the Party, whereas the CP lost Labour one seat to the Liberals in a marginal ward in Liverpool in the recent council elections.

7. The *Militant* public meetings you refer to were mainly in support of elected Labour councillors in the struggle against the Tories. It is unfortunate that instead of implementing the 1984 Labour Party Conference policy by organising public rallies in support of these councillors, the NEC are spending valuable time in conducting attacks against Labour councillors, undermining Labour's position amongst voters.

I want to emphasise that when the *Wirral Globe* article speaks of finding out more about 'their organisation', this is purely the comment of the editor, not the comment of myself or any other *Militant* supporter; nor was it the content of the meeting. Incidentally, the Wallasey meeting was 5 March 1986, not 1985 as you say, which means you took 'evidence' after the NEC inquiry had been officially finished!

8. I readily admit that I participated in the National 21st Birthday rally at the Albert Hall, as did 5000 other labour movement activists. Do you propose to expel all 5000? I also know several political opponents of the *Militant* paper who attended from Merseyside, including political allies of Sean Hughes, right-wing Labour MP for Knowsley South! Do you propose to expel Jack Collins of Kent NUM who spoke at the rally, or any other miners who attended?

9. As a supporter of the general ideas put forward in the *Militant* paper, I certainly welcomed the rally, and see absolutely nothing contrary either to Labour's socialist traditions or Labour's official conference policies in the leaflet advertising the rally. On the contrary, it praises efforts to ˒organise YTS trainees (conference policy) and supports the courageous Liverpool Labour councillors (conference policy).

10. You assert that 'it is a matter of record and beyond dispute' that I am editor of *Mersey Militant*. Your assertion is false, and you completely fail to substantiate it. I can only assume it is one of the pieces of hearsay and gossip provided by opponents of mine during the inquiry—'unspecified hearsay' as the High Court called it.

I am not the editor of *Mersey Militant* nor is there any 'record' of my being so.

11. Your only 'proof' is a series of articles I wrote for *Mersey Militant*. If writing articles is proof of a person being the editor of the paper which publishes them, then Neil Kinnock is editor of the CP's *Marxism Today*, Roy Hattersley is editor of the capitalist *Guardian,* and Joe Ashton MP is editor of a smutty rag called the *Star*!

12. I would challenge the NEC to document anything in the

articles I have written in *Mersey Militant* which is contrary to Labour Party policy, or which is detrimental to the party's position amongst readers.

The articles oppose big rent and rate rises; expose the corruption of big business and the Tories; advocate nationalisation of the banking system; condemn the blatant patronage of the honours list; expose how witch-hunts lose votes for Labour (with facts and figures to prove this); and call on Labour's leadership to turn words into deeds in defence of the working class. What is anti-Labour about any of that?

13. The difference between the articles I have had published by *Mersey Militant* and those which Roy Hattersley gets published in the *Guardian* are firstly political, and secondly financial. He is reputed to earn about £80,000 a year, largely from his journalism: I can assure you that my income keeps me firmly in the lifestyle of the working class!

It seems it is alright for millionaire press baron Robert Maxwell to remain a party member whilst he scuttles around Glasgow in a limousine handing out redundancy notices to print workers, but to write socialist articles for a socialist paper is an expellable offence!

14. The letter I wrote to the *Wirral Globe* states some simple facts, including the fact that the policies advocated in *Militant* have increased Labour's vote in elections. It argues for policies that have been agreed by party and trade-union conferences, such as a 35-hour week, national minimum wage and workers' control of industry. There is nothing 'distinctive and separate' from party policy in this—unless we accept that party policy is to be determined by a caucus of party leaders against the decision of conference.

15. I am a 'spokesperson for *Militant*' in the sense that I support the general policies in that paper, and I am prepared to speak out and say what I believe in. I could just as easily be called a 'spokesperson for socialism' or 'spokesperson for Clause IV, part 4 of Labour's constitution. Marxist ideas have been part of Labour's tradition since the founding of the party, as chairman Harold Laski wrote in his foreword to the 1948 centenary edition of Marx and Engels' *Communist Manifesto*, published by

the Labour Party. There is no political or constitutional basis for expelling Marxists who publicise their views.

16. Jim Mortimer, then General Secretary of the Labour Party said in January 1983 that: 'The NEC's action should not preclude Labour Party members from reading, selling, purchasing, publishing or writing for newspapers, including *Militant.*' Michael Foot said in 1982: 'You cannot suppress ideas by organisation.'

I would appeal to the NEC to heed both these points, made by avowed opponents of *Militant*. I would appeal to you to drop your charges against a socialist who will continue to build the Labour Party as the organised voice of workers and youth, and to concentrate all your energies on expelling the Tory/Alliance class enemies from office, in the pursuit of socialism.

Fraternally,
Richard Venton
13 May 1986

Appendix 7: Letter of Liverpool City Council Labour Group to the NEC

14 May 1986

WE THE undersigned group officers of the Liverpool Labour group have been instructed by the Labour group at its meeting of 13 May 1986 to make the following representation to you in relation to the proposed expulsion of members of this Group from the party.

In particular, we are instructed to refer to allegations against Tony Mulhearn and Felicity Dowling that they have been guilty of 'arrogating to the DLP the improper function of dictating group strategy and action to the Labour group on the Liverpool City Council'.

We do not propose to argue point by point the particulars of the charges which you have put to our comrades regarding relations between the DLP and the Labour group but rather state in general terms the Labour group's understanding of that relationship which has already been expressed in a resolution.

The Group's understanding of their relationship with the DLP is that the DLP was the main policy-making body so far as the Group was concerned. The DLP's function was not to involve itself or interfere with the day to day management of the city council and so far as this group is concerned it has not done so. There is clearly a very grey area in seeking to distinguish between policy on the one hand and strategy on the other hand. Under the party's constitution, the DLP is clearly stated to be the policy-making body of the party whilst the group is charged with responsibility for day to day management.

The Group recognises the value of the widest possible discussion and consultation with delegates from all bodies affected by decisions of the council. Furthermore, in instances where the policies determined by the DLP's policy conferences require clarification or amendment, the group have always felt it to be appropriate to refer such issues back to the policy making body, ie the DLP.

We would also point out that many of the individual instances of which you complain were referred to the DLP at the behest of the Labour group and not by the party officers.

We would also make the point that there are a number of members of this group who are also members of the Liverpool DLP's Executive Committee, apart from Tony Mulhearn and Felicity Dowling. Even if, therefore, there is any substance in any of your allegations regarding the relationship between the DLP and the group, those other comrades are equally guilty with Councillors Mulhearn and Dowling and your prosecution of those two is clearly prejudicial and unfounded.

Finally, we are instructed to refer to a previous decision of the Group, a copy of which we have already sent to you, and a further copy of which is annexed, to the effect that this group will not recognise any expulsion from the party. Any expellees will still retain whatever office on the city council that they now hold and will remain members of the Labour group.

John Hamilton, Leader
Derek Hatton, Deputy Leader
Tony Hood, Secretary
Jim Parry, Chief Whip

Appendix 8: Liverpool NUT's Legal Action (November 1985)

IN OCTOBER 1985 the Liverpool branch of the National Union of Teachers (NUT), together with the Headmasters' Association, went to the high court to have the council's redundancy notices declared illegal (see Chapter 16). On behalf of Jim Ferguson, Liverpool NUT secretary, a learned QC denounced the Council's action as 'unreasonable, irrational, and illegal'. The Council's policy was completely distorted in court, and the QC appointed by council officials, not the councillors, dismally failed to put the council's real case. The three judges predictably ruled that the issuing of the redundancy notices was 'invalid' as 'it stemmed from the city's setting of an illegal rate'. (*Financial Times*, 18 October 1985) The presiding judge was Lord Justice Watkins, notorious for his punative rulings against the NUM during the miners' strike, including the sequestration of the NUM's funds. Another was Lord Justice Wolf, who had recently ruled that Hackney Council's delay in setting a rate was illegal. Later Wolf again ruled against the Liverpool councillors: sitting in the Court of Appeal, despite the fact that he had already declared their July 1985 budget illegal, he rejected their appeal against the District Auditor.

At the NUT's annual conference in April 1986 the Executive attempted to justify the legal action against Liverpool's 'strategy for combatting government restrictions'. (NUT Executive: *1986 Annual Report*, p71) Delegates supporting *Militant* moved the following ammendment, which received a sympathetic hearing and was supported by about a quarter of the delegates:

It is now recognised that it was a serious mistake for the Committee and the Executive to have approved the legal action of the Liverpool Division of the NUT against Liverpool City Council in November 1985. Whereas legal action was not pursued against Avon and Haringey, which made serious cuts in education, Liverpool NUT's action was taken rapidly to the High Court before any real attempt to reach agreement with the Liverpool authority, a Labour council under exceptional pressure to make cuts by central government, had been exhausted. It is clear that the NUT's action in this case was based on a serious misunderstanding of Liverpool council's strategy, which was first to delay making a rate until 14 June and then temporarily to adopt a defict budget to gain more time for the campagn for extra resources from central government to make up the £29 million gap (£117 million gap after penalties) in order to avoid cuts in jobs, services and education. Liverpool Labour council's stand against cuts was especially worthy of NUT support because of the improvements made by the council in education provision. The council carried out a long overdue reorganisation of secondary education, establishing 17 community schools to give every child a decent education. Despite the Department of Education's claim that they were 80 teachers over quota, the council refused to cut teachers and actually improved teacher-pupil ratios. Among other improvements, the council spent £5 million on school refurbishment, and opened 6 new nursery classes.

The NUT's legal action was based on a misunderstanding, in particular, of the mass redundancy notices, issued at the end of September, which the council clearly had no intention of implementing, but which were necessary as a legal expedient and political tactic which by reducing the council's commitments on paper avoided immediate technical insolvency of the authority. It is now clear that the officers of Liverpool NUT failed to explain the real significance of this move to the members, and it is noteworthy that they put no alternative proposals to the Joint Shop Stewards Committee. Later, when it became clear to the Labour Group that, unlike the previous year, it would not be possible to force the government to give Liverpool extra resources, the council retreated to its fall-back policy, under consideration since August, of raising loans from the private sector on the basis of deferred purchase schemes and a small element of capitalisation, which ensured that no redundancies would be necessary. The alternative of implementing the Stonefrost Report would, on the other hand, have meant redundancies, including teachers, as well as an unacceptable combination of rate and rent increases.

Lord Justice Watkin's ruling at the end of the case, that the teachers' redundancy notices were null and void, had no practical effect because of the way the council's strategy had developed. However, the adverse judgement had an extremely damaging effect on the council's campaign, and the consequences of the judgement, had they been pursued as encouraged by the judge to a quashing of the rate, would have been catastrophic for education in Liverpool. 300 to 400 teachers would have lost their jobs, and schools would have had to be closed.

The Court ruled that the issuing of redundancy notices was unlawful as it was the illegal consequence of setting a deficit, which was held to be illegal. The local authority's obligations under the 1944 Education Act was not a major issue in the case. Liverpool council did not accept that a deficit budget was illegal, but because of the speed of the NUT's action had no time to prepare its case on the complicated issues involved. The Court held that 'All that was required was a relatively small reduction in the budget in the region of £26 million. Such a reduction would lead to a great increase which, taken with the spending reduction itself, should bring the council's finances into balance.' The logic of this ruling (which is being appealed by the council) is that the council should have accepted drastic cuts from the start. Rather than fighting to improve education provision in Liverpool, which it succeeded in doing, it should have sacked teachers and closed schools.

Fortunately, after several weeks, the NUT dropped its action, started at the end of the original case, to quash the rate.

It must further be recognised, however, that the NUT's misguided action had severe adverse effects on a Labour council which has demonstrated its exceptional determination to fight cuts. The NUT's action put additional pressure on the council at the height of the budget crisis, and far from helping to resolve it, hindered the council's intense efforts to find an alternative way of protecting jobs and services. Moreover, the NUT's action gave Lord Justice Watkins the opportunity of ruling that a deficit budget is illegal. This is a key issue in the Liverpool (and Lambeth) councillors' appeal against the District Auditors' surcharge and disqualification. Not only did the council not have time to prepare a full case on this issue, but the Labour councillors could not be represented in that action as councillors. It is therefore particularly regrettable that, arising from the NUT's action, Lord Justice Watkin's judgement seriously prejudiced the appeal against the District Auditor of councillors who have put their own jobs, personal property, and livelihood on the line in the battle to defend council jobs and services.

Appendix 9: Should Marxists take legal action?

WHEN FACED with expulsion proceedings in 1982, *Militant's* Editorial Board decided to challenge the NEC's unconstitutional and undemocratic move in the courts. The question was inevitably raised: Should Marxists resort to the capitalist courts? This was answered in an editorial written by Lynn Walsh, published in *Militant* on 12 November 1982, the essence of which is reprinted here (shortened for reasons of space). The position was amply vindicated by events. Without the Editorial Board's legal action, the five would have been summarily expelled following the 1982 Conference, which approved the Register. Instead, the right wing were forced to allow lengthy hearings, which gave *Militant* the opportunity of putting its case to the labour movement. Similarly with the leading members of the Liverpool District Labour Party. The outcome, as far as the right were concerned, was predetermined. But legal action forced the NEC to grant the Liverpool leaders proper hearings, which again provided an opportunity to explain their case for the benefit of Labour's ranks.

Is it justified for socialists to go to the capitalist courts?

That is the question which has been raised in relation to *Militant's* recent statement that we are seriously considering legal action against the NEC if they attempt to go through with expulsions.

Marxists, without having illusions as to the nature of the courts, have never ruled out the use of the law as one form of action. The great teachers of Marxism, Marx himself, Lenin and Trotsky, were all prepared, under certain conditions, to go to the courts.

Marx, in 1860, attempted to take legal action against a certain Herr Vogt, who worked as a paid spy and provocateur within the workers' movement for the French dictator, Louis Napoleon. Vogt tried to discredit Marx and his followers by publishing scurrilous allegations in the German press. Legal action, wrote Marx, was 'decisive for the historical vindication of the party and the future position in Germany.'

In 1936, at the time of the notorious Moscow frame-up trials, Trotsky, then exiled in Mexico, faced a similar situation. One of the right-wing papers of the multi-millionaire Hearst group published, without permission, one of Trotsky's articles. This enabled the Stalinists unscrupulously to accuse Trotsky of 'collaborating with Hearst against the Soviet Union.' Trotsky explained why he was initiating legal action: 'I believe that according to American laws I have the right to sue Hearst for infringing upon my rights as an author and for the great political and moral harm he has caused me with this infringement.'

Labour's right wing are in no position to complain about legal action being taken. They have never hesitated to go to the courts, or use the threat of legal action. Invariably, it has been to prevent the authority and prerogatives of right-wing trade union leaders or officials from being challenged by their rank and file.

Recently, on the other hand, a number of rank and file trade unionists have felt compelled to resort to legal action because all democratic procedures within their unions have been blocked off. The left in the Boilermakers' Society, for instance, has twice challenged recent election results in the courts on the grounds of alleged serious irregularities in the balloting.

The London Central branch of the electricians' union is also currently making a legal challenge to the amalgamation of London branches by the EETPU leadership against the wishes of many rank and file members.

The function of the judges and the courts in capitalist society is to protect private property and defend the power and privileges of the ruling class. This general truth is elementary for Marxists. But it would be too crude simply to conclude that, therefore, socialists should never go to the capitalist courts.

To make juridical institutions effective, to give them authority among the majority of people when the working class enjoys democratic rights, the capitalist class has to put the power of the courts within a general framework of law, legal rights, consistent procedure, and so on.

For the legal machinery to play its role, especially when there is enormous pressure from a labour movement which has fought to establish democratic and legal rights, the courts generally have to appear to uphold impartial justice, administer the law fairly, and to give all sections of society the opportunity to go to the civil courts to settle disputes or put right grievances.

Because of this, it is possible, under some circumstances, for workers and socialists to take some issues to court with the chance of a favourable outcome. If there is a strong case in law, or if arbitrary or oppressive action against certain individuals blatantly contravenes the common law conceptions of 'natural justice', it can be possible, within limits, to get a favourable verdict...

Legal action is a legitimate means of trying to avert undemocratic, unconstitutional measures, of trying to halt summary expulsions and the imposition of a new system of right-wing thought control...

In 1977-8 Newham North East Labour Party was infiltrated by agents of the capitalist class. They were trying to reverse moves by the constituency party to de-select their MP, Reg Prentice, who later defected to the Tories. Lewis and McCormick, who turned out to be financed by the ultra-right 'National Association for Freedom', disrupted the party and tried to use legal action to reverse democratic Labour Party decisions.

Members of Newham NE fought Lewis and McCormick politically, but, quite correctly, they also fought back—successfully—through the courts.

In the Newham case, even the 'class-ridden, bourgeois' courts were forced to recognise the justice of the constituency party's case and condemn the totally alien, undemocratic intervention of Lewis and McCormick. Who would argue that the left should have opposed going to the courts as one part of a campaign to get rid of Prentice and establish the party's right to re-select its MP?

Militant's case, however, is even more significant. It is no longer outsiders trying to disrupt the Party. The right-wing majority on the NEC itself, under the pressure of the capitalist class and its news media, is attempting to trample on the democratic rights of Party members. In this situation, it would be completely wrong to rule out the possibility of going to the courts.

In the long run, of course, it is not the courts who will resolve the issues. We have no illusions in the role of the law in present class society. In the long run it is the rank and file of the labour movement who will decide the issues. We are already confident of their verdict.

For the time being however, the right still controls the NEC and the Party apparatus. They have already shown that they will be ruthless. They are prepared to use every undemocratic manoeuvre and dirty trick in the book. Why should we, then, rule out any legitimate means to struggle to stop them trampling on the democratic rights of Labour's rank and file?

★ ★ ★

The last word can be left to Lenin. In 1913 he was asked by Maxim Gorky whether he was in favour of legal action against a certain Pyatnitsky, the dishonest director of a Petersburg publishing firm. His reply (*Collected Works*, Vol 35, p85) was unequivocal:

"As regards Pyatnitsky, I am for prosecution. There is no need to stand on ceremony. Sentimentalism would be unforgivable. Socialists are not at all against use of the state court. We are for making use of legality. Marx and Bebel made use of the state court even against their socialist opponents. One must know how to do it, but it must be done.

"Pyatnitsky must be prosecuted and no nonsense. If you hear reproaches against you for this—spit in the mugs of those who make them. It is the hypocrites who will reproach you. To give way to Pyatnitsky, to let him off for fear of going to court, would be unforgivable."

Bibliography of Main Sources Quoted or Referred to

Books and Pamphlets

Jim Arnison, *Leo McGree-What a Man...What a Fighter!* Union of Construction Allied Trades and Technicians, 1980.

Jack and Bessie Braddock, *The Braddocks*, MacDonald and Co, 1963.

Noreen Branson, *Poplarism 1919-25 – George Lansbury and the Councillors' Revolt*, Lawrence and Wishart, 1979.

Trevor Carter with Jean Coussins, *Shattering Illusions – West Ind'ns in British Politics*, Lawrence and Wishart 1986.

Michael Crick, *Militant*, Faber and Faber 1984.

Michael Crick, *The March of Militant*, Faber and Faber 1986.

RM Fox, *Jim Larkin-Irish Labour Leader*, International Publishers Inc, New York 1957.

Peter Fryer, *Staying Power-The History of Black People in Britain,* Pluto Press 1984. (This edition 1985).

Ian Gilmour, Sir, *Inside Right*, Quartet 1979

William Hamling, *A Short History of the Liverpool Trades Council*, Liverpool Trades Council and Labour Party 1948.

HR Hikins, *Building the Union-Studies on the Growth of the Workers' Movement on Merseyside*, 1756-1987. Liverpool Toulouse Press 1973.

HR Hikins, *The Liverpool General Transport Strike of 1911*, first published by the Historic Society of Lancashire and Cheshire. Volume 113, 1961, published in this edition by Toulouse Press 1980 and reprinted 1981.

Robert Kilroy-Silk, *Hard Labour*, Chatto and Windus 1986.

Emmet Larkin, *James Larkin Irish Labour Leader 1876-1947*, first published by Routledge and Kegan Paul Ltd 1965, published in this edition by New English Library Mentor Books 1968.

Michael Leapman, *Kinnock*, Unwin Hyman 1987.

Liverpool Black Caucus, *The Racial Politics of Militant in Liverpool-The Black Community's Struggle for Participation in Local Politics, 1980-86,* Merseyside Area Profile Group and Runnymeade Trust 1986.

Liverpool City Council, *Success Against the Odds*, Liverpool City Council Public Relations and Information Unit 1986.

Militant, *Liverpool Fights the Tories*, Militant Publications 1984.

JE Mortimer, *History of the Boilermakers' Society, Volume 2, 1906-39,* George Allen and Unwin 1982.

Professor Michael Parkinson, *Liverpool on the Brink*, Policy Journals 1985.

John Rose, *Solidarity Forever*, Kings Cross Associated Society of Locomotive Engineers and Firemen, 1987.

A Sivanandan, *A Different Hunger-Writings of Black Resistance*, Pluto Press 1982, this edition 1987.

Millie Toole, *Bessie Braddock MP*, Robert Hale Ltd, 1957.

Leon Trotsky, *The History of the Russian Revolution*, first published in England by Victor Gollancz Ltd, in three volumes 1932-33, this volume 1966, subsequently published by Pluto Press in one volume in 1979 and Monad (New York) 1980.

Leon Trotsky, *Their Morals and Ours*

Leon Trotsky, *Writings on Britain, Volume 3*, New Park Publications 1974.

PJ Waller, *Democracy and Sectarianism-A Political and Social History of Liverpool 1868-1939*, Liverpool University Press 1981.

Documents

Committee of Inquiry into the Conduct of Local Authority Business, The Conduct of Local Authority Business, Research Volume 1V, Aspects of Local Democracy, HMSO June 1986.

Press Notice of the Department of Environment and a letter from Patrick Jenkin to David Blunkett.

Liverpool Council Worker.

City of Liverpool NALGO Branch News.

NUPE Liverpool City Branch News.

Labour Party Conference Resolutions etc, 1984-86.

Minutes and Reports of Liverpool Trades Council, 1969-75.

Minutes and Reports of Liverpool Labour Party, 1969-79.

Correspondence between officers of the Labour Party and officers of Liverpool Labour Party and those later facing disciplinary measures, between their legal representatives.

Miscellaneous documents of Liverpool City Council.

Hansard.

Report by Jack Dromey to General Executive Committee of the Transport & General Workers' Union on Budget Settlement of November 1985.

Council correspondence of Tony Mulhearn.

Newspapers and Periodicals quoted

Black Linx, Bournemouth Evening Echo, British Nationalist, Campaign Group News, Caribbean Times, Catholic Pictorial, City Limits, Conservative Newsline, Daily Express, Daily Mail, Daily Mirror, Daily Star, Daily Telegraph, De Waarheid (Holland), The Economist, Evening Standard, Financial Times, Glasgow Evening Times, Glasgow Herald, Guardian, The Independent, Irish Times, Labour Briefing, Labour Herald, Labour Weekly, Liverpool Daily Post, Liverpool Echo, Liverpool Star, London Daily News, London Labour Briefing, Mail on Sunday, Marxism Today, Mersey Militant, Militant, Militant International Review, Morning Star, New Musical Express, Newsline, New Socialist, New Society, News of the World, News on Sunday, New Statesman, Not the Echo!, Liverpool Labour News, NUPE Journal, Observer, Private Eye, Public Service, Scotsman, Seven Days, Sheffield Star, Socialist Fight, Socialist Worker, Socialist Worker Review, Sun, Sunday Express, Sunday Mirror, Sunday People, Sunday Times, Sunday Telegraph, Tidningen (Sweeden), Time Out, The Times, Today, Tribune, Universe, Workers' Vanguard (Nigeria).

Index

Frequently occuring names are only indexed in regard to specific events. All trade unions are referred to by their initials.